MW00639489

The Legacy of
Maimonides
Religion, Reason and Community

Edited by Yamin Levy and Shalom Carmy

Yashar Books, 2006

THE LEGACY OF MAIMONIDES: RELIGION, REASON AND COMMUNITY
Edited by Yamin Levy and Shalom Carmy

Copyright © 2006 Maimonides Heritage Center
www.MaimonidesHeritageCenter.com

All rights reserved. No part of this book may be used or reproduced in any manner whatsoever without written permission from Yashar Books Inc. except in the case of brief quotations in reviews for inclusion in a magazine, newspaper, or broadcast.

Library of Congress Cataloging-in-Publication Data

The Legacy of Maimonides: religion, reason and community / edited by Yamin Levy and Shalom Carmy
Includes index.
1. Maimonides, Moses, 1135-1204. 2. Maimonides, Moses, 1135-1204—Ethics. 3. Philosophy, Jewish. 4. Philosophy, Medieval. 5. Ethics, Jewish. I. Title.
ISBN 1-9331439-14-2

For information and catalog write to Yashar Books Inc., 1548 E. 33rd Street, Brooklyn, NY 11234, or visit our website: www.YasharBooks.com

TABLE OF CONTENTS

Preface

Anniversaries of the birth or death of Maimonides (Rambam) are obvious occasions for appreciations and compilations of articles. So it was in 1904 and then in 1935. People who know no other Jewish jurist or philosopher recognize his name, and some of them feel the need to have opinions about him. The comprehensiveness and authority of his achievement in the most important areas of Torah study—the full range of halakhic discourse and the fundamental issues of theology and philosophy, make every detail of his work of interest to all serious students of Judaism. Since Rambam was a hyper-careful writer, who made no secret of the indirection in his mode of communication, precise reading of his text has become *de rigueur*, and the deliberate ambiguities inserted into crucial passages exert an endless fascination. An historian of Jewish philosophy, some years ago, counted the number of academic articles published annually on Maimonides, and lamented the disproportionate attention he continues to receive, while other medieval writers are, in her opinion, neglected. If this is true of university scholars, under constant pressure to come up with something new, it is even more the case among students of Torah for its own sake, who try to prize originality less than truth, and return again and again to the living sources that have fueled the quest for truth over the centuries.

Thus Yamin Levy's invitation that I join him in preparing the volume before you was, on the one hand, an easy assignment—locating authors and topics of abiding interest to professional and lay readers. On the other hand, however, there is a challenge in procuring discussions informative and stimulating, in a variety of areas, to readers devoted to Rambam, which at the same time can open a window into the laboratory of Maimonides study for those whose familiarity is limited. How can one even attempt to do justice to his multifaceted creativity? How does one focus on Rambam's own work, and yet tell the story of the hundreds of Torah students and academics who have contributed to our understanding of that work? How convey the excitement of plumbing the richness of individual texts without losing sight of general themes? Above all, how does one enter into the purely intellectual and analytic aspects of the Maimonidean corpus while upholding the religious vision without which all study becomes lifeless?

How well the collection of essays we have obtained, some original for this book, others retrieved from relatively inaccessible journals or translated from Hebrew, satisfy our hopes, is for the reader to judge. Let me add a few words, by way of introducing the individual papers that make up the volume.

It is appropriate that the opening essay, and the longest in the book, is by the late Professor Isadore Twersky, dean of intellectual historians working on Rambam, and himself a role model for the combination of Torah and academic scholarship. His subject is the growth of Rambam's reputation and his impact on later Torah scholarship. Rabbi Norman Lamm, for so many years a productive scholar and leader of American Orthodoxy, discusses a question central to religious life—the love of God—drawing on Rambam's halakhic works and the *Guide*. Professor Arthur Hyman, who occupies a prominent place among contemporary interpreters of Maimonides' philosophy, surveys, with his customary concision and clarity, the broad options in the academic scholarship of the 20th century.

My own contribution, and David Berger's, focus on critical questions regarding the ongoing implications of certain Maimonidean doctrines. My article offers a defense of Rambam's robust approach to dogma. Berger explores present day utilizations of Rambam's naturalistic teachings about the messianic age. The late educator and scholar Rabbi Norman Frimer depicts Rambam's influence as a role model for intellectual searchers. His son, the legal scholar Dov Frimer, turns to the details of Rambam's jurisprudence, and produces some unexpected conclusions regarding the halakhic status of non-Jews. Roslyn Weiss devotes her paper to a detailed examination of one text in the introduction to the *Guide*: whether or not one accepts the particulars of her interpretation, she succeeds in communicating the exhilaration of such microscopic study and its more systematic pertinence.

Yamin Levy's essay looks at the general relationship between Rambam's championing of rational thought and the kind of community it fosters. Hayyim Angel surveys many of Rambam's discussions pertinent to Biblical exegesis and their abiding importance for our own study of Tanakh. Elimelekh Polinsky deals with a specific area, honor and respect for parents. His essay, too, exemplifies the integrated study of Rambam's Halakhah and his philosophy. The essays by Moshe Sokolow and Gerald Blidstein, expand the scope of the book. Sokolow demonstrates the significant issues tackled by Rambam in his epistles. Blidstein, much admired for his three analytic and historical monographs on specific topics in Maimonides' jurisprudence, discusses the idea of Oral Law in Rambam. David Shatz aptly closes the volume with an analysis of the last chapters in the *Guide*, casting new light on Rambam's view of human nature, the role of the *mitzvot* and the goal of human existence, while demonstrating yet again the necessity of painstaking microscopic analysis of the text and its literary organization.

The initiative for this project was Rabbi Levy's, and the great bulk of its execution was his, as well. I am honored that he sought my advice and participation in this work. This preface provides the opportunity to express my appreciation for his, and his family's, quarter of a century of loyal friendship. I look forward to working with him in the future.

Shalom Carmy

Foreword

The spirit that propels the effort of those of us involved with the Maimonides Heritage Center is developed from a strong conviction that Rambam's legacy is not only relevant but a compelling religious and philosophic voice in modern man's search for a spiritual community and personal equanimity.

In addition to resonating with the individual's spiritual quest, Rambam's theological and political legacy addresses many of our modern day community's most pressing issues. The reemergence of Rambam's world view can have a potentially profound influence both in the diaspora and in Israel.

Any attempt to describe the impact and influence of Maimonides on Judaism and Jewish culture would ring hagiographic. I therefore quote the measured words of the late Rabbi Isadore Twersky from the first page of his seminal work "Introduction to the Code of Maimonides (Mishneh Torah)":

> Rabbi Moses ben Maimon, known in Hebrew literature as the RaMBaM and in western culture since the Renaissance as Maimonides, is perhaps the most famous and resplendent figure of medieval Judaism. His fame is a direct result of the quality and quantity, scope and originality, magnetism and fascination of his writings. For Maimonides—born in Cordova, Spain (1135/8); died in Cairo (Fustat), Egypt (1204)—was a prolific author of amazing vigor and precision, of intellectual, moral and religious force of analytic sharpness and aesthetic delicacy. This is well known and generally appreciated often with a dash of gratuitous hyperbole. In truth his reputation needs no inflation or exaggeration for his stature is nearly *sui generis* and his commanding influence has

been almost universally recognized. His literary oeuvre was not only remarkably comprehensive but also endlessly repercussive. He wrote epoch-making works in the central areas of Halakha and religious philosophy—an achievement that is unquestionably, almost overpoweringly, characterized by monumentality, using the term very literally. His works representing an unprecedented conjunction of halakhic authority and philosophic prestige, were extensively studied, meticulously annotated, frequently translated and intensively interpreted. Their influence direct as well as indirect reflected through many works in various genres by a host of authors, was global. His mighty historical image assumes heroic proportions rather early in his posthumous career, and it is this heroic figure which dominates the stage.

The Enigma

After Maimonides' death, on the 20th of Tevet 4965 (December 13th, 1204), a public fast was declared, and the mourning communities read the *tokhahah* of Leviticus and repeated the verse "The glory is departed from Israel, for the Ark of God has been taken" (1 Samuel 4:22). The outpouring of emotion and lamentation is hardly surprising as it is further proof of Maimonides' stature as one of the greatest, if not the greatest, Jewish scholars of all time. His profound and pervasive impact on Jewish life and commanding influence on Jewish thought has been universally recognized and continues to influence Jewish scholarship on the highest level.

And because the names Rambam and Maimonides are well-known in Jewish circles—no matter the denomination—it is truly astounding that so few people have any understanding of Rambam's life or philosophical and theological legacy. Over the years, I have run into so many whose knowledge of Maimonides begins and ends with the name of a hospital. The great Maimonidean scholar, Rabbi Yoseph Kafah, in his commentary on Rambam's *Mishneh Torah*, cites countless examples of rabbinic leaders who misunderstood or misinterpreted Maimonides because they were simply unaware of his philosophical and political views.

In some circles Maimonides is described as the pious rabbinic sage, while in other circles he is represented as the forward thinking scientist, and still in other circles he is just another prolific Jewish rabbi. Each of these descriptions is but a simple piece, albeit an important one, in the complex puzzle that encapsulates Maimonides' life, legacy, and everlasting contributions.

Maimonides the halakhist is incomplete without Maimonides the philosopher-theologian, yet any attempt to understand Maimonides the philosopher absent of the traditional halakhic values that he espoused would be describing someone other than the man he actually was. This indeed is his greatness: an authentic description of the "true" Maimonides must integrate the many facets that made up his religious personality with his many secular achievements.

There are so many examples of Maimonides taking original positions or restating positions that did not find expression in the religious political mainstream of his day. The unpopularity or possible controversy of an idea never dissuaded Maimonides from voicing his opinion. Take for example Maimonides' belief that the path to knowing God includes the study of Torah as well as the study of all other disciplines such as natural sciences, physics, and philosophy. Maimonides himself attests to the fact that he studied the books of idol worship, as well as the scientific books of the Greeks and Muslims. This was not a compromise position, as many today still believe, but rather part and parcel of the Jew's educational curriculum. As heir to a tradition that produced philosophically and philologically trained Talmudic scholars who were well versed in Greek science and Rabbinic tradition, Maimonides understood that the road to the "inner chamber of the palace" is paved with the knowledge of various disciplines and that one cannot fulfill the *mitzvah* of loving God without knowledge of the world that He created. Another example of Rambam's refusal to accept the status quo and desire to improve Jewish culture and society despite the confrontations and criticisms he knew he would face was his ruling that a Torah scholar is forbidden from making his pursuit of knowledge an economic enterprise. With this ruling Rambam effectively challenges the entire Geonic and Jewish Medieval establishment.

These are just two of countless examples of religious, theological, and political views Maimonides espoused that were both groundbreaking and controversial, yet true to the spirit and tradition of the Talmudic sages. It is no wonder that Maimonides stirred up significant passion in his lifetime and following his death. It can be argued that the Maimonidean controversy continues today. In 1997, during a Sabbatical in Jerusalem I attended a "spiritual" workshop led by leaders in the mystical and spiritual disciplines of the day. When I asked if Maimonidean thought had a place in their spiritual teachings, one after another responded with a resounding no. One speaker went as far as suggesting that the study of Maimonides would be counter to the goals of the "spiritually enlightened."

The goal of the Maimonides Heritage Center is to educate the greater public about the life and thought of HaRambam, in the hopes that his life's purpose will once again be disseminated beyond the ivory tower. Of the fourteen articles appearing in this volume Rabbi Norman Lamm's, Dr. Arthur Hyman's, Dr. Gerald Blidstein's, Dr. David Shatz's, Rabbi Norman Frimer and Dr. Dov Frimer's are reprints, while Dr. Isadore Twerky's and Dr. David Berger's articles are translations of previously published articles in Hebrew. The remaining six articles are original papers solicited for this volume.

Our challenge as editors was two-fold. We looked for articles of interest, varied and relevant to a readership that does not necessarily have an academic background, and we wanted the presentation to be not only academically sound but also a faithful depiction of the living Rambam. Dr. Isadore Twersky's paper presents an analysis of Rambam's legacy through the prism of comments made by scholars over a period of 700 years. Rabbi Norman Frimer documents Rambam's life, and religious and philosophical legacy as reflected through his works. We included a series of articles that address Rambam's worldview and religious outlook on a range of relevant and intriguing subjects such as: Rabbi Lamm's Maimonides on Love of God, Rabbi Shalom Carmy's discussion on dogma, Dr. David Berger's presentation of Rambam's views on the coming of Messiah, Dr. Dov Frimer's presentation of Maimonides' position on Jewish-Gentile legal relations, Dr. Gerald Blidstein's work on Rambam's attitude to Oral Law, Dr. Elimelekh Polinsky on Rambam's approach of *ta'amei ha-mitzvot* and parent-child relations and my essay on Maimonides and community. Dr. Arthur Hyman's essay is in not only an introduction to the study of the *Guide* but an introduction to Maimonides' methodology in general. Both Rabbi Hayyim Angel's and Dr. Roslyn Weiss' are cutting edge articles on Maimonides the biblical exegete. Dr. Moshe Sokolow introduces our readers to the influence Maimonides had on Jewish communities and Jewish culture through his letters.

At this point a word of gratitude and appreciation is in order. I would like to thank my co-editor Rabbi Shalom Carmy whose friendship and guidance over the years has been, and continues to be, a source of strength and inspiration. My utmost appreciation and deepest gratitude to all those who contributed to this volume. *Yashar koach* to Joel Linsider who translated Dr. Twesky's article and Jonathon Saks for translating Dr. David Berger's article. I thank Rabbi Mayer Twersky for his time and attention in preparing his father's article for publication. Our publisher, Gil Student, deserves special mention for his patience, and encouragement of, this project.

A special thank you to President Richard Joel, Chancellor Norman Lamm, and Dr. Herbert C. Dobrinsky for affording me the platform at Yeshiva University to explore, research, and teach the rich heritage of Sephardic Jewry. Indeed, my intellectual world would be significantly impoverished without my *talmidim*, students, at Yeshiva. I am grateful for my students and thank them for their continuous curiosity, interest and their high expectations.

The Maimonides Heritage Center would not be in existence without the commitment of its supporters and volunteers, and for that I am most grateful.

A word of gratitude to my in-laws Dr. Mel and Goldie Issacs is in order for their constant support and encouragement throughout my career. Over the years, I've shared and sharpened my thoughts about Rambam with Rabbi Reuven and Chaya Grodner.

My father, of blessed memory, always enjoyed receiving my published essays, articles, and books. While he will not see this book in its final version, he did enjoy hearing about its progress. I dedicate my contribution to this effort to his memory. I thank my revered mother Esther Levy for her constant attention and guidance of the Levy clan.

Words will never adequately express my sense of awe and appreciation for my wife Dvorah. Her natural wisdom, combined with her ongoing quest for meaning is humbling. We share life's great joy of raising five wonderful children Amichai, Yedidya, Hananel, Shira and Eliyahu.

Odeh Hashem be-khol levav—I am eternally grateful to the Lord.

Yamin Levy
In Memory of My Beloved Father
Mimon Halevi Ben Alegrina

Some Reflections On The Historical Image Of Maimonides: An Essay On His Unique Place In Jewish History*

Isadore Twersky

> Dedicated to the memory of my teacher and father-in-law, the *ga'on* R. Yosef Dov ha-Levi Soloveitchik, *zz"l*—the Maimonides of our generation

In the Name of the Lord, God of the World[1]

"And in point of fact his activity has resulted, as we see today, in the consensus of the greater part of the population of the earth glorifying him and considering themselves as blessed through his memory." This sentence from the *Guide of the Perplexed* (3:29),[2] which Maimonides wrote about our father Abraham, can certainly be applied to Maimonides himself as well. Rabbenu Moses b. Maimon the Sefaradi has attained a unique status, one unparalleled in the chronicles of great Jewish leaders and scholars. All—or, certainly, nearly all—glorify him and find blessing in his memory and work. Maimonides' words are echoed in a statement by R. Solomon b. Simeon Duran:

> And all the authors who came after him, and the commentators who followed in his steps, Muslim and Christian alike, though criticizing him on a few matters, recognize the splendid glory of his majesty, crave his teaching, and acknowledge that it is proper to glorify him and be blessed through him.[3]

---

* Translated from the Hebrew by Joel A. Linsider. As in the Hebrew original, the author's substantive footnotes are marked with asterisks. Numbered endnotes are used for citations (which appear as parentheticals in the text of the Hebrew original) and for translator's and editor's notes. The rich, idiomatic texture of Prof. Twersky's Hebrew is not easily translated. The translators and editors have done their best to meet this challenge and accept responsibility for any shortcomings in translation.

The historical-national consciousness has pronounced an unambiguous verdict, clear as the noon-day sun: our master, *Rabbenu* Moses, "the great scribe of Israel"[4] occupies his own distinctive place. But how did this come to be? What is his unique image and what is its secret?

We can penetrate the mysteries of this evaluation, uncovering its causes and components, by gathering and analyzing the testimonies that extol and glorify Maimonides. We will discover *sui generis* words of praise that attest to, and simultaneously reinforce, history's verdict regarding a unique personality of exceptional influence, a verdict which continues to reverberate to this day. It is generally recognized that our literature abounds in words of praise—some hackneyed and others seemingly growing out of profound feeling and recognition—and that it contains as well an ample measure of exaggeration and hyperbole. Maimonides himself taught us to steer clear of superficial remarks and not to be taken in by trite rhetoric or grandiloquent titles:

> For such words are merely inflated names, in the manner of nicknames and epithets. And I have seen people in the Land of Israel called "*haverim*" [a title indicating a substantial measure of learning], and in other places called "*rosh yeshivah*" [head of the academy], though they did not engage in Torah study even one day every three months.[5]

A title can become so overblown as to become a joke. With regard to Maimonides, however, we can identify unique praise in distinctive literary formulations, reflecting, and thereby also shaping, a unique historical reality and perception. It is possible to work out a systematic, phenomenological taxonomy of adulatory statements that will help to illuminate his image in history by means of history itself. Indeed, the aim of philology, which aspires to a precise understanding of a particular source or array of sources, is the internal clarification of the meaning of those sources; this yields the genuine meaning, and this constitutes the truth of Torah and wisdom.

I

There is no end to statements that ardently proclaim Maimonides' greatness and commanding influence. Writers who "praise the great rabbi at length, using exaggerated rhetoric"[6] attribute to him every imaginable quality. His genius, erudition, originality, strength of character, and daring are all described with awe and with love; his piety and generosity have been emphasized as well. To quote Nahmanides:

> ...in the degree of his piety, the power of his faith, the force of his modesty, the greatness of his lineage, the generosity of his purse; in his wondrous acts and his awesome words.

So, too, R. Solomon ben Adret (Rashba) in his *Sefer Minhat Kena'ot*: "We have heard of his piety and teachings."[7] R. Menahem ben Zerah, in the introduction to his *Sefer Zedah la-Derekh*,[8] concludes his praise of Maimonides with the comment that "in addition to his wisdom, he was a man of great piety." R. Samuel de Medina (Maharshdam), whose comments will be referred to again later, notes in his collection of responsa that "at several places in his texts, his piety and holiness are apparent."[9] In other words, characterizations of Maimonides and depictions of his personality highlight both his exceptional moral qualities and his exceptional intellectual qualities. All the characteristics enumerated by the sages and their chroniclers as found in persons of worth have been found in and attributed to him; there are examples in abundance, from the pens of Ashkenazim and Sefardim alike, at all time and in all places.

Beyond that, we have more detailed imagery: Maimonides is said to be the diadem of the sages and the crown of the righteous and perfect, the great eagle, the great light, the great voyager, the great guide, the rabbi who instructs, the righteous teacher, the illuminator of darkness, the lamp of Israel, he who illuminates the eyes of the Diaspora, the divine philosopher, the philosopher-genius, exalted above all the sages in his wisdom, the prince and head of all the nation's philosophers, the glory of the rabbis, the master of Torah sages, the crown and circlet of [the Jewish] religion, the master of all treatise-writers, the crowning glory of those possessed of Torah, and a man in whom can be found the spirit of the Holy God.

My purpose here is not to exhaust the list of soubriquets; it is, rather, to provide examples showing their range, color, and tone. To them must be added the poetic lines that describe, characterize, and exalt Maimonides, such as the well-known poem by R. Judah Alharizi: "You are an angel of God, created in the image of God, and if you share our [human] form/it was for your sake that God said 'Let us make a man in Our image, after Our likeness.'"[10]

One could easily compile a book entitled "In Praise of Maimonides" (though one could, of course, append to it a "catalog of indictments" based on the animadversions and criticisms leveled against him). One leafing through this book would find himself touring the length and breadth of

Jewish history and literature and would encounter the greatest writers, sages, scholars, creative thinkers, and critics of every generation.

But it is not these words of praise, however impassioned and effusive, that establish Maimonides' uniqueness and distinctive qualities. We must draw distinctions among the various statements, rigorously and sensitively assessing their worth and their purpose; we must ask what each expression of praise actually seeks to convey. "One said it in these terms; another said it in those terms" (*Shabbat* 5b), and the question pertains to the phenomenology of praise. Words of praise must be regarded with both deference and circumspection: one should not be overly impressed by them, but neither should one be indifferent. One should reflect on their meaning from the posture of "one does not take pride in them, one does not reject them, one does not remove them" (*Hullin* 7b). And, of course, even if the words of praise are identical, not all great scholars uttering them are equal. "...[J]ust as in wisdom, one sage is greater than another,"[11] so, too, with respect to Maimonides, not all words of praise have equal value and weight. What is fundamental is the development and preeminence of a distinctive conception: in many places, under many circumstances, from various viewpoints, and in various literary contexts, people emphasized not only Maimonides' greatness but also his uniqueness. That development will be reviewed and explained below.

R. Aaron ben R. Meshullam of Lunel, scion of an exalted and well-pedigreed family in southern France, well-born and well-schooled, writes as follows to R. Me'ir ha-Levi Abolafia, "the prince of Levite princes," one of the great Spanish sages of the late twelfth–early thirteenth centuries and author of the talmudic commentary *Yad Ramah*:

> For, indeed, since the days of Ravina and R. Ashi, none like Moses [Maimonides] has arisen in Israel, of wondrous might and great insight. And his deeds are greater than those of R. Hiyya, for he established testimony in Jacob and Torah in Israel, by means of his intellect and knowledge, which will never be forgotten by his descendants...[12]

It should be noted that R. Me'ir Abolafia does not allow R. Aaron of Lunel's remarks to pass without comment. He holds him accountable for having demeaned R. Hiyya, especially in view of the Talmud's statement (*Bava Mezi'a* 85b) that even R. Judah the Prince humbled himself before him: "My gut roiled when I heard...about your saying that his achievements were greater than those of R. Hiyya."[13] Nevertheless, he does not question the primary judgment that "since the days of Ravina and R. Ashi, no one [like him] has arisen in Israel;" even his brother, R. Joseph ben Todros ha-Levi—an energetic opponent, as we shall see, of the ascendant rationalism—explicitly incorporated that determination into his own assessment of Maimonides. These two prominent brothers well understood the singular nature of R. Aaron's fervent remarks, sensed that they were not merely a *pro forma* tribute, and considered the point and accepted it. The unique adulation had begun to reverberate.

A contemporaneous view is that of R. Samuel ibn Tibbon, the translator of Maimonides' *Guide of the Perplexed* from Arabic to Hebrew and the apparent recipient of the last letter written by Maimonides.[14] Ibn Tibbon states:

> But after the sages of the Talmud, there are to be found few who were moved to compose a book or write anything on these sciences; rather, it sufficed for them to write about civil laws and religious restrictions. Until God noted the intellectual poverty of His people and the extent of their ignorance of all matters of science, and He raised up for them a redeemer, a wise and discerning man—a "skilled artisan and expert enchanter" [cf. Isa. 3:3]—such that since the days of R. Ashi we have not known one like him to have arisen amongst our people with respect to all matters of wisdom. He is the true sage, the divine philosopher, our master and teacher, Moses, the servant of God, son of the great sage R. Maimon, of blessed memory.[15]

In a letter to the rabbis of France, R. Asher ben R. Gershom protests against their hostility toward Maimonides and accuses them of having abandoned the ways of our Sages and their devotion to wisdom in the broad, authentic sense. He also determines that "none has arisen like him since the time of R. Ashi."[16] That is to say, Maimonides restores the world of the Sages in its perfect equilibrium. Nahmanides, in his famous letter already cited, stops short of formulating his praise this way, but he, too, determines, in almost parallel wording, that "in the entire French and Spanish diaspora, none like him has arisen."[17] R. Yed'ayah ha-Penini of Bedres, who lived during the late thirteenth and early fourteenth centuries, refers to Maimonides at the end of his widely known book Behinat Olam:

> [C]hronologically the last of the *ge'onim*, in importance, the first—the great rabbi and teacher, the Rambam, may the memory of the righteous be for a blessing, who has no peer among all the sages of Israel since the completion of the Talmud.

In his *Iggeret ha-Hitnazlut*, another essay that attracted broad attention and detailed examination over the ages, R. Yed'ayah ha-Penini mentions several thinkers since "the great *ga'on* R. Sa'adyah" and then sums up:

> In sum, he [Maimonides] ascended the ranks of truth in peace and honesty more than we have heard tell about anyone else from the completion of the Talmud until now.

And so this great adulation took root, reverberating ever more loudly from generation to generation. R. Solomon ben Simeon Duran (Rashbash), a North African rabbi and judge and a representative of the final generations of Spanish sages in the fifteenth century, likewise determines, in his short book *Milhemet Mizvah* "that since the days of R. Ashi, no one has arisen like our Rabbi Moses, our great rabbi." Around the same time, R. Moses ben Shem Tov ibn Habib writes, at the end of his commentary on *Sefer Behinat Olam*:

> Do you not see that those weak in intellect and reason have mocked the books of R. Moses ben Maimon, of blessed memory, like whom none has arisen in learning from the days of Ravina and R. Ashi until today?

The comments of R. Isaac ben R. Sheshet (Ribash) seem to point in the same direction, though the precise wording is missing:

> The Rambam, of blessed memory... had learned the entire Torah in full—*halakhah*, *agaddah*, *Tosefta*, *Sifra* and *Sifre*, and the entire Babylonian Talmud and Talmud of the Land of Israel, as we can see from the book *Mishneh Torah* that he authored.[18]

In the sixteenth century, R. Samuel de Medina (Maharshdam) reverted to his predecessors' formulation: "And the treatise [known as] the *Yad [ha-Hazakah*; another name for the *Mishneh Torah*] attests that its author is one like whom there has been none from the time the Talmud was completed until the present."[19] His contemporary, R. Isaac de Leon (author of *Sefer Megillat Ester* on Maimonides' *Sefer ha-Mizvot* with Nahmanides' comments) likewise determines that Maimonides' treatise "is set forth in its entirety with no thorn or thistle, in a pleasing arrangement such as there has not been since the days of Ravina and R. Ashi."

Another chronicler of the time, R. Elijah Kapasli, comments as follows:

> He produced fine rulings on the basis of the entire Talmud...for from the time of Ravina and R. Ashi, the compilers of the Talmud, no one [else] has composed a work on the entire Talmud, from beginning to end.[20]

Only R. Jacob Emden, in his commentary on the Mishnah, appears to limit this expression of esteem for Maimonides, suggesting it applies only to his literary style: "Does it make sense to say that about so insignificant a person [an individual under discussion at that point], particularly making use of Maimonides' wording, which is ten times finer and clearer than the wording of all the treatise writers in Israel since the conclusion of the Talmud?"[21]

A pronounced expansion of this theme appears in the seventeenth century, in R. Joseph Solomon Rofe Delmedigo's *Mikhtav Ahuz*. Delmedigo describes Maimonides as "the treasure of Israel's wisdom" and then adds:

> For since the time of the prophets, none has arisen like him, a leader for the entire House of Israel in the valuable arranging and studying of the Torah and laws of righteousness.

Maharam of Rotenberg had already dubbed the *Mishneh Torah* the "*Urim ve-Tumim*";[22] and R. Me'ir ha-Levi Abolafia was taken aback when told that it was customary for the Jews of Provence to say, when speaking of the *Mishneh Torah*, "Bring out the *efod*."[23]

These words of praise require no detailed internal analysis. What they all have in common is their divergence from the usual literary framework and their being cast as a historical verdict. They provide the basis for the historical conception that depicts Maimonides' image in unique terms elevating him far beyond any normal praise. The starting point is the rabbinic period, the standard of reference is the Talmud, and the special regard for Maimonides is anchored in the recognition that since the completion of the Talmud, there has been no one like Maimonides in his command of the entire Torah. And, in fact, the post-talmudic rabbinic literature confirms that this assessment reflects reality, for that literature lacks any precedent for or parallel to his comprehensive and all-embracing oeuvre.

II

The distinctive, unifying feature of this acclaim—and, it follows, in the historical image of Maimonides and the historical consciousness reflecting it—can be highlighted by a simple but telling comparison with the way in which earlier writers expressed esteem for the great men of the past. How was their adulation of those giants formulated?

Maimonides regarded himself as a student of R. Isaac Alfasi (Rif) and, in the Introduction to his *Commentary on the Mishnah*, remarked that "the [book of] *halakhot* compiled by the great rabbi, R. Isaac [Alfasi], may the memory of the righteous be for a blessing, suffices in lieu of all others, for they include all the practical lessons, rulings, and laws that are needed nowadays." The twelfth-century thinker and chronicler R. Abraham ibn Da'ud extols R. Isaac Alfasi and defines his accomplishments and historical role. Writing in his *Sefer ha-Kabbalah*, a work devoted primarily to tracing the contributions and achievements of Jewish sages through the generations, he says: "and he compiled *halakhot* in the manner of a miniature Talmud, and since the time of R. Hai [*ga'on*] there has been none like him in wisdom."[24] R. Hai was the greatest disseminator of Torah at the end of the geonic period; "he spread Torah throughout Israel more than any of the *ge'onim*; and seekers of Torah from East to West walked by his light...and there were none like him among the *ge'onim* who preceded him, and he was the last of the *ge'onim*."[25] But R. Hai died in 1038 and Rif died in 1103. For purposes of our phenomenology, it is significant that in complimenting Rif for his wisdom and accomplishments, Ibn Da'ud elevates him over anyone in the preceding two or three generations.

That compliment highlights the unusual quality of the praise accorded Maimonides: the formulations applied to him do not speak of Maimonides' uniqueness in the interval since the days of R. Hai or R. Sa'adyah Ga'on or R. Yehudai Ga'on; the comparison is not to the period of the *ge'onim* at all but to the period of the Talmud. Maimonides is raised above all others and placed in the company of the Sages of blessed memory.

To provide a full picture, it is worth noting that traces of the unique view of Maimonides can be found in reference to Rif. For example, R. Zerahyah ha-Levi writes:

> And the wings of his righteous acts, in his treatise on *halakhot*, are spread over his generation and all the ensuing generations, for so fine a treatise has not been produced regarding the Talmud since its conclusion.[26]

We see that the reliable standard for true greatness and for unique, unquestionable spiritual-intellectual standing is the Talmud itself. A sage's distinctive greatness is determined by reference to his proximity to the Talmud and its sages. That is how a fine work or a great talmudic scholar is measured.

The place of Rif is fixed among the great *rishonim*. His compilation is a "miniature Talmud," an authoritative summary of the practical portions of the Talmud, simultaneously playing a scholarly and a practical halakhic role. His remarkable abridgment impelled and inspired further, on-going, in depth study; in R. Judah ha-Levi's poetic words, "the power of the insightful never ceased/ using the understanding they derived from you." The budding conception of Rif's uniqueness is significant not only in its own right, however, but also because it failed to take root. In Maimonides' case, on the other hand, the concept did take root and became the focus of a unique historical assessment of his figure. That is what R. Aaron ben Meshullam intended when he concluded his words of praise for Maimonides (which, as noted, began with the determination that "indeed, since the days of Ravina and Rav Ashi none like Moses has arisen in Israel") with the following comment: "For we have not heard with our own ears, nor have our fathers told us, of the writer of any book written after the writing of the *gemara* like the book *Mishneh Torah.*" R. Samuel ibn Tibbon likewise lauded the book as well as the writer: "There is not to be found in recent times a treatise like it with the wisdom of the Talmud."[27]

Interestingly, the fourteenth-century Spanish sage R. Isaac ben R. Sheshet (Ribash) concludes his words of praise for *Rabbenu* Jacob Ish Tam, the greatest of the Tosafists, as follows:

> The second luminary [is] R. Jacob Ish Tam, like whom there has been none in argumentation since the Talmud was completed. Talmud flows fluently from his mouth; he is a Sinai and an uprooter of mountains[28], grinding one against the other. All wise men will be in awe of his argumentation, the depth of his mind, and the breadth of his understanding.[29]

We thus see that when R. Zerahyah ha-Levi lauds Rif, he praises his work—a summary and abridgment of portions of the Talmud, though not a reworking of the entire Talmud—but not the author. When the Ribash praises *Rabbenu* Tam, he speaks of his mighty intellectual prowess but not of any of his writings. With respect to Maimonides, however, the acclamation is all-encompassing: only his treatise encompassed the entire Talmud, and only he is brought into the circle of Ravina and Rav Ashi.

III

From *ga'on* to *ga'on*—and on to the *ga'on* of modern times, "The Ga'on," R. Elijah of Vilna. It is doubtful that his disciples or other writers could express the full measure of his greatness as a fount of learning, but let us examine what they said of him. R. Hayyim of Volozhin, the Ga'on's faithful and dedicated standard-bearer, sets forth a detailed account of the Ga'on's greatness with respect to both revealed and concealed learning and provides a historical perspective for a proper assessment of his personality. His well known introduction to the Ga'on's commentary on *Sifra de-Zeni'uta* is replete with provocative and instructive stories and fervent words of praise ("the holy pious one," "the one from whom no mystery is concealed"). In the course of "recounting the greatness and wonders of our great rabbi's holy Torah," R. Hayyim determines the Vilna Ga'on's place in history: "The great man was unique; there had been none like him for several generations preceding him." R. Hayyim sees fit to emphasize that for quite some time, several generations, we had not been blessed with a pious and holy *ga'on* like R. Elijah of Vilna.

It is worth noting as well that R. Hayyim (and, in his footsteps, his nephew, R. Abraham Simhah of Amatzislav) assesses the Vilna Ga'on with reference to the belief (held by R. Sa'adyah Ga'on, Maimonides, R. Isaac Luria, and R. Israel Ba'al Shem Tov, among others) in the historical missions assigned to particular individuals in the life of the nation. These exalted individuals are destined by Providence to play certain vital roles in particular historical periods. R. Hayyim writes as follows of the Vilna Ga'on:

> Blessed be He Who keeps His promise to Israel, may His Name be blessed; for we have been promised by His word, may He be blessed, that the true Torah will not be forgotten by the true progeny. And His promise, may His Name be blessed, is what has sustained us and our ancestors…He granted us a blessing through the remnant whom the Lord calls throughout the generations, each generation and its sages, by whose mouths we live and from whose waters we drink. This generation, you see…*

In each generation, the Holy One Blessed Be He calls on a remnant to ensure that the ember is not extinguished and that the hope for ongoing,

---

* R. Jonathan ha-Kohen of Lunel praises Maimonides in similar terms: "Blessed be He Who keeps His promise to Israel, that it will not be forgotten from the mouths of his progeny." (*Iggeret la-Rambam* in *Responsa*, ed. J. Blau, vol. 3, p. 51.) As we know, Maimonides himself relies in various contexts on the reference in Joel 3:5 to "the remnant whom the Lord shall call;" the expression came to serve him as an important and meaning-laden slogan. See, for example, *Guide* 1:34, 2:29 and the Introduction to the *Mishneh Torah*: "A few gather, the remnant whom God calls…and engage in Torah and understand the writings of all the sages." This sort of wording is used to characterize the Vilna Ga'on and other prominent Jews, seen as key players in intellectual and spiritual history.

creative Torah study remains vibrant. The Vilna Ga'on is considered to be one of these few, called upon by God to maintain the Torah within the nation through his wondrous genius.

But it goes no further than that. Although R. Hayyim of Volozhin indefatigably and ceaselessly praises and extols the Vilna Ga'on, he does not elevate him above all the generations. A tendency of that sort does emerge, however, among the Vilna Ga'on's sons, who begin to assign him a status, like that of Maimonides, that transcends time and place. They write that "his wisdom exceeded that of several preceding generations, and from the time of the *savora'im* and the *ge'onim*, none like him has arisen."[30] Similarly, R. Abraham Simhah of Amatzislav writes:[31]

> And even though I wrote earlier that the generations become more and more corrupt and people's spirits diminish…nevertheless there is the wondrous matter of our great rabbi, may his memory be for a blessing, like whom no great scholar, a man encompassing everything,[32] has arisen since the days of the *savora'im* and the *ge'onim*, may their memories be for a blessing.

In our own day, the *Hazon Ish* expressed esteem for the Vilna Ga'on in a manner pertinent to our inquiry with respect to Maimonides. His impassioned words require analysis of their halakhic and historical implications:

> He is regarded as one of the *rishonim* and accordingly disagrees with them forcefully at some points, and he disagrees as well with the Rif and with Maimonides. We assign him a place in the line that includes Moses our Teacher, peace be upon him, Ezra, peace be upon him, R. Judah the Prince, Rav Ashi, Maimonides, and the Ga'on Rabbi Elijah, for Torah was revealed through him as a holy [man] destined for that [role], for he illuminated what had not been illuminated until he came and took his part.[33*]

But despite the Vilna Ga'on's rare accomplishments, awesome knowledge, and vast influence, this trend did not become dominant, and these expressions of praise did not take root. When all is said and done, even

---

* A fervent expression of esteem—though not so fervent as that of the Vilna Ga'on's sons— appears in the approbation by R. Israel Lifschitz (author of the mishnaic commentary *Tif'eret Yisra'el*) to the Koenigsburg 1855 printing of the *Shulhan Arukh*. He writes: "And not for naught is he referred to throughout the Diaspora simply as "the Ga'on;" for it is as if a heavenly voice came forth saying it is true, that he is unique in his generation as one of the earlier *ge'onim*, and all habitations reside together under a single star, such as this one, that rises only once in a millennium."

if we were to say that the Vilna Ga'on is like Nahmanides or like the Rashba—and knowledgeable readers will recognize the significance of the various formulations—the one-of-a-kind nature of the adulation expressed for Maimonides and of his historical image remains in place.

IV

And so we see that a great sage may be hailed as "the great one," "the spokesman," "the unique one," "the emblem," or "the glory" of his generation. The adulation flows from great regard and profound esteem, but it is contained by the chains of history and the limitations of chronology.[34] The wise man and his generation are interwoven with each other.

It is always possible to expand and supplement the words of praise; it depends on the rhetorical talent with which the speaker has been graced by God and his inclination to be expansive or effusive. Consider, for example, the remarks of Maharam of Lublin concerning Maharal of Prague:

> Who can recount his mighty acts, who can speak [adequately] of his wonders, who can extol his wonders? Accordingly, silence is his praise, concealment of his honor is his glory, and brevity in praise is his splendor. Is he not the breath of our life, the precious object of our eyes, the emblem of our generation, the splendor of our Diaspora, the *ga'on*, the great one of Israel, his name a powerful hammer, the light of Israel, the pillar at the right hand, the head of the academy and the Exilarch...[35]

As stirring as these praises are, and for all the extended and exaggerated rhetoric with which they vividly depict an important sage, from a historical point of view they include nothing that uniquely sets their subject apart from the ongoing succession of generations and flow of history. The overlapping laudatory terms flow trippingly off the tongue. Even if we carefully examine the *leitworte* of various recitations of praise—great *ga'on*, renowned *ga'on*, true *ga'on*, *ga'on* of *ge'onim*; rabbi of rabbis, rabbi of Israel, rabbi of all the Diaspora—we find that it is only the words of praise for Maimonides that have a distinctive, historically unique quality.

It should be noted that even encomia for Maimonides are sometimes found to be anchored in circumstances of time and place. A telling example can be found in Nahmanides' famous letter to the Tosafists ("*Terem E'eneh Ani Shogeg*"), a document that, as we have seen, illuminates Maimonides' personality from various angles but also reveals its writer's thoughts and inner feelings:

> And the honor extended to the great rabbi who built a tower of the Talmud has no end…and our long-desolate house of learning will be rebuilt throughout this profane Diaspora, from Spain and the Maghreb to the East; and he was a redeemer and teacher to the glorious one [Israel].

Which is to say: He was the greatest of his generation and worked mightily for the good of his contemporaries. R. Judah Aryeh Modena quotes[36] Nahmanides' fervent words (as did many others, before and since, especially those involved in the first Maimonidean controversy, all the way to R. Zevi Hirsch Chayes[37]) and concludes: "and he went on in his adulation without end." But for all the detailed descriptions of Maimonides' achievements and lengthy expressions of praise, the letter appears, when all is said and done, to be missing something: it lacks the distinctive terminology, such as those in the comments of R. Aaron bar Meshullam, casting Maimonides as a unique figure. Even R. Moses of Coucy, author of the *Sefer Mizvot Gadol* (a work that more or less consistently follows in Maimonides' footsteps), represents this more tempered and limited approach. He writes of Maimonides that "we have heard of none like him in recent generations."[38] Like the praise for the Rif mentioned earlier, these remarks, though appropriate, are embedded in a framework of time and place; they are not limitless.

In addition, of course, to these instances of standard, measured praise, we find that some of the greatest *rishonim*—especially the German and French sages, including R. Moses of Coucy, the Rosh, and a string of sages extending to Marharshal—voiced reservations, directly or indirectly, about the assessment of Maimonides as a one-of-a-kind figure in history. That judgment of uniqueness first appeared in the writings of Maimonides' disciples and may reasonably be assumed, by the very nature of things, to have served a clear ideological purpose. At the same time, the northern European sages acknowledged that Maimonides was certainly a great sage, but maintained that *Rabbenu Tam* and R. Isaac and their circle were greater still "and it is better that we rely on them than on the words of R. Moses [Maimonides]…for they exceeded him in wisdom and number."[39] In explaining why he occasionally demurs from Maimonides' halakhic determinations, R. Moses of Coucy writes:[40]

> And on some points, the Torah's pillars and personalities disagree with his interpretations and rulings; they include *Rabbenu* Solomon ben *Rabbenu* Isaac [Rashi], *Rabbenu* Jacob ben *Rabbenu* Me'ir, and

Rabbenu Isaac ben R. Samuel, from whose waters all the later sages of Israel drink.*

Over the course of time, however, the other assessment—based on an unusual historical notion and a unique historical judgment—came to prevail. All the praises are recited, and all the honorifics recounted, but Maimonides appears, above and beyond them, not merely as one unique in his generation but as one unique in many generations, unparalleled since the sages of the Talmud. Each generation has its sages, and it is well known that a person cannot easily transcend a particular chronological context; but Maimonides, an extraordinary man, a wondrous personality, was elevated beyond time and place and understood to be the sage of all generations. He is associated with the rabbis of the Talmud, with Ravina and R. Ashi.

V

Within this literary-conceptual context, we may be able to properly assess the important adage "From Moses to Moses none has arisen like Moses," the underpinning or the pinnacle of the unique attitude that anchors Maimonides' greatness in a comparison not only to the talmudic sages but even to the master of the prophets himself.[41] During the second half of the thirteenth century, between the time of the first Maimonidean controversy with its banning of the *Guide* and of *Sefer ha-Madda* and that of the second controversy and the banning of the study of philosophy (except for the works of Maimonides himself, which by then were being praised), we see the emergence, in various forms and contexts, of profound and multi-faceted terminology drawing on a comparison between the biblical Moses ("*Mosheh Rabbenu*," "Moses our teacher") and Moses Maimonides ("*Rabbenu Mosheh*," "our teacher Moses").

In a seemingly natural and self-evident way, appearing almost inevitable after the fact, Maimonides' name left its imprint on the collective consciousness and contributed to the establishment and spread of the unique conception of his status and significance and of the profundity, precision, and authoritativeness of his all-encompassing teachings. It followed that people

---

* The reservations about Maimonides in recent times (see, for example, the writings of the Munkaczer Rebbe) rely on this tradition of holding the sages of Ashkenaz in higher esteem. The *ga'on* R. David Friedman, the Rabbi of Karlin, comments (in *Sefer She'eilot David*) that one of the reasons contemporary sages are able to disagree with the *Shulhan Arukh* is R. Joseph Karo's limited reliance on the sages of Ashkenaz. See also R. Zevi Hirsch Chayes, *Tif'eret le-Mosheh*, Introduction, pp. 400-406.

began to play on that name and its implications. In R. Jonathan ha-Kohen of Lunel's letter to Maimonides, we already find the writer saying "hence his name was called Moses, for he drew [people] up with him from the waters of error,[42] to recall the times of old."[43] In the epistle of the sages of Saragossa to the communities of the Aragon, we likewise find "'Moses commanded us a law, an inheritance [*morashah*]' (Deut. 33:4)—it draws [*mosheh*] us from the sea of folly, error, and waywardness."[44] In the important controversy between R. David Kimhi and R. Judah Alfakhar, we find a letter from R. Bahya b. R. Moses to the communities of Aragon in which he mentions, among other things, "the book of the teachings of Moses (*"torat Mosheh"*) the servant of God, that is to say, the mighty hammer, *Rabbenu* Moses b. R. Maimon, may the memory of the righteous be for a blessing."[45] R. Sheshet ha-Nasi, in his letter to the sages of Lunel, comments on "those who adhere to the teachings of Moses, the lamp of the Maghreb, who shines its light on all Israel."[46] The Provençal poet Joseph ha-Azovi similarly says "and Moses after him, the man of God."[47] At the beginning of the fifteenth century, R. Ephraim Alnako notes: "This man Moses, like Moses, received Torah from Sinai; and his words are free of all contaminants, pure and clean, the words of the living God. [48*]

The plot thickened. In his letter to R. Isaac ha-Rofe regarding the renewed controversy, R. Hillel of Verona writes: "Do you not think that *Rabbenu* Mosheh [Maimonides] would have been almost [Moses'] deputy in the generation of [the biblical] Mosheh *Rabbenu*?" Later on, he reiterates his view: "What would you say of *Rabbenu* Mosheh, who was second to Mosheh *Rabbenu*?"[49] In *Mikhtav al ha-Rav ha-Moreh*, printed as an appendix to *Sefer Minhat Kena'ot*[50]—a letter pertaining to the renewed controversy at the end of the thirteenth century—we read: "There is a pearl in the mouth of one who calls him the second Moses." And Maimonides' great disciple, R. Joseph ibn Kaspi, declares, in his testament to his son, "And even more so the *Guide*, written by our teacher Moses, a father in Torah and a father in wisdom, [51] and who for us is greater than Moses."[52] In *Sefer ha-Sod*, ibn Kaspi refers to "the perfect teacher, whose name is the same as that of his master, in his book called *Mishneh Torah*."[53]

The adage "From Moses to Moses none has arisen like Moses"

---

* R. Judah Alfakhar, the probing and pointed critic of Maimonidean philosophy, understood and was not pleased by this literary-conceptual development: "And they appeared to elevate *Rabbenu* Moses of blessed memory above the prophets and place him at the head of all who are called" (*Kovez Teshuvot ha-Rambam*, part 3, p. 2 col. 4.)

sums up and embodies the exceptional esteem accorded to Maimonides' remarkable image and mighty oeuvre; it is an unprecedented and highly resonant literary coinage. There is reason to believe that the maxim took wing during the period under discussion (late thirteenth-early fourteenth centuries), for R. Shem Tov, the author of *Sefer ha-Emunot*, refers to it as widespread and popular. R. Shem Tov was a sharp-witted polemicist who judged Maimonides harshly; naturally, he is distressed at the maxim's popularity:[54]

> And it is surprising that the man is regarded as the great one of the ages, to the point that they say of him, in their foolishness, "From Moses to Moses none has arisen like Moses."*

But he was not the only one. R. Joseph Ya'abez, an expellee from Spain who mounted a comprehensive and probing criticism of Jewish philosophical thought as it had developed there, also knew of the adage, writing that "it has been widely said of him that from Moses to Moses none has arisen like Moses." He, too, was troubled by the slogan, rejecting it forcefully and clearly, though without biting polemic. In the course of his assessment, in which he expresses both praise and condemnation, he adds: "If you challenged him on the basis of R. Moses [Maimonides], will you not challenge me on the basis of Moses our teacher, peace be upon him?"[55] Elsewhere, in recounting the greatness and piety of R. Joseph Hiyyun (whom he characterizes, it is worth noting, as "an eminent elder,...replete with Torah like one of the *amora'im*"), R. Joseph Ya'abez reports as follows: "After he would clearly explain the rabbi's [Maimonides'] meaning, he would say: this is the meaning of *Rabbenu* Mosheh [Maimonides], not the meaning of [the biblical] Mosheh *Rabbenu*."[56] In the sixteenth century, a scribe copying *Sefer Sha'ar ha-Shamayim* by R. Isaac ibn Latif (written in 1238) inserts, toward the end of the introduction: "Said the writer: I have heard it said, 'from Moses to Moses none has arisen like Moses.'"

This "thing heard to be said" circulates more and more widely and takes root as an adage; at the same time, it begins to be used in reference to other sages, frequently in comparison to Maimonides himself. For example, Maharshal, who could praise R. Moses Isserles (Rema) but also

---

* That the adage had already taken root in its original form and context is further established by the fact that some writers applied it as well to others named Moses. As early as the fourteenth century, it was said of R. Moses Butril. See A. Jelinek, *Beit ha-Midrash* 6: 141-143). We will see further below how this secondary usage became more widespread.

challenge him, says of him: "In that opinion, it is fitting to say of you, 'From Moses to Moses none has arisen like Moses.'"[57] Over the course of the generations, the adage was applied to R. Moses Cordovero, R. Moses Hayyim Luzzatto, R. Moses Sofer (the *Hatam Sofer*) and even to Moses Mendelssohn and Moses Montefiore. R. Hayyim Joseph David Azulai (the Hida) interprets the adage in light of the fact that Jews tended not to use the name Moses during the Second Temple Period and the time of the talmudic sages: "I found written in a book that there is to be found no *tanna* or *amora* named Moses, and that is a wonder and a mystery, and that is as people say, 'from Moses to Moses, none has arisen like Moses.'"[58]

The explication of names cited by R. Hayyim Vital[59] in the name of R. Isaac Luria is well-known. But the path we have taken here shows that the adage is not merely a rhetorical flourish nor was it created in a vacuum. Rather, it is an emblem or an ingredient, a summary or a pinnacle of the development we have been considering; it embodies a clear trend and a specific historical conception. It is a historical judgment on history, a verdict of uniqueness. It means that Maimonides freed himself of the bonds of time and the bounds of space and was elevated to eternal life in the national consciousness. No one like R. Moses Maimonides has arisen in Israel since his time—a wondrous figure who occupies a place of honor in his own historical sphere.

It follows from this that the name "Moses" opened the door to wordplay on the name. Maimonides' disciples delighted in it (under the rubric of "your praiseworthiness is consistent with your name"), while his detractors recoiled from the distinctive praise it embodied, correctly seeing it as an unconventional conception. As early as the start of the thirteenth century, we find R. Joseph b. Todros ha-Levi, brother of R. Me'ir ha-Levi, joining in the chorus of praise:

> The mighty tamarisk/Who magnified Torah and glorified it/Great in counsel and abounding in deed…and of all the Diaspora sages the wonder and the sign/All his actions wonderful and awesome/ whose coin extends throughout the world/And whose name is greater than all.[60]

He concludes with the unique assessment that was then beginning to take root (and which had first appeared, as noted above, in R. Aaron b. Meshullam's letter to R. Me'ir ha-Levi) that "none like him has arisen since the days of Ravina and R. Ashi, the great rabbi, our Rabbi Moses."

At the same time, however, he argues that Maimonides is not beyond criticism, and if "the rabbi R. Solomon who dwells on the mountain" (that is, in the city of Montpelier) rains arrows on him, he is not to be disparaged for doing so or accused of

> speaking against God and his servant Moses and adjudicated a wayward elder, who disputed the words of the teacher; should all the unclear words of Moses' book be regarded as *halakhah* from Sinai?[61]

R. Joseph b. Todros ha-Levi represents those who opposed the unquestioning elevation of Maimonides and his books above and beyond all criticism. There is no reason to disparage his critics and to call them (in the words of R. Y. Alharizi) "little foxes attacking vineyards."[62] The position of the detractors had a practical impetus: they were prepared to grant Maimonides a unique position in history, but they wanted to avoid a situation in which he would enjoy immunity from criticism sufficient to preclude all halakhic or ideological challenges to him. As we know, Maimonides himself ruled that the gates of interpretation were not closed;[63] those who opposed excessive praise of Maimonides strongly felt that neither were the gates of criticism closed—not even against Maimonides himself.

These concerns, it seems fair to assume, likewise underlie the initial objections to the title *Mishneh Torah*, a subject I dealt with in various articles many years ago. Some sages opposed the title, in which they saw a hubristic expression of or aspiration to exclusive halakhic authority. They applied all manner of nomenclature to the work, but avoided the name coined by the author himself. Rabbinic literature (as distinct from general historical or literary writings) speaks of "the Treatise," "Maimonides' Book," "the wording of R. Moses," "the writing of the rabbi, Maimonides," "the great treatise by the rabbi, may his memory be for a blessing"—any term except "*Mishneh Torah*." At the end of the thirteenth century, the very time when the author's name was becoming the focus of exaggerated formulations of praise, the name of his book—*Mishneh Torah*—was almost entirely suppressed; even Maimonides' disciples declined to use it. It was at that time that the subtitle "*Yad ha-Hazakah*"[64] first appeared; it seems to have been a coinage of the Exilarch in Damascus, R. Jesse ben Hezekiah, who wrote in his epistle of "his honored books, precious to all who know religion, the *Yad ha-Hazakah*, which he called *Mishneh Torah*, and the *Guide of the Perplexed*."[65] Still, the bitter turned sweet: when all is said and done, the change in name can be seen as an additional dimension to the unique array of praises lavished on the writer.

In short, the adage in all its forms spread, the concept took root (despite a certain degree of reservation), and Maimonides' unique image continued to take shape in the historical consciousness.

VI

In the seventeenth century, R. Hayyim Ya'ir Bachrach (author of *Havvot Ya'ir*) brought it all together:

> For is there anyone who does not see and understand from his treatises the great extent of his grasp of the entire Torah together with all seven sciences, to the point that they said of him "from Moses to Moses...," as the great rhetorician concluded his book, *Behinat Olam.*[66]

At exactly the same time, R. Judah Aryeh Modena worked the adage into the following statement:

> The lamp of Israel, the treasure chest of wisdom, the rabbi, the guide, may his memory be for a blessing, of whom they correctly said [except for prophecy] "From Moses to Moses none has arisen like Moses."[67]

He goes on to explain: "For the first wrote for us the written Torah, and the second—the oral Torah."[*]

The author of *Havvot Ya'ir* was preceded by R. Elijah Kapasli; in the passage from *Seder Eliyahu Zuta* referred to above, he blends the two formulations:

> He produced a fine [set of] ruling[s] from throughout the entire Talmud, and called it *Mishneh Torah*...and there has been none like him among all the decisors who preceded him, nor will there be such a one after him. For since the days of Ravina and R. Ashi, the compilers of the Talmud, there has been no one to compose a work on the entire Talmud from beginning to end, as did the man Moses, more modest than any man. Hence the adage "From Moses to Moses none has arisen like Moses."[68]

---

[*] This blending of the two distinctive lines of praise—the historical judgment on the one hand and the symbolic significance of the name on the other—seems to have already been suggested by the author of *Sefer Alilot Devarim* (*Ozar Nehmad*, vol. 4, p. 184); he writes "For I have sent to you, after the completion of the Talmud, a man in whom there is the spirit of God; and his name is the same as his teacher's."

R. Elijah, to be sure, offers a similar assessment of R. Yed'ayah ha-Penini's apologetic letter, "a truly choice epistle...before it there was no such epistle, nor will there again be such a one after it;"[69] but the difference between the two contexts is readily apparent. Note that R. Elijah combines and highlights three basic ideas: Maimonides' standing as unique and unmatched since the days of Ravina and R. Ashi, the extravagant adage that "from Moses to Moses...," and a decisive determination that there will be no future composition like the *Mishneh Torah* (see further on that below). R. Solomon He'elma likewise writes "Our teacher Moses ben Maimon, of whom it is said, 'From Moses to Moses.'"[70] The adage spread far and wide and appears from time to time as a refrain in important literary contexts.

It is interesting that this historical sense was not far from Maimonides' own self-perception. Not for naught does he determine, unhesitatingly and unreservedly, that:

> None before me since our holy Rabbi [Judah the Prince, compiler of the Mishnah] and his holy circle have set out like me to issue halakhic rulings with respect to the entire Talmud and all the laws of the Torah.[71]

In the Introduction to the *Mishneh Torah* as well, Maimonides sees his work as encompassing "all those works...from the days of our holy Rabbi until today." His bond is not to Ravina and R. Ashi but to R. Judah the Prince, of whom he said, "We have none greater in wisdom than our holy Rabbi."[72] And history turned out to apply that very judgment to him: since the time of the Talmud, we have no one greater in wisdom than R. Moses Maimonides. But some, knowingly or unknowingly, used that same wording against him; that may explain the words of R. Yehiel Nissim of Pisa, the great antagonist of philosophy, who issued the following declaration regarding Maimonides' *Mishneh Torah*:

> He left out no scriptural verse, mishnah, talmudic statement, *halakhah*, *aggadah*, no large or small matter. [There was nothing that] he did not probe deeply, as can be seen from his great composition, called *Mishneh Torah*, which is unmatched in Israel from the days of our holy Rabbi [Judah the Prince] until today.

It need not be emphasized that when all is said and done, it is not merely the adulation that matters. As important as the one-of-a-kind praise may be, actions are even more important: the constant study of and engagement with Maimonides' works, and the on-going connection to him and his teachings. All manner of students and readers unceasingly benefit from his teachings. Even where they are unaccompanied by express words of praise, the facts speak loudly: the unspecified references to "the rabbi" or to "the rabbi's great treatise" or to "Maimonides in his great treatise" lack honorifics but show actively that "not so my servant Moses" [i.e., he is unique. Cf. Num. 12:7]. No other author merited unique praise of this sort, and no other work attracted such on-going, driving attention.

Consider, for example, the number of responsa collections that are organized according to the sequence of books and chapters in the *Mishneh Torah*. R. Moses Hayyim Luzzatto writes that the *Yad ha-Hazakah* must be studied, with its commentaries, from beginning to end.[73] The disciples of R. Moses Sofer tell that "at the end of Holy Sabbath, his practice was to study Maimonides' *Yad ha-Hazakah* in sequence." The history of rabbinic literature teaches that many of the best people sensed that "one who wishes to become wise should engage with Maimonides' *Mishneh Torah*; for there is no subject [greater] than it; and it is like a flowing stream."[74] Everyone appears to have internalized the final sentence of *Hilkhot Kiddush ha-Hodesh* (Laws of Sanctifying the New Month), where Maimonides emphasizes, in moving terms, his desire for all-encompassing wholeness:

> Thus we have explained it...so that all will be known to those who understand and they will not have to set out to pursue it in other books. Ask it of God's book and read it; nothing will be missing (cf. Isa. 34:15).

And so, students from then until now have diligently "asked it of God's book," the book known as Maimonides' *Mishneh Torah*.

VII

Let me now briefly note seven weighty issues connected to our subject.

(1) Now that we have taken this evidence and determined its significance (an exercise in the phenomenology of praise, as already noted), we must emphasize that the secret of Maimonides' unique greatness, historical success, and continuing, overpowering influence is rooted in one basic fact of enormous importance and wide consequence: his teaching, which excelled in its originality, was all-encompassing as well. The entire Torah, in its broadest and most exhaustive sense, was

incorporated into his teaching, as we have just seen in the responsum by the author of *Havvot Ya'ir*: "the great extent of his grasp of the entire Torah." That fact was repeatedly stressed in the writings of *rishonim* and *ahronim* alike. It will suffice to cite the fulsome rhetoric of R. Solomon ben Simeon Duran:

> And if one would boast of the glory of his Torah learning, recognize that he [Maimonides] is the father to us all. There was no realm that was beyond him. Babylonian Talmud, Talmud *Yerushalmi*, *Tosefta*, *Mekhilta*, *Sifra*, *Sifrei*, *Sifra Rabba*, *Sifra Zuta*—his eye saw all of it, and his ear similarly heard and understood the novellae, compositions, and praises of the *ge'onim*, and the Sages' *midrashim*.[75]

This is the root of the concept that elevated Maimonides beyond time and place and projected him into the circle of the talmudic Sages of blessed memory. This notion was formulated and disseminated by Maimonides' admirers in the area of rational religious thought. As the harsh criticism and bitter polemic that initially greeted Maimonides' work subsided, the concept, anchored in Maimonides' original and comprehensive achievements in the field of rabbinic literature, came gradually to be accepted by Jewish sages of all stripes. Here, too, Maimonides' self-awareness coincides with the image woven into historical consciousness. Maimonides himself emphasized over and over that he wanted to produce a work "from which nothing would be missing."[76] Comprehensiveness is the common denominator of every comment regarding his great enterprise. Not in vain did he tend to refer to the *Mishneh Torah* as "our great work, dealing with all the laws of our Torah."

Maimonides taught us that learning must be all-encompassing and that in no event should interrelated areas be divided: written Torah and oral Torah, matters pertinent to the present age and matters not needed now as a practical matter, *halakhah* and philosophy—all areas of knowledge, Torah and science, as they emerge from all sources of knowledge. He tore down artificial barriers between permanent and temporary, analysis and action, interior and exterior, and he declined—in principle and as a practical matter—to divide the Torah into discrete packets or scrolls.[77] He drew on all the riches of Torah and of wisdom, "he weighed and investigated all matters of the Torah,"[78] and he set forth clearly everything for everyone. Accurately, straightforwardly, yet startlingly, he said of his work, as already noted, "Ask it of God's book and read it; nothing will be missing"[79] (Isa. 34:15)—an audacious declaration that resounded in Jewish literature.

Maimonides' impression of innovation, profundity and originality, embodied in the comprehensiveness of his scholarly enterprise, was not lost on his contemporaries and successors. Since the sages of the Talmud, no one had dealt with the entire Torah in an original, organized, and deeply penetrating way, and there was little prospect of that effort being repeated. Interestingly, one of his recent commentators cautiously observes that "before him, there was none like him, and there has been none like him since, to this day."[80] In contrast, one of his earliest commentators, the Me'iri, asserted with full confidence that "before him, there was none such...and after him there will be none such."[81] And R. Judah Alharizi has cited the comment of that "Never again will there arise one like this prince."[82] Even R. Elijah Kapasli determined, as already noted, "there has been none like him among all the decisors who preceded him, nor will there be such a one after him." As far as we know, no one has attempted to repeat Maimonides' achievements or compete with his effort. R. Hasdai Crescas, at the beginning of his book *Or ha-Shem*, announced his intention to compose a comprehensive work like the *Mishneh Torah*, and Joseph Solomon Rofe Delmedigo proudly declared in *Sefer Novelot Hokhmah* that

> I have confidence in God [that I will] produce a book of great value that will be of more use to the masses than Maimonides' *Yad ha-Hazakah*, and its renown will not depart from among the Jews until the coming of the redeemer.

But neither of them carried out his intention, and Me'iri's comment remains fully valid. History's one-of-a-kind judgment continues in full force and effect, its rationale unabated; and the laudatory adage is as fresh as when it was first uttered. The treatise remains unique and unrivaled.

(2) The comprehensive originality that characterizes Maimonides' enterprise has a distinctive dimension warranting special emphasis; it is summed up in *Havvot Ya'ir*'s observation, noted above, regarding "the great extent of his grasp of the entire Torah together with all seven sciences." Maimonides consistently and rigorously declined to distinguish between laws currently in effect, such as those related to *shofar* and *lulav*, and laws not now in effect, such as those related to sacrifices; and he likewise rejected forcefully any attempt to detach all such laws from the Account of the Beginning (*ma'aseh bereishit*) and the Account of the Chariot (*ma'aseh*

merkavah), which he decisively and prominently identified with natural science and metaphysics, respectively. "These matters [natural science and metaphysics] are referred to throughout the Talmud as *pardes*."[83] The Oral Torah in its total perfection encompasses "the great thing and the lesser thing."[84]

Maimonides' yearning was for "the science of Law in its true sense;"[85] that is, *halakhah* and philosophy in tandem, bound up with each other, "the principles of Torah and the bases of the principles of Torah"[86] yoked together. The Torah is a hendiadys, and it may not be sundered. Maimonides interpreted the Talmud and summarized Israel's laws and practices, but it was also he who established the principles of faith and forcefully insisted that Jews energetically and devotedly study those principles in depth, each person in accordance with his ability. The Torah simply may not be compartmentalized. The spiritual ideal hovering before his eyes, which he hoped would come to pass in the time of the Messiah, was that "Israel be free [to engage] in Torah and its wisdom… they will be…great sages who know concealed matters, and they will attain knowledge of their creator to the extent mankind is capable."[87] In short, he appears as a halakhist craving knowledge of God, love of God, and service of God, and so his religious-ethical image took shape. His powerful yearning for spiritual experience entranced and excited his contemporaries and all who have come since.

Maimonides' teachings are grounded on the express recognition that the details of *halakhah* and the fundamentals of belief are bound together in a natural and vital way and must forever remain so in Jewish consciousness. The emphasis on that point requires recourse to the spiritual; more precisely, to the spiritual strain within Judaism, which incorporates principles of the highest importance in Maimonides' teachings. That is the central idea later to be embodied in the concept of "soul of the Torah" or "interiority of the Torah," corresponding to "perfection of the soul" or "perfecting the soul," the fundamental idea that comprehending the interiority of the Torah is a precondition to perfecting the soul, and that doing so is what the Torah and the commandments intend.

Around the time the *Mishneh Torah* was published, we find sages directing their attention to the duality within Maimonides' unified teachings. R. Jonathan ha-Kohen of Lunel writes:

> And in the mystery of the Talmud God gave him a well-taught tongue. He traversed the sea of understanding and triumphed,

knowing how to sustain the weary, taking the greatness of the Torah to the extreme,[88] teaching to distinguish between holy and profane and between impure and pure, traversing river and stream in the Torah of God, immersed in the wellspring of belief in Torah, sowing the seed of holiness, tearing the kingdom of impurity from himself... the explanation in the *Mishneh Torah* illuminated the dark reaches of the world, and it explained great and hidden things.[89]

R. Abraham, Maimonides' son, constantly emphasizes the need to combine involvement with "the principles of our religion, which are the unity of the Creator and His sanctity" with the study of "the deliberations of Abayye and Rava, the parry and riposte, the problem and its resolution." He directs attention to the fact that

> my father and teacher of blessed memory, dealt with this matter at length in his treatise, for it is the essence of Torah and the foundation of fear, love, and service [of God]. And he explained [the point] and brought several proofs, [arrived at both] through reason and through the words of the Torah, the prophets, and the Sages, as he wrote in his books that clarify knowledge, the *Guide of the Perplexed* and *Sefer ha-Madda*... These treatises by my father and teacher of blessed memory—the great treatise that he composed in the holy tongue and is called *Mishneh Torah* and the treatise that he composed in the language of Ishmael [Arabic] and called *Guide of the Perplexed*...have spread all across the sea and to many places, and they have been useful to Israel in the precision of their belief and the light of their wisdom.[90]

The comments of R. Isaac ibn Latif are particularly important in this regard:

> Until the *ga'on Rabbenu* Moses son of *Rabbenu* Maimon arose...and worked to prepare a single comprehensive treatise. And his first intention there was to explain the principles of unity and the roots of faith...and that was also the intention of the first Talmud...and the second intention set by the *ga'on* of blessed memory was to compile everything that followed clearly from these matters, that is, the subject matter of the Talmud and the necessary corollaries of the first principles, without setting out to mention this one's rationale or that one's opinion but only the clear opinion in accordance with which the *halakhah* was determined.[91]

So, too, should we understand the remarkable words of R. Sheftel Horowitz, at the beginning of his book *Shefa Tal*:

> My masters and teachers, God's holy ones and servants of the Most High...the great rabbi...whose steps never stumbled, wherever he

ventured, that is, the rabbi, *Rabbenu* Moses ben Maimon, may the memory of the righteous and holy be for a blessing, and the great rabbi, the holy light…, that is, *Rabbenu* Moses Cordovero, may the memory of the righteous and holy be for a blessing, of both of whom we may say "from Moses to Moses none has arisen like Moses"—the one in divine philosophy and the other in divine *kabbalah*; they were worthy and caused the masses to be worthy.

What Maimonides and R. Moses Cordovero shared—enabling the pious Kabbalist R. Sheftel Horowitz to apply the well-known adage to both of them despite their conspicuous and profound differences and the differing contents of their analytical-religious teachings—was their engagement with meta-halakhic matters, with the Torah's interiority, each in accord with his conception and principles.*

This emphasis is an important component of Maimonides' distinctiveness as the archetypical comprehensive sage, the master of the entire, comprehensive teaching, directing highly focused attention toward the most elemental of all the elements, the knowledge of God.

(3) In this connection, we must speak for a minute of the *Guide of the Perplexed*, the crowning glory of Jewish philosophical literature, a book that symbolizes the pinnacle of Jewish religious thought and the goal of its aspirations. Maimonides' disciples, who remained devoted to philosophical inquiry and yearned to disseminate religious rationalism, saw this composition as a splendid achievement and held it in esteem as "great in stature and usefulness."[92] R. Jonathan ha-Kohen of Lunel said of it, "Let not a wise man exalt in his wisdom (Jer. 9:22) but in understanding and knowing it [that is, the *Guide of the Perplexed*]." R. Joseph ibn Kaspi forcefully and fervently declared "Since God's Torah, nothing has been written like it." It is important to note that here, too, Maimonides himself determined that "no book at all has been written regarding them [that is, these philosophical matters] within our nation during the time of this exile;"[93] he thus saw himself as reestablishing anew the importance of philosophical thought as an honored and essential component of the Oral Torah. His disciples followed suit and went even further in setting his philosophical work as the pillar of all religious thought. In doing so, of

---

* See also the instructive comments of R. Joseph Karo (*Kesef Mishneh* on *Hilkhot Yesodei ha-Torah* 4:13): "For the subject treated in the Account of the Chariot is the Creator, may He be exalted, in the view of both the sages of *kabbalah* and the sages of [philosophic] inquiry.

course, they sought to grant the *Guide* the same standing as the *Mishneh Torah*, as a work departing from the flow of history and moving to a plane that transcends time and space.

In any event, the *Guide* rounded out the perfection and comprehensiveness of Maimonides' intellectual enterprise and bolstered his image as one who encompassed all of Judaism—its laws and its beliefs alike. The *Guide*, with all its ramifications, adds an important building block to Maimonides' structure and promotes the concept of its author as a one-of-a-kind phenomenon. Maimonides, who managed to restore lost dimensions of the Torah and to uncover broad halakhic areas that had been closed and neglected, unambiguously proclaimed as well his belief that philosophy was vital to religion. He taught man to aspire to broaden the scope of his intellectual cognition, making full use of the capacity he was given. Maimonides sensed and stressed that Judaism's intellectual content had been denigrated and its philosophical bases damaged; and he saw a need to correct that situation. He was "the sage who encompassed what was encompassed within the two sorts of perfection." It is extremely important to note and firmly emphasize that the two perfections are reflected in the *Mishneh Torah*; that great treatise incorporates both the principles of law and the fundamentals of belief, a blending of *halakhah* and thought that includes, in concentrated form, its author's speculative teachings. No artificial divide should be erected between the talmudic and the philosophical; both are evident in the *Mishneh Torah* (and even in the *Commentary on the Mishnah*).

Maimonides' disciples regarded his two treatises, and the sources of information on which they depend, as complementary, together embodying the pinnacle of perfection. That assessment is nicely reflected in R. Hayyim Ya'ir Bachrach's concise statement quoted earlier: "For is there anyone so blind as to not see and understand from his writings the great extent of his grasp of the entire Torah together with all seven sciences, to the point that they said of him...." That is, what justifies the distinctive motto "From Moses to Moses none has arisen like Moses" is Maimonides' having been a comprehensive sage, one who joins Torah and philosophy and draws on all the treasures of Torah and science. R. M. Alshakar, in rejecting the attack on Maimonides by R. Shem Tov, author of *Sefer ha-Emunot*, gives prominence to this overpowering command of Torah and philosophy together and stresses that this mastery is dependent on extra-Talmudic sources of information: "and it is known that these and similar matters cannot be apprehended by a person solely from the Talmud, but require many preliminaries from the intellect." In other words, this, too, is a decisive component of Maimonides' perfection.

It is noteworthy that many worthy people of all sorts—philosophers and kabbalists, Hasidim and advocates of the Musar movement, preachers and writers, and, most prominently, halakhists—disregarded Maimonides' guidance and studied the *Guide* piecemeal, drawing from it whatever individual ideas they wished. Brilliant insights, original explanations of Scripture, sharp analysis and engaging commentary—all were gleaned from his writings and used in Jewish thought and literature. Even those who distanced themselves from his method and his way took advantage of the light of his inspiration. Readers throughout the ages, to this very day, consistently turned to Maimonides, seeing in him a superior teacher, a fount of wisdom and sensitivity, of speculative and philosophical openness and breadth, of clear theological rigor and consistently pure morality, of tradition and devotion, of innovation and depth; a man of Halakhah and of faith, one "whose soul demanded to find out acceptable words."[94] His teaching, in all its details and innovations (if not always in all its generalizations and principles) was conceived as *philosophia perennis*, a system having eternal elements in that it deals with eternal subjects.[*]

On the other hand, those who objected to philosophy saw the *Guide* as seriously flawed, a deviant work better not to have been written. Maimonides was not spared denunciation and scorn, murmuring and hostility, slings and arrows. As we know, the *Guide* and *Sefer ha-Madda* were sentenced to be burned less than thirty years after Maimonides' death. (The common fate of the two works provides evidence that even their denigrators recognized their unity and the well-rounded quality of their author's teaching.) History plays no favorites, and Maimonides received more than his share of attention from all manner of sharp critics. It is clear that the *Guide* generated in some readers an attitude of hostility, and its author was well aware of the prospects and risks of that happening. Even with respect to the *Mishneh Torah*, Maimonides accurately foresaw[95] that the inclusion within it of "fundamentals of belief" would fan the critical flames and augment the reservations harbored by many about his monumental work, and that

---

[*] It is instructive to review the leading texts of Hasidism as well as the basic texts of the Musar movement, to see the extent to which Maimonides is used selectively and strategically, consistent with the notion of *philosophia perennis*.

opponents would attack its formulation of the fundamentals of belief. But he never retreated, and the compositions appeared as he had planned.

In assessing Maimonides' image, however, we must note that just as the *Guide* alone could not have created or sustained the unique conception we have set out to reconstruct and describe, neither did it have the capacity to negate or weaken it. All the varied critiques of the *Guide* could not diminish the assessment of Maimonides' greatness that was based on his great treatise dealing with all the laws of the Torah. In kabbalistic circles, for example, we encounter: (1) those who forcefully rejected Maimonides' speculative teachings; (2) those who attempted to construct a bridge between *kabbalah* and philosophy and show that the two systems really are one; (3) those who, despite their intense opposition to religious rationalism, nevertheless defended Maimonides, distanced him from his translators and disciples (who had been accused of distorting and deviating from his words), and distinguished between him and philosophy in general; and (4) those who in effect transformed Maimonides into a kabbalist and argued that, in any event, his philosophical teachings have no force. But the attitudes of these varied groups toward the *Mishneh Torah* do not differ substantially; all assign it primacy, and all acknowledge its uniqueness: none like Maimonides had arisen before, and after him none has arisen (or will arise).

The biting opponents became advocates; and along with their gentle dissents or blatant disdain, their specific detailed criticisms or general opposition in principle, they praised his mighty Torah-scholarship enterprise. "And recent scholars have already raised strong claims against him and beaten this opinion of his on the head," writes R. Isaac Arama;[96] the author of *Shenei Luhot ha-Berit* (*Shelah*) says that "the sages of truth have already beaten him on his head."[97] But these beatings, strong and firm enough on their own, did nothing to diminish his stature. As the *Maggid* said to R. Joseph Karo, "But the Torah defends itself." Moreover, these opponents themselves did not rest content with abstract praise; they often grounded their novellae and analyses on his words. It is told that R. Jonah of Gerona, a great halakhist and sharp opponent of Maimonides during the fierce and tragic first Maimonidean controversy of the early thirteenth century, at the end of his days "would mention *Rabbenu* Moses' treatise in connection with each and every *halakhah*, saying '*Rabbenu* Moses wrote thus in his composition, and his words seem proper to me.'"[98] In the heat of the controversy, Rashba recounts:

And who honors the Rabbi and his words more than we? We have made for him a throne to sit on at the head; we say to him, "our master, please teach us;" we constantly mention his name in the study halls and his holy opinions. Through us, his words will ascend on wings of eagles; though our interpretations, his lips speak from the grave.[99]

We may say that Rashba's words are equally valid for his great teacher Nahmanides, his great student the Ritva, and all who follow them. "The Rabbi's Treatise" became a pillar of Talmud study and of profound delving into the Oral Torah. In other words, the denunciations ceased, and even in times of raging tempers, engagement with the *Mishneh Torah* continued and became more intense and more profound.

Particularly instructive are the remarks of R. Shem Tov ben Shem Tov in *Sefer ha-Emunot*; he is mentioned by R. Judah Aryeh Modena as one of Maimonides' principal adversaries and denigrators, along with R. Me'ir ibn Gabbai. R. Shem Tov sallies forth in his book against "the fraudulent ideas to be found among the philosophers, such as the author of the book *Guide of the Perplexed*;" yet he calmly includes, in the same work, a sentence such as: "And the great rabbi, who built a mighty tower and fortress of the Talmud,[100] built as a citadel and filled with pure gold of Ophir [cf. Isa. 13:12] from *Sifra*, *Sifre*, *Tosefta*, *Mekhilta*, and the entire Babylonian and Jerusalem Talmud." In another passage, in which he replicates this praise for the *Mishneh Torah*, he comments, "And if criticisms alighted on some of his opinions, so, too, did criticisms alight on those greater and more praiseworthy than he." In other words, criticism does not diminish the greatness of a man and his *oeuvre*. The Italian Kabbalist R. Elijah Hayyim Guinzano states explicitly that "my wish is to defend him for having done wonderfully in creating his talmudic treatises." Similarly, in the eighteenth century, R. Aviad Sar Shalom Basilea, one of the *me'assefim*,[101] not of Mendelssohn but of the camp of great Kabbalists who profoundly criticized Maimonides' philosophical thought, publicly declares of the *Mishneh Torah*: "No treatise as fine as it has been produced anywhere in Israel's dispersion."[102]

Despite the murmuring that recurs from time to time, we see a unique tendency to stand up for Maimonides' work. Even those who impeach and find flaws in his philosophical teachings soften their criticism, defend him, and attribute to him proper intentions and pure, refined motives. They apply to him the rule, which he had invoked in his own defense, that "It is time to do something for the Lord, for they have infringed Your Law,"[103] or they say that all his actions, including those of which they disapprove, were for the sake of Heaven. The comments of Maharal, one of Maimonides' greatest detractors, typify this approach:

> And I say that because in the generation of the Rabbi, of blessed memory, they were attracted to the thinking of gentile wise men on whom the light of the Torah had not shone, they being the philosophers, and if he had not interpreted Scripture for them in accordance with their views, there was a risk of something even worse—that, God forbid, they might not have left room for Scripture—and for that reason, he explained Scripture to them in accordance with their thinking.[104]

He later says: "And even here it appears that Maimonides of blessed memory wrote these things to draw the people's hearts to the Torah, as we have seen before."*

We see reflected here a widespread historical notion that Maimonides' involvement with philosophy was largely, if not exclusively, apologetic; that it was directed outward or conditioned on an external challenge. According to this view, Maimonides became involved in philosophy because of the needs of the time, but that involvement, though positively regarded because of his historical circumstances, should not be considered a binding precedent for future generations.

As an aside, it is worth noting that even the intra-philosophical criticism, seen for example in the writings of *Rabbenu* Nissim of Gerona, R. Hasdai Crescas, R. Isaac Abarbanel, R. Joseph Ya'abez, R. Isaac Arama, and others, did not diminish Maimonides' greatness or centrality. And even the various modern critiques of Maimonides as philosopher, raised by the schools of Mendelssohn, Formstecher, R. Samson Raphael Hirsch, Hermann Cohen, or Franz Rosenzweig, or by Peretz Smolinskin and his circle or Ze'ev Ya'avez and others in eastern Europe, have had no bearing on the recognition that his enterprise was unique. If you find scholars of competing views who agree on Maimonides' greatness, you can anticipate a determination confirming his uniqueness.

---

* R. Hasdai Crescas likewise observes (*Or ha-Shem*, Introduction): "And the Rabbi's intention here was proper." See also *Sefer ha-Tashbez*, part 1, topic 63, p. 23b, end, where R. Simeon b. Zemah 'Duran notes: "or, perhaps, the Rabbi, of blessed memory, exaggerated here ... to give support to those grasping at straws...as he does in all his essays to strengthen weak hands and faltering knees, which his words will raise up."

(4) The unprecedented comprehensiveness of Maimonides' writings means that they deal with an abundance of subjects not previously treated. For various reasons, some related to the temper of the times and some to the sages' own inclinations, the study of Torah and of science had narrowed in scope since the completion of the Talmud, and essential portions of the Torah fell into neglect during the generations preceding Maimonides. Maimonides restored the crown of Torah to its former glory, reviving the study of many areas in a manner clearly marked by his consummate originality.

This all-encompassing originality manifests itself in many details and novellae. It is tied to a breathtaking, pervasive creativity that enthralled ensuing generations, who found it a rich source of stunning illuminations and provocative concepts. Since no one had preceded Maimonides in these areas, his words instantly became the point of departure for those who followed; but he shed new light as well even on matters that had previously been examined. He made the *Mishneh Torah* a home for all of Torah and all of science and became a ubiquitously leading voice, an anchor for many later discussions. Every inquiry of his, every formulation, every summary and every innovation became a pillar of *halakhah* and of thought, a literary and conceptual focus of Torah wisdom, a spur to profound learning and ongoing creativity. Every spark given off by his hammer ignited a blazing torch. One could say of him that "he had no teacher and no instructor" (using his own formulation in the first chapter of *Mishneh Torah, Hilkhot Akum*), but he was the teacher of many others who learned from him and did as they saw him do.

Subjects such as repentance, charity, wisdom, ethics, prayer, fasting, and honoring the Sabbath and taking pleasure in it; sacrifices, the sanctity of the Land of Israel, the sanctity of Jerusalem, the sanctity of houses in walled cities, ritual purity and impurity, sanctifying the New Moon, and the Sanhedrin; love, fear, faith, sanctification of God's name, joy, religious intent, knowledge of God, *imitatio dei*, theodicy, and true religion; legal conditions, acquisition of property, engaging in business, compulsion, vows, drawn water, sabbatical year treatment of loans and land, robbery and lost property; rejoicing on festivals, hospitality, *mazah* guarded against leaven from the time the grain is harvested, recounting the Exodus from Egypt, writing a Torah scroll; love for one's fellow, love for a stranger, love for a woman, love for all of God's creatures; prophet, high priest, king, stranger, resident alien, Abraham our father, Moses our teacher,

King David, the King Messiah; disqualified priests, disqualified sacrifices, disqualified witnesses, commandment fulfilled through a transgression, questioning of witnesses; the bases of the Oral Torah, interpretation of *aggadah*, rationales for the commandments, interpretation of the written Torah, kingship, messianism, the world to come, prophecy, miracles, free will, divine providence, the fundamentals of belief—these subjects (and many others) cannot be approached without taking account of all of Maimonides' works and, first and foremost, of the *Mishneh Torah*. They are an imposing citadel, a source of endless inspiration.

It is said of Plato that whichever way we turn, we encounter him on the way back. I have my doubts that this can be truly said of Plato (notwithstanding Whitehead's famous observation that the history of Western philosophy is a series of footnotes to Plato). But the adage certainly applies to Maimonides, whose place it aptly describes. He is a presence every way we turn, facilitating our every inquiry; wherever we go, we see his footprints. Even those who fragmented his comprehensive and orderly teachings acknowledged that he encompassed all. Masters of Scripture, *mishnah*, or *gemara*; halakhists, aggadists, philosophers, kabbalists and ethicists—all have been warmed by his glow or by the sparks he threw off. But the principal, fundamental point is that the world of *halakhah*, in its widest and deepest sense, was broadened and expanded by him.

(5) A secondary factor underlying Maimonides' uniqueness follows from his path-breaking completeness, is intertwined with it, and even fortifies it. I am referring to his precise writing style and the express demands he makes of his readers as they study his words.

Time and again, Maimonides emphasized the precision and meticulousness of his writing. Everything is deliberate and exact; each idea is formulated with great care, every juxtaposition of distinct subjects is calculated, every sentence is written with due consideration, every example cited has significance, and every word fills a specific need. Nothing was written by chance, by inadvertence, or solely for rhetorical effect.

The extreme meticulousness and intense attentiveness demanded of every author are described by Maimonides in his *Iggeret ha-Shemad* as follows:

> Among the things you should know is that a person should not speak and discourse publicly until he has gone over what it is he wishes to say one, two, three, or four times, reviewing it well; and

only after should he speak. And so said [the Sages], peace be upon
them, and they cited proof from the wording of Scripture (Job
28:27-28): "Then He saw it and enumerated it; he readied it and
probed it," and only after that did He speak. This refers to what a
man must say orally; but regarding what a man plans to inscribe
with his hand and write in a book, it would be fitting that he first
review it a thousand times, were it only possible.

We may assume these words guided him as he wrote. And can it be that
R. Joseph b. Todros ha-Levi had this passage in mind when he described
Maimonides' prose in these terms: "He saw and enumerated it; readied it
and probed it."

Maimonides says of himself "I did not write it however it came to me;
rather, it was after contemplation and due consideration and examination of
correct and incorrect opinions."[105] Elsewhere he says "None of it was attained
without my having exerted great effort in clarifying it in all its aspects."[106]
The following sentence is typical: "For the diction of this Treatise has been
chosen not haphazardly, but with great exactness and exceeding precision."[107]
Maimonides' tribute to brevity likewise proclaims the premise that every word
must count; his concentrated, carefully honed style, pure and incandescent,
reflects the principle that "when speaking words of Torah or words of science,
a person's words should be few and their content abundant"[108] or that "among
the signs of a sage is brevity, and among the signs of a fool is verbosity."[109]
Maimonides uses the resonant phrase *"Kab ve-naki"* [used to describe a
sage's rulings as few in number but always authoritative][110] to accentuate his
consistent quest for concentrated, carefully honed, on-target writing, worded
clearly and concisely:

> All our treatises are *kab ve-naki*. Our intention is not to increase the
> size of the books or to spend time on something unproductive.[111]

This meticulousness and care in writing imply a corresponding attribute with
respect to reading. Maimonides emphatically demands that *quid pro quo*:

> Review these words of mine many times, contemplate them well;
> and if your mind assures you that you understand our point from
> one reading or ten, God knows that reassurance is a falsehood. Do
> not hasten it.[112]

And elsewhere:

> And if you wish to have all-encompassing knowledge, contemplate
> our words on that matter from beginning to end and examine them
> well. And do not read them hastily and superficially; rather, read
> them calmly and reflectively.[113]

In response to a question by R. Samuel ha-Levi, head of the Academy, he comments, "He should have regarded the precision of our wording."[114]

Maimonides' dreams for his great treatise were not realized, and the work did not become established as the nation's book of dispositive rulings. But history proved kinder to his requests and directions regarding precision and detail: scholars accepted his guidance and even augmented it. Everyone drew practical and academic conclusions from his precisely controlled language and lent an attentive ear to catch every nuance suggested by it. The need to read closely became axiomatic in studying Maimonides' works. He came to be widely depicted as one who placed crowns on the words of the Torah, and sages throughout the generations interpreted and drew conclusions from each and every jewel and facet of those crowns. Every variation in wording, whether large or small, every detail of terminology, expression, enumeration, or classification—all of them merited attention. He became teacher and goad, instructor and prod. Even his silence taught lessons: major principles of Torah were derived from his deletions, omitted examples, and silence in one context regarding rulings made in another. Maimonides' carefully formulated and consummately refined words were processed through the minds and pens of scholars of all schools, and all of them interpreted those measured words, drawing from them inspiration and guidance, abstract halakhic analysis together with practical halakhic rulings.

Moreover, Maimonides' achievements were so great and so natural that many perspectives, components, and illuminations included in his oeuvre were instantly accepted and taken as self-evident, as a "clear, plausible, correct"[115] consensus. His great treatise incorporates a plethora of novellae, but because he could blend his source material and his original contributions so naturally and with such creative elegance, one can hardly tell that the source material has been digested and reworked. The novellae are incorporated within the sources, as if they were openly and explicitly stated within them. We must recall that while Maimonides repeatedly and forcefully stressed the innovative character of his work with respect to form, structure, and scope, he tended to obscure the innovative qualities of his exegesis and reasoning. He regarded it as preferable not to highlight his independent exegeses and original insights, instead presenting his ideas as simple and conventional, avoiding any self-glorification. He concealed his vast and creative scholarship and presented his words so as to make them appear self-evident from the source material, subject to no challenge or reservation, doubt or hesitation.*

In effect, one can say that where Maimonides curtailed his comments, the sages of succeeding generations explained them at length in various ways. His innovations burst forth and proclaimed "Explain me!" and Maimonides' students heeded the call, again and again explaining, interpreting, and finding new meaning.

Inference and interpretation went hand-in-hand; that is the basis for the comment of R. Samuel of the House of Kal'i in the mid-sixteenth century: "One can [draw inferences by] read[ing] his works closely and engaging in fine argumentation over them, just as one can do with the *Gemara* itself."[116] R. Wolf ha-Levi of Baskowitz went a step further, stating "I know, to be sure, that he did not intend this understanding, but the spirit of the Lord spoke within him and caused his tongue to speak," and later, "Is there anything not alluded to in *Mishneh Torah*? For the spirit of the Lord spoke in him and caused his tongue to speak."[117] We see here a tendency on the part of commentators not merely to discover sources that may be hidden from the eye but to propose all manner of new interpretations and even to attribute to Maimonides opinions, intentions, and rationales that clearly never entered his mind, on the premise that it is proper to do so when dealing with this one-of-a-kind treatise.**

Maimonides knew that his great treatise would be subjected to criticism, but he believed as well that after some time had gone by, it would be accepted throughout Israel "and they would have recourse to no other book of *halakhah*."[118] But while the treatise was accepted by the

---

* When asked why he had included a particular physical flaw in his enumeration of those rendering an animal unfit to eat (*Hilkhot Shehitah* 8:16)—a flaw having no explicit source or precedent—he calmly replied: "As for your remark that you see no reference in the composition to anyone having included that flaw, there are many things that the exegetes failed to mention because they did not pay attention to them; but when a person understands such matters, they will make sense" (*Responsa*, Responsum 315, p. 585.). Which is to say, it is necessary to deduce or reconstruct the exegesis embodied or concealed within the ruling. And, in fact, he concealed a great deal of excellent exegesis within his rulings.

** It is worth noting that R. Menahem Mendel of Vitebsk (*Sefer Peri ha-Arez* [Jerusalem, 1969], 200, *Parashat Lekh-Lekha*) speaks of the *Guide* in similar terms: "And Maimonides of blessed memory rationalized the commandment of circumcision as a way to weaken the sexual urge. And the truth is that he, of blessed memory, uttered from his holy mouth true words related to supernal matters even though he did not intend them.

nation, it was not necessarily seen as the final word concerning practice but as the end of talmudic analysis and as a source of perennial challenge, under the rubric of "the words of the Sages are like prods." The decisive fact from a historical perspective is that, be the reasons what they may, the treatise's vitality continued to renew itself and grow stronger on its own.

(6) The end of this process, through which the close reading and analysis of the *Mishneh Torah* were sharpened even beyond what Maimonides had demanded or expected, was the transformation of the treatise from a book of rulings into an exegetical work. That transformation seems to have begun soon after the book's appearance and circulation, and an account of its evolution from the end of Maimonides' life to our own day would depict a pivotal religious-literary story of great importance. For now, it suffices to mention the explicit evidence in the comments of R. Menahem ha-Me'iri toward the end of the thirteenth century, in which he provides fascinating information about how Torah was studied in his milieu and speaks of the exegetical role of the *Mishneh Torah*:

> As God lives, it often happened that I thought I had attained the true understanding of a halakhic matter, but when I pursued knowledge about the ruling in the works of the early writers, and especially in the works of the Rabbi of blessed memory [Maimonides], which served me as the final probe and final guidance[119] regarding all the treatises that provide rulings, I sensed within myself that I did not have a proper grasp of the passage's meaning.[120]

In other words, even as outstanding a talmudic interpreter as R. Menahem ha-Me'iri felt obliged to go back and restudy passages in light of Maimonides' rulings. Consideration of Maimonides' writings provokes and encourages one to return to the talmudic text, skeptical of the conventional interpretation and eager to consider alternative readings.* "But for his treatise about the Torah, we would not have full understanding of the Talmud."[121]

---

* R. David b. R. Reuben Bonfid, one of Nahmanides' disciples, notes at the end of a comprehensive give-and-take: "That is the proper order of the entire passage, and the interpretation by Rashi, of blessed memory, does not succeed, and I learned this from the words of R. Moses b. R. Maimon, of blessed memory." We see that R. David reconstructed his interpretation of the entire passage (*Pesahim* 86) on the basis of Maimonides' ruling in *Hilkhot Korban Pesah* 9:6. See the novellae of R. David b. R. Reuben Bonfid on Tractate *Pesahim* (Jerusalem, 2000), 338. This incident does not appear exceptional; rather, it is typical of the method of study taking shape.

This observation embodies the clear recognition that the *Mishneh Torah* is not only a vast work of practical *Halakhah* accompanied by a Hebrew translation of portions of the Talmud; it is also, in effect, a comprehensive and original commentary on the Talmud. Each summary or suggested ruling reflects exegetical perspectives, particular assumptions, latent analytical steps, new proofs, non-routine determinations, and unexpected conclusions—all of them requiring study, for they are both a stimulus and a challenge to probe deeply and with originality. Once again, the Me'iri's words resound in our ears:

> And it is apparent to all who understand that in places too numerous to be counted the merit of his treatises and interpretations and their complete perfection in accordance with the truth can be perceived only by one who strives to see how they treat each matter dealt with in the *gemara*, after going over the [talmudic] passage and seeing how he explicated it.[122]

It must be emphasized that Maimonides' greatness does not depend on absolute agreement with him, in the manner of the talmudic interpretation of "And the Lord was with him" (1 Sam. 16:18) to mean "the *halakhah* is everywhere in accordance with his view."[123] Entire communities, to be sure, accepted the *Mishneh Torah* as exclusively authoritative, as we learn from comments by Rashba, Rosh, Ran, Ribash, Tashbez, and others. Even earlier, R. Isaac ibn Latif determined that the treatise had been instantly accepted as a pillar of halakhic ruling: "And the treatise spread to the ends of the Earth, and the Jews heeded it, doing everything as Moses had commanded, and they have articulated laws and instruction in accordance with him going back thirty years from today."[124] Later, R. Hayyim Benvenisti wrote, "All Israel, from East to West, have walked by the light of that treatise."[125] With specific reference to the Jews of Yemen, R. Jacob Saphir commented, "Their principal study is of the *Yad* by Maimonides, of blessed memory, and they determine their laws and practices exclusively in accordance with the opinion of Maimonides, of blessed memory, and they do not diverge from him either toward greater stringency or greater leniency, for only him did they accept as their teacher and judge."[126]

But Maimonides' universally recognized distinctiveness does not rest on full agreement of this sort. We find objections and annotations, disagreements and reservations, comments beginning with "this is not," "he erred in this...," or "one might ask..."; and we find objections (by, for example, Maharal and Maharshal) to his decisional tendencies in general and his *Mishneh Torah* in particular. None of that, however, detracts from his distinctiveness. Rashbash nicely summed up, in the sentence quoted at the beginning of this journey, that fruitful and vital interplay between criticism and esteem:

> And all the authors who came after him, and the commentators who followed in his steps, Muslim and Christian alike, though criticizing him on a few matters, recognize the splendid glory of his majesty and crave his teaching...

All who have studied Maimonides, whether long ago or more recently, have sought to understand the *Mishneh Torah*, plumb its deep meanings, and discover the exegetical underpinnings of its rulings. The following generalization seems fair: The earlier writers were more inclined to "vindicate the righteous one," to defend Maimonides, respond to criticisms, dismiss objections, resolve challenges, clarify the obscure, and "uphold his opinions through the give and take of argument,"[127] all under the rubric of "you are indeed a great scholar, for you have upheld the words of the Sages."[128] The later writers, in contrast, sought primarily to comprehend (and reconstruct) Maimonides' unseen exegetical moves and to explain the numerous disagreements between him and those who differed with him either directly and explicitly or through divergent practical rulings. The *Neziv* described this with memorable directness:

> And our recent rabbis, of blessed memory, favorably regarded Moses, that is, Maimonides, of blessed memory, and wanted very much to understand his opinion, in various places where his way was more exalted than the conventional understanding of the matter as explicated by Rashi, Tosafot, and other commentators. And they already know his great power, even when he is not arguing actively; and he was absorbed in the word of God, that is, *halakhah*, in his wondrous treatise...and not one thing, not one detail, eluded him in the two Talmuds and in every other source or spring from which he drew. Accordingly, they found themselves obliged to slant his opinion by means of close reading and argumentation, extensive or limited, in accordance with the reader's ability...and so, there is no good way to "vindicate the righteous one" other than by saying from the outset that the meaning of the talmudic passage differed in his view from that of his teachers, using a formulation hedged with roses.

In our own day, this theme was stressed by the *ga'on*, R. Yosef Dov Soloveitchik, *zz"l*, in his account of his father's lessons:

> My father and teacher always spoke about Maimonides. And

this was his practice: he would open the *gemara* and read the passage. Then he would say something along the lines of "that is the interpretation of R. Isaac and the Tosafists; now we'll look at Maimonides and see that Maimonides did not interpret it as they did and that he diverged from the simple path."[129]

From one point of view, Maimonides represents an instance of the rabbinic declaration "when he speaks, all are struck dumb."[130] But that was so only briefly; for they soon resumed speaking, deploying the power of what they had learned, and they understood the challenge posed to them by Maimonides' words. Maimonides did not close off the wellsprings of wisdom; rather, he opened them widely, for people learned from him and studied his teachings in depth, thereby gaining strength. Many agreed with R. Menahem ha-Me'iri's statement that "nothing should be added to or taken away from him;"[131] still, in the nature of things, they did add and take away in the course of fruitful, in-depth study. Hundreds and thousands of essays were focused on Maimonides' great treatise; almost every talmudic study and analysis encounters it.

(7) Moreover, knowingly or not, Maimonides stirred and encouraged not only the exegetical process but also the critical enterprise. He provided a justification for criticism, for the fundamental dialectic of authority and autonomy, and he prominently adhered to the fundamental principles that "perfection is God's alone"[132] and "wisdom is greater than the wise man,"[133] as well as the slogan he himself coined: "Accept the truth from whoever expresses it."[134] That justification follows from the fact that Maimonides treated his predecessors the same way: he was the emblem of intellectual daring, and others treated him with similar daring, despite his greatness and authoritativeness. The audacity to disagree with "the great eagle" represented intellectual freedom; as such, it serves as an important force in the development of halakhic and conceptual literature, in all its effervescent freshness.

The Rashba's concise comments on the matter are directly on target:

> I today am the least in all areas of knowledge. Yet even the rabbi, R. Moses wrote [on various matters] in his book and was challenged in thousands of places by two great rabbis, R. Abraham and R. Moses ha-Kohen of blessed memory, and, in fact, one of them must have erred in his ruling, either the rabbi the author or the rabbis who came after him. So who am I that I should not err in one or more rulings?[135]

In his commentary on the mishnaic statement "Who is wise? He who learns from every man," R. Joseph Hiyyun defends the intellectual liberty that underlies criticism, as he considers the standing and fate of Rashi and Maimonides:

> And whom do we have as great in Torah as Rashi, yet his grandson *Rabbenu* Tam disagreed with [some of] his words and nullified them, adducing persuasive arguments and forceful proofs for doing so. And so, too, many disagreed with the Ram[bam], of blessed memory, despite his being one who illuminated the eyes of all Israel.[136]

Particularly striking is this passage in the introduction, by the author's son, to R. David ha-Kohen's book *Migdal David* (on Tractate *Gittin*):

> For it is not at all surprising that humans will err, for they are made of dust; and from Moses to Moses none has arisen like Moses b. Maimon, of blessed memory, yet the Rabad nevertheless responded to him. [137]

And, once again, the author of *Havvot Ya'ir* summed up the matter with characteristic brevity in his critique of Maimonides' listing of the laws regarded as having been given to Moses at Sinai ("*halakhah le-Mosheh mi-Sinai*"):

> And even the greatest of the prophets erred and overlooked a *halakhah*, but his merit was not on that account diminished, God forbid; for who is so blind as not to see and understand from his treatises the great extent of his grasp of all matters?

And in *Ta'am Zekeinim* we find the following written:

> Let it not be a wonder in your eyes and do not be surprised how the Rabbi of blessed memory overlooked all the questions and objections that I have posed against his words. For, in truth, several matters were hidden from those who were great paragons of wisdom, and only later were they revealed to their students.

An on-target slogan is that of R. Menahem Lonzano, who writes, in the context of some critical remarks, "let not the reader be surprised, for I have no obligation to honor him more than the true God is honored."[138]

CONCLUSION

Maimonides is the focus of a dynamic literary reality that adjures the reader to leave room for questioning and challenge, for examining and inquiring, for criticizing and supplementing. It follows that Maimonides' variegation is itself variegated. First and foremost, he erected a spacious literary-conceptual structure, the King's palace. To it was added a multi-faceted bounty of exegetical streams, rising like a stream flowing through the ages. This variegation is the product not of any vagueness in Maimonides' language or obscurity in his style; on the contrary, it results from luminous formulations, great intelligence, and exalted, authoritative language that stirs and excites heart and mind. Readers of the treatise could always find something new in it, in the manner of "any time a man thinks about them, he finds them palatable."[139] Maimonides himself noted in the Introduction to the *Guide* that every reader will derive benefit from the book, each in accordance with his ability, concepts, and aspirations; and that observation is even more applicable to the *Mishneh Torah*, which was intended, the author declares, for both "young and old."* In other words, Maimonides himself was aware of fruitful dialectical elements in his oeuvre. This effervescence added an important element to that oeuvre, one with numerous consequences; its tones resonated in the ears of readers and students.

Finally, it should be noted that an additional layer of distinctiveness is provided by Maimonides' international reputation, which began to spread even during his lifetime and immediately following his death. R. Sheshet ha-Nasi, R. Jonathan ha-Kohen, R. Jacob Antoli, R. Menahem ha-Me'iri, R. Joseph ibn Kaspi, and the Ritva all tell of Maimonides' renown among gentile sages. "He was a banner to the nations" and "a witness to the entire world;" "he is praised even amongst the nations." In our day, R. Abraham Isaac ha-Kohen Kook spoke of "the brilliance of his light, extending across the span of civilized humanity in general."[140]

In the wake of this concept, it is clear that everyone will want to claim a place on Maimonides' family tree. Esteem and approval, authoritativeness and the quest for authority are all intertwined. If Maimonides, in fact, is one-of-a-kind, truly unique in history, and if his scholarly image hovers above history, everyone will try to link up with it, to find or invent some connection or proximity to him. Every development, every movement, every conceptual stirring will try to find an anchor within his thought, broadening the scope of his vast influence.

---

* Consider what Maimonides says as an aside in *Hilkhot Kiddush ha-Hodesh* 11:5—"Lest a gentile or Jewish sage who has studied Greek wisdom contemplate these matters that I am dealing with." He sensed that various types of readers, including gentile sages, would turn to his composition.

The ongoing influence itself is a source of value: special importance attaches to one who occupies a place at the energy source of eternal existence rather than at the shifting periphery.

Influence has many aspects. It can be clear and direct, more or less objective; or it can be ongoing, developing and expanding over the ages. It is as if history continues to take shape even after the death of the influential person, and the line between studying his teachings in depth and making use of those teachings becomes blurry. Some study Maimonides and some use him. If he is so esteemed and so authoritative, every effort will be made to appropriate him for the benefit of some opinion, point of view, or movement, even if the acquisition involves a change of name and form.* This influence is without limit, for it is open to all; and it is rooted in the reconstruction and rewriting of history, in an approach to the past guided by ideology. Maimonides' influence flows like a rising stream, like waters with no end.

---

[1] A quotation from Gen. 12:18 and 21:33, found in numerous manuscripts as a superscription to sections of the *Mishneh Torah—editor's note.*

[2] Pines trans., 515.

[3] Rashbash, *Sefer Milhemet Mizvah*, 21.

[4] *Sotah* 13b. In *Sotah*, the soubriquet is applied to the biblical Moses, *Mosheh Rabbenu.* The author here applies it to Maimonides, *Rabbenu Mosheh—translator's note.*

[5] *Commentary on the Mishnah*, *Bekhorot* 4:4. Cf. *Hagigah* 5b.

[6] R. Moses Nahmanides, "*Terem E'eneh*," An Epistle to the Rabbis of France, in *The Writings of Nahmanides*, ed. H. D. Chavel (Hebrew), vol. 1, p. 340.

[7] *Responsa Rashba*, ed. H. Z. Dimitrovsky, vol. 2, ch. 110, p. 784.

[8] R. Menahem ben Zerah, *Zedah la-Derekh* (Warsaw, 1880), 6.

[9] *Responsa Maharshdam*, *Yoreh De'ah*, sec. 192.

[10] R. Judah Alharizi, *Sefer Tahkemoni*, ed. Toporovski, part 50, p. 388.

[11] *Hilkhot Yesodei ha-Torah* 7:2.

[12] *Kitab al-Ras'il* (Paris, 1871), 30.

[13] Ibid., 15. R. Me'ir Abolafia goes on to say that "if you say he is a man and there is none

---

* A prominent example is Maimonides' influence in the generation of the *me'assefim* and early Enlightenment: Maimonides' teachings did not suit them, but his symbolism was so great and so profound that they were forced to identify with him and identify him with their movements.

in Israel like him now, he is as you say."

[14] Ibn Tibbon had in his possession a copy of the *Mishneh Torah* edited from Maimonides' own manuscript, and R. Me'ir Abolafia consulted him when he needed to verify a reading, as recounted by R. Menahem ha-Me'iri. *Kiryat Sefer*, 46.

[15] Commentary on Ecclesiastes, ms. Parma 272, p. 7a.

[16] *Kerem Hemed* 5, 9.

[17] Nahmanides, *Terem E'eneh*, 340.

[18] *Responsa Ribash*, sec. 45.

[19] *Responsa Maharshdam, Yoreh De'ah*, sec. 192.

[20] *Seder Eliyahu Zuta*, 165.

[21] *Lehem Shamayim, Pe'ah* 7:2.

[22] The mechanism on the High Priest's breastplate through which he received divine communications. *Responsa Maharam* (Lvov, 1860), sec. 426.

[23] The High Priest's breastplate. *Kitab al-Ras'il*, 16.

[24] *Sefer ha-Kabbalah*, ed. G. Cohen, 62. These words are repeated verbatim by R. Menahem ben Zerah in his *Zedah la-Derekh*, 6.

[25] *Sefer ha-Kabbalah*, 43.

[26] R. Zerahyah ha-Levi, Introduction to *Sefer ha-Ma'or* on the Rif.

[27] Ms. Parma 272, p. 9.

[28] A rabbinic image for one who is both erudite and highly skilled in argumentation—*editor's note.*

[29] *Responsa Ribash*, sec. 394.

[30] *Sefer Tavnit ha-Bayit*, Introduction.

[31] Introduction to *Midrash Rut he-Hadash* with collected comments of the Vilna Ga'on.

[32] Cf. *Sotah* 47b. The word here translated "great scholar" is *eshkol* which, by play on words, is taken to imply "one who encompasses everything" (*ish she-ha-kol bo*)—*translator's note.*

[33] *Kovez Iggerot*, part 2, sec. 32.

[34] That limitation may appear implicitly as early as in the Book of Ben Sira (44:1), which states "I will praise pious men, our fathers in their generations." We should also note Maimonides' comment that "'He was wiser than all men' (1 Kings 5:11, said of Solomon)—but not [wiser] than Moses, for in saying "than all men," he means to say than all men of his generation" (*Guide* 3:54).

[35] *Responsa Maharam Lublin*, sec. 51.

[36] *Ari Nohem*, 4.

[37] *Tif'eret le-Mosheh*, Introduction, pp. 400-401.

[38] *Sefer Mizvot Gadol*, Introduction.

[39] *Responsa Rosh* 94:5; Maharshal, *Yam shel Shelomoh, Hullin*, Introduction; see also *Responsa Havvot Ya'ir*, sec. 192.

[40] *Sefer Mizvot Gadol*, Introduction.

[41] See in this regard the comments of R. Joseph Delmedigo quoted above.

[42] Cf. Ex. 2:10, the etymology of biblical Moses' name—*editor's note.*

[43] *Responsa*, ed. Y. Blau, vol. 3, p. 51.

[44] *Kovez Teshuvot ha-Rambam*, part 3, p. 5.

[45] Ibid., part 3, p. 6.

[46] JQR 25:427.

[47] *Ke'arat Kesef*, 30.

[48] *Sha'ar Kavod* 5, 3.

[49] *Kovez Teshuvot ha-Rambam*, part 3, p. 14.

[50] Pressburg, 1838.

[51] See Maimonides' explanation of these terms in *Guide* 3:54 and his comments in *Mishneh Torah, Hilkhot Aveil* 13:10.

[52] *Zava'ot Ge'onei Yisra'el* (ed. Abrahams), 148.

[53] *Sefer ha-Sod*, 4.

[54] *Sefer ha-Emunot*, ch. 2, p. 14b.

[55] *Or ha-Hayyim*, ch. 9.

[56] Ibid., ch. 12.

[57] *Responsa Rema*, 60:67.

[58] Hida, *Shem ha-Gedolim*, "R. Mosheh Ga'on."

[59] E.g., *Sefer ha-Gilgulim*, 78.

[60] In the original Hebrew, the couplets are rhymed—*translator's note.*

[61] See *Yeshurun*, ed. Kaback, 8 (1875): 39.

[62] Cf. Song of Songs 2:15. *Takhkemoni*, part 46.

[63] *Guide* 2:25.

[64] Lit, "the mighty hand." The numerical value of *yad* is fourteen, the number of major divisions of the work—*translator' note.*

[65] *Kovez Teshuvot ha-Rambam*, part 3, p. 21b.

[66] *Responsa Havvot Ya'ir*, sec. 192. The reference, of course, is to R. Yed'ayah ha-Penini, who wrote "Like whom there is none among all the sages of Israel since the completion of the Talmud."

[67] *Ari Nohem*, 4.

[68] *Seder Eliyahu Zuta*, 165.

[69] Ibid., 170.

[70] *Sefer Merkevet ha-Mishneh*, Introduction.

[71] Letter of Maimonides to R. Pinhas ha-Dayyan.

[72] *Hilkhot Aveil* 13:10.

[73] *Sefer Derekh Hokhmah* .

[74] See *Bava Batra* 75b.

[75] *Milhemet Mizvah*.

[76] *Sefer ha-Mizvot*, Introduction.

[77] See *Eruvin* 54a and *Gittin* 60b

[78] R. David b. R. Samuel ha-Kokhavi, *Sefer ha-Batim*, 27.

[79] *Mishneh Torah, Hilkhot Kiddush ha-Hodesh*, end.

[80] R. Y. Kafah, *Sefer ha-Madda*, 9.

[81] Me'iri, *Beit ha-Behirah, Berakhot*, Introduction, p. 25.

[82] See the passage published by S. M. Stern, "R. Judah Alharizi in Praise of Maimonides," in *Hagut Ivrit be-Eiropah*, 100.

[83] *Hilkhot Talmud Torah* 1:12. [*Pardes*, literally an orchard, came to be a reference to the manifold ways, including the esoteric, in which the Torah can be interpreted and the wisdom associated with those interpretations—*translator's note*.]

[84] *Hilkhot Yesodei ha-Torah* 4:13; *Guide* 1:71.

[85] *Guide*, Introduction.

[86] *Commentary on the Mishnah, Hagigah* 2:1, end.

[87] *Hilkhot Melakhim* 14:5.

[88] Lit. "until David exceeded." Cf. 1 Sam. 20:41—*translator's note*.

[89] *Responsa of Maimonides* (ed. Blau), vol. 3, pp. 51-52. (The Hebrew consists mostly of rhymed couplets—*translator's note*).

[90] *Milhemot ha-Shem*, 49, 52-53.

[91] *Sefer Sha'ar ha-Shamayim*, Introduction, p. 123.

[92] R. Shem Tov.

[93] *Guide*, Introduction.

[94] *Guide*, Introduction (Pines trans., p. 4). Cf. Eccl. 12:10.

[95] Letter to his student Joseph b. Judah, *Iggerot ha-Rambam*, ed. D. Z. Bennett, 51.

[96] R. Isaac Arama, *Akeidat Yizhak*, part 57.

[97] *Shelah, Kelal Kevod Elokim Hester Davar.*

[98] Letter of R. Hillel of Verona to R. Isaac b. Mordecai.

[99] *Minhat Kena'ot*, c. 52 in *Responsa Rashba* , ed. H. Z. Dimitrovsky, vol. 2, p. 479.

[100] The expression calls to mind Nahmanides' comments in his epistle *"Terem E'eneh."*

[101] The term, borrowed from the name of the first Hebrew-language journal of the Enlightenment period (*Ha-Me'assef*) usually refers to adherents of the Enlightenment movement in the time of Moses Mendelssohn. R. Aviad Sar Shalom Basilea (c.1680-1749) lived during part of that period—*translator's note.*

[102] *Sefer Emunat Hakhamim*

[103] *Guide*, end of the Introduction to Part 1 (Pines trans., p. 16), citing Ps. 119:126.

[104] *Derekh Hayyim*, commentary on *Pirkei Avot* 6:10.

[105] *Commentary on the Mishnah, Sanhedrin, Perek Helek*, 217.

[106] Ibid., *Toharot*, Introduction, p. 37.

[107] *Guide*, Introduction to Part I (Pines trans., p. 15).

[108] *Hilkhot De'ot* 2:4.

[109] *Commentary on the Mishnah, Avot* 1:16.

[110] *Yevamot* 49b.

[111] *Ma'amar Tehiyat ha-Meitim.*

[112] *Commentary on the Mishneh, Sanhedrin, Perek Helek*, 217.

[113] Ibid., *Hagigah* 3:2.

[114] *Responsa*, Responsum 310, p. 574.

[115] *Mishneh Torah*, Introduction.

[116] *Responsa Mishpetai Shemu'el*, sec. 114.

[117] *Seder ha-Mishnah*, beginning.

[118] Letter of Maimonides to R. Joseph b. R. Judah,51.

[119] Lit., "hoe"; cf. *Avodah Zarah* 19b and *Bava Mezi'a* 86b.

[120] *Beit ha-Behirah, Berakhot*, Introduction, p. 28.

[121] R. Sa'adyah ibn Dan'an, *Seder ha-Dorot, Hemdah Genuzah*, 30.

[122] Introduction, p. 28.

[123] *Sanhedrin* 93a.

[124] *Sha'ar ha-Shamayim*, Introduction.

[125] *Kenesset ha-Gedolah, Orah Hayyim*, Introduction.

[126] *Even Sappir* 1, 53a.

[127] *Merkevet ha-Mishneh*, Introduction.

[128] *Nega'im*, c. 9, end.

[129] *Ish ha-Halakhah – Galui ve-Nistar*, 230.

[130] *Hagigah* 14a.

[131] *Beit ha-Behirah*, Introduction, p. 25.

[132] Nahmanides, *Milhemot ha-Shem*.

[133] R. Isaiah di Trani, *Responsa*, sec, 61.

[134] *Shemonah Perakim*, Introduction.

[135] *Sefer Minhat Kena'ot*, letter 72, in *Responsa Rashba*, ed. H. Z. Dimitrovsky, vol. 2, c. 46, p. 453.

[136] *Milei de-Avot*; it is interesting to compare the words of R. Joseph Colon, *Responsa Maharik*, sec. 171.

[137] Salonika, 1597.

[138] *Sefer Derekh Hayyim*, 32.

[139] *Eruvin* 54b.

[140] *Kovez ha-Rambam*, 3.

MAIMONIDES ON THE LOVE OF GOD*

Norman Lamm

Immediately after the profession of divine unity in the *Shema*, the Torah introduces us to one of the fundamental precepts of Judaism, namely, *ahavat Hashem*, the Love of God: "Thou shalt love the Lord thy God with all thy heart and all thy soul and all thy might"(Deut. 6:4). It is readily understood that so powerful and central a theme in religion in general, and especially in Judaism,[1] has engaged the attention and careful scrutiny of almost every Jewish thinker.[2] Certainly, we expect the subject to be treated by Maimonides, and our expectations are not disappointed. No serious consideration of any aspect of Jewish thought or philosophy can or may avoid considering the views of Maimonides.

Before proceeding to the more analytic interpretations of our key verse, all of which concern the nature of the Love of God, it is appropriate to mention a midrash that gives an entirely different "spin" to the commandment to "love the Lord thy God." The *Sifre* takes the verb *ve-ahavta*, "and thou shalt love," in the causative sense:

> Another explanation of, "Thou shalt love the Lord thy God":
> *Cause* Him to be beloved by humans, even as your father Abraham did, as it is written, "(And Abram took Sarai his wife, and his brother's son Lot and all the substance that they had gathered) and the souls that they had gotten in Haran" (Gen. 12:5).[3]

In an old and well-known midrash, "the souls that they had gotten in Haran" is interpreted by the Sages as referring to the proselytes whom Abraham and Sarah had brought from paganism to monotheism.[4] Hence, to love God means to act so as to make Him beloved of others.

---

* Originally published in Maimonidean Studies 3, ed. Arthur Hyman (New York, 1995), 131-142.

In a parallel text in the Talmud, this same theme is recorded elaborately:

> Abbaye cited a *baraita*: "'Thou shalt love the Lord thy God' means that because of you the Name of Heaven will become beloved." [This means] that if a person studies Scripture and Mishnah and attends on scholars of the Torah, and his business dealings are honest, and he speaks pleasantly with people (*im ha-beriyyot*)— what do people say about him? [They say:] "Happy is his father who taught him Torah; happy is his teacher who taught him Torah; woe to those who have not studied Torah. Have you seen so-and-so who studied Torah? How beautiful are his manners! How refined are his deeds"![5]

The *Sifre* and the Talmud see the Love of God as a functional and societal as well as a personal and affective commandment: we are to live and act so that others, whether Jews or non-Jews, believers or non-believers (note the use of *beriyyot*, literally "creatures," and thus the word for human beings in general), turn to Him in love.

That we have here not only a charming homily but also an important principle is evident from the space that Maimonides devotes to it: he mentions the passage from *Sifre* and expands on it in his *Sefer ha-Mizvot*, where it takes up fully one half of his description of the *mizvah* of the Love of God. To love God, says Maimonides, is to be impelled to bring others to know Him and to love Him.[6] But while this provides us with an important and inspiring insight, it does not touch directly on the content of the precept of the Love of God.[7] It is that to which we must now turn our attention.

The *locus classicus* of the Maimonidean view on *ahavat Hashem* is the passage in his immortal code, the *Mishneh Torah:*

> What is the way to attain the Love and Fear of God? When a man contemplates His great and wondrous deeds and creatures, and sees in them His unequaled and infinite wisdom, he immediately (*miyad*) loves and praises and exalts Him, and is overcome by a great desire to know the great Name. As David said, "My soul thirsts for God, for the living God" (Psalms 42:3). And when he considers these very matters, immediately (*miyad*) he withdraws and is frightened and knows that he is but a small, lowly, dark creature who, with his inferior and puny mind, stands before Him who is perfect in His knowledge. As David said, "When I consider Thy heavens, the work of Thy fingers…What is man that Thou art mindful of him?" (Psalms 8:4,5). Thus do I explain many great principles concerning the actions of the Master of the Worlds, [namely,] that they provide an opportunity for a wise person to love God. As the Sages said

concerning Love, "as a result of this you will come to know Him by Whose word the world came into being"[8]

There are several ideas in this passage that are worthy of notice and require careful attention.

First, there is, according to Maimonides, a common origin, even method, for the two religious emotions of Love and Fear: the contemplation of the cosmos. Such deep reflection on creation leads to two apparently divergent religious effects: *ahavat Hashem* and *yir'at Hashem*. The two, Love and Fear, are different but they are fundamentally linked to each other; one cannot discuss, let alone understand, the one without the other.

Second, Love and Fear differ in that each is the mirror image of the other. Love of God is a centrifugal motion of the self as man, overwhelmed by the wisdom revealed in the marvels of creation, seeks to reach outward and upward towards the Creator to better know Him. Fear of God is the precise opposite. Overwhelmed by the greatness of the Creator, man traumatically realizes his own unimportance, his marginality, and his very nothingness; in a centripetal psychological motion he pulls inward and retreats into himself.[9]

Third, there is an implicit relationship between Love and Fear. The first reaction to the contemplation of Nature is, instinctively and impulsively, Love. But this reaching out in a cognitive quest for the Creator is, intuitively and instinctively, countered and curtailed by the limiting impulse of Fear. The use of *miyad*, which we above translated in its usual sense of "immediately," once with regard to Love and again with regard to Fear, must, I believe, be taken in this sense of an intuitive reaction, one that is *immediate* in the sense of being un-mediated.

The role of intuition is significant in the works of Maimonides. In the Introduction to the *Guide* he speaks of momentary flashes of intuition—unmediated by any act of ratiocination—as the mode of apprehension of both metaphysical knowledge and prophecy. This epistemology, of course, presents a problem because of Maimonides' high esteem for metaphysical deduction and clear, logical analysis. Julius Guttmann, who raises this issue, offers no solution.[10] The most obvious answer, however, is provided by a close reading of our key passage. Here, Maimonides does not speak of the intuitive (*miyad*, "immediately") reaction as the first response to Nature, but the second. The love of God comes about after one "contemplates" the wonders of creation and "sees" in them the infinite wisdom of the Divine, and only then does he "immediately" love Him, etc. The same pattern holds for the Fear of God; when man "considers" these matters, the wonders of creation, he "immediately" withdraws into himself in fear, etc. What we have here is a two-step process: first one studies Nature, *then* this evokes for him the latent intuitive response of the appropriate religious emotions. Hence, the study of natural science leads to the intuitive reaction of Love and Fear to the creation. It is left for the philosopher to elaborate these responses in the language of metaphysics. This philosophical elaboration, too, involves a flash of insight, but it is different from the Love and Fear reaction; it is, as it were, a "normal" epistemological act and one which must then be set down according to all the rules of metaphysical argument.

Fourth, despite the fact that Love is immediately limited by the emotion of Fear, Maimonides obviously agrees with the Sages that "one who acts out of Love is greater than one who acts out of Fear."[11] Thus, he concludes the *halakhah* with a comment on Love only, that the Creator does certain things in order to grant man the opportunity (or will) to love Him. Fear serves a vital but ancillary role to Love; it is the latter which remains the most significant and valuable religious quality.

Let us return to the first idea in the Maimonidean passage, the common origin of Love and Fear in the contemplation of the divine wisdom in His creation. While Maimonides here focuses on the creation or Nature as the object of man's contemplation in order to arrive at Love, he elsewhere elaborates on the object of such contemplation. In *Hilkhot Teshuvah* 10:6 he presents his severely rationalistic view of the Love of God, and declares it to be proportional to one's *knowledge* of Him: "One loves the Holy One only with the mind, thus knowing Him; for Love is in accordance with knowledge, whether little or much." This is followed by the advice to attend to intellectual immersion in the various branches of wisdom which lead to the knowledge of God (and, thus, to love of Him):

> Therefore must a man set aside [time] to understand and comprehend the [various branches of] wisdom and learning which impart to him knowledge of his Creator, depending on man's capacity to understand and apprehend, etc.

It should be noted that the branches of "wisdom and learning" are not necessarily limited to the natural sciences, although they certainly include them. Maimonides unquestionably intended that the immediate reaction to nature must be lead to and be shaped by proper and correct metaphysical speculation.

The study of Nature (which, as mentioned, is the prerequisite for the intuitive reactions of Love and Fear) is far less esoteric than metaphysical speculation. The Talmud *requires* one who is capable of studying geometry and astronomy to do so, and "one who knows how to calculate the cycles and planetary courses but does not do so, of him Scripture says, 'but they regard not the work of the Lord, nor have they considered the work of His hands' (Isaiah 5:12)."[12] We find no Talmudic encouragement of the study of philosophy as such. But Maimonides raises philosophy to the highest rung in the religious life, higher than that of the natural sciences. Thus, after introducing chapter 2 of *Hilkhot Yesodei ha-Torah* by describing the source of Love and Fear, Maimonides undertakes to teach the reader about matter and form, the angels, the nature of divine knowledge, divine unity, etc. All this, he says (2:11), is included in the term *ma'aseh merkavah*, the highly esoteric study of the "divine chariot." The next two chapters deal with astronomy and physics. "All these matters are only a drop in the bucket and profound, but not as profound as [the matters taken up in] the first two chapters." The latter two chapters are referred to as *ma'aseh bereshit*, literally, the account of creation, which, while it is not popular fare, is not as recondite and restricted as is the study of *ma'aseh merkavah* (4:10, 11).[13] Hence, the study of Nature is available, even required, of those who have the talent for it, but not for all others, while the study of metaphysics is clearly reserved for those who have both the aptitude and the spiritual preparation for it.[14]

In his *Sefer ha-Mizvot*, the canvas is broadened even further: "For He has commanded us to love Him; and that [means] to understand and comprehend His *mizvot* and His actions."[15] Here Maimonides includes not only "His actions"—which may well embrace the divine guidance of history as well as His governance of Nature—but also "His *mizvot*," His commandments. This may be an indirect reference to the study of Torah, repository of the commandments, as a source of inspiration to the Love of God. This is stated explicitly (in his own name) by the author of *Sefer ha-Hinukh*, who usually follows Maimonides: "That is, along with reflection in Torah necessarily comes a strengthening of Love in the heart."[16]

There is further indication that in this passage from his *Sefer ha-Mizvot* Maimonides did indeed intend that study of Torah is a source of *ahavat Hashem;* it was not added as a mere afterthought. The reason for this assertion is a proof-text from the *Sifre*. He writes, following the lines we mentioned above:

> This is the text of the *Sifre*: It is said, "thou shalt love the Lord thy God." But [from this] I do not know *how* one loves Him; therefore is it said, "And these words which I command thee this day shall be in thy heart" (Deut. 6:6)—as a result of this you will come to know Him by Whose word the world came into being.[17]

The antecedent of "as a result of this" is obviously "these words," and this undoubtedly refers to the words of Torah (or, at the very least, the words of the *Shema*) and not to the contemplation of Nature.

Here we face a dilemma in the exegesis of Maimonides' thought. Is Nature, the divine creation of the cosmos, the sole object which, when contemplated, leads to the Love and Fear of God—or is the Torah, the direct revelation of the divine Will, equally a source of Love and Fear? In the two passages from his legal code, the *Mishneh Torah*, he clearly stipulates Nature as the source of such inspiration which leads to the Love and Fear of God. Yet in his *Sefer ha-Mizvot* he mentions both the commandments (using two synonyms) and His works, i.e., Nature.

Which, then, according to Maimonides, is the primary object the contemplation of which leads to Love—Nature (and metaphysics which follows upon and elaborates the Love and Fear responses to Nature) or Torah and *mizvot*? Is there perhaps a double focus, with each holding equal value? Is the *Sefer ha-Hinukh* offering a valid interpretation of Maimonides' view or is the author of this work imposing his own view, one with an apologetic slant?

Viewing all the major passages in which Maimonides discusses the Love and Fear of God, we find the following: In the *Mishneh Torah* he mentions only Nature as the source of the two fundamental religious emotions. This is despite the effort by some to find justification for the inclusion of Torah alongside Nature as the source of Love and Fear by reading this into the closing phrase of Maimonides in *Hilkhot Yesodei ha-Torah*, cited above, or as an addition to it.[18] In the *Sefer ha-Mizvot* he posits both Torah and Nature, with emphasis on the former.

We now turn to his major philosophical work, the *Guide of the Perplexed*, and are not at all perplexed that our guide, Maimonides, identifies the contemplation of Nature as the source of the emotions of Love and Fear.

The two most important passages in the *Guide* appear in Part III. In Chapter 28, he tells us that the Torah, "in regard to the correct opinions through which the ultimate perfection may be attained," ideas such as God's existence, unity, and power, spoke only in general and apodictic terms, without going into much detail:

> With regard to all the other correct opinions concerning the whole of being—opinions that constitute the numerous kinds of theoretical sciences through which the opinion forming the ultimate end are validated—the Torah, albeit it does not make a call to direct attention toward them in detail as it does with regard to [the opinions forming ultimate ends], does so in summary fashion by saying, "To love the Lord" (Deut. 22:7). You know how this is confirmed in the dictum regarding love: "With all thy heart and with all thy soul and with all thy might" (Deut. 6:5). We have already explained in *Mishneh Torah* that this love becomes valid only through the apprehension of the whole of being as it is and through the consideration of His wisdom as it is manifested in it.[19]

Here, then, Maimonides posits Nature—its study and philosophical elaboration—as the source of Love, as he did in the various passages in the *Mishneh Torah*.[20]

In Chapter 52 of Part III of the *Guide*, Maimonides distinguishes between two categories of commandments: the practical ones, the do's and the don'ts of Scriptural legislation, and the "opinions" or theological propositions taught by the Torah. The former lead to Fear of God, the latter to Love.

> As for the opinions that the Torah teaches us—namely, the apprehension of His Being and His unity, may He be exalted—these opinions teach us love, as we have explained several times. You know to what extent the Torah lays stress upon love: "With all thy heart and with all thy soul and with all thy might." For these two ends, namely, love and fear, are achieved through two things: *love* through opinions taught by the Torah, which include apprehension of His being as He is in truth, while *fear* is achieved by means of all actions prescribed by the Torah, as we have explained.[21]

We have, then, in the *Mishneh Torah* and the *Guide of the Perplexed* the assertion that Nature and the correct philosophical ideas resulting from its contemplation are the sources of Love, while the *Sefer ha-Mizvot* adds, and appears to emphasize, Torah and the commandments. Is this a trivial inconsistency, or are the apparent contradictions deliberate, and can Maimonides be made consistent and coherent? I believe that the latter is the case, and the principle is one that characterizes much of Maimonides' thought, namely, the distinction between the masses and the learned elite.[22]

The average man is expected to observe all the actional commandments—the *halakhah*—in all their details. These actions, plus the summary of otherwise profound philosophical ideas concerning God that the Torah offers ever so briefly, are enough to give this average person the wherewithal to conduct his life in an orderly, moral, and civilized manner and with an awareness of the basic ideas that distinguish Judaism. The *mizvot* will guide him or her onto the right path, consistent with such person's intellectual capacity. The elite, however, whose curiosity and intellectual ability raise them beyond the ordinary, are expected to strive for a far higher standard, much beyond the limits set by the Torah for the masses. Such a person must aspire to understand the most refined concepts of the Deity and His attributes.[23]

Now, in the *Sefer ha-Mizvot*, which—as its very name indicates—deals with an enumeration of the commandments, Maimonides is writing for ordinary Jews who wish to observe what is required of them and what is within their ability to understand. Hence, the very *mizvot* which are such a person's principal connection to the service of God—the behavioral commandments plus the outline the Torah offers of the major concepts of the Deity—are the source of his or her Love of God. To the extent that such a person's ability permits, Nature and its reflection of the imponderable wisdom of the Creator are also available to him.[24] But his primary source for religious inspiration is the commandments and, of course, the Torah of which they form a part. This explains the passages cited in Maimonides' "popular" work.

However, the *Mishneh Torah* offers seeming resistance to our thesis. After all, this is Maimonides' principal halakhic work; it is meant for all Jews equally, and hence here he ought to confine the source of Love to Torah and *mizvot* and omit the contemplation of the cosmos and its consequent requirement of metaphysical speculation. But it so happens that the two passages in this work in which Maimonides discusses Love and Fear are those in which the context calls for a standard different form the popular one. In *Hilkhot Yesodei ha-Torah* his goal is to impart, in non-technical terms and in a manner accessible to the non-philosopher, the theological foundations of Judaism. However, although the information is simplified for the masses, the subject matter remains intrinsically so difficult and so intellectually demanding that even in its pedagogically simplified form it constitutes a formidable intellectual challenge. Maimonides maintains that it is a key to understanding the divine governance of the universe[25] and that it forms the essential content of the *ma'aseh merkavah*—the exegesis of Ezekiel's vision of the divine chariot which the Sages declared an esoteric study,[26] rather than halakhic discourse which is accessible to all, "young and old, men and women."[27] Hence, it is to be expected that here Maimonides will point to the contemplation of Nature as the source of the intuition that leads to both Love and Fear. Moreover, since the context of these first chapters of *Hilkhot Yesodei ha-Torah* concern matters scientific and metaphysical—such as matter and form, the essentials of Ptolemaic astronomy, and spiritual beings—it stands to reason that the source assigned to Love and Fear will be Nature rather than the commandments and the Torah.[28]

The context of Maimonides' discussion in *Hilkhot Teshuvah* demonstrates that Maimonides is using an alternative definition of Fear—the conventional one, that is—as opposed to the more sophisticated version as presented at the beginning of *Hilkhot Yesodei ha-Torah*. Chapter 10 of *Hilkhot Teshuvah* is devoted to the distinction between those who observe the laws for their own sake and those who do so for ulterior motives—such as the desire for reward or the fear of punishment. The latter—which includes "the ignorant, women, and children"—operate out of Fear, which, of course, is a lower form of religious devotion; whereas the former do so out of Love.

> What is the proper kind of love? When one loves God with very powerful, great, and overflowing love, such that his soul is bound up in the love of God and he is constantly absorbed in it, as if he were love-sick and his mind is never free of that woman, being constantly absorbed in [that love] whether sitting or standing, whether eating or drinking.[29] It is well known that the love of the Holy One does not become bound up with the heart of man until he thinks about it constantly and properly and abandons everything in the world except for it; as we were commanded, "with all thy heart and with all thy soul." One loves the Holy One only with the mind, thus knowing Him, for love is in accordance with knowledge. If little [knowledge] then little [love], if much [knowledge] then much [love]. Therefore must a person dedicate

himself to understand and comprehend the [branches of] wisdom
and learning which inform him about his Creator according to his
capacity to understand and comprehend...[30]

This form of Love goes beyond the Fear described in *Hilkhot Yesodei
ha-Torah*; it is a higher level, and, hence, one that can come only to a
person who is prepared "to understand and comprehend the [branches]
of wisdom and learning," Maimonides' term for both natural science and
metaphysical thinking.

And, of course, in the *Guide*, his often esoteric philosophical *magnum
opus*, we expect to find the higher standard of the elite predominate, as
we most certainly do. We see then, that when Maimonides was writing
for a general audience, as in the *Sefer ha-Miẓvot*, he included Torah
study and the performance of the Commandments along with scientific
and philosophic contemplation as the source of Fear and Love of God,
since most members of the general audience would be capable only of
the former. When writing for the intellectual elite, as in the *Guide for
the Perplexed* and in the particular section of the *Mishneh Torah* where
he discusses Love and Fear of God, he includes only philosophic and
scientific study. Hence, Maimonides was consistent in his identification
of Nature or Torah and *miẓvot* as the object of thought, which leads to
Love of God.

---

[1] "All the Torah is included in the commandment to love God, because he who loves the
King devotes all his thoughts to doing that which is good and right in His eyes." *Sefer
Miẓvot Gadol* (Venice ed., reprinted in Jerusalem, 1960), Pos. Com. 3, p. 96b.

[2] The most comprehensive work on this subject is that of Georges Vajda, *L'amour de Dieu
dans la Théologie Juive du Moyen Age* (Paris, 1957).

[3] *Sifre, va-Ethanan, piska* 32, ed. Louis Finkelstein (New York, 1969), 54.

[4] *Gen. Rab.* 39:14, ed. Yehuda Theodore and Chanoch Albeck (Jerusalem, 1965), 378 f.

[5] *Yoma* 86a. My translation (based on Soncino ed., *Yoma* 427).

[6] *Sefer ha-Miẓvot*, ed. Rabbi Hayyim Heller (Jerusalem, 1946), Pos. Com. 3, p. 35f.

[7] In general, the Talmud and Midrash are more behavioral and practical in their
interpretation of the commandment to love God, whereas the philosophically inclined
Rishonim tended to a more affective and mystical view, but the line should not be drawn
too tightly. See Louis Jacobs, *A Jewish Theology* (New York, 1973), 154.

[8] *Hilkhot Yesodei ha-Torah* 2:2

[9] This analysis of Love and Fear of God should be compared with the 19th century
Protestant thinker Rudolf Otto who, in *The Idea of the Holy* (translated by John W.

Harvey [New York, 1958]) 12-40, wrote of two reactions to Nature; the first is *fascination* with the divine wisdom implicit in Nature and the second is *terror* as man retreats before the *Mysterium Tremendum*. I do not know if Maimonides influenced him directly, but he certainly preceded him in this almost identical formulation.

[10] See his *Philosophies of Judaism*, trans. David W. Silverman (Philadelphia, 1964), 156f.

[11] *Nedarim* 31a.

[12] *Shabbat* 75a. See Saul Lieberman, *Hellenism in Jewish Palestine* (New York, 1950), 180-193, on the Talmud's positive attitude to the need for scientific knowledge for the proper observance of certain *mizvot*; and pp. 100-114 on the ban on studying Greek "wisdom."

[13] See further in my *Torah Umadda: The Encounter of Religious Learning and Worldly Knowledge in the Jewish Tradition* (Northvale, N.J., 1990), 77-81 on Maimonides' views on the study of the sciences and philosophy as part of *pardes*.

[14] See too R. Isaac Simcha Hurewitz, *Yad Levi* (Commentary to Maimonides' *Sefer ha-Mitzvot*) *Shoresh* 1, no. 40 (Jerusalem, 1927), 18a, b.

[15] *Sefer ha-Mizvot*, Pos. 3. This follows the Heller edition; the Kafah translation has slight but insignificant variations.

[16] *Sefer ha-Hinukh* 417, ed. Hayyim D. Chavel (Jerusalem, 1952), 529.

[17] See note 3, above.

[18] The same uncertainty about the correct interpretation of the *Sifre* will be noticed in the comment of R. Naftali Zevi Yehuda Berlin ("The Neziv," 1817-1893) in his *Ha'amek Davar* to Deut. 6:7, especially in the addendum to this commentary taken from the author's manuscript. In the commentary proper he cites the *Sifre* and takes it clearly to imply that the study of Torah is the means to achieve the Love of God. In the addendum, however, he concedes that the plain sense of the *Sifre* passage would indicate that the contemplation of the creation and Nature are the vehicles to *ahavat Hashem*, and that Maimonides, in the above passage from *Hilkhot Yesodei ha-Torah*, supports that understanding. However, see below note 20.

[19] *The Guide of the Perplexed*, trans. Shlomo Pines (Chicago, 1963), 512-513.

[20] The Neziv adds that one cannot derive *ahavat Hashem* from the study of Nature alone; such exclusive contemplation may well lead to an appreciation of the greatness of the Creator, but hardly to *loving* Him. It may be compared to one who knows that another person is great and worthy of love, but who does not know him personally, so that even if he sees him he cannot love him because he does not truly know him. So, too, the study of natural science can lead to love only if it is preceded by the study of Torah; for then, to continue the analogy, one knows the other person directly and can then learn to love him. Note the intellectual honesty and also the breadth of Neziv's own approach—he points to the inadequacy of Nature as a source of *ahavat Hashem* without disqualifying it altogether, and recommends that only study of science and Torah together provide the entrée to Love of God, with Torah taking priority over science. This is a point he makes often; see e.g., *Ha'amek Davar* to Deut. 4:2. Such breadth and intellectual capaciousness, with the accompanying sensitivity to complexity and to subtle nuances, should not be confused with the kind of ambivalence that bespeaks an inability to make up one's mind for fear of making the wrong choice. For more on the attitude of Neziv on this issue, see my *Torah*

Umadda, 40-41, 44, and 72, n.2. Also see Hannah Katz, *Mishnat ha-Neziv* (Jerusalem, 1990), 109-116; however, her use of the term "ambivalent" for Neziv's breadth of scope and sensitivity to complexity is unfortunate because it implies indecisiveness which clearly was not part of Neziv's personality.

[21] *Guide*, 630.

[22] In the very beginning of the *Guide*, Introduction to Part I (Pines trans. 8f.), Maimonides holds that the deeper understanding of the Torah, which he identifies with philosophic truth, was available to the intellectual elite, and was not to be revealed to ordinary folk. However, this does not result in disdain for the benighted masses; the latter are granted, in simple and uncomplicated fashion, certain basic truths, such as the incorporeality of God. Thus, Maimonides (like Onkelos) held that the figurative interpretation of biblical anthropomorphisms and anthropopathisms must be taught to all Jews regardless of intellectual sophistication or lack thereof.

[23] The elite, however, must continue to abide by the actional commandments along with the masses; their higher aspirations and deeper understanding are not a dispensation to do away with the obligations that devolve upon all other Jews. Everything in the life and writings of Maimonides rejects the notion, sometimes proposed, that the elite are beyond the law.

[24] See above, n. 13.

[25] *Hilkhot Yesodei ha-Torah*, 2:2, end.

[26] Ibid., 4:10. See above, n. 13.

[27] Ibid., 4:13.

[28] See the commentary to Maimonides' *Sefer ha-Mizvot* by R. Hananiah b. Menahem, *Kin'at Soferim* (Livorno, 1740), Pos. Com. 3.

[29] *Hikhot Teshuvah* 10:3.

[30] Ibid., 10:6.

INTERPRETING MAIMONIDES[*]

Arthur Hyman

Dedicated to the memory of Dr. Samuel Belkin, *zz"l*, who, in building Yeshiva University, built an institution hospitable to traditional Jewish learning and modern scholarship.

Maimonides' *Guide of the Perplexed* is a difficult and enigmatic work that many times perplexes the very reader it is supposed to guide. Its technical subject matter, the elitist audience for which it was composed, its allusory and contradictory style, and its apparently eclectic philosophical foundations have challenged a long line of interpreters who attempted to clarify the details of Maimonides' views and to determine his overall philosophic orientation. This line of interpreters, which extends from Maimonides' days until our very own, may, in fact, be said to have been started by Maimonides himself. For when, in his *Ma'amar Tehiyyat ha-Metim*, Maimonides reaffirmed his belief in the literal meaning of the resurrection of the dead against charges that he denied this principle, he became the first interpreter of his own views.

In this brief paper I shall undertake a three-fold task. I shall begin by analyzing some of the features of the *Guide* of which any interpreter must take account. Then I shall describe some aspects of the interpretation of Maimonides by modern scholars, showing that modern interpreters may be divided into two basic groups. And finally, I shall make two suggestions concerning further research that may help to clarify Maimonides' views.

[*] This paper was delivered as a lecture at the 1973 annual meeting of the American Academy for Jewish Research, and published in Gesher 5 (New York, 1976), 46-59.

I

By his own admission, Maimonides did not compose a purely philosophic work, thereby setting himself apart from the philosophic tradition of his day. Unlike his Islamic predecessors—Alfarabi, Avicenna, Ibn Bajjah—and his contemporary Averroes, who composed commentaries on Aristotle's works, *summae* of his views, and philosophic treatises of their own, Maimonides had no intention to add to the philosophic literature of his day or to become an innovator in the realm of philosophic speculation. This was already clear from his early program in the *Commentary on the Mishnah*, according to which he had in mind to write a "Book of Prophecy" and a "Book of Correspondence," devoted respectively to an account of prophecy and an exposition of difficult Midrashim.[1] More explicitly, he writes in the *Guide, 2, 2*:

> Know, that my purpose in this Treatise of mine was not to compose something in the natural science [physics], or to make an epitome of notions pertaining to the divine science [metaphysics]...For the books composed concerning these matters are adequate...If however, they should turn out not to be adequate with regard to some subject, that which I shall say concerning that subject will not be superior to anything else that has been said about it.[2]

If the *Guide* is not a work of purely philosophic speculation, what then are the subjects with which it deals? Maimonides foregoes characterizing the contents of the *Guide* by means of a single word or phrase, describing them instead in three-fold fashion. In the Introduction to the *Guide*, he first states that it is the purpose of his work to explain the equivocal, derivative, and amphibolous terms appearing in the Scriptural texts and to clarify Scriptural parables which are obscure. Then again, he describes the subject matter of the *Guide* by the rabbinic terms *Ma'aseh Merkavah* and *Ma'aseh Bereshit*, which in all of his works he identifies with physics and metaphysics. Finally, he states that the *Guide* is devoted to "the science of the Law in its true sense" (*hokhmat ha-Torah al ha-emet*), "the secrets [of the Law]" (*ha-sodot*), and "the mysteries of the Law" (*sitrei Torah*). That the secrets of the Law discussed in the *Guide* are not co-extensive with the totality of physical and metaphysical knowledge may be gathered from an incidental enumeration that Maimonides himself provides. In a chapter advocating the moderate intellectual enlightenment of the masses (*Guide* 1,35), he states emphatically that the secrets and mysteries of the Law must be concealed from them, and he lists such secrets: divine attributes, creation, God's governance of the world and His providence for it, divine will, apprehension, knowledge, names, and prophecy and its various degrees. Comparing this list with the topics forming the subject matter of the *Guide*, one discovers that it contains all the topics of the work with the exception of the section, at the end of the book, devoted to the reasons for the commandments *(ta'amei ha-mizvot)*. From these observations one may conclude that, whatever else the *Guide* may be, it is a book of Scriptural exegesis devoted to the secrets of the Law. The purpose of Maimonides' exegesis remains, however, still to be determined.

Just as the *Guide* is restricted to a limited subject matter, so is it restricted to a limited audience. Maimonides wrote for Jews, and for Jews of a special kind at that. That the work was not written for pure philosophers is clear from what has been seen so far as well as from the fact that most of the subjects discussed in the *Guide* are of little interest to those concerned with pure philosophic speculation. Nor is the work addressed to the masses, to those who are beginners in speculation, or to those scholars who are only engaged in the legal study of the Law— although all of these may derive some benefit from the work. To whom, then, is the *Guide* addressed?

Maimonides, in his Introduction, describes the addressee of the *Guide* as someone who is "perfect in his religion and character," that is, someone who is a devoted Jew and who, at the same time, has "studied the sciences of the philosophers and come to know what they signify." The reader so described has been perplexed by the conflict between the literal meaning of Scriptural terms and parables and what he has learned in the philosophical disciplines. He is concerned that were he to follow the teachings of philosophy he would have to renounce the foundations of the Law, and were he to accept literally the Scriptural terms and parables, he would have to sacrifice the discoveries of his mind. Once again, it remains to be seen how Maimonides resolves the perplexity of his reader.

The literary character of the *Guide* imposes further difficulties of interpretation—difficulties occasioned by halakhic considerations as well as principles of philosophic prudence. The *Mishnah* in *Hagigah* 2:1 enjoins the public teaching of *Ma'aseh Bereshit* and *Ma'aseh Merkavah*, stressing that *Ma'aseh Bereshit* may be taught to only one person and *Ma'aseh Merkavah* only to one who is wise and able to reason for himself. Maimonides in *Mishneh Torah, Hilkhot Yesodei ha-Torah* 2:12 and

4:2 codifies this mishnaic principle as binding law, and this presents him with a problem in writing the *Guide*. For if *Ma'aseh Bereshit* and *Ma'aseh Merkavah* are identical with physics and metaphysics, how can he write a book devoted to these topics, especially since presenting one's views in writing is public teaching *par excellence?*

Aware of this dilemma, Maimonides justifies his writing the *Guide* in three-fold fashion. First, he invokes the Biblical verse: "It is time to do something for the Lord, for they have infringed Thy Law" (Ps. 119:126). This is the same verse that had been used to justify the writing down of the *Mishnah*, another work the writing down of which had been legally enjoined. To the Biblical verse he adds as additional justification the rabbinic saying "Let all thy acts be for the sake of Heaven" (*Avot* 2:17).

Maimonides takes cognizance of the halakhic injunction in the literary form of his work as well. He begins the *Guide* with an Introductory Letter, addressed to a former student, Joseph ben Judah ibn Sham'un, whom he had previously tested to make sure that he was wise and able to reason for himself. Since the work has the form of a personal communication addressed to someone who has fulfilled the qualifications of the *halakhah*, the writing of the *Guide* cannot, strictly speaking, be said to be public teaching.

Maimonides, however, was well aware that his work would become available to the community at large (certainly aided by Samuel Ibn Tibbon, who translated the *Guide* into Hebrew), and so he had to look in still another direction to justify writing the *Guide* in accordance with *halakhah*. This he did by using methods of contradiction. After enumerating in the Introduction to the *Guide* seven types of contradictions that appear in books and compilations, Maimonides states explicitly that he will use two of these in his work. One of these is the use of contradictions for pedagogic reasons, the other to conceal one's true opinions. Concerning the latter he writes:

> In speaking about very obscure matters it is necessary to conceal some parts and to disclose others. Sometimes in the case of certain dicta this necessity requires that the discussion proceed on the basis of a certain premise, whereas in another place necessity requires that the discussion proceed on the basis of another premise contradicting the first one.

There has been no greater challenge to interpreters than to locate these contradictions and to discover how they may be resolved.

We have so far spoken about problems occasioned by the subject matter of the *Guide*, the audience to which it is addressed, and the method of contradiction which Maimonides uses, but there is one further aspect of the work which invites the interpreter's attention: the overall orientation of Maimonides' philosophic views. It is a commonplace among the students of Maimonides that he was an Aristotelian in his philosophic orientation, but hardly anyone has clarified what kind of Aristotelianism he embraced. This question becomes acute once it is realized that two types of Aristotelianism were current in Maimonides' days—that of Avicenna and that of Averroes. Avicenna's Aristotelianism manifested a strong Neoplatonic coloration and it had a certain theological bend. By contrast, Averroes' Aristotelianism was of a more naturalistic kind. Averroes undertook to restore the true Aristotelian teachings by cleansing them of Neoplatonic accretions, and he accused Avicenna of having capitulated to theological considerations on certain points. Hence, one may contrast the theologically colored Aristotelianism of Avicenna with the more naturalistic one of Averroes. What kind of evidence does Maimonides provide for assessing his position on this philosophic controversy?

Maimonides mentions both philosophers in his writings. He mentions Averroes in a well-known letter to Samuel Ibn Tibbon, the first Hebrew translator of the *Guide*, as well as in a letter to Joseph ben Judah, the addressee of the *Guide*. Scholars agree that Maimonides became acquainted with the views of Averroes too late to consider them in his *Guide*.[3] However this does not preclude that Maimonides' Aristotelianism may have been of an Averroean kind, since Maimonides associated himself with Andalusian Aristotelianism—an Aristotelianism which was naturalistic in its orientation.

Maimonides also mentions Avicenna in the letter to Samuel Ibn Tibbon, but while he recommends Averroes without any reservation, he attaches some strictures to the study of Avicenna. Comparing Avicenna and Alfarabi he writes: "Though the works of Avicenna manifest great accuracy and subtle study, they are not as good as the works of Abu Nasr al-Farabi."[4] This somewhat negative opinion must be balanced by the observation that in the continuation of this passage Maimonides advocates the study of Avicenna's works and that on a number of crucial philosophic issues on which Avicenna and Averroes held conflicting opinions he follows Avicenna's views. Thus, for example, he follows

Avicenna (against Averroes) in stating that essential attributes applied to God must be understood as negations and in recognizing the validity of the proof of the existence of God known as the proof from necessity and contingency.

With these backgrounds in mind, we can now proceed to a discussion of some aspects of modern interpretations of Maimonides.

II

The modern study and interpretation of Maimonides may be divided into two periods. The first of these extends from the 1840's until the early 1930's; the second from the early 1930's until today. Of the studies which appeared during the first of these two periods one may single out Scheyer's *Das Psychologische System des Maimonides* (1845) and Rosin's *Die Ethik Maimonides* (1876), but scholars would probably agree that the Arabic edition and annotated French translation contained in S. Munk's *Le Guide des Egarées* (1856-66) mark the high-point of the scholarly accomplishments of this period. Research during this period was hampered by the lack of adequate editions of the parallel Arabic texts and by the absence of monographic studies devoted to the Islamic philosophers on whom Maimonides drew. Thus, for example, Scheyer, in his study of Maimonides' psychological teachings, had to rely on citations in the Hebrew commentaries on the *Guide* for his knowledge of Maimonides' Islamic philosophic antecedents.

The turning point came in the early 1930's with the appearance of Julius Guttmann's *Die Philosophie des Judentums* (1933), Leo Strauss' seminal *Philosophie und Gesetz* (1935), and H. A. Wolfson's magisterial studies. The Arabic texts of Maimonides' Islamic predecessors now started to appear, as did monographs on their thought.

While Maimonides scholarship during the second period was devoted primarily to articles and monographs on specific problems within Maimonides' thought, certain trends in the overall interpretation of his position started to emerge. There were some scholars, primarily Strauss, Pines, and, more recently, Berman, who proposed what may be called the naturalistic interpretation of Maimonides; there were others, primarily Julius Guttmann, H. A. Wolfson and the present writer, who tended toward a more harmonistic interpretation.

The pioneering study of the naturalistic interpretation was Leo

Strauss' *Philosophie und Gesetz*—a work, judging by the footnotes, partially influenced by Leon Gauthier's *La Théorie d'Ibn Rochd (Averroès) Sur Les Rapports de la Religion et de la Philosophie* (1909), which Strauss describes as a *"Meisterhafte Analyse"* of Averroes' *Fasl al-Maqal*.[5] Gauthier's work, together with Strauss' own research on the political writings of Alfarabi, brought Strauss to emphasize the political dimensions of Maimonides' thought and the esoteric nature of his exposition.

Strauss pointed out that Maimonides (like the Muslim Aristotelians) followed Aristotle in his physical and metaphysical views, but his political teachings were Platonic. Through the intermediacy of Alfarabi, Maimonides accepted the Platonic notion that the ideal state consists of three classes of men, each one of which performs the function for which it is fit. (It should be noted that Maimonides reduces these classes to two— the elite, literally "the perfect ones," and the masses.) The ideal state can only come to be when there exists a philosopher-king who combines the virtues of the philosopher and the statesman. Pagan societies never produced a philosopher-king, so the ideal state was never found among them. By contrast, the advent of the Scriptural prophets, particularly Moses, created the possibility of the ideal state and the ideal law. Manifesting an interest in the political function of the prophet more than in the psychological processes productive of prophecy, Strauss and those who follow his approach point out that Moses, for Maimonides, becomes the embodiment *par excellence* of Plato's philosopher-king and that the state that Moses founded and the Law he brought are the embodiment of the Platonic ideal.

Strauss continued his studies of Maimonides in "The Literary Character of the Guide for the Perplexed,"[6] and in his "How to Begin the Study the *Guide of the Perplexed.*"[7] Strauss' insistence on the esoteric character of the *Guide*, his detailed analysis of its literary structure, and his painstaking investigation of its dominant themes imply a certain theory concerning Maimonides' overall views. The position of Strauss and those who follow his interpretation may be gathered from their account of two characteristic Maimonidean topics—prophecy and prophetic knowledge, and creation. From Maimonides' account of these two topics it appears, at first glance, that he believes that the prophet possesses knowledge beyond the natural knowledge attained by philosophers and that the world was created. But it may be asked: are these Maimonides' real views? Might it not be the case that Maimonides' overt statements are simply an exoteric exposition, while in his esoteric views he maintains that there is no special prophetic knowledge and that he agrees with the Aristotelians that the world is eternal?

Strauss' answer to the question appears to have undergone a change as his researches progressed. In his early *Philosophie und Gesetz* he seems to have accepted that Maimonides is the proponent of special prophetic knowledge and of creation,[8] but one gains the impression that in his later "The Literary Character of the *Guide for the Perplexed*" and "How to Begin the Study of the *Guide of the Perplexed*" he moved toward the naturalistic interpretation of Maimonides' views. While Strauss' allusive style makes it somewhat difficult to locate his views with precision, S. Pines defends the naturalistic orientation of the *Guide* in a more overt fashion. Pines, in fact, speaks of the "naturalistic aspect" of Maimonides' thought and he ascribes to him "a certain naturalistic hard-headedness."[9]

Pines' stance receives clarification from his interpretation of a passage appearing in the Introduction to the *Guide*. In this passage, Maimonides states that the knowledge of the "Secrets of the Law" comes to select individuals, the prophets, like bolts of lightning and that Moses received this kind of knowledge in pre-eminent, singular fashion. At first glance one gains the impression—and this is the opinion of most of the commentators—that Maimonides describes here a kind of intuitive illumination that only prophets can attain. Pines, however, interprets the passage in another fashion. Citing a passage from Ibn Bajjah's *Risalat al-Ittisal,* Pines explains that while it is true that Moses alone was the recipient of the highest kind of intuitive knowledge, this knowledge was within the natural powers of the human mind. Thus, Pines concludes his interpretation by stating:

> When Maimonides borrowed part of his imagery from Ibn Bajja, he must have been aware that all his readers who were more or less familiar with the main philosophic texts of his time, would tend to identify the man receiving the lightning flashes with the highest type of philosopher and not, as the passage might suggest, with the prophets.

If it is then correct that Strauss and his followers see in Maimonides primarily a philosopher committed to a naturalistic interpretation of Aristotle's views, what is the purpose of Maimonides' scriptural exegesis in the *Guide* and how does he resolve the perplexities of his reader? The answer to this question is that the *Guide* is a transitional book. The reader for whom the work was written is a believing and practicing Jew who, having studied the philosophical sciences, has become perplexed by the literal meaning of Scriptural terms and parables. To this reader Maimonides wants to show that the judicious, esoteric interpretation of Scripture reveals that the secrets of the Law are identical with the pure philosophic teachings. This was a position which Averroes had also taken. But in spite of this philosophic orientation, Maimonides, unlike Spinoza later on, requires that the philosopher must observe the commandments of Jewish Law. For while the practices contained in the Law have only a secondary function in producing the contemplative state, which, for Maimonides, is the goal of human life, they are necessary for the stability of the state, of which even the philosopher has need.

Let us now turn briefly to the second exegetical trend—that which has been described as the harmonistic interpretation. Whereas Strauss and his followers emphasize the political dimensions of Maimonides' thought, these merit less attention in the researches of scholars following the harmonistic trend. Guttmann in his *Philosophie des Judentums* barely mentions Maimonides' political views, and his account of prophecy concentrates on the psychological processes of the prophet rather than on his political function. This is not simply due to the fact that this work appeared before Strauss' *Philosophie und Gesetz*. In the Hebrew version of Guttmann's work, which appeared in 1950, not only did Guttmann see no need to revise his earlier views, he in fact argued against Strauss' thesis in a footnote.[10] While Guttmann's reaction to Strauss has so far been largely a matter of conjecture, a posthumously published work by him has helped to explicate his views. In his *Philosophie der Religion oder Philosophie des Gesetzes?*[11] Guttmann shows his appreciation of Strauss' study of the political and legal dimensions of Maimonides' thought, but reiterates at the same time his conviction that theoretical philosophic concerns lie at the center of Maimonides' thought. In a salient passage, Guttmann writes:

> Auch wenn man Strauss den schleehthinnigen Primat des Gesetzes zugeben wollewere es doch nur das Recht des Philosophierens, das im Gesetz begründet ist. Ihre sachliche Grundlegung vollzieht die Philosophie selbst, und ihr innerer Aufbau wird dureh den sachlichen Zusammenhang ihrer Probleme bestimmt.[12]

It is similarly interesting to note that H. A. Wolfson, who has written on many aspects of Maimonides' thought, did not devote a study to his political views. Instead, proponents of the harmonistic trend turned their attention to Maimonides' physical, psychological, and metaphysical views out of the apparent conviction that these topics provide the most important issues of the *Guide*.

While proponents of the harmonistic interpretation are aware of Maimonides' use of contradictions, they do not place this principle at the center of their interpretation of the *Guide*. Hence, they take Maimonides at his word when he affirms his belief in creation, when he makes prophecy in some way dependent on the will of God, and when he holds that prophets can acquire knowledge which is not available to the philosopher. H. A. Wolfson expresses this point of view when he writes:

> They both [Halevi and Maimonides] agree that God acts with free will and that in His action there is therefore an element of grace and election, opposing thereby the view which they both attribute to Aristotle and to the philosophers in general that God acts by the necessity of His nature.[13]

Guttmann speaks in a similar vein when he writes: "Even with regard to speculation the prophet transcends the pure philosopher, for cognition rises in him to speculative heights that surpass the boundaries of that which can discursively be grasped."[14]

What, then, according to the harmonistic interpretation is the complexion of Maimonides' thought and what is the purpose of the *Guide*? H. A. Wolfson, in his first published study, answered this question by felicitously describing Maimonides as an Aristotelian, though with limitations. By that he meant that "[it was Maimonides' aim] to show that Scriptures and Talmud, correctly interpreted, strictly harmonize with the philosophical writings of Aristotle."[15] However this harmonization is limited in the sense that the human mind has only a limited capacity for truth. Beyond that—in areas such as creation, prophetic knowledge and so forth—Scripture provides a truth not available to the unaided human intellect. In writing the *Guide* it was Maimonides' task to show that Scripture, properly interpreted, contains the truths of Aristotelian physics and metaphysics but that, in addition, it provides knowledge which man cannot attain by his own natural powers. In somewhat different language, Guttmann makes the same point when he writes.

> Maimonides' theistic Aristotelianism made room for the creator-God of the Bible within his philosophic outlook, thereby effecting metaphysically a real synthesis between Biblical religion and Aristotelianism.[16]

III

Confronted by these two divergent interpretations, what is the contemporary interpreter to do and can he ever hope for a resolution of this dilemma? Isadore Twersky has given expression to the interpreter's problem when he writes in his *Maimonides Reader:* "This dialectic and these difficulties [of the *Guide*] continue to befuddle and divide students of the *Guide* concerning Maimonides' true intention and actual religious stance. There is little agreement among scholars in this area."[17]

Having studied Maimonides consistently for decades, I have no clear-cut answer to our question. My own preference is for the harmonistic interpretation, though I cannot close my eyes to the merits of the naturalistic school.[18] I want to conclude, however, with two suggestions for future Maimonides' studies which, to my mind, will help to clarify our problem.

My first suggestion is to investigate anew Maimonides' psychological doctrines. Admittedly this is not easy, since his discussion of psychological topics is rather scant. But we now have good editions of psychological writings of Alfarabi, Avicenna, Ibn Bajjah, and Averroes which will undoubtedly be of help. Specifically, the nature of the illuminative experience described in the Introduction of the *Guide* should once again be investigated. My second suggestion is to probe further the relation of Maimonides' teachings to those of the Ash'arite Ghazali. While it is evident that Maimonides' stance is quite different from that of Ghazali, scholars have suggested that what has been called Ghazali's occasionalism may have had some influence on Maimonides' thought. An answer to the question "What is the correct interpretation of Maimonides' thought?" may lie at the end of a long road, studies such as those suggested might help to move us along the way.

---

[1] Cf. *Guide*, I, introduction.

[2] English citations are taken from S. Pines' translation of the *Guide*.

[3] See S. Pines, "Translator's Introduction," *Guide of the Perplexed* (Chicago, 1963), lix-lxi, cviii and H. A. Wolfson, *Crescas' Critique of Aristotle* (Cambridge, Mass., 1929), 323.

[4] A. Marx, "Texts by and about Maimonides," *JQR*, n. s., XXV (1934-35): 380.

[5] Strauss, 70, n. 1.

[6] In S. W. Baron, ed., *Essays on Maimonides: An Octocengennial Volume* (New York, 1941); the article also appeared in Strauss' *Persecution and the Art of Writing* (Glencoe, I.L., 1952).

[7] In S. Pines' English translation of the *Guide* (Chicago, 1963).

[8] pp. 76-79.

[9] "Translator's Introduction," xcvii and cix.

[10] *Ha-Philosophiah shel ha-Yahadut*, 394, n. 476b; *Philosophies of Judaism*, 434, n. 125.

[11] *Proceedings*, The Israel Academy of Sciences and Humanities, V (Jerusalem, 1974), 6.

[12] Ibid., 168 [23].

[13] "Hallevi and Maimonides on Prophecy," *JQR*, n. s., XXXII (1942): 345.

[14] *Philosophie des Judentums*, 195, my own translation.

[15] "Maimonides and Halevi: A Study in Typical Attitudes towards Greek Philosophy in the Middle Ages," *JQR*, n. s., II (1912): 307.

[16] *Philosophie des Judentums*, 205, my own translation.

[17] 21, note.

[18] See my "Some Aspects of Maimonides' Philosophy of Nature," *La Filosofia della Natura del Medioevo*, (Milan, 1966), 209-218 and "Maimonides' Thirteen Principles," *Jewish Medieval and and Renaissance Studies*, ed. A. Altmann (Cambridge, M.A., 1967), 119-144.

THE SOVEREIGNTY OF DOGMA: RAMBAM AND/OR THE MISHNAH

Shalom Carmy

The Problem

Like so many philosophers, Aristotle defined man as a thinking animal. If philosophers of our time are less given to such essentialist concepts, and both secular and religious thinkers insist on the importance of non-intellectual components in human existence, it is nonetheless impossible to limit spiritual and religious life to mere behavior. Rambam, more than any other Jewish thinker, integrated the life of the mind within the comprehensive framework of codified Torah.

As is often the case with Rambam, the rationale for his inclusions and omissions is not made explicit. The three centuries that followed Rambam's enumeration of the principles of faith precipitated a substantial literature on dogma, criticizing, defending and offering alternatives to the classic list he proposed in his commentary to the Mishnah, in the introduction to the chapter "All Israel have a Share in the World to Come" (*Perek Helek*) of Tractate *Sanhedrin*. R. Hasdai Crescas, R. Yosef Albo and R. Isaac Abarbanel are among the most famous participants in this debate.

I do not propose to survey their work, nor do I wish to compare Rambam's famous formulation in the Mishnah commentary with classifications of normative belief found in his later books, such as the catalogue of heresies in "Laws of Repentance" chapter 3 and *Guide to the Perplexed*. Instead we will start from two fairly obvious questions concerning the relation between the *mishnah* and Rambam's conclusions:

1) How did Rambam get from the *mishnah*'s three principles to his own thirteen?

2) The *mishnah*'s list of dogmas is negative: it is denial of the principles that excludes one from the World to Come. Rambam's list is positive: in order to merit a portion in the World to Come, the believer must subscribe to the requisite beliefs. What justifies Rambam's move to this stricter demand?

After forty years, Professor Hyman's article is still the best treatment of these questions.[1] Clearly the list of thirteen principles is an expansion of the *mishnah*'s three. The dogmas pertaining to the existence of God, His unity, incorporeality, eternity, and unique worthiness of worship correspond to the *mishnah*'s exclusion of the "*Apikoros*," who denies divine involvement in the universe, from the World to Come. The next four—belief in prophecy, in the unique status of Moses, in the completeness of the Mosaic revelation and its unchangeability—elaborate upon the *mishnah*'s principle of Torah from Heaven. The last four, referring to divine omniscience, reward and punishment, the coming of the Messiah and resurrection of the dead, are rooted in the *mishnah*'s insistence on belief in resurrection as a Torah doctrine.

Regarding the second question, Hyman explains that true belief, for Rambam, is intrinsically connected to immortality of the soul. It is by means of true belief that human beings constitute their "acquired intellect" and it is this metaphysical entity that becomes immortal. Therefore, in order to merit a portion in the World to Come, it is not sufficient for a person to avoid heretical belief. He or she must adhere to true beliefs. Here Rambam's philosophical perspective affects his rewriting of the *mishnah*.

On further analysis, our answer to the first question—the suggestion that Rambam is expanding the *mishnah*'s list—is open to two interpretations. Perhaps Rambam would maintain that the author of the *mishnah* in fact intended Rambam's elaborated version but, for some reason, perhaps a laconic style, the *mishnah* did not spell out the thirteen principles. Another possibility is that Rambam would concede that although the author of the *mishnah* presumably had in mind only the three principles set down, he allowed for Rambam's expansion as a legitimate formulation of the *mishnah*'s legal message. Insofar as the content of Rambam's thirteen principles, despite its general similarity to the language of the *mishnah*, is not logically entailed by the *mishnah*, the second approach seems more plausible. We are then left wondering how Rambam would justify his assertion of the expanded version as normatively defining the intellectual standard for partaking of the World to Come.

The same problem is even more troublesome with respect to our second question. Offhand there is a sharp difference between requiring a positive belief in a doctrine and merely proscribing the denial of a true doctrine. We have little difficulty imagining individuals who have not thought about Rambam's principles, and hence neither affirm nor deny them. Our late Cartesian heritage inculcates doubt as a desirable intellectual orientation and tends to admire, at least in theory, the skeptic who keeps himself aloof from real assent, holding beliefs at arm's length, or gazing upon them as one paring his fingernails; in its post-modern devolution, the actual truth of religious doctrine is treated, with a shrug of the shoulders, as a matter of no importance. Taken literally, the *mishnah* does not exclude such individuals from the World to Come; Rambam does.

For those who wish to deny, or minimize, the place of normative belief in Judaism, Rambam is thus cast in the role of the villain. From their perspective, the requirement of correct belief separates Orthodox Judaism from the rest of the Jewish people, and thus undermines Jewish unity and cooperation. It is not my purpose in this brief article to discuss whether this is the case—though I agree with David Berger's observation that those who deviate from Orthodoxy in their beliefs almost always deviate in their behavior as well, so that an exclusively behavioral definition is hardly more inclusive than one that does not omit intellectual commandments. Nor do I wish to belabor the fact that even those who minimize the importance of belief recognize, willy nilly, that Judaism is incompatible with certain beliefs; even those who accept Jewish agnosticism or atheism blanch at the idea of Jewish-Christian syncretism.

My purpose in this brief article is to supply a rationale for Rambam's expansion, and transformation, of the *mishnah*'s list. I am not building on implicit hints in Rambam's own texts because, in this area, I have not identified such unarticulated arguments. The plausibility of my story is thus rooted in its plausibility as an account of how dogma ought to be formulated. Furthermore, my account bears significant similarity to the way we think about the formulation of halakhic principles. Hence I expect my proposal about Jewish dogmatology to resonate with readers who have thought seriously about the unfolding of halakhic deliberation. For such persons, my approach may seem obvious to the point of triviality.

Formulating Dogma

The premise underlying my explanation is simple: it is that the believer in Torah begins with the "raw material" of doctrine, as provided by revelation. Reflection on this raw data eventually leads to normative formulas. Initial formulations of this reflection will often seem coarser grained than later stages of the process. At the very least, each formulation provokes questions about the precise meaning of terms, or about the relationship between the particular doctrine being presented and other propositions that are part of the network of beliefs, and so forth. Advanced stages of reflection are likely to be more abstract and richer in detail. Though no intellectual principle or law is totally free of indeterminacy, successive attempts at formulation successfully redefine and delimit the areas of uncertainty.

Illustrations from the realm of *halakhah* are myriad. Frequently, the *Tanna'im* state a law in concrete terms; it is only in later discourse that the law is reformulated as a general principle. Thus, earlier sources[2] imply that R. Shimon and R. Yehudah disagreed about whether it is permissible to drag a bench over the ground on Sabbath, given the likelihood of making a groove. It is only the later discussion that discovers in this dispute a universal debate about responsibility for the unintended consequences of an act (*davar she-eino mitkavven*). Later students of *halakhah* refine the full ramifications of these principles through a variety of case applications and conceptual analysis. If the original historical figures in the discussion, like the baffled Moses whom *Hazal* depict attending the school of R. Akiva,[3] cannot recognize the language or trace the intricate implications of their primeval positions, this is the way of *Torah she-Be'al Peh*, ever more sophisticated in its tools, forever loyal to the raw material of revelation.

The same is true of theological reflection. I submit that, for Rambam, the *mishnah* recorded the raw material at the base of Jewish theology, the recognition that certain beliefs are central and necessary for Judaism. As noted, these pertained to the nature of God, Torah, and reward and punishment. Rambam did not take the specific clauses in the *mishnah* to be the ultimate formulations of Jewish belief. Insofar as he believed that he had refined the instances of unacceptable belief enumerated by the *mishnah*, he provided a more elaborate menu of heresy, which expanded the three principles into thirteen. And insofar as he believed that he had attained more precise articles of faith than were available to his predecessors, and so could provide his community with a more adequate regimen of belief, he was also prepared to judge normative a positive adherence to these beliefs, rather than mere avoidance of error.

One necessary condition for the greater rigor of Rambam's dogmatology, compared with that of the *mishnah*, is thus the intellectual possibility of achieving such exactitude. A second condition would be the desirability of mandating such precision. A thinker who did not consider rightness of belief, regarding these questions, to be a matter of grave importance, might have been satisfied to allow more vagueness in formulating their obligatory nature. In addition to his confidence that he had made progress in identifying the essential doctrines of Jewish theology, Rambam clearly held that some of his principles, such as the incorporeality of God, must be thoroughly internalized, in conformity with his philosophical teachings.

Learning from Ahad Ha'am

This year is not only the 800th anniversary of Rambam's death; it is also the centenary of the 700th anniversary. Among the literary productions that honored his memory in 1905, the famous essay *Shilton ha-Sekhel* ("The Sovereignty of Intellect"), by the highly influential Ahad Ha'am, remains part of our cultural background. I would like to utilize his article to make a point about Rambam's dogmatic orientation.

Ahad Ha'am was a secularist; he believed in Jewish culture. As a cultural Jew, he found Rambam's intellectualism a source of inspiration for his own rationalism. This is a primary theme in his tribute to Rambam. At the same time, Ahad Ha'am was not an advocate of cultural or intellectual activity detached from the needs of the Jewish people. It is this combination of free-thinking and social responsibility that made him the indispensable writer and editor of his time. Ahad Ha'am does not want to create the impression that Rambam was the kind of rootless intellectual he rejected. And so he observed that Rambam adopted belief in resurrection of the dead as one of his thirteen principles, even though this doctrine did not sit well with the medieval Aristotelian metaphysics that attracted him.

Indeed, except for the Introduction to *Perek Helek*, Rambam avoids discussing bodily resurrection, to the point that he was questioned about the omission. In his Epistle on Resurrection of the Dead, Rambam admits that it is not his favorite doctrine. For a philosopher who valued the activity of the intellect above that of the body, immortality of the soul, which plays a more conspicuous role in Rambam's thought,[4] has all the advantages with none of the drawbacks connected to the notion of an eternally functioning body.

Why then did Rambam preach corporeal resurrection? Ahad Ha'am says he did it to satisfy the masses, who favored tangible bodily survival over the elitist spiritual reward so dear to Rambam and his enlightened fellow philosophers. The moral, according to Ahad Ha'am, is that the ideal Jewish intellectual ought to condescend to popular taste rather than insist uncompromisingly on the truths of reason. This lesson, of course, befits the outlook of cultural Zionism.

The lesson, for those who take Rambam at his word, is that normative Jewish belief is more than the projection of an individual thinker's philosophy. However much a thinker molds the raw material of revelation and normative tradition in the light of his or her philosophical orientation—and it is neither necessary nor possible to deny the way in which Rambam's philosophical views influenced his interpretation of the data supplied by the Torah—there comes a point where intellectual honesty and religious integrity demand a humbling of one's own intellectual inclinations and convictions in the face of what one recognizes as the authentic voice of the tradition.

---

[1] "Maimonides' Thirteen Principles" in Alexander Altmann ed., *Jewish Medieval and Renaissance Studies* (Cambridge, M.A.: 1967).

[2] Cited in *Shabbat* 46b; *Beiza* 23b, *inter alia*.

[3] *Menahot* 29

[4] See *Hilkhot Teshuvah* 8-10 for a prominent example within *Mishneh Torah*.

Some Ironic Consequences of Maimonides' Rationalist Approach to the Messianic Age

David Berger

Rationalism and messianic activism are conceptual strangers. The rationalist views the world as ever following its natural course. The typical messianic activist views it as teetering on the edge of fundamental change that will topple the order of the Creation, or perhaps more accurately, restore that order to its ideal form. The rationalist perspective is hostile even to the activist who anticipates a naturalistic messianic age that is "no different from the current world except with regard to our subjugation to [foreign] kingdoms" (*Talmud Bavli, Berakhot* 34b; *Sanhedrin* 99a) since even such an activist seeks to hasten the end, while the sober and skeptical view of the rationalist reminds him that Jewish history is replete with messianic disappointment. He believes in the coming of the anticipated day, but even if the deeds of the Jewish people can help speed its arrival, he understands those deeds as the ordinary performance of *mizvot*, and not classic messianic activity. Both the psychology of the rationalist and his logic dictate his fundamental opposition to messianic activism.[1]

And yet, it is not only the case that rationalism and messianic activism sometimes coexist; inevitably, and against the will of those who uphold the banner of messianic rationalism, the rationalist orientation produces views that serve as the impetus for active messianism and provide a means of defense for messianic phenomena of even the most hysterical sort. As if impelled by a demon, the skeptical thinker extends

---

* This is an English translation of an article that originally appeared in *Maimonidean Studies* 2 (1991).

decisive support to movements that are thoroughly inimical to his mode of thought.

I

One example of this phenomenon is set forth without reference to its implicit irony in Gerson Cohen's essay on the messianic postures of Ashkenazic and Sephardic Jews. Cohen suggests that it was precisely the rationalistic worldview of the Sephardim that generated optimism regarding the possibility of penetrating the secrets of history, and thus, some Sephardic intellectuals succumbed to the temptation of eschatological calculation. Even though these thinkers themselves were not caught up in messianic movements, they created an atmosphere charged with messianic tension, which made the masses more receptive to a variety of messiahs.[2] Cohen's thesis is intriguing, but it cannot be accepted with certainty both because the messianic movements in question were not particularly significant and because it is possible to offer other tenable explanations for Sephardic messianism.[3]

Another example of this phenomenon whose sharp irony has not been previously noted derives from the most famous messianic passage in the writings of Maimonides—the description of the messianic process that appears at the end of "The Laws of Kings":

> Do not suppose that the Messianic King must produce signs and wonders, bring about new phenomena in the world, resurrect the dead, and the like. This is not so… If a king will arise from the House of David who studies the Torah and pursues the commandments like his ancestor David in accordance with the written and oral law, and compels all Israel to follow and strengthen it and fights the wars of the Lord—this man enjoys the presumption of being the Messiah.. If he proceeds successfully, builds the Temple in its place, and gathers the dispersed of Israel, then he is surely the Messiah (*Mishneh Torah*, "Laws of Kings" 11:3).

In the following chapter, Maimonides adds the following:

> As to all these matters and others like them, no one knows how they will happen until they happen, because they are impenetrable matters among the prophets. The Sages too had no tradition about these issues; rather, they weighed the Scriptural evidence, and that is why they differed about these matters. In any event, neither the sequence of these events nor their details are fundamental to the faith, so that no one should occupy himself and spend an inordinate

amount of time studying the *aggadot* and *midrashim* that deal with these and similar matters, nor should he make them central, for they lead to neither love nor fear of God. Nor should one calculate the end.... Rather, one should wait and believe in the general doctrine as we have explained (*Mishneh Torah*, "Laws of Kings" 12:2).

It is evident that Maimonides' purpose, which he formulates here almost explicitly, is to moderate and dissipate messianic tension.[4] One who understands that the statements of the rabbinic sages regarding these matters can be mistaken will not direct most of his energy toward the study of the *midrashim* that describe the redemptive process and will thus not succumb to the dangerous messianic temptation. But this practical purpose is not the only consideration that motivated Maimonides' assertion. There can be no doubt that his repudiation of signs and wonders and his rejection of confident reliance upon rabbinic *aggadot* derive from a fundamental rationalist perspective. He believed, however, that the philosophical approach and the practical objective go hand-in-hand. To provide further security, he went on to propose standards necessary for establishing not only messianic certainty, but even presumptive messianic status. Not everyone who wants to lay claim to the mantle can come and do so.[5]

And yet, not only was this rationalist approach inadequate to stem the tide of burgeoning messianism, under certain circumstances it actually helped fan the flames of a messianic movement by depriving its opponents of their primary weapon. In the absence of an existing movement, it may be that Maimonides' approach could convince certain types of readers to refrain from plunging into messianic activity,[6] but when messianic movements already have a solid footing, this rationalist approach brings about results diametrically opposed to those that Maimonides expected.

In the presence of a real messianic pretender whose followers affirm with certainty that the process of redemption is already upon us, what evidence is available to non-believers who wish to demonstrate beyond doubt that this is not the Messiah, nor is this the beginning of the redemption? If the figure in question is neither an ignoramus nor a heretic, the only option is to demonstrate that specific conditions that should already have been met at this stage have in fact not been fulfilled. There is simply no other argument that can refute the messianic claim with certainty.

And now, along comes Maimonides to inform us that the Messiah need not perform a single sign or wonder, and that even the rabbinic descriptions of the messianic process are not authoritative. If so, the non-believer's sole method of providing an absolute refutation of the messiah has been taken away from him. In the throes of the enthusiasm and psychological upheaval marking a powerful messianic movement, the certainty of the believer will surely wield greater force than the tentative rejection expressed by the denier. Under these conditions, even the criteria required to establish the status of presumptive Messiah offer little assistance to the skeptic. First, someone who has not yet attained the status of presumptive Messiah could still conceivably turn out to be the Messiah; thus, even one who argues that these criteria have not been met cannot rule out the possibility that the figure in question is destined to be the redeemer. Moreover, it was precisely Maimonides' rationalistic approach that compelled him to choose standards that are not so difficult to achieve—at least in the eyes of a believer. Thus, before Shabbetai Zevi's apostasy, his followers were convinced that he was a king of Davidic ancestry who studied the Torah and pursued the commandments, that he compelled all Israel to follow and strengthen it, and that he fought the wars of the Lord if only in a spiritual sense. Similarly (after due allowance for the deep differences between the movements), just such an explicit argument can be found in publications of some circles in the Habad movement, who see all the virtues enumerated by Maimonides in the personality and deeds of the Lubavitcher Rebbe.[7] It is very difficult for a rationalist to establish pre-messianic requirements that someone who is not the Messiah would find absolutely impossible to fulfill, especially since the criteria are, by their very nature, designed to characterize an individual who could ultimately turn out not to be the Messiah.

If we now turn our attention to the largest messianic movement in the history of Judaism, we will see that we are not dealing with a merely abstract possibility. One who carefully reads *Sefer Zizat Novel Zevi* by R. Jacob Sasportas, the primary opponent of Sabbateanism before the apostasy, will realize that the Maimonidean ruling from the "Laws of Kings" was the major stumbling block that he faced, preventing him from presenting his rejection of Shabbetai Zevi's messianic claim in unequivocal terms. It is true that Sasportas continually relies on the words of Maimonides as his basis for rejecting a confident affirmation of the Sabbatean faith, and this reliance is legitimate and even convincing for those who are prepared to be convinced. However, his frequent assertion that the Sabbateans deny the validity of Maimonides' position obscures the true historic impact of this Maimonidean passage on the raging controversy regarding the Messiahship of Shabbetai Zevi.

Scholem, for example, writes that while Nehemiah Cohen relied on sources such as *Sefer Zerubavel* and *Sefer Otot ha-Mashiah*[8] to refute the claim of the messianic pretender, Sasportas relied upon Maimonides and the plain meaning of Biblical texts.[9] This is correct. Nonetheless, it is absolutely clear that if Maimonides had ended his "Laws of Kings" after Chapter 10 without ever writing the last two chapters on the Messiah, Sasportas would have presented his objections to Sabbateanism on the basis of the plain meaning of Scripture and other sources such as the *Zohar* without any need for the Maimonidean position. Even more so – and this is the main point – had Maimonides not written these final two chapters, Sasportas would have presented his rejection of Shabbetai Zevi's Messiahship not tentatively but with absolute conviction. Anyone who relies upon the passage in the *Mishneh Torah* for anti-Sabbatean purposes must also accept its authority with respect to the view that we have no definitive knowledge of the messianic process. Maimonides' position proved to be a minor and almost negligible impediment to the Sabbatean movement; its primary impact was to lend the movement major and almost definitive support.

Let us examine several illustrations from *Sefer Zizat Novel Zevi:*

> And if those who rebel against the rabbis' words [i.e., the Sabbatean believers] will say that our sages have not hit upon the truth, and, as Maimonides said, all these matters cannot be known by man until they occur, then I too agree. But I will not discard the tradition of our sages, all of whose words are justice and truth, before the messianic fulfillment. And if after that fulfillment, it turns out that their statements still do not accord [with the actual course of events], then the Messiah himself will argue on their behalf... And if you have acted out of piety by believing [in Shabbetai Zevi], you have in fact placed yourselves in the straits of serious doubt... Either way, I am innocent and bear no iniquity... Have you heard me declare in public that this is all lies and falsehood? Rather, I have told all those believers who have asked me that it is possible [that he is the Messiah], although it is a distant possibility until he has performed a messianic act.[10]

And in another passage:

> None of his initial deeds accord with the words of Rabbi Simeon bar Yohai in [*Zohar*] *Parashat Shemot*, and God forbid that we

should say, like the ignorant among the masses, that none of our sages hit upon the truth. And though Maimonides stated in the above mentioned passage that no one will know these matters until they occur, he nonetheless agrees that until that time, we are to remain rooted in the tradition of our sages.[11]

It is clear from these passages that were it not for the Maimonidean ruling, the followers of Shabbetai Zevi would have been at a loss to account for the lack of congruence between what they saw as reality and the depiction of the redemptive process in rabbinic texts and the *Zohar*. It is also clear that Sasportas would have taken advantage of this lack of congruence to refute the Sabbatean messianic claim categorically. Indeed, after the apostasy, we find a letter by R. Joseph Halevi denying Shabbetai Zevi's Messiahship on the basis of passages from the Talmud and the *Zohar* that are no less relevant to the period before the apostasy, and he does so without any need for additional arguments relying upon Maimonides.[12] The importance of Maimonides for the Sabbateans themselves is manifest in the words of Nathan of Gaza, who falls back upon the Maimonidean passage even after the apostasy of his master:

> And though we have found no hint of this matter in the explicit words of the Torah, we have already seen how strange the sages' words are regarding these matters, so that we cannot fully understand anything they say in their context, as the great luminary Maimonides has also testified; their words will be understood only when the events actually unfold.[13]

I would not venture so far as to say that the success of the Sabbatean movement would have been impossible if not for the Maimonidean ruling, but there can be no doubt that we are witness here to a sharp and highly significant irony.

It is particularly interesting that Maimonides himself encountered the problem that we have been examining when he composed his *Epistle to Yemen*. The *Epistle*'s assertion that the Messiah *will* be recognized by signs and wonders results from the need to reject the messianic mission of a specific individual by establishing clearcut criteria. Thus, the discrepancy between the "Laws of Kings" and the *Epistle* on this point also demonstrates the tension between rationalism and the requirements of anti-messianic polemic during a confrontation with a real messianic movement.[14]

II

Until now we have concerned ourselves with messianic activism of an extreme sort that did not arise out of rationalism but used it effectively as a protective shield. Now we will turn to more moderate messianic manifestations that derive in no small part from the naturalistic conception of the redemption, which continues to provide them with inspiration to this day. Thus, the ironic connection between the restrained messianism of the rationalist and messianic activism is by no means restricted to the Middle Ages and the beginning of the modern period; it extends into the modern age, leaving its mark on Religious Zionism both in the nineteenth century and in our own day. This irony arises from deep within messianic rationalism and is rooted in its very essence. On the one hand, the naturalistic conception of the redemption tends to prevent messianic delusions as well as behavior that deviates from the realm of the normal. But on the other hand, the very nature of the naturalistic conception encourages activism. If the Messiah is not destined to appear with the clouds of heaven, if it is necessary to fight the wars of the Lord in the plain sense of the word, if the Temple is not destined to descend fully assembled from the heavens, if it is necessary to re-institute *semikhah* (the direct chain of rabbinic ordination between master and pupil deriving from Sinai) and the *Sanhedrin* before the arrival of the redeemer, then human activity is needed to help realize the messianic hope. This conclusion appears so clear and unavoidable that some scholars and thinkers view Maimonides as a guiding spirit for religious Zionism.[15]

It seems to me that despite the logic inherent in this claim, Maimonides had no such intentions. He advises his readers simply to "wait." The Maimonidean positions that are capable of generating messianic activism derive solely from rational and halakhic considerations. For example, the determination that *semikhah* must be re-instituted by an act of the rabbis in the land of Israel before the redemption can occur is based on a verse from Isaiah in conjunction with the quintessential Maimonidean position that the *halakhah* will not change at the End of Days and that miracles are to be left out of the messianic process.[16] This approach precludes Maimonides from describing a *Sanhedrin* composed of rabbis without *semikhah*, or of proposing, as did certain rabbis after him, that *semikhah* would be re-instituted with the return to earth of the prophet Elijah (who certainly had *semikhah*) from his place in the heavens.

There is no intention on the part of Maimonides to encourage actions expressly designed to bring the redeemer. Nevertheless, Jacob Katz's important essay showed how his position led to the famous attempt to re-institute *semikhah* in sixteenth-century Safed out of explicit messianic motivations.[17]

Similarly, Maimonides' determination that the Third Temple will be built by human hands, a determination that was so important to R. Zevi Hirsch Kalischer in his proto-Zionist polemic, certainly did not stem from a desire to encourage messianic activism. The view that the Third Temple will fall intact from the heavens appeared in marginal sources, and Rashi introduced it into the center of Jewish messianic consciousness only as a consequence of a serious difficulty in a Talmudic passage in tractates *Sukkah* and *Rosh ha-Shanah*. There, the Talmud states that the origin of a particular rabbinic prohibition lies in a concern arising out of the possibility that the Third Temple might be built at night or on a holiday. Rashi raises an objection based on another Talmudic passage that unequivocally prohibits building the Temple during these times, and he resolves the contradiction by concluding that the Third Temple will not be built by human hands.[18] Although from a purely exegetical standpoint there is no better answer than the one offered by Rashi, a commentator who has been influenced by rationalism will be unwilling even to consider such a possibility. For this reason, R. Menahem ha-Meiri does not even mention Rashi's explanation, and instead he forces himself to manufacture a suggestion that we are concerned about the prospect of an error by the rabbinic court, which out of love for the Temple may allow it to be constructed during times when it is forbidden to do so.[19] That is to say, ha-Meiri is prepared to express concern about an error by a rabbinic court presumably functioning under the supervision of the Messiah himself so that he will not have to entertain the notion of buildings dropping out of the sky. Despite the rationalist motivation, which has nothing to do with messianic activism, the position that the Third Temple would be built by human hands—as well as related naturalistic approaches—had a greater potential to generate such activism than the approach that looks forward to miracles in which human beings play no active role.

As I have noted, there are scholars who do not see the irony in this situation because they attribute to Maimonides a conscious, though moderate, activist intention. I see no evidence for this motivation in his writings, and I am not willing to create such a Maimonidean position based on logical considerations alone, when his explicit directive is simply to wait.[20] On the other hand, scholars who have dealt with Maimonides' influence on messianic developments before the rise of Zionism tend to view his stand as a successful attempt to thwart messianic activism. As we have seen, this position too is highly questionable. It seems to me that we stand before an ironic paradox with significant consequences. The rationalist, while striving to moderate the messianic drive, will sometimes unwillingly enhance it.

---

[1] I have used the term "rationalist" to refer, following Nahmanides' formulation, to someone who tends to maximize nature and limit miracles, and who reacts skeptically toward beliefs that lack plausible evidence. It should be understood that the term carries no fixed definition, and when referring to medieval thinkers, one must utilize standards appropriate to that period.

[2] Gerson D. Cohen, "Messianic Postures of Ashkenazim and Sephardim" in *Studies of the Leo Baeck Institute*, ed. Max Kreutzberger (New York, 1967), 56-115.

[3] For another explanation, see my article, "Three Typological Themes in Early Jewish Messianism: Messiah Son of Joseph, Rabbinic Calculations, and the Figure of Armilus," *AJS Review* 10 (1985): 162, n. 82.

[4] Cf. Amos Funkenstein, *Teva, Historia, u-Meshihiyyut ezel ha-Rambam* (Tel-Aviv, 1983), 57: "The purpose of the substantial attention that Maimonides dedicated to the messianic era was to prevent the proliferation of messianic movements seeking to hasten the End, and thus, following his forerunners who advocated a realistic messianism, he refrained from painting the Messiah in overly concrete colors. To do so would give an opening to anyone who wanted to come and proclaim himself the Messiah." We shall see as we proceed that the last part of this passage requires fundamental rethinking.

[5] The importance of the category of presumptive Messiah in preventing the spread of messianic movements is highlighted in Aviezer Ravitsky's analysis, "Ke-fi Koah ha-Adam: Yemot ha-Mashiah be-Mishnat ha-Rambam," in *Meshihiyyut ve-Eskatologiyyah*, Zvi Baras, ed. (Jerusalem, 1983), 205-206, and in David Hartman's introduction to A.S. Halkin and D. Hartman, *Crisis and Leadership: Epistles of Maimonides* (Philadelphia, 1985), 191. On Maimonides' moderate approach to events in the messianic era, see Gershom Scholem, *The Messianic Idea in Judaism* (New York, 1971), 24-32.

[6] Though, as we will see, even this assumption needs to be substantially qualified.

[7] See M. Zelikson, "Kol Mevasser Mevasser ve-Omer," *Kovez Hiddushei Torah: ha-Melekh ha-Mashiah ve-ha-Ge'ullah ha-Shelemah* (1983), 14-17. See also: "Mihu Yehudi: Shabbat ha-Gadol—ve-ha-Hishtammetut ha-Gedolah," *Kfar Chabad* (1984), 53, at the end of the essay.

[8] These were popular works depicting an apocalyptic drama preceding the messianic age.

[9] Gershom Scholem, *Shabbetai Zevi ve-ha-Tenuah ha-Shabbeta'it bi-Yemei Hayyav* (Tel Aviv, 1957), 557-559.

[10] Isaiah Tishbi, *Sefer Zizat Novel Zevi le-Rabbi Ya'akov Sasportas* (Jerusalem, 1954), 104.

[11] Ibid., 119. The reference to *Zohar Parashat Shemot* points to an extensive and detailed description of events during the course of the messianic process that should have already occurred, at least in part, by that point in the Sabbatean movement. See *Zohar*, Part II, 7b and following.

[12] Ibid., 190-191, and cf. 195.

[13] Ibid., 260. See Scholem, *Shabbetai Zevi*, 628.

[14] See: Maimonides, *Iggerot*, ed. Yosef Kafah (Jerusalem, 1972). There is some plausibility in Kafah's attempt to harmonize the assertion in the *Epistle* with Maimonides' position in the *Mishneh Torah*. See Kafah's notes *ad loc*. Nonetheless, the emphasis in the *Epistle* is certainly different from the impression given by the "Laws of Kings."

[15] For this general conception from different perspectives and with different degrees of emphasis, see Joel L. Kramer, "On Maimonides' Messianic Postures" in *Studies in Medieval Jewish History and Literature II*, ed. Isadore Twersky (Cambridge, MA, and London, 1984), 109-142; Aryeh Botwinick, "Maimonides' Messianic Age," *Judaism* 33 (1984): 425; Menachem Kellner, "Messianic Postures in Israel Today," *Modern Judaism* 6 (1986): 197-209; Shubert Spero, "Maimonides and the Sense of History," *Tradition* 24:2 (1989): 128-137.

[16] Maimonides, *Perush ha-Mishnayot, Sanhedrin* 1:3; cf. *Hilkhot Sanhedrin* 4:11. This example is cited by several of the authors in the previous footnote. See also Funkenstein, *Teva, Historia, u-Meshihiyyut*, 64-68.

[17] Jacob Katz, "Mahloket ha-Semikhah bein Rabbi Ya'akov Beirav ve-ha-Ralbah," *Ziyyon* 15 (1951): 28-45.

[18] Rashi, *Sukkah* 41a s.v. *i nami; Rosh ha-Shanah* 30a s.v. *la tserikha*. Cf. Tzvi Hirsch Kalischer, *Derishat Ziyyon*, Israel Klausner ed. (Jerusalem, 1964), 144-147.

[19] Ha-Meiri, *Beit ha-Behirah, Sukkah, ad loc*.

[20] For reasons that may be scholarly and may be personal, I do not assert that Maimonides' own posture would have necessarily compelled him to oppose the messianic motif in religious Zionism, especially after the development of the larger movement out of other considerations; my remark at the beginning of this essay about movements that are "thoroughly inimical to [the rationalist's] mode of thought" refers to Sabbateanism and other classic messianic movements. Still, the encouragement of messianic activism, even of the moderate type, played no role in Maimonides' consciousness, but emerged willy-nilly out of his rationalist position.

On the other hand, the attempt to use Maimonides to prove that there is no messianic significance in the establishment of the State of Israel runs afoul of the problem we pointed out in the first half of the essay. Proponents of this position customarily point out that Maimonides mentions the ingathering of the exiles only after the appearance of the Messiah and the rebuilding of the Temple ("Laws of Kings" 11:4). But Maimonides himself pointed out in his "agnostic" ruling ("Laws of Kings" 12:2) that the order of these events is not central to the faith. When I mentioned this to Zalman Alpert of the Yeshiva University Library, he graciously directed me to the exchange between Amnon Shapira and Dov Wolpe, *Ammudim* 413, 415, 416 (1980): 211-214, 291-295, 345-347.

MAIMONIDES: A MAN FOR ALL AGES[*]

Norman E. Frimer

Some years ago, a renowned American teacher, addressing a college audience in the Midwestern United States, asked the students how many could identify such historic figures as Isaiah, Plato, Dante, and Schiller. The positive response was immediate and enthusiastic. He then inquired how many could recognize such popular figures of the early twentieth century as Daniel Knight, Pearl White, Theda Bara, Arthur Roche, and Maxwell Bodenheim. The hands raised were hesitant and few in number. He then hastened to point out that the former had lived in various parts of the world, anywhere between two hundred and almost three thousand years earlier, while the latter consisted of heroes and heroines of the arts in their own country whose names had been magical to their own parents or grandparents, only a few decades earlier. Why, then, this glaring difference? Because, he underscored, the men and women of transient fame, whom he entitled "contemporaries," spoke only to the moment; they streaked across the sky with a moment's brilliance, like a falling meteor, only to be buried, together with their gifts, in oblivion. The Isaiahs and the Dantes, on the other hand, grappled with perennial social and spiritual issues of human existence. Consequently, their writings and teachings spanned time and space, speaking to the hearts and challenging the questing minds and souls of every generation. No wonder they have survived as "everlasting modernists."

[*] This paper was given at a convocation of the Hebrew Theological College of Chicago and was then published in *Annual Volume of the Council of Young Israel Rabbis in Israel*, vol. 1, ed. Rabbi Emanuel B. Quint (Jerusalem, 5747 [1987]), 3-12. It was subsequently republished in the author's *A Jewish Guide for Religious Meaning* (Hoboken, N.J., 1993), pp. 86-92.

In light of this intriguing definition, Moses ben Maimon remains, particularly for the informed Jew, the modernist *par excellence*. No Orthodox Jew, for example, can offer up his daily prayers without declaring Maimonides' Thirteen Fundamentals of the Jewish Faith or its poetic paraphrase found in *Yigdal*. No student of Torah can peruse the classical *Ethics of the Fathers*, particularly during the summer months, without encountering Maimonides' classic introduction, the *Eight Chapters*—in essence a monograph on the philosophy of ethics—and now and again referring to his *Commentary* proper. What Jewish Scholar would dare begin studying a tractate of the Talmud without carefully examining the brilliant and pithy essays—for that's what they are despite their deceptive brevity—of his *Commentary to the Mishnah*? What yeshivah student with any claim to thoroughness can bypass the *Mishneh Torah*—an indispensable guide lending a *yad hazakah*, a firm and unwavering hand, to those who would wind their way through the labyrinth of Talmudic legal sources? For such writings as these and many more, the Rambam stands as an intimate, if not daily, teacher and companion.

What about the rest of the Jewish community, among whom, problems of faith notwithstanding, there are many restless pursuers of truth? Can Maimonides speak to these searchers?

Some individuals of stature are considered great because they have found the right answers to the dilemmas of living. With deep insight they have been able to furnish mankind with life-directing and helpful responses to its confused search. Others, however, have earned our lasting indebtedness because they have daringly posed penetrating questions. In either case, these giants were blessed not only with unprecedented prescience and clarity of thought, but with the unrelenting courage to define the confusion of man and society, and thereby help to chart a renewed search. Because they dared to ask aloud the crucial, although unpopular, questions and to propose pioneering but well-thought-out paths, they spurred and directed their generation, and those beyond, toward creative discovery and purpose. People could once again dare to seek and hope.

Maimonides was, uniquely, a genius at both.

Let me give a homely but telling illustration from my own experience of his capacity and contribution as the Great Questioner. A group of young people had gathered in our home to participate in a study session. The discussion progressed in a freewheeling manner, but in the course of the evening veered unexpectedly toward the question of faith and religion in our times. Slowly but inexorably, the doubts that gnawed at their spiritual innards, the questions and challenges which the more pious believers had probably considered too heretical to reveal to their revered teachers, began to pour forth. Fortunately, Maimonides' *Guide of the Perplexed* was easily at hand and without disclosing the author of the volume, I began to read aloud some critical selections from the text: What proof was there for the existence of God? Who created evil, if God is all-good? Are the laws and teachings of the Torah reasonable for man? Can one explain prophecy and divine revelation? If God is all-knowing, how can man possess free will? These and many more questions, posing difficulties and dilemmas to the *ma'amin*, the Jewish believer, flowed from the printed pages. Their curiosity was heightened when they learned that these ponderings had come directly from the writings of the Rambam, who had obviously faced these challenges far more sharply and with greater learned audacity than they could ever have mustered.

In the protective assurance of Maimonides' penetrating questions, these contemporary Joseph ibn Aknins gradually began, during the late hours of that night, to find their religious equanimity. At times, when a young person is inescapably assailed by spiritual struggles, what he may often most earnestly need is the chance to be able to articulate his doubts and to be allowed to battle them through for himself. For young people to know that the great Maimonides, too, had passed over the dread ford of Jabbok, had wrestled, Jacob-like, with the very angels of the Almighty One, and had nevertheless emerged triumphant in his faith, was a healing balm to their hearts and an anchor to their storm-buffeted spirits.

But Maimonides also proffered some vital answers, valid even for later ages!

Despite the increasing modesty and moderation of scientific claims in recent decades, one of the philosophic and theological issues which invariably appears on the intellectual agenda of modern man, and particularly that of the Jew, is that of the confrontation between religion and naturalism. Earnest scholars have not ceased to ponder such questions as: What is the genuine source and criterion of truth? Is it human reason? Is it divine revelation? Can the two be legitimately bridged? This subject was grappled with in the days of R. Moses ben Maimon even more heatedly than in our own day. Consequently, even though Aristotelian cosmogony is now dated and medieval physics outmoded, the metaphysical issue had lingered on with us, albeit less vocally. It was to this challenge that Maimonides directed a double-edged response, cutting across major segments of our intellectual world.

To the rationalists, both of his and of our own day, who enthrone man and reason, the Rambam would impress the fact that there is a limit at which the human intellect stops. We do not yet know the number of stars in the sky, and we are utterly ignorant of how many kinds of animals, minerals, and plants there are.

Furthermore, Maimonides would argue that reason cannot be relied upon to provide even the educated, thinking man, let alone the average, unphilosophic person, with those truths by which they may regulate their daily thoughts and beliefs, their emotions and actions.

> We are like those who, though beholding frequent flashes of lightning, still find themselves in the thickest darkness of the night...others are in the condition of men, whose darkness is illumined not by lightning, but by some kind of crystal...and to them even this small amount of light is not continuous, but now it shines and now it vanishes....The multitude of ordinary men... never beheld the light even for one day, but walk in continual darkness.[1]

Albert Einstein, though not a traditionalist in any sense, agreed with Maimonides on this basic point when he epigrammatically asserted: "Science without religion is blind." How unfortunate it is, then, that despite our awareness that there has been placed into our hands a knowledge so potent that its abuse or misuse can annihilate the world in one fell swoop, we do not match that awareness with a recognition of the powerful need to translate religious truths into effective patterns of living. It has been well said that science can be a wonderful servant, but a terrifying master. Science that is blind becomes science gone mad.

But if Maimonides would strive vehemently to rescue faith for the man of reason, he would strive no less vehemently to salvage reason for the contemporary man of faith.

In times of severe human crisis, when man stands at the brink of an abyss, he all too frequently deserts reason as an instrument of guidance, hurling himself headlong into the fraudulently alluring clutch of instinct and emotion. At the very moment when sober and solid thinking is an indispensable weapon in the battle against fear and paralyzing panic, man rejects that very gift of God which makes him uniquely man.

Our own day has seen too many examples of such default to unreason, both in the political and social arena, to require any further belaboring. What is utterly disturbing, however, is to see the sanctuary of religion (not excluding Judaism) being invaded by the onslaught, and in some areas by the embrace, of obscurantism, anti-intellectualism and faith motivated by fear.

To this, Maimonides would not keep silent.

> ...the intellect...was granted to man as the highest endowment. ...With reference to this gift the Bible states that "man was made in the image and likeness of God" (Gen. 1:26). On account of this gift of intellect man was addressed by God, and received His commandments, as it is said: "And the Lord God commanded Man" (Gen. 2:16).[2]

Torah need not and cannot be authentically joined to irrationalism, nor need faith be the result of groveling despair. On the contrary, science must be wedded to religion and reason must become a partner to revelation; both bring the wellsprings of God's eternal truth. Consequently, a life of obedience to the *mizvot* of the Torah and one guided by the dictates of reason are not incompatible. Just as Maimonides was the great mediator in his day, so must we aspire to build such models for our own age.

For me, however, the Rambam's most lasting contribution is the model of his own personality. "Religion," the saying goes, "cannot be taught, but must be caught." To which I would add, "it cannot be caught save from contagious personalities." In moments of solitude, I have often thought that a major reason for the current indifference to the word of God is the dearth of men of God whose very magnetic presence and towering example call smaller mortals to emulate their selfless dedication to the will and love of God. For our basically and spiritually impoverished age, then, how compelling and inspiring looms the personality of a R. Moses ben Maimon.

He was foremost an aristocrat of the intellect, one whose creativity could be stemmed neither by persecution nor by his interminable flight from the fanatic fury of the Moslem Almohads. But to this nobility he added the ingredient of love, an unquenchable love for his brethren—a quality which prevented an intellectual aristocracy from being corrupted into immoral snobbery and social contempt. Thus, when the Jewish residents of Yemen turned to him for guidance after being cynically given the choice between apostasy and exile, how patient was his instruction and how understanding his admonitions! As he writes in his *Epistle to Yemen:*

> Put your trust in these true texts of Scripture, brethren, and be not dismayed by the succession of persecutions of the enemy's ascendancy over us, or the weakness of our people. These trials are designed to test and purify us....It behooves you, all my fellow countrymen in the Diaspora, to hearten one another, the elders to guide the youth, and the leaders to direct the masses....Give the assent of your community to the Truth that is immutable [the Torah], and to the postulates of the true faith that shall never fail.[3]

His love of God both required and generated a love for all men as well. Despite personal and familial suffering at the hands of the Moslems, as well as the ravages inflicted by the Christians upon the Jewish people, Maimonides could write with all religious truth and philosophic objectivity in his *magnum opus*, the *Mishneh Torah*, that he saw these daughter religions as divine instruments in God's ultimate scheme of world redemption, whose task it was to bring the message of God's unity to the heathens.[4]

Finally, Maimonides was a child of two civilizations, knowing intimately the travail of living successfully in both, an experience so much akin to our own. Yet he shunned the easy or glib solution. He refused to dilute his faith, nor would he retreat from the struggle into self-imposed isolationism. Plunging into the very heart of the conflict, he forged an enduring and masterful partnership out of its seething antinomies. He was astronomer and mathematician, physician and philosopher, savant and scientist, logician and theologian. But perhaps the greatest tribute came from the lips of Etienne Gibson, a non-Jewish philosopher, who wrote on the eight-hundredth anniversary of his birth, "The best way to pay Maimonides the homage we owe is to accept him simply for what he really was—a man of God."[5]

Few men have been endowed with his rich genius. Fewer still have been able to exploit this godly gift as a blessing to our people and for all mankind. But it is given unto all of us to warm our soul by the fires of these divinely kissed spirits and thereby, from this spiritual kinship, to capture into our very beings a spark of their godliness.

This is the priceless legacy of Maimonides for our age.

---

[1] *Guide for the Perplexed,* trans. M. Friedländer (London, 1904; reprint, ed., New York, 1956), Introduction (p. 3).

[2] *Guide* 1:2.

[3] *Crisis and Leadership: Epistles of Maimonides,* trans. A. Halkin, discussions by D. Hartman (Philadelphia, 1985), 102-103.

[4] *Hilkhot Melakhim u-Milhemotehem* 11:2, in uncensored editions.

[5] E. Gibson, "Homage to Maimonides," in *Essays on Maimonides: An Octocentennial Volume,* ed. S. W. Baron (New York, 1941), 35.

ISRAEL, THE NOAHIDE LAWS AND MAIMONIDES: JEWISH-GENTILE LEGAL RELATIONS IN MAIMONIDEAN THOUGHT*

Dov I. Frimer

One area of Jewish law and life deemed most sensitive and problematic throughout large portions of Jewish history concerns the relations between Jew and Gentile. Moreover, its existential nature and potential impact for the Jewish people at large and the Diaspora community in particular makes the thorny character of this subject obvious and present to all classes and individuals.

Jewish sensitivity to the issue finds its expression already in Tannaitic sources.[1] Yet, for various reasons—many of which have been examined by Professor Jacob Katz in his classical work *Exclusiveness and Tolerance*[2]—few halakhic authorities, even to this day, have provided us with an all-encompassing, working, *legal* model for Jewish-Gentile relations.[3] I emphasize the word "legal" for it is this aspect which most perturbs us today, both ideologically as well as pragmatically. Preferences and distinctions based on religious identification are well understood and readily accepted in today's society, even by those outside our faith community, when reserved for the uniquely ceremonial and ritualistic spheres of religious life. However, such criteria for the distribution and dispensation of justice, while perhaps tolerated by the medieval mind,[4] violate the temper of contemporary man.[5]

---

* This article originally appeared in *Jewish Law Association Studies II*, ed. B.S. Jackson (Atlanta, 1986), 89-102. The author wishes to express his indebtedness to his colleague and close friend Dr. Joshua Rosensweig. Many of Dr. Rosensweig's insights and comments have been incorporated into the body of this paper.

Probably the most dramatic and courageous attempt at providing Jewish Law with such a legal model belongs to R. Menahem ha-Me'iri, active in Provence at the turn of the fourteenth century. He rooted all of Jewish-Gentile legal relations in the firm concept of comity[6]—a principle commonplace to modern jurisprudence in the area of Conflicts of Law. It is the Me'iri's contribution which lies at the heart of Katz's abovementioned work and analysis; we confidently refer the reader to that source.[7] Interestingly, Professor Katz contends[8] that the *philosophical* underpinning of the Me'iri's approach flows from the writings of R. Moses Maimonides. It is our belief, however, that Maimonides himself had already conceived of a comprehensive *legal* model by which to guide Jewish-Gentile relations, a model which, while different from that of the Me'iri, can, nonetheless, adequately serve the legal and intellectual needs of the twentieth century halakhist living in an open and pluralistic society.

As is well known, Jewish Law does not obligate Gentiles to perform all 613 *mizvot* of the Torah. Yet, Halakhah requires all nations of the world to live by the Seven Noahide Laws.[9] It is these seven laws which Judaism perceives as the bare and basic minimum necessary to sustain and preserve a lawful and humane society. Maimonides codified these Noahide laws in his *Mishneh Torah, Hilkhot Melakhim* chapters 9-10. Of special interest are Rambam's historical remarks through which he introduces this section:

> Adam was commanded six *mizvot*...[proceeding to enumerate them]. Noah was proscribed, in addition, from eating the limb of a live animal...totaling seven. So it remained throughout the world until the time of Abraham. When Abraham came, he was commanded in addition to the others, the *mizvah* of circumcision. In Egypt, Amram was further given commandments until Moses our teacher came along who finally completed the Torah.[10]

R. Joseph Engel,[11] one of the keenest Talmudic minds of the latter-day period, took careful note of Rambam's "theory of evolution" of commandments:

> It is clear from the language of Maimonides that the Seven Noahide Laws are still incumbent upon us,[12] drawing their authority from their pre-Sinaitic obligation. The Torah [which was later given to Israel] merely complemented those laws by commanding new *mizvot* not yet given.[13]

Thus, according to Maimonides, not only are the Seven Noahide Laws obligatory upon the Gentile nations of the world, but in this very form[14] upon the Jewish people as well.[15] This radical notion, namely that the Jews as well are bound by the Seven Noahide Laws, can be traced to a *Baraita* recorded in the Babylonian Talmudic tractate of Sanhedrin:[16]

> Ten commandments were given to the People of Israel at Marah:[17] The seven which the Children of Noah had accepted upon themselves, to which were added the *miẓvot* of Laws, the Sabbath, and Honoring one's Father and Mother.

This *Baraita* clearly establishes that the Jews were commanded the Seven Noahide Laws at Marah and are incumbent upon all of Israel to perform. However, the deeper legal significance of this event is spelled out in a responsum by the great medieval halakhic authority R. Solomon ben Samson Duran (Rashbash),[18] who was asked the following question:

> Why were the Jews commanded at Marah ten *miẓvot*: the seven Noahide Laws, the Sabbath, Laws and Honoring One's Parents? After all, the Jews were already required to fulfill the Seven Noahide Laws. The author of the *Baraita*, consequently, needed only to state that the Jews were given three *miẓvot*.

To which the Rashbash responded:

> The Rabbis have already stated[19] that any *miẓvah* which was given to the Children of Noah and not repeated at Sinai is obligatory upon Israel alone and not upon the Children of Noah. Those commandments, however, which were give to the Children of Noah and repeated at Sinai are intended for both the Children of Noah as well as for the Children of Israel. Consequently, if not for the fact that the Seven Noahide Laws were commanded once again[20] to the Israelites at Marah,[21] the Children of Noah would have been free of their observance; only the people of Israel would have been so bound. Now, however, that these seven commandments were repeated at Marah both the Children of Noah as well as the People of Israel are obligated to fulfill them and let the righteous rejoice.[22]

Thus in the eyes of the Rabbis, the entire world—Jews and non-Jews alike—is governed by the Seven Noahide Laws. One may correctly conclude that these laws were commanded of *all* the children of Noah and are truly universal in nature, binding together the totality of mankind.

On the other hand, however, the Torah was given to the People of Israel at Sinai—a Torah that is unquestionably of a particularistic character.[23] Furthermore, there can be no doubt that a Jew owes obedience first and foremost to the laws of the Torah. When then, one may rightfully ask, are Jews to be guided by the Seven Noahide Law rather than by the 613 *miẓvot* of the Torah? Two possibilities come to mind. Firstly, a Jew may find purpose in turning to the Seven Noahide Laws for direction in those areas of lacunae which are not expressly covered by the edicts of the post-Sinaitic period. Let us take, for example, suicide or the indirect causation of murder. Although applying to Jews, Maimonides[24] cites as his sources and proof-texts for these crimes Biblical verses[25] which are to be found in God's proscription to Noah.[26] While the legal ramifications of this thesis are quite fascinating, a more complete treatment of this aspect of the topic must await a separate paper.

What concerns us now is the second area where the Noahide Laws may possibly control Jewish behavior, that of Jewish-Gentile legal relations. It would appear that the Seven Noahide Laws could perhaps provide that set of uniform principles necessary to govern adequately the legal interactions between Jew and non-Jew. The Noahide Law, with its universal quality and its legal flexibility especially in civil and monetary matters, might well serve as a sort of *"Jus Gentium* of Jewish Law."[27] According to this perspective the post-Sinaitic commandments are viewed as essentially tribal, determining primarily the relationships between Jew and fellow Jew. At the same time, the broader Seven Noahide Laws govern both the interactions between Gentile and Gentile as well as those between Jew and Gentile. It is our contention that a close look at the writings of Rambam would reveal that such is, indeed, his position. Let us examine a few of the relevant passages found in *Mishneh Torah*. We will begin with the subject of murder.

In *Hilkhot Rozeah* 4:11 the Rambam rules: "However, the gentiles[28] with whom we are not at war[29]...it is forbidden to cause[30] their death." Maimonides in *Hilkhot Avodah Zarah* 11:1 extends this ruling even to a case of true idol worshippers. While a Jew is enjoined from saving an idolator found already in a perilous situation, Rambam reminds us that we are, nonetheless, forbidden from directly bringing about the idolator's death.

What is the Biblical injunction[31] upon which this prohibition of murder is based? One's first instinct is to run to the verse "Thou shalt not murder."[32] This possibility—at least as far as Maimonides is concerned[33]— must be eliminated. Rambam, in the very opening words of *Hilkhot Rozeah*, limits the application of this injunction solely to the murder of a Jew: "He who kills a single Jewish person,[34] transgresses a negative commandment, as it is stated: 'Thou shalt not murder.'"

From where, then, did Rambam draw the prohibition of a Jew

murdering a non-Jew? Invoking the principle laid down by Maimonides himself, that Jews as well are obligated by the Seven Noahide Laws, the solution becomes obvious: the universal Noahide injunction against homicide prohibits not only a non-Jew from killing a Jew but also a Jew from murdering a non-Jew.[35]

Another interesting example can be found by investigating the *halakhah* regarding intermarriage. It is a well established doctrine of Jewish Law that there can be no *"Kiddushin"*—roughly translated as betrothal—between a Jew and non-Jew.[36] Scholars generally assume that this implies total rejection of *connubium* between Jews and Gentiles.[37] However, Rambam does not accept this prevalent position. As R. Joel Sirkes[38] has indicated,[39] Maimonides does recognize a concept of marriage—*"Hatnut"*—between Jew and Gentile, albeit within highly restricted parameters. R. Sirkes, though, gives no indication as to what may have prompted Rambam to adopting this maverick stance.[40]

It seems to us that Rambam's conclusion regarding intermarriage is a natural by-product of his assumption that Jews are still bound by the Seven Noahide Laws. One of the Noahide Laws is the prohibition against adultery.[41] Adultery, by definition, is predicated upon the existence of a legally recognized marriage. To the extent that the Noahide Laws recognize marriage and its legal consequences,[42] so too must Rambam accept intermarriage[43] between a Jew and a non-Jew.[44]

One final illustration is found in the case of robbery. The Babylonian Talmud in tractate *Bava Kamma*[45] differentiates between *"oshek"*—withholding money belonging to a Gentile—which may be permitted, and the actual robbery of a Gentile, which is definitely prohibited. The Talmud is forced into making this distinction by the Torah's[46] own language: "Thou shalt not withhold money (*"Lo ta'ashok"*)from thy fellow Jew."[47] Nonetheless, in apparent disregard for the Talmud's seemingly expressed position on the matter, Maimonides, in a sweeping statement, remarks: "The Law of the Torah prohibits us from robbing anything—even from a Gentile idolater it is forbidden to rob him or withhold his money."[48]

The commentators[49] have taken note of this difficulty in Rambam's position and struggle to find an adequate solution. What makes matters even more problematic is the realization that Maimonides[50] himself has defined the commandment of "Thou shalt not rob"[51] as proscribing exclusively a robbery from a Jew:

He who robs from his fellow Jew (*"havero"*)[52] that which is worth at least a *perutah* transgresses a negative commandment, as it states: "Thou shalt not rob."[53]

It seems curious, therefore, that on the one hand Maimonides should prohibit the robbing of a non-Jew as "Torah Law," while at the same time exclude such a robbery from the scope of "Thou shalt not rob."

Once again, though, we believe that these incongruities find their resolution in the principle stated above. Although the post-Sinaitic prohibitions of "Thou shalt not withhold money from thy fellow (Jew)" and "Thou shalt not rob" are limited in their application to cases between Jew and Jew, still such acts are forbidden between Jew and Gentile as a result of the pre-Sinaitic prohibition of *gezel*[54]—robbery—included in the Seven Noahide Laws.[55]

Until this point we have attempted to demonstrate the universal character and application of the Seven Noahide Laws. Yet, it is not this quality alone which makes these laws so appropriate for governing Jewish-Gentile legal relations. The flexibility of the Noahide Law, especially in the area of civil and monetary matters, is also an important ingredient. This feature is highlighted by Maimonides' understanding of the Noahide commandment of *dinim*— laws.

There is a difference of opinion between Maimonides and Nahmanides regarding the proper definition of *dinim*. Maimonides maintains that *dinim* requires of a non-Jewish society to set up a working court system whose function it is to enforce the other six Noahide Laws.[56] Nahmanides,[57] however, has a broader conception of this *mizvah*. For Ramban, *dinim* includes not only the establishment of a court system to enforce the other six commandments but also the adjudication of all money matters in their various forms. The *Aharonim*[58] are quick to point out, however, that one should not conclude from this debate that Maimonides believes that Gentile courts lack "Halakhic" authority or permission to rule on civil monetary matters. Such a conclusion would be mistaken; Maimonides merely categorized these cases under the heading of *gezel*. This contention musters strong support from the extremely broad formulation utilized by Rambam in his definition of the Noahide prohibition of *gezel*, encompassing not only formal robbery but all analogous situations where monetary rights have been violated.[59]

Regardless of the classification, the scholars are in dispute as to the legal sources which should be utilized in forming the normative basis for non-Jewish laws in these areas. One group of Aharonim[60] posits that the Gentile nations—like the Jews—must turn to the rules of the Torah with regard to all such monetary matters. When a non-Jewish judge decides a civil dispute even between two non-Jewish litigants the judge is to do so in accordance with Jewish Law. A second group of authorities,[61] however, reject such a notion out of hand. They maintain in its stead that the Gentiles are empowered to legislate and adjudicate laws in accordance with their own individual concepts of law.

Without passing judgment on the merits of the various positions, Maimonides—as contemporary halakhic scholars have correctly commented[62]—is clearly fixed in the latter camp.[63] Evidence for this is deduced from Rambam's *Hilkhot Melakhim*, in which he comments:

> Two Gentiles who come for judgment before Jewish judges:[64] should both litigants desire the application of Torah Law so be it. If, however, one should oppose the application of Jewish Law then the court should not impose it upon him but rather judge in accordance with their Gentile Law (*dineihen*). [65]

This notion of adjudication in accordance with Gentile Law—"*dineihen*"— clearly indicates a recognition by Rambam of the legitimate existence of non-Jewish legal systems different and distinct from that of post-Sinaitic Torah Law.[66]

By coupling this pluralistic approach with our thesis that Jewish-Gentile legal relations are governed by the Seven Noahide Laws, we discover another intriguing result. Should there be a monetary dispute between Jew and non-Jew, the relevant law to the case as a whole would, in fact, be the Noahide Law. However, inasmuch as the Noahide Law with regard to monetary matters refers in turn to the personal law of the litigants, the applicable law of the Jewish litigant *within the context of the Noahide Laws* is the post-Sinaitic Torah Law. Thus, when hearing a civil case where one party is Jewish and the other Gentile, the court, in choosing which legal system to apply, is confronted with a classical situation of Conflicts of Law. The halakhic approach to this problem deserves its own intensive treatment, one that is beyond the scope of this paper.[67]

One last brief thought. If we are correct in our assertion that in the Maimonidean model relations between a Jew and a Gentile are governed—from the Jewish legal viewpoint—by the Seven Noahide Laws, would we not expect as well that much of the legal contacts between the Jewish nation and a Gentile nation also be determined by the Noahide Laws? In other words, should not the halakhic principle of *Dina de-Malkhuta Dina*[68]—"The Law of the Land is Law"—also, to some large extent, be defined by the content of the Noahide Laws? This interdependence between *Dina de-Malkhuta Dina* and the Seven Noahide Laws is generally attributed to Rashi.[69] There are some *Aharonim*,[70] however, who contend that Maimonides is of a similar stance. While their proofs and demonstrations are open to debate, such a conclusion would certainly set well with the thesis presented in this paper.

Indeed, both the universality and flexibility of the Seven Noahide Laws provide an adequate and appropriate framework for Jewish-Gentile legal relations. The recognition of this fact by Maimonides is merely one more testimony to his genius for conceptual structure and order. One can hardly doubt the accuracy of Professor Isadore Twersky's description of the *Mishneh Torah* as being a "tightly structured and multi-dimensional work, unmistakably marked by vastness of erudition, subtlety of discernment, delicacy of interpretation, fastidiousness of classification, and sensitivity of formulation."[71]

---

[1] *Sifre, Deut.* 344 (ed. Finkelstein, 401; *Bava Kamma 38a; Yerushalmi Bava Kamma* 4:3 (4b)). As to the historical background and significance of the incident related, see Moshe David Herr, "The Historical Significance of the Dialogue Between Jewish Sages and Roman Dignitaries," in *Studies in Aggadah and Folk-Literature* (Scripta Hierosolymitana, Vol. 22) ed. Joseph Heinemann and Dov Noy (Jerusalem, 1971), 123-150, at 132-133 and sources cited therein.

[2] (New York, 1962), esp. chap. 5, at 48-63.

[3] A rather intriguing explanation for the seemingly anti-Gentile sentiment sometimes expressed in Jewish law can be found in *Responsa Divrei Hayyim* (by the Rebbe of Sanz, Rabbi Hayyim Halberstam, Galicia, 1793-1876), *Yoreh De'ah*, sec. 30. Cf. Moshe Meiselman, *Jewish Woman in Jewish Law* (New York, 1978), 43-44.

[4] See Katz, *supra* n.2, at 54-58, and sources cited therein.

[5] See the comments of Rabbi Jehiel Jacob Weinberg in Marc B. Shapiro, "Scholars and Friends: Rabbi Jehiel Jacob Weinberg and Professor Samuel Atlas," *The Torah U-Madda Journal* 7 (1997), 105 at 112.

[6] See for example *Beit ha-Behirah, Bava Kamma* 37b (ed. Schlezinger, 122). See also Michael Guttmann, "The Term 'Foreigner' (*nokhri*) Historically Considered," *Hebrew Union College Annual* 3 (1926): 1-20; Isaac Allen, *Comparisons Between Talmudic and American Law* (Tel Aviv-New York, 1960), Heb. Sec., 23.

[7] *Supra* n.2, esp. at Chap. 10, 114-128. See also his *Halakhah and Kabbalah* (Jerusalem,

1984), 291-310, and *Tarbiz* 48 (1979): 374-376; Israel Ta-Shma, *Tarbiz* 37 (1978): 197-210; 49 (1980), 218-219; Ephraim E. Urbach, *"Shitat ha-Sovlanut shel R. Menahem ha-Meiri— Mikorah u-Migbeloteha,"* Perakim be-Toledot ha-Hevrah ha-Yehudit bi-Yemei ha-Beinayim u-Be' et ha-Hadashah* (Jerusalem, 1980), 34-44. The profound impact of the Meiri's approach on Jewish legal thought can be appreciated by merely scanning the writings of numerous halakhic scholars of recent generations. See, for example: *Torah Temimah*, Ex. 21:35, no. 277, Lev. 25:14, no. 83; Rabbi Joseph Eliyahu Henkin, *Perushei Lev Ivra* (New York, 1981), 116, reprinted in *Kitvei ha-Gri Henkin* I (New York, 1980), 207b; and in *"Kez ha-Yamin,"* ha-Darom 10 (5719), 5-9, at 7-8, reprinted in *Teshuvot Ivra*, 115, in *Kitvei ha-Gri Henkin* II (New York, 1989), 230-231; R. Jehiel Jacob Weinberg in Shapiro, *supra* n. 5 at 118; Rabbi Dr. Simon Federbush, *Mishpat ha-Melukhah be-Yisra'el*, 2nd ed. (Jerusalem, 1973), 59; Rabbi Ben-Zion Meir Hai Uziel, *"ha-Akum ve-ha-Nakhri be-Dinei Yisra'el,"* ha-Torah ve-ha-Medinah 4 (5712), 9-21; Rabbi S. Turk, *"Hazalat Akum mi-Mitah,"* ha-Pardes 51:3 (December, 1976): 17-20; Rabbi Yehuda Gershuni, *Kol Zofyikh* (Jerusalem, 5740), 315-320, 326. Note also the sources cited in these references. See in addition: *Keneset Hagedolah, Hoshen Mishpat* 425, *Hagahot Beit Yosef*, end of no. 12; *Responsa Noda be-Yehudah*, Introduction to *Mahadurah Kama*, "Author's Apology;" *Gilyon Maharsha, Yorah Deah*, 159:1. Cf., however, Rabbi Zevi Yehuda Kook in his notes to Federbush, (ibid., 237), p. 59, line 12 and p. 59, end of footnote 14. See also Shneur Zusha Reiss, *"Dinei Akum bi-Zeman ha-Zeh,"* Talpiot 3 (5707-5708): 623-624; sources cited by Shapiro, *supra* n. 5 at 121, note 47.

[8] *Supra* n.2, at 199-222. See also *Halakhah ve-Kabbalah, supra* n. 7 at 299-300. In general, Maimonides also had a great impact on Me'iri's halakhic thinking. See R. Dov Berish Zuckerman, *Be'urei ha-Rambam 'al fi ha-Me'iri* (Jerusalem, 5744).

[9] *Tosefta Avodah Zarah* 8:4 (ed. Zuckermandel, 473); *Sanhedrin* 57a-b; Maimonides, *Hilkhot Melakhim* 9:1. These norms are generally accepted to include: 1. a requirement of the establishment of a system of civil law, and prohibitions against, 2. blasphemy, 3. idolatry, 4. murder, 5. robbery, 6. sexual immorality, and 7. the eating of flesh torn from a living animal. For a concise review of this topic in English, see Saul Berman, *"Noahide Laws: The Principles of Jewish Law,"* ed. Menachem Elon (Jerusalem, 1975), 708-710. I would also refer the reader to the intriguing study published in English by Aaron Lichtenstein, *The Seven Laws of Noah* (New York, 1981).

[10] See and compare *Exodus Rabba* 30:9.

[11] Poland, 1859-1920.

[12] I.e., the Jews.

[13] *Beit ha-Ozar* (Pietrokov, 1903), Part 1, Principle 1, sec. 7, 9. See also pp. 10, 16.

[14] Except, of course, in those cases where the Torah expressly changed the law from its pre-existent form, e.g., in punishment and procedure. See Rabbi Z. H. Chajes, *Torat Nevi'im* in Vol. 1 of *Kol Sifrei Maharaz Hayes*, (Jerusalem, 1958), chap. 11, 71. This is in keeping with the principle "When the Torah was given the law was changed." See *Shabbat* 135a; Maimonides, *Hilkhot Avel* 1:1; *Hidushei Maharaz Hayes*, Shabbat, *ad loc.*; Moshe Potolsky, "The Rabbinic Rule, 'No Laws are Derived from before Sinai,'" *Diné Israel* 6 (1975): 195-230, at 208-212.

[15] This would also appear to be the opinion of Rabbi Judah ha-Levi in his *Kuzari*, Part I, sec. 83, where he states: Up to this time (i.e. the Exodus from Egypt) they had only a few laws

which they had inherited from Adam and Noah. These laws were not abrogated by Moses but rather increased by him." See *Ozar Nehmad, ad loc.,* s.v. *ve-lo.* See also: Rabbi Moshe Mordekhai Epstein, *Levush Mordekhai, B.K., Mahadurah Tinyana,* end of Chap. 14, and Rabbi Shlomo Fisher, *Bet Yishai,* Vol. 2, Sec. 107 who support this view. *Cf.,* however, Rabbi Y.Z. Gustman, *Kuntrese Shi'urim,* B.M., Discourse 12, sec. 3-4, who rejects such an idea.

It appears that this may have in reality been at the center of an extensive tannaitic dispute. See *Mekhilta, Yitro,* Chap. 8 (ed. Horowitz-Rubin), 232; *Mekhilta de-Rabbi Shimon bar Yohai, Yitro,* 20:13 (ed. Epstein-Melamed), 152; *Yalkut Shimoni, Shemini* 11:2, sec. 535, sv. *zot; Lev. Rab.* 13:2; *Torah Shelemah,* vol. 2, Gen. 9:6, 468-469, footnote 36. See also *Mekhilta, Mishpatim,* Chap. 1 (246); *Mishnat Rabbi Eliezer,* Chap. 16 (ed. Enelow, 308); *Midrash ha-Gadol, Mishpatim* (ed. Margulies, 454-455); *Be'er Sheva, Hor.* 8b; *Torah Shelemah,* vol. 17, Ex. 21:1, 3, footnote 6.

Note in addition the language of the *Zohar, Noah,* sec. 260 (Sulam-Hazohar edition, vol. 3, 92). The final word *"Kehada"* seems to imply an understanding which corresponds to that of Maimonides. I wish to express my gratitude to my father, Rabbi Dr. Norman E. Frimer, for bringing this *Zohar* to my attention.

[16] *Sanhedrin* 56b; *Horiot* 8b. My father, Rabbi Dr. Norman E. Frimer, correctly suggests that Maimonides may have also drawn support from *Exodus Rabba* 30:9: "...but to Israel He gave them all."

[17] Immediately prior to Sinai. See Ex. 15:22-26. Note esp. verse 25.

[18] North Africa, 1400-1467.

[19] *Sanhedrin* 59a.

[20] Rabbi Reuven Margoliyot, *Margoliyot ha-Yam, Sanhedrin* 56b, no. 23, based upon the Rashbash and Rabbi Engel, emphasizes that the three *mizvot,* the Sabbath, Laws and Honoring One's Parents, were not merely added on to the already existent Seven Laws commanded to Noah; rather the Seven Noahide Laws were themselves actually repeated and recommended to the Israelites at Marah. Cf. *Sanhedre Ketanah, Sanhedrin* 56b, who is of the opinion that the Seven Noahide Laws were *not* repeated at Marah.

[21] Maimonides, in his commentary to *Hullin* 7:6 (ed. Kafah, 212), is most emphatic in asserting that the Jewish people observe the *mizvot* because they were given through Moses and not due to any prior obligation placed upon the Children of Noah or the Patriarchs. It is clear, however, from the Rashbash that the Marah experience would most certainly be included within the scope of "G-d's commandments through Moses." There is no reason to assume that Rambam would disagree. See *Hagahot Maharaz Hayes, Sanhedrin* 56b. *Margoliyot ha-Yam,* ibid., nos. 23, 29 (Rabbi David Cohen, in personal communication, finds support for this position in *Horiot* 8a-b.). Maimonides does proceed to explain that Jews observe the prohibitions against eating the limb torn from a live animal or the nervus ischiadicus, as well as the commandment of circumcision, solely because they were "commanded at Sinai." However, as Rabbi Chajes (ibid.) notes, that is merely because these *mizvot* were not among those given at Marah. No normative conclusion can be extracted from these very specific examples. Furthermore, it would appear that Maimonides himself includes Marah under the rubric of "Sinaitic Legislation," as he writes in his "Response to Joseph Ibn Gabir," *Letters of Maimonides,* trans. and ed. Leon D. Stitskin (New York, 1977), 86 at 89, which reads: "The Torah enjoined by Moses is in its totality a revelation by God. If it contains ancient laws, as the Noahide laws and the

sign of the covenant, we are not bound by them because they were observed in ancient times but because of the later Sinaitic Legislation vouchsafed exclusively to us." See also Potolsky, *supra* n. 12, at 197-199, 213-215.

[22] *Responsa ha-Rashbash,* Chap. 543.

[23] See *Rambam, Hilkhot Melakhim* 8:10, 10:9-10; *Yam Shel Shelomoh, Bava Kamma* 10:18.

[24] *Rambam, Hilkhot Rozeah u-Shemirat Nefesh* 2:2-3.

[25] Gen. 9:5-6.

[26] See *Bava Kamma* 91a; *Genesis Rabba* 34:5 (ed. Theodor-Albeck, 324).

[27] Gedalyahu Alon, *Toledot ha-Yehudim be-Erez Yisra'el bi-Tekufat ha-Mishnah ve-ha-Talmud* (Tel-Aviv, 1958), Vol. 1, 346 translated into English by Gershon Levi and entitled *The Laws in their Land in the Talmudic Age* (Jerusalem, 1984), Vol. 2, 555; José Faur, "The Fundamental Principles of Jewish Jurisprudence," 12 *New York University Journal of International Law and Politics* (1970): 225-235, at 226. See also Simon Schneebalg, "The Philosophy of Jewish Law—A Reply to Professor Faur," *ibid.* 13 (1980): 381-392, at 384-387.

[28] *"Ha-Goyim."* This is obviously the correct version, as is evident from an examination of all early texts of the *Mishneh Torah.*

[29] This proviso is based upon *Masekhet Sofrim* 15:7 (ed. Higger, 281-282). See *Kesef Mishneh, ad loc.; Beit Yosef, Yoreh De'ah* 158, *Hoshen Mishpat* 425:12 ("Expurgations by the Censor"). See also *Tosafot, Avodah Zarah* 26b, s.v. *"ve-Lo Moridin;"* Rashba, *Avodah Zarah* 26b; Rabbenu Bahya, Ex. 14:7; *Shulhan Arukh,* 158:1.

[30] *"Ein mesavevim"* – indicating that even indirect causation is prohibited. See below n.31.

[31] It appears from the language of Maimonides that this injunction is indeed biblical. See *Beit Meir* 17:63; *Resp. Bet Yehuda, Yoreh De'ah,* chap. 4. This ruling would correspond with the *Mekhilta, Mishpatim* Chap. 4 (ed. Horowitz-Rabin, 263) and *Mishnat Rabbi Eliezer,* Chap. 9 (ed. Enelow, 167). See Maimonides, *Hilkhot Roze'ah u-Shemirat Nefesh* 2:11; *Kesef Mishneh, ad loc.; Meshekh Hokhmah,* Ex. 21:14; Turk, *supra* n. 7, at 18-19. Furthermore, there seems to be no concrete basis for distinguishing between the direct causation of death and the indirect causation of death. See *Bah, Yoreh De'ah* 158; *Orah Meshor, Yoreh De'ah.* 158, note 1; *Responsa Yam ha-Gadol, Hoshen Mishpat,* end of Chap. 94; Turk, ibid., at 17-19. See also *Responsa Temim De'im,* Chap. 203; *Beit ha-Behirah, Sanhedrin* 57b (ed. Sofer, 226-227). *Cf. Taz, Yoreh De'ah.* 158, note 1.

A propos, see *Beit Yosef, Yoreh De'ah 158,* s.v. *"u- Moshe Rabbenu."* Rabbi Joseph Karo's inference from *Tosafot* is highly questionable. The author of the *Tosafot* cited is none other than Rabbi Isaac the Elder. This can readily be ascertained from the signature found at the conclusion of our *Tosafot* as it appears—in almost identical language—in the *Tosafot Rabbenu Elhanan, Avodah Zarah* 26a: "M"R" = *"Me-divrei Rebbe"* where "Rebbe" is undoubtedly Rabbi Isaac the Elder. See Ephraim E. Urbach, *Ba'alei ha-Tosafot* (Jerusalem, 1955), 212. It should also be noted that the *Tosafot Rabbenu Elhanan* "are the primary source for our *Tosafot"* on *Avodah Zarah.* See Urbach, ibid., 507. This identification can further be supported from the parallel citation of *Tosafot* in *Perush Talmidei Rabbenu Yonah, Avodah Zarah* 26a, where the name of "Our Rabbi Isaac" is clearly given.

The position of Rabbi Isaac the Elder on our subject is unequivocally expressed in his abovementioned responsum published in the *Temim De'im.* This stance, however, runs directly counter to Rabbi Karo's understanding of "Rabbi Isaac's" *Tosafot*. Moreover, the fuller version of the *Tosafot* as found in the *Perush Talmidei Rabbenu Yonah* is in complete accord with *R"i's Temim De'im* formulation. We would conclude, therefore, that any explanation of our *Tosafot* which is contrary to the *Temim De'im*, and the *Perush Talmidei Rabbenu Yonah*, must be deemed erroneous.

[32] Ex. 20:13; Deut. 5:7.

[33] Cf. *Ra'avan*, the end of *Bava Kamma* 91a; *Hinukh*, Commandment 34 (ed. Chavel, 91). See the comments of Rabbi M. M. Kasher in his additions to *Torah Shelemah*, Vol. 16, Chap. 20, the end of sec. 2. However, see as well the *Minhat Hinukh*, ad loc. and on Commandment 93. Note also *Sefer Yere'im*, Chap. 248.

[34] "*Adam me-Yisra'el*"—This is the correct text. It had been changed by the censor, as already noted by Rabbi Shabse Frankel in his introduction to the Frankel edition of the *Mishneh Torah* (Jerusalem, 1975), *Zemanim*, 12. *See also Dina de-Hayai*, Negative Commandment 260; *Minhat Hinukh*, Commandment 34. Cf. Dr. Abraham Arazi in his "popular commentary" to Maimonides ad. loc. (Jerusalem), footnote 3, and Rabbi Yehudah Amital, "A Letter," *Kesher Tefutsot* (published by Yeshivat Har Ezion), No. 2 (Passover, 1983:) 5 at 7, who were obviously unaware of the correct text.

[35] Although the prohibition is the same, the punishment and procedure are different. See Maimonides, *Hilkhot Rozeah u-Shemirat Nefesh* 2:11, based on *Mekhilta*, supra n. 31; *Mekhilta de-Rabbi Shimon bar Yohai*, *Mishpatim* 21:14 (ed. Hoffmann, 125); *Sifre Zuta*, *Mas'ei* 35:24 (ed. Horowitz, 333); *Mishnat Rabbi Eliezer*, supra n. 31. See also Maimonides, *Hilkhot Melakhim* 9:14, based on *Sanhedrin* 57b. This is in consonance with our comments in n. 13 supra.

[36] *Kiddushin* 68b; Maimonides, *Hilkhot Ishut* 4:15.

[37] See for example: Benzion Schereschewsky, *Family Law in Israel*, 2nd ed. (Jerusalem, 1974), 80; J. David Bleich, "The Prohibition Against Intermarriage," *Journal of Halacha and Contemporary Society* Vol. 1 No. 1 (Spring, 1981): 5-27, at 10, reprinted in his *Contemporary Halakhic Problems* (New York, 1983): Vol. 2, 271-272.

[38] Poland, 1561-1640.

[39] *Bah*, *Even ha-Ezer* 16, s.v. *Um"sh derekh ishut*. See also *Arukh ha-Shulhan, Even ha-Ezer* 16:1.

[40] Some latter-day scholars, however, have followed Maimonides' lead. See for example *Responsa Shevut Ya'akov*, Part 1, Chap. 20 (regarding the selling of one's *hamez* to his Gentile wife); *Responsa Zera Avraham*, Chap. 24, sec. 5-6; *Sha'arei Tohar* (Volk), Vol. 5, Chap. 32, Sec. 4.

[41] *Hilkhot Melakhim* 9:5, 7.

[42] See *Responsa Shevut Ya'akov*, supra n. 40.

[43] As to the effect of this type of approach on the possible recognition of a civil marriage between two Jews, see Issachar Meir Mazuz, "Civil Marriage and their Consequences," *Shenaton ha-Mishpat ha-Ivri* 3-4 (1976-1977): 233-270, at 243, 261-262, and the sources cited therein. See in addition *Responsa Seridei Esh*, Vol. 3, Chap. 20, sec. 3, Chap. 22 (My thanks to Professor Aaron Kirschenbaum of Tel-Aviv University Faculty of Law for bringing this last source to my attention); *Responsa Mishneh Halakhot*, Vol. 9, Chap. 278, secs. 1-2.

[44] Curiously, however, the majority of scholars are of the opinion that according to Maimonides there would be no criminal offense of adultery for sexual intercourse between a Jewish male and a married Gentile female. See *Hilkhot Melakhim* 8:3. They attribute this ruling to a *lex specialis*. See *Sanhedrin* 52b; *Sha'ar Hamelekh, Hilkhot Isurei Bi'ah* 12:2; *Avne Melu'im*, E.H., Chap. 16, Sec. 1 (1) and (3); *Resp. Zikhron Zvi* (Horowitz), Vol. 1, Chap. 24, s.v. *"Ve-Hene"*; *Sha'are Tohar, supra* n. 40, s.v. *"U-kenir'eh."* Cf., however, the *Lehem Mishneh*, ad loc., who holds that even according to Maimonides there would be criminal adultery under such circumstances. See also *Torah Temimah*, Ex. 21:35, note 277, Lev. 20:10, note 22, who implies that there may be a distinction between Gentiles who observe the Seven Noahide Laws and those who do not. Under any circumstances, however, there would exist a rabbinic prohibition against such conduct. See *Sha'ar ha-Melekh*, ibid.

[45] *Bava Kamma*, 113b.

[46] Lev. 19:13.

[47] *"Re'ekha"*—lit. "thy comrade." This phrase is generally understood by the Rabbis to imply "thy fellow Jew." See *Bava Mezia* 111b; *Yerushalmi Bava Mezia* 9:11 (12b).

[48] *Hilkhot Gezelah va-Avedah* 1:2. See also *Hilkhot Geneivah* 1:1.

[49] *Kesef Mishneh, ad loc.; Yam Shel Shlomo, supra* n. 21. *Responsa Hakham Zevi*, Chap. 26; *Yeshuot Ya'akov, Even ha-Ezer*, Chap. 26; *Hatan Sofer*, Vol. 2, *"Sha'ar Hamakneh ve-ha-Kinyan ve-ha-Shetarot,"* Chap. 28, note 2; *Responsa Hut ha-Meshulash* (Rabbi Hayyim of Volozhin), Chap. 14; *Even ha-Azel* (by R. Isser Zalman Meltzer, 1870-1954), ad loc.

[50] Cf. *Ra'avan, supra* n. 33.

[51] Lev. 19:13.

[52] See *Hut ha-Meshulash, supra* n. 49, s.v. *"Umah;" Even ha-Azel, supra* n. 49.

[53] *Hilkhot Gezelah va-Avedah* 1:1.

[54] Legally, withholding money and theft are the same crime. See *Bava Mezia* 111a ("Whatever is *oshek* is also theft"). As such they are both included under the broad category of "theft" as found in the Noahide Laws. See *Hilkhot Melakhim* 9:9; *Mishmeret Hayyim* (Regensberg), Chap. 39 (at 152). Dr. Joshua Rosensweig suggests that this analysis may explain why Maimonides coupled the injunction against a Jew stealing from a Gentile together with that of withholding a Gentile's money in one single phrase: "...it is forbidden to steal from him or withhold his money": *supra* n. 48. This formulation is in contrast with that found in Maimonides' discussion of these injunctions vis-à-vis a fellow Jew. In this latter context the Rambam clearly distinguishes and differentiates between theft and withholding, listing each in a separate section: *supra* n. 48 at sec. 3 (theft)—4 (withholding). Maimonides was obviously being true to the legal sources and nature of the respective prohibitions.

[55] In *Hilkhot Geneivah* 1:1, however, Maimonides explicitly includes theft from a Gentile in the Sinaitic prohibition of "Thou shalt not steal." See Rabbi Abraham Ticktin, *"Kuntres be-Inyane Gezel Akum," Ve-Zot le-Yehudah* (Jerusalem, 1977), 147-158, at 150 and sources cited therein. Why did not the Rambam merely rely on the power of the prohibition found in the Noahide Laws—as he did by robbery? What forced Maimonides to insert the theft of a non-Jew's property also within the parameters of the Sinaitic injunction? This matter as yet requires further examination. See also *Even ha-Azel, supra* n. 49, s.v. *"Akhen."*

[56] *Hilkhot Melakhim* 9:14

[57] Gen. 34: 13 (ed. Chavel, Vol. 1, 191-192). See also Nahmanides' comments to Root 14 of Maimonides' *Sefer Hamizvot* (the very end).

[58] *Responsa Hatam Sofer*, Vol. 6, Chap. 14; *Mishpat ha-Melukkah*, Chap. 9, Sec. 14 (at 345); *Mishmeret Hayyim, supra* n. 54 (at 151).

[59] See *Hilkhot Melakhim* 9:9. This position may find its antecedent in the writings of Nahmanides, Gen. *supra* n. 55. See *Margoliyot ha-Yam, Sanhedrin*, 56b, no. 9; Lichtenstein, *supra* n. 9, at 36-38.

[60] *Responsa Rema*, Chap. 10; *Responsa Hatam Sofer, supra* n. 58.

[61] Rabbi Jacob Anatoli (1194-1246, Father-in-law of Rabbi Samuel Ibn Tibbon) *Malmad ha-Talmidim* (Lyck: 1886), *Noah* (12a) and *Mishpatim* (71a [end]), quoted also by *Margoliyot ha-Yam, Sanhedrin* 56b, no. 9; Rabbi Nathan Mez (Teacher of Rabbi Moses Sofer), *Binyan Shelomoh, Sanhedrin* 56b; *Ha-Amek She'elah, She'iltah* 2,note 3; *Arukh ha-Shulhan ha-Atid, Hilkhot Melakhim* 79:15; *Mishpat ha-Melukhah*, Chap. 10 Sec. 12; Rabbi M. M. Kasher, *Addendum to Torah Shelemah*, Vol: 17, Chap. 1 (pp. 217-222); Rabbi Ahron Soloveichik, *Parah Mateh Aharon, Ahavah, Hilkhot Milah* 1:6 (pp. 118-119) and the sources cited therein. See also Samuel Atlas, *Pathways in Hebrew Law* (Heb., New York, 1978), 22. In general, see Rabbi Eliezer Yehuda Waldenberg, *Hilkhot Medinah* (Jerusalem, 1952-1955), Vol. 1, Gate 1, Chap. 1 (pp. 2-9); Vol. 3, Gate 10, Chap. 2 (pp. 230-232).

[62] *Margoliyot ha-Yam, Sanhedrin* 56b, nos. 10-11; *Einayim la-Mishpat, Sanhedrin* 56b, no. 5; *Hilkhot Medinah*, Vol. 1, ibid. at secs. 2-3 (pp. 2-5) and Vol. 3, ibid., at sec. 2 (pp. 231-232); *Mishmeret Hayyim, supra* n. 54; *Responsa Yehaveh Da'at*, Vol. 4, sec. 65, note at p. 313; *Parah Mateh Aharon, supra* n. 61. Note also that Rabbi Jacob Anatoli, ibid., was generally an ardent follower of Maimonidean thought. See Umberto (Moses David) Cassuto, "Jacob Ben Abba Mari Ben Samson Anatoli," *Encyclopedia Judaica* (Jerusalem, 1972), Vol. 2, 927 at 928.

[63] It is interesting to note that there is a group of important scholars who maintain that the position of *Rema* and *Hatam Sofer* cited in n. 60 *supra* is only in the absence of expressed legislation by the Gentile legislature. Then, according to these scholars, Jewish Law is to be applied. Should, however, there be proper legislation relevant to the issue, then all would agree with Maimonides and his school that the Gentile legislation should be enforced. See *Helkat Yo'av, Mahadurah Tinyana*, Chap. 14 (end); *Keter David Kama*, Chap. 18; *Responsa Minhat Yizhak*, Vol. 4, Chap. 52, no. 3; *Responsa Yehaveh Da'at*, ibid.

[64] "*Dayanei Yisra'el.*" See MS The Royal Library of Stockholm (Catalogue 6, Rdl 1)— 1549. I am indebted to my friend and colleague Dr. Berahyahu Lifshitz of The Hebrew University Faculty of Law who made me aware of this proper reading. See his "The Rules Governing Conflict of Laws Between A Jew and A Gentile According to Maimonides," *Mélanges à la Mémoire de Marcel-Henri Prévost* (France, 1982), 179-189, at 184-185.

[65] *Hilkhot Melakhim* 10:12. See also *Hilkhot Nahalot* 6:9.

[66] Our discussion, here, has centered around civil and monetary matters. We have not been able to conclusively ascertain whether the same degree of flexibility is afforded by Jewish Law to the Gentile courts in the other areas of Noahide Law. See Nahmanides, *Sefer ha-Mizvot, supra* n. 55; Rabbi Joab Joshua Weingarten, *Resp. Helkat Yo'av*, Vol. 1, Chap.

14 (end); *Margoliyot ha-Yam, Sanhedrin* 56a, no. 27 and 56b, no. 11; Rabbi J.E. Henkin, *Perushei Lev Ivra, supra* n. 8, at 125, in his *"Kez ha-Yamin", supra* n. 8, at 8, footnote, and in his *Teshuvot Ivra,* Chap. 95 (1) in *Kitve ha-Gri Henkin* 2 (New York, 1989), 172.

[67] See *Hilkhot Melakhim, supra* n. 65; see *Hilkhot Nizkei Mamon* 8:5. These rulings may perhaps be explained as based upon the principles of *lex fori.* However, in order to prevent "forum shopping," the Jewish court will not allow the Gentile to succeed beyond the limits of his own personal law. See at length Lifshitz, *supra* n. 62, at 179-189. See in addition R. Uziel, *supra* n. 6, at 16-17. Note also *Even ha-Azel, Hilkhot Nizke Mamon, ad loc.; Mishpat ha-Melukhah, Hilkhot Melakhim, ad loc.* In general, see: *Beit ha-Behirah,* supra n. 6; *Arukh ha-Shulhan ha-Atid, Hilkhot Melakhim* 80:14; *Torah Temimah, Ex., supra* n. 7; *Levush Mordekhai,* supra n. 15; *Hazon Ish, Hilkhot Melakhim ad loc.* And *Hilkhot Nizkei Mamon ad loc.;* Rabbi M. M. Kasher, *supra* n. 61.

[68] *Gittin* 10b; *Bava Batra* 55a; *Rambam, Hilkot Gezeilah va-Aveidah* 5:11-18, *Hilkhot Zekhiyah u-Matanah* 1:15.

[69] *Gittin* 9b (top). See Shmuel Shilo, *Dina de-Malkhuta Dina* (Jerusalem, 1974), 59-60; Menachem Elon, *Ha-mishpat ha-Ivri* (Jerusalem, 4th ed., 1988), I, 60-61 esp. footnote 59.

[70] *Even ha-Azel, supra* n. 67, and again in *Hilkhot Malveh ve-Loveh* 27:1; *Mishpat ha-Melukhah, supra* n. 67, See Shilo, *supra* n. 69, at 82-83. See also *Responsa Ez Hadar,* Chap. 1; *Responsa Mishpat Kohen,* Chap. 13 and notes *ad loc.;* Rabbi M. M. Kasher, *supra* n. 61 (pp. 218-219, 221-222). See also *Or Sameyah, Hilkhot Melakhim,* 3:10, and *Hemdat Yisra'el* (Pietrokow: 1927), *Kuntres Ner Mizvah,* Negative Commandment 71 (pp. 75-76), who view the law of even a Jewish king *(din melekh)* as analogous to the Noahide Laws.

[71] Isadore Twersky, *Introduction to the Code of Maimonides ("Mishneh Torah")* (New Haven and London, 1980), 517.

Four Parables about *Peshat* as Parable

Roslyn Weiss

In his Introduction to the *Guide for the Perplexed*, Maimonides alerts his readers to a method he will be employing throughout the work. He will, he says, deliberately contradict himself in order to conceal his true beliefs, revealing them only in occasional "flashes" and only to his most attentive readers. It is the thesis of this essay that Maimonides employs this method even in the Introduction itself, and, moreover, that he does so precisely when he explains how the Torah conceals *its* views. Just as the words of the Torah and the books of the Prophets have a literal sense (*peshat*) under which lies a hidden meaning, so, too, the words of Maimonides have a *peshat* under which lies a hidden meaning precisely when he deals with this issue.

In his Introduction, Maimonides presents four parables to clarify the relationship between the Torah's *peshat*, on the one hand, and its secret truth, on the other. The first parable is that of R. Hanina,[1] and is found in *Shir ha-Shirim Rabba* 1:1:8.

> To what were the words of the Torah to be compared before the advent of Solomon? To a well the waters of which are at a great depth and cool, yet no man could drink of them. Now what did one clever man do? He joined cord with cord and rope with rope and drew them up and drank. Thus did Solomon descend from one parable to another and from one word to another until he understood the meaning of the words of the Torah.[2]

Maimonides explains in this way that Solomon came to understand "obscure matters."

Immediately upon concluding the first parable Maimonides proceeds to the second, also found in *Shir ha-Shirim Rabba* 1:1:8:

> Our Rabbis say: A man who loses a *sela* or a pearl in his house can find the pearl by lighting a taper worth an *issar*. In the same way this parable in itself is worth nothing, but by means of it you can understand the words of the Torah.[3]

I shall refer henceforth to the first parable about the waters of a well as R. Hanina's parable and to the second parable about the lost pearl as the Rabbis' parable. Both these parables say in essence the same thing, namely, that there is something precious—cool waters or a pearl—that is beyond reach. What is needed in order to gain access to this precious commodity is something—ropes or a taper—that has only instrumental value. What is new, however, in the Rabbis' parable is that it explicitly states that the taper lacks intrinsic worth. From this parable Maimonides concludes that "the internal meaning of the words of the Torah is the pearl whereas the external meaning is worth nothing."

After these two parables Maimonides presents a third one, this time a parable of his own invention. Although this third parable is his own, Maimonides nevertheless proffers it as if it were merely a fuller account of the words of the Rabbis. He says:

> ...and they [the Rabbis] compare the concealment of a subject by its parable's external meaning to a man who let drop a pearl in his house, which was dark and full of furniture. Now this pearl is there, but he does not see it and does not know where it is. It is as though it were no longer in his possession, as it is impossible for him to derive any benefit from it until, as has been mentioned, he lights a lamp—an act to which an understanding of the meaning of the parable corresponds.

Despite Maimonides' pretense that this restatement of the Rabbis' parable is nothing but a paraphrase of it, the restatement in fact constitutes a new and distinct parable that I shall call Maimonides' parable. Indeed, the differences between the Rabbis' parable and Maimonides' version of it are quite striking. First, in the Rabbis' parable, the house in which the pearl is lost is simply a house. In their parable there is no description of the house. In Maimonides' parable, however, the house in which the pearl is lost is dark and full of furniture. Second, in the Rabbis' parable, the *peshat* is the taper, and the secret, deeper meaning is the pearl. In Maimonides' parable, by contrast, the house full of furniture is the *peshat*, and rather than being instrumental in finding the pearl, it is obstructive: it makes it more difficult to find the pearl. Third, the lamp in Maimonides' parable is not the counterpart of the taper in the Rabbis' parable. Whereas the taper in the Rabbis' parable is the *peshat*, the lamp in Maimonides' parable that one must light if one is to find the pearl is the intellect's power of understanding.

Maimonides, then, changes quite substantially the Rabbis' parable. Although the *peshat* in the Rabbis' parable has no intrinsic value it does have instrumental value; it is the light that helps the seeker find the pearl. In Maimonides' parable, it is not only that the *peshat* has no intrinsic value; it has negative value. The *peshat* is the analogue of the dark house full of furniture that *conceals* the pearl, that makes it difficult to find the pearl. In Maimonides' parable, then, but not in the Rabbis', there is a need for something other than the *peshat* to enable the seeker to find the pearl—the lamp that will help him is his intellectual understanding. Just as the lamp enables the seeker of the pearl to avoid the furniture and to penetrate through the darkness to the pearl, so the intellect enables the seeker of truth to avoid the *peshat* and penetrate through to the truth hidden beneath it. Rather than being a help in the discovery of the hidden truth, the *peshat* in Maimonides' parable is a liability.

The reader who fails to attend sufficiently carefully to Maimonides' parable will surely miss, as Maimonides no doubt intends him to, the differences between it and the Rabbis' parable. Indeed, he will assume that both say roughly the same thing. The fact is, however, that the two parables contradict one another. The conclusion of Maimonides' parable is that *peshat* gets in the way of finding the truth; the conclusion of the Rabbis' parable is that it helps the seeker to find it.

If indeed these last two parables are radically different from one another, it is important to determine which of them Maimonides prefers. It seems clear that he must prefer his own; had Maimonides been satisfied with the Rabbis' parable, why would he have replaced it with another? The only reason Maimonides could have had for replacing the Rabbis' parable with his own is that he could not accept theirs. He apparently does not think that *peshat* helps those who seek the deeper hidden truths of the Torah to find them, but thinks, on the contrary, that *peshat* is an obstacle that prevents one from grasping the truth.

Another indication that Maimonides regards *peshat* as a hindrance to truth may be found earlier in the *Guide*,[4] where Maimonides lays out the book's two purposes. The first purpose of the *Guide*, Maimonides says, is to explain certain problematic words in the Torah in order that a religious man who has studied Torah and also has delved into philosophy will not become confused on their account. The second purpose is to clarify the hidden parables in the Torah, that is, the parables that do not announce themselves as parables.[5] A person who reads them is prone to confusion. According to Maimonides, there are two ways of dispelling the confusion. One way is to elucidate the parable's meaning. But the second way—and it is this one that is most interesting and most significant—is simply to inform the reader that the parable is a parable. The recognition alone that something is a parable is sufficient to remove the confusion.

What Maimonides seems to be saying here is that it does not matter what the parable means; all that matters is that the parable be seen as a parable. Why? Presumably because once the reader who wants to know the truth sees the parable for what it is he can disregard it. Since the parable to be disregarded is the *peshat*, the *peshat* cannot be like the taper that illuminates the truth. It can only be like the dark house that obstructs the understanding and impedes the penetration to truth. (A point similar to this one will appear when we consider Maimonides' treatment of the next and final parable, the parable of the golden apple.)

Let us turn now to the final parable found in the Introduction. The source for the final parable is not a midrash but rather a verse from Proverbs (11:25): "A word fitly spoken is like apples of gold in settings of silver filigree." Maimonides praises these words of Solomon as particularly apt. For, Maimonides says, every well-constructed parable has both a *peshat* and a hidden meaning—both are beautiful, but the hidden meaning is even more so, just as gold is more beautiful than silver.[6]

From Maimonides' praise of this final parable it certainly appears that he sees value even in the *peshat* which, he says, is as beautiful as silver. In other words, his words seem to warrant the inference that *peshat* actually has intrinsic value. And Maimonides goes on to contend that *peshat* must contain within itself something that "indicates to someone considering it what is to be found in its internal meaning."[7] It would seem, then, that Maimonides thinks that the settings of silver filigree, like the taper in the Rabbis' parable, have instrumental value with respect to the hidden truth, for they point to it. Indeed, were we to stop reading at this point, or had Maimonides stopped writing at this point, we could conclude that in the final analysis Maimonides believes that *peshat* has both intrinsic and instrumental value; on the one hand, it is as beautiful as silver and, on the other, it points beyond itself to the deeper truth it contains.

Maimonides, however, does not stop here, and if one continues to read and to think about what one is reading one will see that it is impossible to take Maimonides at his word when he writes that *peshat* points to the existence of a hidden meaning just as settings of silver filigree, a sort of silver net containing fine apertures, reveal a golden apple. For, as Maimonides goes on to say, when one looks at the apple from afar or without devoting to it perfect attention, one thinks it is made of silver; only someone who has a sharp eye and who devotes to the apple his full attention sees what is inside the silver filigree, namely, an apple of gold.

Is it the silver filigree that helps the discerning individual to recognize that a golden apple lies within? Or is it rather the case that the discerning individual must peer through the *apertures* in the filigree if he is to see the golden apple within? It seems clear that the filigree actually tricks those who do not have keen vision, hiding the golden apple from them. Moreover, it provides no help whatsoever to the one who does see and recognize what is within. The latter, after all, has to disregard the deceptive filigree; he must look not at it but through it.

If, then, Solomon's dictum meets with Maimonides' approval, it can only be because what it really teaches is that *peshat* does *not* lead to the apprehension of truth. We must still note that the apple parable does not merely repeat Maimonides' parable but rather takes a further step in discrediting *peshat*; it charges *peshat* with being deceptive. Whereas the dark house full of furniture in Maimonides' parable was a hindrance to the finding of the pearl, neither the dark house nor the furniture it contained could possibly be mistaken for the pearl. Not so in the case of the apple: whoever fails to appreciate that the silver overlay is filigree-work thinks—mistakenly—that the apple itself is silver.

If Maimonides thinks that *peshat* hinders the attainment of truth and is deceptive, why, we must wonder, does he attribute to it the intrinsic value of silver? By doing so does he not assign positive value to *peshat*, even if the value he assigns to it is less than the value he assigns to the Torah's deeper, hidden truth?

What becomes clear as Maimonides continues is that although he does not think that *peshat* has instrumental value in the sense that it leads to truth, he does think that the Torah's literal sense is valuable in that it enhances human associations; it improves moral character and social and political relations among people. *Peshat* is, therefore, beautiful in its own way, as beautiful as silver. But insofar as it is useless for discovering truth, it is like the dark house full of furniture in Maimonides' parable and not like the taper in the Rabbis' parable or the ropes in R. Hanina's. It is important to remember that at the same time that *peshat* improves social relations it also conceals the truth from ordinary people and even fools them; it causes them to believe that *it* is the truth and that there is no deeper and more genuine truth.[8]

It is worthwhile at this juncture to cite another place in the *Guide* where Maimonides compares silver to gold. In *Guide* 1:59, Maimonides relates a story from the Talmud[9] in which it is told that there was a certain *sheliah zibur* who, when he led the congregation in prayer in the presence of R. Hanina, prayed as follows: "God who is great, mighty, and revered, princely, powerful, feared, and strong." R. Hanina, the story goes, admonished the *sheliah zibur* for his additions to the standard prayer and said: "Have you finished praising the Lord? As it is, we would not be permitted to utter the first three words of praise—great, mighty, and revered—had Moses not said them in the Torah (Deut. 10:17) and had the Men of the Great Assembly not subsequently redacted them into the prayer service. Yet you extend the praises and add all of these?" Following his admonition, R. Hanina proceeded to offer the following parable: "To what is this situation to be compared? To a king of flesh and blood who had one million gold coins and was praised for having silver ones—is this not rather an insult to him?" Maimonides comments on this parable at the end of the chapter as follows:

> R. Hanina did not say: "To what is this situation to be compared? To a king of flesh and blood who had one million gold coins and was praised for having one hundred coins," for were that the case, this parable would have indicated only that the perfections of the Exalted One are greater than those that were attributed to him, but nevertheless of the same sort. But the matter is not so...but the wisdom of this parable lies in that it says...that what we consider to be perfections are nothing with respect to Him, may He be exalted, but are in fact defects with respect to him. Therefore R. Hanina said: "It is an insult to Him."[10]

If we transfer the Maimonidean view concerning the relationship between silver and gold in this story to our passage, we can say that the settings of silver filigree are worth nothing with respect to truth—indeed, that they are defects with respect to truth—but that their value is limited to social and moral matters alone. It is not, in other words, that *peshat* is only somewhat less valuable than the truth that lies hidden beneath it, a mere quantitative difference, but rather that its value lies elsewhere, a qualitative difference, and that with respect to truth it is not only of no value but is actually detrimental.

There is yet another textual indication of Maimonides' true view with respect to the value of the literal sense of the Torah. At the end of his treatment of this matter,[11] he returns to a point that he had made earlier.[12] As we saw earlier, Maimonides said that it suffices for a person who wishes to dispel his confusion when studying Torah to recognize that the *peshat* is a parable, and that he need not understand the parable's meaning. And now he says something quite similar:

> In some matters it will suffice you to gather from my remarks that a given story is a parable, even if we explain nothing more: for once you know it is a parable, it will immediately become clear to you what it is a parable of. My remarking that it is a parable will be like someone's removing a screen from between the eye and a visible thing.[13]

Because *peshat* hinders the apprehension of truth, it is sufficient for the reader to recognize that it is a parable, for then he will know that what he must do is look away from it or disregard it. If the parable is indeed "a screen between the eye and a visible thing," it is just like the silver net or the house full of furniture that must be sidestepped if one is to reach the golden apple or the pearl. The parable is unlike a taper that enhances one's vision as in the Rabbis' parable, for were the seeker to discard the taper that would make matters worse: he would not then succeed in finding the pearl.

What I hope to have shown up to this point is: (1) that the parable of the golden apple is close to Maimonides' parable and far from the Rabbis' parable; (2) that the parable of the golden apple removes from *peshat* any instrumental value with regard to the apprehension of truth; (3) that, nevertheless, the parable of the golden apple concedes that *peshat* has value—though not from the point of view of truth; (4) that from the point of view of truth, the parable of the golden apple shows that not only does *peshat* not have value but that it is likely to fool the unwise or undiscerning man because it presents itself as if it is the truth; and (5) that both in Maimonides' parable and in the parable of the golden apple Maimonides hides his views from the hasty and careless reader who is not sufficiently attentive to what he reads. Such a reader will believe that Maimonides' parable and even the parable of the golden apple somehow restate in other words the point of the Rabbis' parable, when in fact Maimonides' parable, as well as the parable of the golden apple, contradict the main point of the Rabbis' parable. Whereas the Rabbis' parable maintains that *peshat* has instrumental value with respect to the discovery of truth, both Maimonides' parable and the parable of the golden apple deny it any such value.

In the remainder of this essay I shall do two things. The first is to consider another approach—that of Abarbanel—to the matter of the glaring differences between the Rabbis' parable and that of Maimonides. The second is to try to show how, when Maimonides treats other topics in the *Guide*, *peshat* indeed functions for him like a net of silver filigree enclosing a golden apple.

I. Abarbanel's Approach

In his commentary on the *Guide for the Perplexed*, Abarbanel seeks to explain why Maimonides presents his own parable as a mere explanation or clarification of the Rabbis' parable when on the face of it the parables differ considerably from one another. According to Abarbanel, since the Rabbis' parable appears in the *midrash* right after that of R. Hanina, Maimonides felt compelled to quote both, thinking it inappropriate to quote the one but not the other. But, says Abarbanel, it immediately became clear to Maimonides that the Rabbis' parable is problematic. It is very difficult to read the Rabbis' parable and believe that when they spoke about a taper that is intrinsically worthless and of only instrumental value that they were referring to the Torah's *peshat*. For one thing, how could *peshat* be of value for understanding "the words of the Torah," when *peshat* is itself "the words of the Torah"? For another, if the parable contains within itself that of which it is a parable, how can it be worthless? And for yet a third, if the parable contains within itself that of which it is a parable, how can the parable be likened to the taper and how can what it contains be likened to the pearl? After all, the pearl is not contained within the taper! According to Abarbanel, then, Maimonides proposed a parable of his own in order to avoid these difficulties in the Rabbis' parable while securing his view that *peshat* is a parable that contains within itself the Torah's secret, deeper, truth.

According to Abarbanel, Maimonides sought to resolve the first difficulty by saying that the expression "the words of the Torah" refers to the secret internal meaning of the words of the Torah rather than to the literal words of the Torah. Thus, even if the parable is the *peshat*, it is possible to say that the parable helps one to reach "the words of the Torah." Maimonides sought to address the second difficulty by saying that the parable is not completely devoid of intrinsic value but is only devoid of intrinsic value from the perspective of its being a parable. From the point of view of its containing within itself the deep hidden meaning of the Torah, however, *peshat* does indeed have value. And with respect to the third problem, Maimonides' solution, according to Abarbanel, is that in the Rabbis' parable it is not the taper that is the analogue of *peshat* but the house, since, after all, there is a house in the Rabbis' parable as well. Did they not say: "A man who loses a *sela* or a pearl in his house..."? Indeed, says Abarbanel, what role would the house play in the Rabbis' parable if the taper is the analogue to *peshat*? Would not the house then be wholly superfluous? According to Maimonides, then, Abarbanel contends, the *peshat* contains the Torah's secret meaning in the same way that the house contains the pearl, *peshat* is dark and difficult to penetrate in the same way that the house is dark, and the *peshat* is full of words in the same way that the house is full of furniture. Just as the pearl is in the house though no one can see it, so is the hidden sense of the Torah unseen. And if one should ask how the house helps one to find the pearl as, according to the Rabbis, the *peshat* is supposed to help one find the deeper meaning of the text, the answer is (says Abarbanel in Maimonides' name) that the house protects the pearl and thus increases the seeker's chances of finding it. And if one should ask what then is the role of the taper if it is not the analogue of *peshat*, the answer is that it is like the lamp in Maimonides' parable, that is, the intellectual apprehension of the truth.

At the end of his treatment of this matter, Abarbanel reveals his own view that the dicta of R. Hanina and of the Rabbis in *Shir ha-Shirim Rabba* 1:1:8 do not deal at all with the relationship between *peshat* and the true meaning of the Torah or its hidden sense. Abarbanel concludes that Maimonides simply erred here. In these midrashic dicta, Abarbanel contends, the subject is a teacher who composes parables and metaphors in order to explain to his students the meaning of the text.

There can be little doubt that Abarbanel is right in his understanding of the purpose of R. Hanina's and the Rabbis' parables. But is he also right when he says that Maimonides "erred" and was unaware of the true intent of these *midrashim*? Is it credible that Maimonides actually thought that the *midrashim* in question deal with the relationship between *peshat* and the Torah's deeper sense? Surely not. Maimonides frequently uses prooftexts to support a position of his while knowing full well that, when taken in their most obvious sense, these sources offer no such support.[14]

But perhaps Abarbanel is right to think that Maimonides creates difficulties for himself which he then resolves by way of his own parable because he "feels compelled" to cite the Rabbis' parable. This, too, however, seems unlikely, for Maimonides tends to cite precisely what he wishes to cite—neither more nor less. Indeed, there are several other passages in the very same *midrash* that Maimonides decides not to quote. For example, Maimonides does not quote the *midrashim* that precede R. Hanina's, for most of them make the point that Solomon was skilled in the composition of parables and metaphors that would help others to understand a Torah that was otherwise closed to them. He also fails to quote the dictum in that very place that says that "until Solomon arose there was no parable (*dugma*)"—for if there were no parables before Solomon composed them, it would appear that the Torah contains no parables. Maimonides even neglects to quote the whole of R. Hanina's dictum, which says in the middle: "They all began to draw and to drink." And Maimonides omits the dictum of R. Yudan that completes the passage: "...to teach that anyone who speaks words of Torah in public merits having the holy spirit rest upon him. And how do we know this? From Solomon, who, by speaking words of Torah in public, merited having the holy spirit rest upon him with the result that he composed three books: Proverbs, Ecclesiastes, and Song of Songs." Why does Maimonides omit this passage? Probably because he realized that the point of it is that Solomon composed parables for the sake of teaching Torah to others—and not because he saw in *peshat* a means by which he himself might penetrate to the depths of Torah. Considering how many parts of *Shir ha-Shirim Rabba* 1:1:8 Maimonides does not quote, it is difficult to believe, like Abarbanel, that he quotes the Rabbis' parable because he felt "compelled" to do so. But once we reject Abarbanel's premise, there remains little reason to accept his analysis of Maimonides' supplementary parable. Moreover, Abarbanel's analysis is problematic. First, the Rabbis' parable states that, "by means of it [the parable] you can understand the words of the Torah." Yet if, as Abarbanel states, the parable is the house and not the taper, then the house ought to be the means by which one can see the pearl. But surely one sees the pearl by means of a taper and despite the house. And second, Abarbanel does not address the matter of why the taper in the Rabbis' parable is worth but an *issar*. Indeed, if, as Abarbanel contends, the taper in the Rabbis' parable is the counterpart of the lamp in Maimonides', should it not, like the intellectual apprehension that is the analogue of the lamp, be more valuable than that? Indeed, Maimonides never suggests in his parable that the *lamp* has little or no value. If, as it now seems, the reason Maimonides cites the Rabbis' parable is not that he felt compelled to do so, why, then, does he cite it? It appears that Maimonides carefully chose just those parables that would enable him to arrive slowly and step-by-step at the parable that best captures the relationship between *peshat* and the Torah's hidden truths. The first step in this progression is represented by R. Hanina's parable, according to which *peshat* has instrumental value for the attainment of truth. The second step is represented by the Rabbis' parable, according to which *peshat* has instrumental value but is itself worthless. Maimonides' parable constitutes the third stage, according to which *peshat* hinders the attainment of truth, so that the only way to attain truth is by way of one's intellect. The fourth and last stage is the parable of the apple, in which *peshat* not only hinders the attainment of truth but actually fools those who are not sufficiently discerning and causes them to believe that the *peshat is* the truth. Nevertheless, according to the fourth parable, *peshat* has in itself social/political/moral value.

II. The Parable of the Golden Apple and Maimonides' Treatment of *Peshat* in Other Places in the *Guide*

As we explore Maimonides' treatment of *peshat* in the *Guide*, it will be helpful to bear two things in mind. The first is that Maimonides excludes matters of *halakhah* from the general principle that *peshat* conceals a deeper truth. He says explicitly:

> I do not think that anyone possessing an unimpaired capacity imagines that the words of the Torah referred to here that one contrives to understand through understanding the meaning of parables are ordinances concerning the building of tabernacles, the lulav, and the law of four trustees. Rather what this text has in view here is, without any doubt, the understanding of obscure matters.[15]

The second is that Maimonides identifies two types of parables that appear in *Tanakh*. There are, he says, on the one hand, parables in which every word is significant, and, on the other, parables in which the parable as a whole has a meaning but in which no special meaning attaches to each word within the parable. In the latter case, the additional words serve to beautify the parable or even on occasion to conceal the parable's point. Moreover, the form of the parable is dictated by the requirements of the *peshat* and not by the requirements of the deeper meaning. Maimonides cautions his readers that in parables of the second type one is not to search for meaning in each word and one is not to expect it to be possible to understand all parts of the parable in accordance with its deeper, hidden sense.

In order to see how the parable of the golden apple in settings of silver filigree expresses Maimonides' sense of the relationship between *peshat* and the depths of Torah, we shall consider two examples, one a story and the second a dogma, from the *Guide for the Perplexed*.

The story of Adam in the Garden of Eden, taken in its literal sense, teaches that when Adam ate from the tree he became wise. He came to understand something he hadn't understood previously, namely, the difference between good and evil. According to Maimonides (*Guide* 1:2), however, it is necessary to understand the matter in a wholly different way. It is hardly likely, Maimonides claims, that Adam benefited after his sin and because of his sin. When Adam ate from the Tree of Knowledge, Maimonides reasons, his level of wisdom must actually have diminished. Indeed, it was before he sinned that he had intelligence, for Scripture says of him that he was created "in the image of God and after His likeness" (Gen. 2:16). Moreover, he received a commandment from God, something that is impossible for a beast devoid of intelligence.[16] For Maimonides, before the sin Adam's intelligence enabled him to distinguish between truth and falsehood; this was a complete perfection. After and because of the sin, however, Adam lost a part of his intelligence and now knew only to distinguish between good and evil. At first Adam was "just short of *Elohim*" (Psalms 5:6), but now the man and the woman are, in the words of the serpent, like *Elohim*, that is, like judges, rulers, or leaders who can "discern good from evil."[17] They are not "knowers of falsehood and truth" or "apprehenders of falsehood and truth." When their eyes were opened Adam and Eve did not "see" something new, but "knew" something new, namely, that they were naked; they regarded something as shameful that they did not so regard previously.[18]

It is clear that what Maimonides sees in the text of Genesis could not emerge from a superficial reading. An ordinary reader sees the "silver" and has no sense that there is any "gold" beneath it. What is the silver? The belief that people become godlike when they distinguish good from evil, the belief that what matters to God and is characteristic of God is moral goodness rather than truth and necessity. There can be no doubt that the belief that God is concerned with matters of good and evil and that it is in their moral sensibilities that human beings resemble Him is beneficial to society and to moral life generally. But the real truth, the gold, is that God has no moral qualities and, to the extent that human beings resemble God at all, they resemble Him in their intellects rather than in their moral nature.[19]

How can one get to the truth, to the gold, when all one is given is the story in Scripture, the silver? How did Maimonides get to it? First, it is clear that it was not the *peshat* that helped him. On the contrary, the *peshat* was the source of the confusion rather than its solution. If Maimonides somehow arrived at the truth, it can only be because his "lamp," that is, his intellect, enabled him to detect apertures in the story that he could then look through. Since he understood that it could not be the case that Adam derived benefit from his sin, and since by way of this understanding he could "see" the defects in the story's *peshat*, he was able to go on to see the truth behind the façade. Maimonides had to look away from the *peshat* that hinders and deceives, and penetrate with his lamp, with his intellect, to the hidden truth.

This story is a parable of the second type that Maimonides identifies, for the continuation of the parable actually contradicts the lesson of its beginning. The lesson of the parable's beginning is, of course, that Adam was created with the intellect to discern truth from falsehood. But later on we read: "And the Lord God said: Behold, the man is become as one of us, to know good and evil" (Gen. 3:22). If the knowledge of good and evil signifies a lower level of intelligence and a descent from the divine level of knowing truth and falsehood, how could God Himself say that man is now like Him in knowing good and evil? Maimonides surely thinks that the Torah here conceals the truth that it had flashed for but a moment. Anyone who is insufficiently attentive will fail to grasp the truth that vanishes almost as soon as it is revealed. The silver filigree quickly covers up the golden apple.

Let us turn finally to a central Maimonidean dogma. Maimonides maintains that God is incorporeal. This is the truth; it is the golden apple. God has no body and also no qualities associated with the body. But how would a person who reads the Torah know that God has no body? Does not the *peshat* of the Torah incline the reader to believe in God's corporeality? And how indeed could the *peshat help* the reader to conclude correctly that God is incorporeal? Nevertheless, the Torah has the value of silver, social and moral value, because it permits simple people, those who are unable to grasp the idea of existence that is not bodily, still to believe in the existence of God. According to Maimonides, had the Torah not attributed corporeality to the Creator, ordinary people would have been unable to believe in Him. Moreover, Maimonides points out, the Torah took care not to assign to God senses and organs that are shameful or that imply deficiency or imperfection. Apparently, then, *peshat* (the silver) helps ordinary people to believe that God exists and that He is perfect (beliefs that are necessary for living a moral life), but at the same time conceals from them the full truth that God has no body, senses, or passions.[20] Indeed, how could a passionless God, a God who neither gets angry nor feels pity, inspire ordinary men to do good? If, then, the Torah does not reveal the truth about God, how does Maimonides get to it? Surely not by studying Torah. Maimonides had to turn away from the *peshat* and use the "light" of his own intellectual apprehension in order to penetrate through the darkness to the truth.

In the above two examples, both in the story of Adam and in the matter of God's incorporeality, the apertures in the silver net open themselves up to the reader whose developed intellect cannot abide the irrational elements in the *peshat*. In both cases Maimonides sensed that something in the *peshat* defies reason. This realization enabled him to free himself from the *peshat* and to see the truth. The truth, then, is found by way of the human intellect that is capable of apprehending it without the help of the Torah, which, in its literal sense, is actually a hindrance to the apprehension of truth. In the final analysis, *peshat* is a parable that obstructs the hidden truth.[21] The hidden truth can only be found independently of the literal words of the Torah—in the intellect and understanding of a man.

---

[1] Maimonides does not mention R. Hanina by name, and, as we shall see, Maimonides presents the four parables as if they were essentially the same.

[2] *Guide*, 1:11. Unless otherwise indicated, translations, occasionally modified slightly, are from Moses Maimonides, *The Guide of the Perplexed*, trans. Shlomo Pines, 2 vols. (Chicago, 1963).

[3] *Guide*, ibid.

[4] *Guide*, 1:6.

[5] Hence, Maimonides cannot be speaking of Solomon's parables.

[6] *Guide*, 1:12.

[7] *Guide*, ibid.

[8] On one occasion Maimonides speaks of views that improve social relations as "correct" opinions (*Guide* 3:28), although he had earlier asserted unequivocally that they are false (see especially *Guide* 1:55).

[9] *Berakhot* 33b, *Megillah* 25a.

[10] My translation.

[11] *Guide*, 1:14.

[12] Ibid., 1:6.

[13] Ibid. 1:14.

[14] A case in point is *Guide* 1:54, where Maimonides interprets "and He will surely not acquit" (*ve-nakkeh lo yenakkeh* – Ex. 34:7) as "He will not destroy utterly." Maimonides cannot fail to be aware that the sense he assigns to this expression cannot be its straightforward sense, particularly since when the same expression appears in the Decalogue, the verse reads: "Because God will not acquit (*lo yenakkeh*) him who takes His name in vain" (Ex. 20:7). It is impossible in this latter context to take *yenakkeh* as "will destroy." Although Maimonides, in order to support his reading of Ex. 34:7, quotes Isaiah 3:26: "And she will be destroyed (*ve-nikkatah*), and will sit upon the earth," nevertheless, the root *nkt* that there means destroy certainly does not mean destroy either at Ex. 20:7 or at Ex. 34:7.

[15] *Guide*, 1:11.

[16] It is not clear why it is not sufficient for the receipt of a command that a man be able to do or to refrain from doing what he is commanded. Why must he have the intelligence to be able in addition to distinguish between truth and falsehood?

[17] The term "God" (*Elohim*) appears several times in the story of Adam and Eve and, according to Maimonides, it has senses other than "God." The serpent uses the expression, "For *Elohim* knows that on the day that you will eat from it, your eyes will be opened and you will be like *Elohim*, knowers of good and evil" (Gen. 3:5). In *Guide* 1:2 Maimonides quotes Onkelos, who understands *Elohim* in this verse to mean judges or rulers or leaders.

[18] According to Maimonides, the word *va-tipakahnah* ("and they were opened") generally signifies a new understanding and not simply the ability to see anew.

[19] See *Guide* 3:51.

[20] According to Maimonides, Onkelos tries in his translation to remove all corporeality

from God. But, from Maimonides' point of view, were Onkelos to succeed, he would succeed too well, for what would then happen to the faith of ordinary people in God?

21 In *Guide* 2:25, where Maimonides says that one must accept literally the words of the Torah either if there is no demonstration to the contrary or if a foundation of the Torah is at stake, it is not advisable to take him at his word. As we have seen, he does not, after all, accord to *peshat* the value of truth. The Torah, he thinks, speaks to the common man. Moreover, Maimonides says twice in his Introduction that the account in Genesis of the Creation is a parable and does not express the secret truth, a truth that is not to be uttered explicitly (*Guide* 1: 8, 9).

Maimonides on Creating an Inclusive Community

Yamin Levy

Each individual possesses something unique, rare which is unknown to others; each individual has a unique message to communicate, a special color to add to the communal spectrum. Hence when lonely man joins the community, he adds a new dimension to the community awareness. He contributes something no one else could have contributed.

> Joseph B. Soloveitchik, "The Community," *Tradition* 17:2 (1978): 10

...[W]e should never alienate or despise the Shabbat violators, but, on the contrary, draw them near and inspire them to perform *mizvot*. As our sages indicated: "A willful transgressor who enters the synagogue to pray should not be disgraced but on the contrary be received with courtesy."

> Maimonides, *Iggeret ha-Shemad*

Once I have recognized the thou and invited him to join the community, I *ipso facto* assumed responsibility for the thou. Recognition is identical with commitment.

> Soloveitchik, ibid., page 18

R. Judah spoke: Hear, O Israel, this day thou art become a people unto the Lord thy God. Now was it on that day that the Torah was given? It is however to teach you that the Torah is as beloved everyday to those who study it as on the day it was given at Sinai.

> *Berakhot* 63b

Introduction

The Maimonides Heritage Center was founded on the premise that the "Great Eagle" Maimonides is not only in harmony with modern man's spiritual sensibilities but is indeed the most relevant Jewish thinker in modern man's struggle back to tradition. Eight hundred years after his death, the influence and impact of Maimonides' writings, as well as what we know about his personal life and his religious passion, affords us the spirituality that many have sought in religious existentialism and mystical texts.

Maimonides also speaks to some of the overriding political and communal issues of the contemporary Jewish community today. R. Norman Lamm formulated our generation's greatest challenge as follows:

> To concentrate solely on our physical survival with no thought to our cultural and religious tradition or, conversely, to focus our loyalties exclusively on our spiritual legacy even if it means alienating vast numbers of Jews who may be indifferent to it— this is the primal sin of our times. Jews without Judaism, Judaism without Jews—either one is treason, because each of these is a prescriptions for the end of the story of both Israel and Torah.[1]

The political implications of Maimonides' Halakhic thought are especially critical. A clear presentation of Maimonides' religious and Halakhic epistemology can be an avenue to bridge the gap between the religious, the secular, and the indifferent. Maimonides affords the twenty-first century Jewish community in the Diaspora and in Israel the spiritual and political answers it seeks in order to ensure the Jewish people remain a unified and pertinent entity.

The need to create a spiritually sensitive "community" is especially urgent in Israel. Contrary to the predictions of the nineteenth and twentieth century earlier thinkers who anticipated a melting pot where minority cultures assimilate, the modern state of Israel has become an arena where ethnic variety, individuality, and pluralism have found expression within the national society. This in itself would not pose a problem were it not for the tensions, animosity, and even outright hostility among various ideologies both within and beyond the range of religious groupings. This clearly poses a crucial and urgent challenge: How do we as a people, with different ideologies, lifestyles and religious and cultural backgrounds, come together to create a community?[2] In the view of Jonathan Woocher,

> At the very heart of the mystery of Jewish survival throughout the ages, in magnificent denial of the normal laws of history that decree the death sentence on people that lose their homeland, is the idea of community.... the sense of a profoundly shared

destiny, a shared purpose, a shared history and customs, a shared responsibility.[3]

One of our strengths as a people has always been the ability to draw on a shared past and the promise of a national destiny. Is there a place in our theology for substantive dialogue among those who share a land but not necessarily a common belief in a historical past, or commitment to a shared destiny? In this essay I will propose that Maimonides' exposition of basic Jewish theological principles and *mizvot* can serve as a guide toward reaching all members of our community and bringing the fragmented parts together in unity of direction and responsibility.

Self Perception

The thesis I am about to present requires a short discussion on the ways that Jews collectively perceive themselves in relation to God and, consequently, in relation to the rest of the world. One element of that collective perception is the concept of the election of Israel, on which the late Talmud scholar Ephraim E. Urbach astutely noted two different views in rabbinic literature. The first view, which he calls *nizhit* (eternal or absolute), sees the chosesnness of Israel as conceived together with the creation of the world. It assumes that the people of Israel are chosen because they possess an intrinsic distinction and that their election is not contingent on anything they do or fail to do. The second view he calls *yahasit* (relative), according to which the election of Israel is linked to certain stipulations and conditions. In this approach, the people are both elected and electors, in the sense that they "chose" as well as have been "chosen."[4]

Urbach attributes the idea of *behirah nitzhit*, the eternal or absolute election of Israel, to R. Akiva and his disciples. He hears the essence of this message in R. Akiva's well-known dictum: "Beloved are Israel who are called God's children... Beloved are Israel because the vessel through which the world was created was given to them."[5] That is, both Israel and Torah are primordial entities.[6] It then follows that both Israel and Torah are in truth eternal and not temporal. This belief was very attractive to a range of later Jewish theologians and scholars, finding its fullest expression in the works of Yehuda Halevi. By way of the *Zohar* and the schools of mystics, it also spread widely through popular writings.

The second view, that Urbach calls *behirah yahasit*, is attributed to the *Tanna* R. Eliezer Ben Azariah. R. Eliezer cited the verse "Thou hast avouched the Lord this day... and the Lord has avouched thee this day" (Deuteronomy 26:17-18) and expounded it:

> The Holy One blessed be He, said to Israel: You have made Me a unique object of your love in this world, so I shall make you a unique object of My love in this world. You have made Me a unique object of your love in this world as it is written "Hear, O Israel, the Lord our God, the Lord is One," and I shall make you a unique object of My love as it is written "Who is like unto Thy people Israel, a nation, one in the earth" (I Chronicles 17:21).[7]

That is, God was chosen by Israel before God chose the people of Israel. An identical view can be attributed to R. Ishmael in his teaching: "And ye shall be holy unto Me...when you are holy you are Mine."[8]

On the election of the Jewish people, Maimonides chose this second and less popular view.[9] As Menachem Kellner asserts persuasively, Maimonides does not assign any special ontological status to the Jewish people.[10] Maimonides does make reference to *behira*, election by God, but only in regard to liturgical traditions and the preservation of certain Talmudic formulations.[11] He does not suggest that God chose the Jewish people for qualities that distinguish them from the rest of humanity, nor does he give any theological significance to that concept.

This stance has many and dramatic implications that Kellner, in his study of Maimonides, examines. It seems clear that Maimonides downplays any special character of the Jewish people and sees no difference between Jew and gentile except in their theological choices. He rejects the concept that Jews are beneficiaries of a special Divine providence or prophecy.[12] Rather, Jew and Gentile are equally capable of achieving human perfection. This concept explains why Maimonides was so welcoming to proselytes.[13] Kellner's thesis also places in context Maimonides' belief that in the End of Days the distinction between Jew and gentile will dissolve.[14]

In the next section, I will apply Kellner's research further and argue that an appreciation for Maimonides' position on the election of Israel as a backdrop for the analysis of Maimonides' religious epistemology might afford us, the Jewish community of the twenty-first century, the religious and theological outlook necessary to engage co-religionists who might lack faith in God, a belief in traditional revelation, and in a shared destiny.

Self Expression

Interestingly, there is a relationship between how one understands the election of the Jewish people (*behirah*) and *ta'amei ha-mizvot*, applying reasons to the commandments. Regarding *ta'amei ha-mizvot*, Maimonides insists in numerous places that "every commandment and prohibition in these laws is consequent upon wisdom and aims at some end."[15] All the commandments are useful and even necessary for helping us achieve human perfection[16] and creating the ideal society. Based on this premise Maimonides goes to great lengths in the *Guide* to expound the reasons for the commandments. This is indeed consistent with his position on *behirah*. For him, *behirah* of the Jewish people is a dynamic process initiated by man seeking out his or her Creator. In presenting *ta'amei ha-mizvot*, Maimonides actually presents a model that by its very nature encourages dialogue and engages all members of the community in the religious quest. Man chose God because His law and creations are perfect and wise, and a relationship is forged from human intuition. Man then rationally communicates that choice and the values of his religious experience to others who may or may not be committed to the same kind of belief. Maimonides uses as a proof-text a verse on rationally communicating to the nations of the world the Divine wisdom of Torah: "*Ki hi hokhmatkhem u-vinatkhem le-einei ha-amim* (For she is your wisdom and knowledge in the eyes of the nations)" (Deut 4:6).

In contrast, those who insist that *behirah* of the Jewish people is absolute and that God chose the Jew because he or she is intrinsically special, regardless of human participation at all, will likely view the nature of *mizvot* in absolutist and fundamentalist terms as well. The Jew observes the *mizvot* because they are God's commandments. The transcendental nature of the relationship is not only its source but also the way it is expressed. The process of uncovering the reason and purpose for the commandments becomes irrelevant and even discouraged. One observes *mizvot* because that is what God wills. Fulfilling God's will for no reason or purpose actually becomes the highest form of religious expression.

Maimonides rejected such a position not only as contrary to the Torah's intended political goals[17] but also as a malady of the individual's soul:

> There is a group of human beings who consider it a grievous thing that causes should be given for any law; what would please

them most is that the intellect would not find a meaning for the commandments and prohibitions. What compels them to feel thus is a sickness that they find in their souls, a sickness to which they are unable to give utterance and of which they cannot furnish a satisfactory account. For they think that if those laws were useful in this existence and had been given to us for this or that reason, it would be as if they derived from the reflection and the understanding of some intelligent being. If, however, there is a thing for which the intellect could not find any meaning at all and that does not lead to something useful, it undoubtedly derives from God; for the reflection of man would not lead to such things.

It is as if, according to these people of weak intellects, man were more perfect than his Maker; for man speaks and acts in a manner that leads to some intended end, whereas the deity does not act thus, but commands us to do things that are not useful to us and forbids us to do things that are not harmful to us. But He [God] is far exalted above this; the contrary is the case—the whole purpose consisting in what is useful for us, as we have explained[18] on the basis of its dictum: *for our good always, that He might preserve us alive as it is at this day* (Deut. 6:24). And it says: *Which shall hear all these statutes and say: Surely this great community is a wise and understanding people* (Deut. 4:6). Thus it states explicitly that even all the statutes will show all the nations that they have been given with wisdom and understanding.[19]

Explaining Jewish law exclusively in terms of faith can become a way of escape for one who does not want to engage the outside world in understanding his way of life. Those whom Maimonides diagnoses with "sickness of soul" make use of *mizvot* to create a community of isolated individuals whose common language is generally dogmatic and absolute. The more they separate themselves from the non-believers, the more deeply they experience the fullness of the *mizvah*. If non-comprehension is indeed the highest expression of religious fervor, then actions that seem the least comprehensible will also seem to be the supreme demonstration of religious faith.

For Maimonides, the ultimate goal is the creation of an inclusive, orderly, and just society that gives the individual the necessary opportunity to achieve human perfection. True inclusion is possible only if one is able to explain the nature of one's actions and beliefs in terms and concepts that can be understood to a diverse public.[20] Maimonides' polemic against those who do not subject the truth of Jewish thought and philosophy to universal rational criteria makes sense in the context of an ultimate goal that will otherwise not be achieved. That goal, of course, is community.[21]

In the introduction to *Perek Helek* of Sanhedrin, Maimonides again discredits those whose religious outlook is exclusive and communicated in absolute literalist terms.

> You must know that the words of the sages are differently interpreted by three groups of people. The first group is the largest one. I have observed them, read their books, and heard about them. They accept the teachings of the sages in their simple literal sense and do not think that these teachings contain any hidden meaning at all. They believe that all sorts of impossible things must be. They hold such opinions because they have not understood science and are far from having acquired knowledge. They possess no perfection which would rouse them to insight from within, nor have they found anyone else to stimulate them to profounder understanding. They, therefore, believe that the sages intended no more in their carefully emphatic and straightforward utterances than they themselves are able to understand with inadequate knowledge. They understand the teachings of the sages only in their literal sense, in spite of the fact that some of their teachings, when taken literally, seem so fantastic and irrational that if one were to repeat them literally, even to the uneducated, let alone sophisticated scholars, their amazement would prompt them to ask how anyone in the world could believe such things true, much less edifying.
>
> The members of this group are poor in knowledge. One can only regret their folly. Their very effort to honor and to exalt the sages in accordance with their own meager understanding actually humiliates them. As God lives, this group destroys the glory of the Torah of God, say the opposite of what it intended. For He said in His perfect Torah, "The nation is a wise and understanding people" (Deut. 4:6). But this group expounds the laws and the teachings of our sages in such a way that when the other peoples hear them they say that this little people is foolish and ignoble.
>
> The worst offenders are preachers who preach and expound to the masses what they themselves do not understand. Would that they keep silent about what they do not know, as it is written: "If only they would be utterly silent, it would be accounted to them as wisdom" (Job 13:5). Or they might at least say, "We do not understand what our sages intended in this statement, and we do not know how to explain it." But they believe they do understand, and they vigorously expound to the people what they think rather than what the sages really said. They, therefore, give lectures to

the people on the tractate *Berakhot* and on this present chapter,
and other texts, expounding them word-for-word according to
their literal meaning.[22]

There is, indeed, a psychological and spiritual security in living only
with others who think and behave the same way and share a common
spiritual language. It can be unsettling to recognize the theological
implications of Maimonides' ideal, in which one must constantly move
between the inclusive and the particular, always trying to find a way of
integrating disparate needs into one's life. This raises the critical need of
finding a shared language between those who observe *halakhah* because
they believe in revelation and those who do not believe in revelation but
want to understand the value of *halakhah* as a way of life.

Shared practice and customs are essential ingredients needed to
create an inclusive community, and so Maimonides would have the
educated Jew go forth into the world and impart his religious experience
and spiritual life to others in commonly intelligible terms. It is a cornerstone
of Maimonidean thought that the Jew has a mandate to communicate the
wisdom of the Divine message in words that can be understood by all.
Maimonides' endeavor of giving reason for the *mizvot* had less to do with
how the law was practiced and more to do with knowing God through
Torah and nature. Yeshayahu Leibowitz formulated this point by stating
that *ta'amei ha-mizvot* is not a pursuit of knowledge as much as it is a
pursuit for knowledge of God.[23]

Recognition

Maimonides offers a model for building bridges through
communication. The edifice of Jewish law takes on greater significance
when the observant individual is capable of sharing his inner spiritual life
with others for the sake of building community. The Jew should be capable
of elucidating the nature of his observance without having to validate the
significance of his actions solely in terms of faith. *Halakhah* and Jewish
philosophy need not isolate the practitioner from full participation in a
universal culture of mankind. Indeed, cognitive isolation would be too
great a price to pay for a commitment to a particular way of life.

Some of the most fundamental *mizvot*, love of God, for example, can
be ideally observed only with recognition of the need to move beyond
traditional disciplines toward understanding of the universal. Thus,

to fulfill the *mizvah* of love of God one must master the natural world, including knowledge of mathematics and physics.

> And what is the way that will lead to the love of Him and the fear of Him? When a person contemplates His great and wondrous works and creatures and from them obtains a glimpse of His wisdom which is incomparable and infinite, he will straightway love Him, praise Him, glorify Him, and long with an exceeding longing to know His great Name; even as David said, "My soul thirsts for God, for the living God" (Ps. 43:3).

> And when he ponders these matters, he will recoil frightened, and realize that he is a small creature, lowly and obscure, endowed with slight and slender intelligence, standing in the presence of Him who is perfect in knowledge. And so David said "When I consider Your heaven the work of Your fingers—what is man that You are mindful of him?" (Ps. 8:4-5).

> In harmony with these sentiments, I shall explain some large, general aspects of the works of the Sovereign of the universe, that they may serve the intelligent individual as a door to the love of God, even as our sages have remarked in connection with the theme of the love of God, "Observe the universe and hence you will realize Him who spoke and the world was."[24]

> It is known and certain that the love of God does not become closely knit in a man's heart until he is continuously and thoroughly possessed by it and gives up everything else in the world for it; as God commanded us, "with all your heart and with all your soul" (Deut. 6:5).

> One only loves God with the knowledge with which one knows Him. According to the knowledge will be the love. If the former be little or much, so will the latter be little or much. A person ought therefore to devote himself to the understanding and comprehension of those sciences and studies which will inform him concerning his Master, as far as it lies in human faculties to understand and comprehend...[25]

The greatest scholars of Judaism, including those of the twentieth century, use insights from disciplines beyond the range of the specifically Jewish. Maimonides' own intellect was shaped not only by the work of his rabbinic predecessors but also by the ideas of gentile philosophers and scholars. In a letter to Samuel ibn Tibbon, who was translating *Guide of the Perplexed*, Maimonides refers to Aristotle, whom he describes as "the roots and foundations of all works in the sciences." He also makes reference to Alexander of Aphrodisias and Themistius, and to the Muslim philosophers Averroes and al-Farabi, with the comment on the latter that his "writings are faultlessly excellent—one ought to study and understand them." Truth reigns supreme based on its content and not on the appeal or authority of its author.[26]

A student of Maimonides learns to appreciate and value of the culture of others, in a context that seeks integration rather than polemics.[27] This is in itself a novel attitude, for as Jacob Katz strongly argues in his seminal work *Exclusiveness and Tolerance*,[28] the traditional Jewish position was one of separatism and of intolerance of the non-Halakhic and the secular.

Actualization

Maimonides was heir to a tradition and culture absolutely committed to *halakhah*, yet he could appreciate the possibilities of dialogue with those of different ideas and cultures.[29] This illustrates how an inclusive attitude can indeed be rooted in a profound passion for one particular belief and way of life. In his philosophy, shared values can be achieved by a variety of means. If this is so, then the Halakhic and the non-Halakhic Jew and even the gentile can share a common teleology, even with their disparate ways of seeking its fulfillment. Maimonides even asserts that the aim of Halakhah is to shape a healthy soul, and that is also the aim of the Aristotelian system. This would give *halakhah* and Aristotelian ethics a common goal and approach to the nature of virtue.[30]

Maimonides begins Chapter Four of the *Shemonah Perakim* with a discussion of virtue based upon moderation:

> Good deeds are such as are equi-balanced, maintaining the mean between two equally bad extremes, the too much and the too little. Virtues are psychic conditions and dispositions which are midway between two reprehensible extremes, one of which is characterized by an exaggeration, the order by deficiency. Good deeds are the product of these dispositions. To illustrate, abstemiousness is a disposition which adopts a mid-course between inordinate passion and total insensibility to pleasure. Abstemiousness, then, is a proper rule of conduct, and the psychic disposition which gives rise to it is an ethical quality; but inordinate passion, the extreme of excess, and total insensibility to enjoyment, the extreme of deficiency, are both absolutely pernicious. The psychic dispositions, from which these two extremes, inordinate passion and insensibility, result— the one being an exaggeration, the other a deficiency—are alike classed among moral imperfections.

The perfect Law which leads us to perfection—as one who knew it well testifies by the words "the Law of the Lord is perfect restoring the soul; the testimonies of the Lord are faithful making wise the simple" (Ps. 19:9)—recommends none of these things (such as self-torture, flight from society, and so forth). On the contrary, it aims at man's following the path of moderation in accordance with the dictates of nature, eating, drinking, enjoying legitimate sexual intercourse, all in moderation, and living among people in honesty and uprightness, but not dwelling in the wilderness or in the mountains, or clothing oneself in garments of hair and wool, or afflicting the body.

The Law even warns us against these practices if we interpret it according to what tradition tells us in the meaning of the passage concerning the Nazirite, "And he [the priest] shall make an atonement for he has sinned against the soul" (Num. 6:11). The rabbis ask, "Against what soul has he sinned? Against his own soul, because he has deprived himself of wine. Is this not then a conclusion a *minori ad majus*? If one who derives himself merely of wine must bring an atonement, how much more incumbent is it upon who denies himself every enjoyment."

Maimonides explains how habitual actions form character:

Know, moreover, that these moral excellences or defects cannot be acquired, or implanted in the soul except by means of the frequent repetition of acts resulting from these qualities, which, practiced during a long period of time, accustoms us to them. If these acts performed are good ones, then we shall have gained a virtue; but if they are bad, we shall have acquired a vice. Since, however, no man is born with an innate virtue or vice, as we shall explain in Chapter VIII, and, as everyone's conduct from childhood up is undoubtedly influenced by the manner of living of his relatives and countrymen, his conduct may be in accord with the rules of moderation; but, then again, it is possible that his acts may incline toward either extreme, as we have demonstrated, in which case, his soul becomes diseased. In such a contingency, it is proper for him to resort to a cure exactly as he would were his body suffering from an illness.

Halakhah is presented as a system designed to reach these goals:

The Law did not lay down its prohibitions or enjoin its commandments except for just this purpose, namely, that by its disciplinary effects we may persistently maintain the proper distance from either extreme. For the restrictions regarding all the forbidden foods, the prohibitions of illicit intercourse, the forewarning against prostitution, the duty of performing the legal marriage rites—which, nevertheless, does not permit intercourse at all times, as, for instance, during the period of menstruation and after childbirth, besides its being otherwise restricted by our sages and entirely interdicted during the daytime, as we have explained in the tractate *Sanhedrin*—all of these God commanded in order that we should keep entirely distant from the extreme of the inordinate indulgence of the passions, and, even departing from the exact medium, should incline somewhat toward self-denial, so that there may be firmly rooted in our souls the disposition for moderation.

Likewise, all that is contained in the Law concerning the giving of the tithes, the gleaning of the harvest, the forgotten sheaves, the single grapes, and the small bunches in the vineyards for the poor, the law of the Sabbatical year and of the Jubilee, the giving of charity according to the wants of the needy one, all these approach the extreme of lavishness to be practiced in order that we may depart far from its opposite, stinginess, and thus, nearing the extreme of excessive prodigality, there may become instilled in us the quality of generosity.

If you should test most of the commandments from this point of view, you would find that they are all for the discipline and guidance of the faculties of the soul. Thus, the Law forbids revenge, the bearing of a grudge, and blood-revenge by saying, "You shall not avenge nor bear any grudge" (Lev. 19:18); "you shall surely unload with him [the ass of him who hates you]" (Ex. 23:5); "you shall surely help him to lift them up again [your brother's ass or ox which has fallen by the way]" (Deut. 22:4). These commandments are intended to weaken the force of wrath or anger. Likewise, the command, "You shall surely bring them back [your brother's ox or lamb which has gone astray]" (Deut. 22:1), is meant to remove the disposition of avarice.[31]

Maimonides also presents his theory on the nature of ethics in the *Mishneh Torah*. Here, too, as in the *Shemonah Perakim*, he begins by establishing a concept of virtue based upon moderation. For this principle his source is not the Talmud or rabbinic authority, but one outside of the tradition.

To cultivate either extreme in any class of disposition is not the right course, nor is it proper for any person to follow or learn it. If a man finds that his nature tends or is disposed to one of these extremes or if one has acquired and become habituated to it, he should turn back and improve, so as to walk in the way of good people, which is the right way. The right way is the mean in each group of dispositions common to humanity; namely, that disposition which is equally distant from the two extremes in its class, not being nearer to the one than to the other.[32]

In *Hilkhot De'ot*, Maimonides identifies God's attributes, such as mercy and graciousness, with the virtuous actions of a healthy soul:

> We are bidden to walk in the middle paths which are the right and proper ways, as it is said, "and thou shalt walk in His ways" (Deut. 28:9). In explanation of the text just quoted, the sages taught, "Even as God is called gracious, so be thou gracious; Even as He is called merciful so be thou merciful; Even as He is called Holy, so be thou holy." Thus too the prophets described the Almighty by all the various attributes "long-suffering and abounding in kindness, righteous and upright, perfect, mighty and powerful," and so forth, to teach us, that these qualities are good and right and that a human being should cultivate them, and thus imitate God, as far as he can.... And as the Creator is called by these attributes, which constitute the middle path in which we are to walk, this path is called the Way of God and this is what the patriarch Abraham taught his children.[33]

Maimonides here presents his students with a remarkably progressive notion that the goals of Jewish law are in certain ways similar to those of other universal systems. According to him, the very goal of perfection of the soul achieved through *halakhah* and imitation of God's moral attributes becomes intelligible in terms that are not based on revelation or commitment to *mizvot*. This suggests that the goals of Halakhah can be achieved by those outside the covenant[34] through a means other than Halakhah. This premise permits the observant individual a meaningful interaction with those of different beliefs, assumptions, and way of life. This approach makes it possible for students of Jewish law who subscribe to certain principles of faith to cooperate, aspire and create with those outside their own religious and belief milieu in a language independent of Halakhah.

Responsibility

It has been observed and documented that Maimonides had a unique approach to the nature of *halakhah* in a conceptual sense. He understood Jewish Law in political terms,[35] as a means toward creating a society and building a community. He distinguishes between the prophet and the legislator; the patriarchs were limited to prophecy as master teachers of monotheism, who knew God and inspired others in that knowledge through rational inquiry and deliberations,[36] whereas Moses was both prophet and legislator, bringing the Law to the community and engaging it in a Covenant with God that is henceforth the way for the people to bind with one another through their relationship with God. This theme is often reiterated in the writings of Maimonides.[37]

> You need to know the following: everything that we are warned against or observe today we are obligated to observe because God commanded Moses [at Sinai] and not because God commanded the prophets that preceded Moses. For example we do not eat *ever min ha-hai* [meat that was ripped off a live animal] because God prohibited the descendants of Noach, but rather because Moses legislated this law according to the word of God at Sinai. Similarly we do not perform circumcision because God commanded Abraham to circumcise himself and his household but rather because God commanded us through Moses to circumcise our male children like Abraham did. Similarly we must observe the prohibition of eating the sciatic nerve (of an animal) not because it was commanded to Jacob our forefather but rather because it was among the 613 commandments given to Moses at Sinai.[38]

Halakhah became authoritative only after the acceptance of the Covenant at Mount Sinai.[39] To be effective in the formation of a community or a nation, the people must collectively and willingly accept the law as proposed by God, presented by Moses and legislated by future Jewish courts of law. The Covenant is then the guide to a just society for a people living in their own land, and *halakhah* gives the individual a meaningful place within that society.

For Maimonides, *halakhah* is best fulfilled through observance within the context of an organized community. The individual should not pursue private contemplation outside of the community, but rather find personal realization through participation in building a community while erecting it upon the Covenant and *halakhah*. Through the Torah and its law, God presents Man with a guide or road map for perfecting himself. While God could, of course, do this instantaneously through a miraculous transformation of the human being, the method of choice was the long and patient process where man will exercise his free will and transform himself. Maimonides presents a model for a Halakhic community developed through stages of education and a process that leads to transformation.

> As for your question: What was there to prevent God from giving us a Law in accordance with His first intention and from

procuring us the capacity to accept this?—you lay yourself open to an inference from this second question. For one may say to you: What was there to prevent God from making them march "by the way of the land of the Philistines" and procuring them the capacity to engage in wars so that there should be no need for this roundabout way with "the pillar of cloud by day and the pillar of fire by night?" (Ex.13:22).

Also you lay yourself open to a third question as an inference, a question regarding the reason for the detailing of promises and threats with regard to the whole Law. One may say to you: Inasmuch as God's first intention and His will are that we should believe in this Law and that we should perform the actions prescribed by it, why did He not procure us the capacity always to accept this intention and to act in accordance with it, instead of using a ruse with regard to us, declaring that He will procure us benefits if we obey Him and will take vengeance o us if we disobey Him and performing in deed all these acts of benefiting all these acts of vengeance? For this too is a ruse used by Him with regard to us in order to achieve His first intention with respect to us. What was there to prevent Him from causing the inclination to accomplish the acts of obedience willed by Him and to avoid the acts of disobedience abhorred by Him, to be natural disposition fixed in us?....

There is one and the same general answer to all these three questions and to all the others that belong to the same class: Though all miracles change the nature of some individual being, God does not change at all the nature of human individuals by means of miracles. Because of this great principle it says: "O that they had such an heart as this" (Deut. 5:26), and so on. It is because of this that there are commandments and prohibitions, rewards and punishments.

We have already explained this fundamental principle by giving its proofs in a number of passages in our compilations. We do not say this because we believe that the changing of the nature of any human individual is difficult for Him, may He be exalted. Rather, is it possible and fully within the capacity of God. But according to the foundations of the Law, of the Torah, He has never willed to do it, nor shall He ever will it. For if it were His will that the nature of any human individual should be changed because of what He, may He be exalted, wills from that individual, sending of prophets and all giving of a Law would have been useless.[40]

Maimonides presents God as a Teacher, constructing a Halakhic community with the people of Israel as the students. The classroom is

Mount Sinai, at the historical moment of the revelation of the Law. The purpose of the lesson is to transform the student into a *"mentsch."*

Many things in our Law are due to something similar to this very governance on the part of Him who governs, may He be glorified and exalted. For a sudden transition from one opposite to another is impossible. And therefore man, according to his nature, is not capable of abandoning suddenly all to which he was accustomed. As therefore God sent Moses our Teacher to make out of us "a kingdom of priests and a holy nation" (Ex. 19:6)—through the knowledge of Him, may He be exalted, accordingly to what He has explained, saying: "To you it was shown that you might know" (Deut. 4:35), and so on; "Know this day, and lay it to your heart" (Deut. 4:39), and so on—so that we should devote ourselves to His worship according to what He said: "

And to serve Him with all your heart" (Deut. 11:13), and: "and you shall serve the Lord your God" (Ex. 23:25), and: "And Him shall you serve" (Deut. 13:5); and as at that time the way of life generally accepted and customary in the whole world and the universal service upon which we were brought up consisted in offering various species of living beings in the temples in which images were set up, in worshiping the latter, and in burning incense before them – the pious ones and the ascetics being at that time, as we have explained, the people who were devoted to the service of the temples consecrated to the stars:

His wisdom, may He be exalted, and His gracious ruse, which is manifest in regard to all His creatures, did not require that He give us a Law prescribing the rejection, abandonment, and abolition of all these kinds of worship. For one could not then conceive the acceptance of (such a Law), considering the nature of man, which always likes that to which it is accustomed. At that time this would have been similar to the appearance of a prophet in these times who, calling upon the people to worship God, would say: "God has given you a Law forbidding you to pray to Him, to fast, to call upon Him for help in misfortune. Your worship should consist solely in meditation without any works at all." Therefore He, may He be exalted, suffered the above-mentioned kinds of worship to remain, but transferred them from created or imaginary and unreal things to His own name, may He be exalted, commanding us to practice them with regard to Him, may He be exalted.

Thus He commanded us to build a Temple for Him: "And let them make Me a Sanctuary" (Ex. 25:8); to have an altar for His name: "An altar of earth you shall make to Me" (Ex. 20:24); to have the sacrifice offered up to Him: "When any man of you brings an offering to the Lord" (Lev. 1:2); to bow down in worship before Him; and to burn incense before Him. And He forbade the performance of any of these actions with a view to someone else: "He that sacrifices to the gods shall be utterly destroyed" (Ex. 22:19), and so on; "For you shall bow down to no other god" (ibid, 34:14). And He singled out priests for the service of the Sanctuary saying "That they may minister to Me in the priest's office" (Ex. 28:14).

And because of their employment in the Temple and the sacrifices in it, it was necessary to fix for them dues that would be sufficient for them; namely, the dues of the Levites and the priests. Through this Divine ruse it came about that the memory of idolatry was effaced and that the grandest and true foundation of our belief – namely, the existence and oneness of the Deity – was firmly established, while at the same time the souls had no feeling of repugnance and were not repelled because of the abolition of modes of worship to which they were accustomed and than which no other mode of worship was known at that time[41].

Here, Maimonides shows the Divine Teacher who with loving patience places the students at the center of His task, with *halakhah* as the curriculum. He takes His students along a spiritual journey, whose starting point is where the students at that moment stand in their development. He accepts their regulations, and that the progress will take time. He addresses them in a language they can grasp: *Dibra Torah bi-leshon benei adam*.

To build community through *halakhah*, there must be mutual acceptance among the various groups within that community. To that end, one who has absorbed the Halakhic way of life and acquired knowledge of the Torah should imitate the love and patience exemplified by the Divine Teacher of Maimonides' exposition.

Unity

Maimonides chose the road that is less traveled and that presents the most dangers. To introduce impressionable minds to ideas and practices outside of *halakhah* and to encourage intellectual openness is to put commitment to our tradition in jeopardy.[42] It takes a special strength to withstand the challenges and temptations of the outside world. In the introduction to his *Guide*, he warns the reader of the risks of exposure to a range of intellectual disciplines. The encounter with the world outside transforms the student's world, and even his relationship with the familiar texts of Jewish tradition will take on a new dimension.

> The human intellect having drawn him on and led him to dwell within his province, he must have felt distressed by the externals of the law and by the meanings of the above-mentioned equivocal derivative or amphiboles terms, as he continued to understand them by himself or was made to understand them by others. Hence he would remain in a state of perplexity and confusion as to whether he should follow his intellect, renounce what he knew concerning the terms in question and consequently consider that he had renounced the foundations of the law. Or he should hold fast to his understanding of these terms and not let himself be drawn on together with his intellect, rather turning his back on it and moving away from it, while at the same time perceiving that he had brought loss to himself and harm to his religion.[43]

In an ideal world made up of intellectually sophisticated people, Maimonides would have us not only confront differing traditions, ways of life, and outlooks but also welcome them. The nature of such an outlook would force us to rethink our own beliefs and practices, which entails tension between continuity and change, between relegating some things to the past and adopting others. We do not live in an ideal world, and for most such activity is remote at best. Yet in the epistemology of Talmudic thought, while there is an implicit high regard for past and precedent, it is presented along with exploration of new insights in the light of emerging ideas. For this, the student/teacher is one who struggles and agonizes over religious issues and, having experienced the pangs of doubt, can go on to inspire others.[44] This is undoubtedly a process that involves continuous self-scrutiny and humility. The more love we show others, the greater, more intense and passionate our own fear of heaven must grow. Indeed the risks are worth the cause.

---

[1] Norman Lamm, *Seventy Faces: Articles of Faith*, Volume 1 (Hoboken, N.J., 2002), 125

[2] I use the term community both in its colloquial sense and in a figurative sense suggesting a combination of religious, cultural, political and geographical purpose.

[3] Jonathan Woocher, *Sacred Survival: The Civil Religion of American Jews* (Bloomington, I.N., 1986), 67-71.

[4] Urbach Ephraim, *Sages*, 528-529. See also, Solomon Schechter, *Some Aspects of Rabbinic Theology* (New York, 1936), 59-60. Two other important compilation of essays on the subject include *Ra'ayon ha-Behirah* ed. Shemuel Almog and Michal Had (Jerusalem) especially Gerald Blidstein's article, as well as Michal Had's article. See also *A People*

Apart: Chosenness and Ritual in Jewish Philosophical Thought, ed. Daniel H. Frank, (New York, 1993) especially the articles by David Novak and Menachem Kellner.

[5] *Avot* 3:14.

[6] Urbach notes the Hellenistic precedent to this idea in *Hazal,* p. 469, citing Ezra 6:56-59. See also, H.A. Wolfson, *Philo,* 2 Vols. (Cambridge, M.A., 1947) I:18; Louis Ginzberg, *The Legends of the Jews* (Philadelphia, 1938) 6:30, note 177.

[7] *Hagigah* 3a and *Berakhot* 6a.

[8] *Mekhilta de-R. Ishmael, Mishpatim* 20; also *Sifre* Deut. 26.

[9] One should note that the absolutist attitude toward *Behirah* has elicited comments like Arnold Toynbee's suggestion that *Behirah* is an example of Jewish arrogance: "The most notorious historical example of idolization of an ephemeral self is the error of the Jews ... they persuaded themselves that Israel's discovery of one true God had revealed Israel itself to be God's chosen people." *Study of History,* Volume 4 (1961), 262.

[10] Menachem Kellner, *Maimonides on Judaism and the Jewish People* (Albany, N.Y., 1991).

[11] See for example *Mishneh Torah Tefillah,* 7:10, 12:5; *Shabbat* 29:2.

[12] In a number of places Maimonides defines human perfection in terms of intellectual perfection. See for example *Hilkhot De'ot* 3:2, *Teffilin* 6:13, *Guide* 1:2 1:30, 3:8, 3:27, 28, 51, 54. See also Kellner's book *Maimonides on Human Perfection* as well as David Shatz's article published in this volume. See also Ya'acov Levinger, "Human Among The Gentiles According To Maimonides," *Hagut II: Bein Yisrael li-Amim* (Jerusalem, 1978): 27-36. On Providence and prophecy see *Hilkhot Yesodei ha-Torah* 7:1, which opens with a statement that God causes Man, in the generic sense, to prophesize. See also *Guide* 2:32-38; 3:17, 18. An important work on Maimonides' view on Providence is Zvi Diesendruck, "Samuel and Moses Inb Tibbon on Maimonides' Theory of Providence," *HUCA* 11 (1936): 341-366; and Avraham Nuriel, "Providence and Guidance in the Guide of the Perplexed," *Tarbiz* 49 (1980): 346-355. See also Rabbi Joseph B. Soloveitchik's *Ish ha-Halakhah* and especially Shalom Carmy's "Tell Them I've Had A Good Enough Life," in *Jewish Perspectives on the Experience of Suffering,* ed. Shalom Carmy, (New York, 1999).

[13] See Maimonides' letters to Obadia the Proselyte found in Y. Shilat, *Iggerot ha-Rambam,* Volume 1, 231-241. It is also found in Blau's edition of *Teshuvot ha-Rambam* (Jerusalem, 1958) nos. 293, 436, and 448. English translations may be found in Franz Kobler, *Letters Through The Ages* 1 (London, 1952): 194-197. Also Isadore Twersky, *A Maimonides Reader* (New York, 1972) 475-476. Other texts include *Hilkhot De'ot* 6:4; *Shabbat* 20:14; *Isurei Bi'ah* 13:1-4; *Bikkurim* 4:3; *Melakhim* 8:10.

[14] Maimonides' position on converts is dramatically opposed to that of Yehuda Halevi and the *Zohar.* For Maimonides position of the ultimate conversion of the gentiles in the messianic era, see *Hilkhot Melakhim* 11:1.

[15] *Guide* 3:26 also 3:28, 31, 49. For an excellent study on Maimonides' approach to *ta'amei ha-mizvot* see Isadore Twersky's *Introduction to the Code of Maimonides* (*Mishneh Torah*) (New Haven, 1980), 374-430.

[16] *Guide* 3:27.

[17] See note **35.**

[18] *Guide* 3:27.

[19] *Guide* 3:31. All translation of the *Guide* are from Shlomo Pines edition and translation (Chicago, 1963).

[20] The noted scholar Gershom Scholem, in his seminal work, *Major Trends in Jewish Mysticism*, 28-29, draws a completely different conclusion. He wonders how Maimonides expected anyone to remain religious and observant of the law if he demanded that the law to be philosophically scrutinized. Maimonides viewed Jewish law in the highest regard and proved that it can and should be scrutinized by all disciplines. Indeed, Jewish Law according to Maimonides is most fully exercised in a context of disciplines that go beyond the scope of *halakhah*.

[21] For Maimonides, being a part of the covenantal-community is essential to the spiritual life of the believing Jew. A Jew's daily relationship with God is structured by communal participation. Heresy is not only a denial of God but a denial of the historical and political realities of ones community. The holidays are all based on a relationship between God and a particular people. A convert to Israel must identify himself with the national destiny of the Jewish people. *Hilkhot Issurei Bi'ah* 14:1-5. See also *Hilkhot Teshuvah* 2:8 and *Iggeret Teiman* on his being prepared to endanger one's own well-being for the welfare of the community.

[22] Isadore Twersky, *A Maimonides Reader* (New York, 1972), 407.

[23] Yeshayahu Leibowitz, *The Faith of Maimonides*, trans. John Glucker (1989), 15 –25. See Maimonides *Mishneh Torah, Hilkhot Me'ilah* 8:8 and Twersky's essay on this law in *Introduction to the Mishneh Torah*, 407-408.

[24] *Hilkhot Yesodei ha-Torah* 2:1; see also *Guide* 1:26, 33, 46.

[25] *Hilkhot Teshuvah* 10:6; see also Norman Lamm in this issue.

[26] See *Hilkhot Kiddush ha-Hodesh* 18:25 and Guide 1:71; 2:11. Maimonides argues that there was always a philosophic tradition that was transmitted orally. See also Maimonides commentary on *Avot* 5:7 and his understanding of Elisha Ben Abuya's apostasy in Guide 1:32. This is a theme that David Hartman develops extensively in his book, *Maimonides: Torah and Philosophic Quest* (1976).

[27] For Maimonides, truth was the ultimate criteria. Loyalty was to reason, not to authority. See Pines, "The Philosophic Sources," 57-59.

[28] Jacob Katz, *Exclusiveness and Tolerance* (New York, 1962). For a more recent discussion on the issue, see Aviezer Ravitsky in *Hazon Nahum*, ed. Jeffrey Gurok and Yaakov Elman, (New York,, 1997), 359-391.

[29] See Jose Faur, *In the Shadow of History: Jews and Conversos at the Dawn of Modernity* (Albany,1992), especially introduction. This essay is not about patrimonial descent or the validity of a certain marriage or divorce documents. I am interested in the opportunities presented for dialogue in the way Maimonides formulates his Halakhic and theological philosophy.

[30] For a discussion on the differences between Aristotelian and Maimonidean ethics, see Eliezer Schweid, *Iyunnim be-Shemonah Perakim* (Jerusalem, 1969), 63. See also Leo Strauss, "Notes on the book of Knowledge," in *Studies in Mysticism and Religion* (Jerusalem,

1967), 277-278.

[31] Twersky, *Reader*, 367-376.

[32] *Hilkhot De'ot* 1:3-4.

[33] Ibid. 2:5-7.

[34] I emphasize that this point only applies to a non-Jew because a Jew is bound by a bilateral covenant entered into by God and the Jewish people at Sinai and Arvot Moab.

[35] See *Guide* 1:54; 11:36-40; 3:34, 41. Also the introductory comments of Shlomo Pines to his translation of the *Guide*, lxxxvii-xcii; Leo Strauss, *Persecutions and the Art of Writing*, 7-21; Julius Guttman, *Philosophies of Judaism*, trans. David Silverman (New York, 1966), 203-205; Guttman "*Philosophia Shel ha-Da'at o Philosophia Shel ha-Hok*," *Proceedings of the Israel Academy of Sciences and Humanities*, Vol. 5:9 (1975): 188-207; Twersky, *Introduction to Mishneh Torah*, 455, n. 239.

[36] *Hilkhot Avodah Zarah*, Chapter 1.

[37] See *Hilkhot Avodah Zara* 1:1, *De'ot* 1:7, *Guide* I:63; 2:39.

[38] *Commentary on Mishnah*, Hullin 7:6.

[39] Leibowitz, ibid, also Faur, "Understanding the Covenant," *Tradition* 9 (1968).

[40] *Guide* 3:23.

[41] Ibid.

[42] The fact that Maimonides did not believe that one must first master the entire Torah before engaging in other disciplines is a subject that is beyond the scope of this essay. Relevant passages include *Hilkhot Yesodei ha-Torah* 4:13, the comments of the *Kessef Mishneh*, and *Hilkhot Talmud Torah* 1:12.

[43] *Guide*, Introduction, pages 5-6.

[44] Works like the *Guide*, the *Mishneh Torah*, and countless letters of significant theological import were clearly written by an individual who was spiritually sensitive and understood the nature of religious and theological struggles. We have been jaded by the countless "*Gadol* Hagiographies" published by popular Jewish presses intended on inspiring their readers with "cookie cutter stories" that describe the lives of *gedolim* in perfect and shining terms and do not reveal their human side. For an excellent short editorial on this see Emanuel Feldman's piece in *Jewish Action* (Summer 2002): 72-73.

Rambam's Continued Impact on Underlying Issues in *Tanakh* Study*

Hayyim Angel

I.

The balance of Rambam as a philosopher and as an exegete continues to be debated by Rambam scholars.[1] Students of Rambam consider his writings as their primary source of inquiry. Students of *Tanakh*, in contrast, view Rambam as one great interpreter among many others, with *Tanakh* standing at the center of all discussions. Regardless of how Rambam's own methodology ultimately will be understood, however, he exerted an extraordinary influence on later biblical commentary. Rambam developed principles in his *Guide* and other writings, including: 1) we must understand the nature of revelation, God and prophecy; 2) we must understand that *Tanakh*, as the revealed word of God, is by definition compatible with science and rational thought;[2] if the literal reading of a biblical text appears to run counter to that logic, the text must be understood allegorically; 3) we must consider the historical setting of *Tanakh* when interpreting biblical narratives, and even when seeking the reasons behind some of the *mizvot*.

Later commentators raised questions about Rambam's principles. What is considered "rational"? How much may one (or *must* one) go beyond the literal reading of a biblical text? What are the limits of contextualizing the Torah, given that it is an eternally relevant and binding covenant? Some of Rambam's ideas became widely accepted in later biblical exegesis. Others drew intense criticism, particularly when they appeared to contradict

---

* I am indebted to my father, Rabbi Marc D. Angel, and to Professor Menachem Kellner of the University of Haifa for reading earlier drafts of this essay and for recommending several important revisions and references.

biblical passages or when they placed too much weight on the historical context of the Torah. Exegetes often accepted Rambam's philosophical arguments in principle but limited their application to instances where they fit the plain reading of the biblical text. In this essay, we will examine a few of the underlying issues in *Tanakh* study on which Rambam has left a lasting mark, and consider how later interpreters balanced Rambam's ideas with the biblical text.[3]

II. Principles of Prophecy:[4]

A. *Nevi'im* vs. *Ketuvim*

Although the Talmud[5] delineated a tripartite division of *Tanakh*, Rambam was the first authority to discuss *why* some books were included in *Nevi'im* (Prophets), whereas others were in *Ketuvim* (Holy Writings). People who had attained full visionary prophecy wrote the books included in *Nevi'im*. In contrast, the authors of the psalms, wisdom, and historical narratives canonized in *Ketuvim* wrote while in a conscious state; God guided those authors' writing with "divine inspiration".[6] Many later rabbinic commentators adopted Rambam's viewpoint.

Abarbanel, however, struggled to find a correlation between the textual record and Rambam's hypothesis. In his introduction to the Early Prophets, Abarbanel leveled several questions against Rambam, including: a) Chronicles seems quite similar to Samuel and Kings; why should the former be in *Ketuvim* while the latter are in *Nevi'im*? b) According to the Talmud,[7] Samuel composed Ruth, and Jeremiah wrote Lamentations. Why were these books excluded from *Nevi'im*, given that prophets composed them? c) Psalm 18 is virtually identical to the psalm in II Samuel 22. It is unlikely that David composed the Samuel version through prophecy, while composing Psalm 18 under the lesser influence of divine inspiration.

In his biblical commentary, Abarbanel seems to have accepted Rambam's division, albeit with further elaboration. Elsewhere, however, it appears that he rejected Rambam's theory; R. Joseph Ya'abez reports that after Abarbanel finished discussing Rambam's position on this issue, he remarked, "*zo kavvanat Rabbenu Moshe, lo kavvanat Moshe Rabbenu*"—this is the intent of our Rabbi Moses (i.e., Rambam), not the intent of Moses our teacher (i.e., the Torah).[8] In any event, Rambam played a seminal role in inspiring further discussion of this important topic.[9]

Aside from its significance for understanding the nature of *Tanakh*, Rambam's theory also became important for interpreting individual passages. For example, King Solomon received prophetic visions, and later was criticized for sinning despite having received two revelations:

> At Gibeon God appeared to Solomon in a dream by night; and God said, "Ask, what shall I grant you?" (I Kings 3:5).

> The Lord appeared to Solomon a second time, as He had appeared to him at Gibeon. The Lord said to him, "I have heard the prayer and the supplication which you have offered to Me. I consecrate this House which you have built and I set My name there forever" (I Kings 9:2-3).

> The Lord was angry with Solomon, because his heart turned away from the Lord, the God of Israel, who had appeared to him twice (I Kings 11:9).[10]

Rambam maintained that Solomon had only attained the level of divine inspiration, not full prophecy.[11] This assertion was consistent with his position explaining why Song of Songs, Proverbs, and Ecclesiastes (all composed by Solomon) are in *Ketuvim*.

Abarbanel[12] criticized Rambam for contradicting explicit biblical texts. While conceding that Song of Songs, Proverbs, and Ecclesiastes may have been composed with divine inspiration (and not full prophecy), the verses in Kings use the language of prophetic revelation. Rambam was imposing his philosophical system onto the text by insisting that Solomon did not receive full prophecy. Abarbanel thus was willing to accept Rambam's philosophical analysis, but limited its application in text interpretation.

B. Critiquing Biblical Heroes

Religious students of *Tanakh* view biblical heroes as exalted beyond our comprehension, yet human enough to guide our lives by example. Traditional interpreters must offer a fair reading of the biblical text while maintaining proper reverence for biblical heroes, especially when considering the apparent failings of righteous characters in *Tanakh*.[13]

Rambam explained that character flaws create barriers in one's relationship to God, and this principle applies even to prophets:

> It is not, however, an indispensable requirement that a prophet should possess all the moral virtues, and be entirely free from every defect, for we find that Scripture testifies in reference to Solomon,

who was a prophet[14]...although we know that he had the moral defect of lust, which is plainly evident from the fact that he took so many wives...Even David—a prophet...we find guilty of cruelty, and, although he exercised it only against the heathens, and in the destruction of nonbelievers, being merciful towards Israel, it is explicitly stated in Chronicles that God, considering him unworthy, did not permit him to build the Temple, as it was not fitting in His eyes, because of the many people David caused to be killed...We find, also, that Elijah gave vent to his anger, and although he did so only against unbelievers, against whom his wrath blazed up, the sages declared that God took him from the world...Likewise, we find that Samuel feared Saul, and that Jacob was afraid to meet Esau. These and similar characteristics were so many partitions between the prophets (peace be unto them!) and God.[15]

This principle has far-reaching relevance when interpreting many prophetic narratives.

At the same time, Rambam often justified the actions of biblical heroes, even when not specifically warranted by the biblical text. For example, although Samson and Solomon married women of non-Jewish origin, Rambam emphatically maintained that those women had converted first.[16]

With regard to Samson's wives, Radak[17] accepted Rambam's presumption of premarital conversion, since the biblical text never explicitly condemns Samson for intermarrying. In the case of Solomon, though, where the narrative explicitly censures his intermarriage (I Kings 11:1-3), Radak[18] rejected Rambam's position and insisted that Solomon sinned.

C. Prophetic Fitness

Rambam maintained that individuals must reach the loftiest spiritual and religious levels in order to attain prophecy.[19] In contrast, R. Yehudah Halevi[20] believed that prophecy is a divine gift; were God to deem it necessary, anyone could receive a prophetic message.

Abarbanel[21] marshaled Amos' autobiographical comment about his career in support of *Kuzari*:

> Amos answered Amaziah: "I am not a prophet, and I am not a prophet's disciple. I am a cattle breeder and a tender of sycamore figs. But the Lord took me away from following the flock, and the Lord said to me, 'Go, prophesy to My people Israel'" (Amos 7:14-15).

According to Abarbanel, Amos considered himself objectively unfit for prophecy, but God had elected him for a particular mission to the people. A prophet's mission to his people—not his personal perfection—is the defining characteristic of biblical prophecy. Abarbanel concluded that Rambam derived his conception of prophecy, which focuses on the individual, from Greek philosophy, and that this understanding is inconsistent with Jewish thought.

Seeking to narrow the gulf between the views of Rambam and *Kuzari*/Abarbanel, Malbim[22] suggested that, as a general rule, a prophet must attain the lofty levels described by Rambam. If God has an urgent message, however (as was true in the case of Amos), God will grant prophecy to the most righteous person available.

D. Particular Styles of Prophets

> Rava said: All that Ezekiel saw Isaiah saw. What does Ezekiel resemble? A villager who saw the king. And what does Isaiah resemble? A townsman who saw the king.[23]

Referring to Ezekiel's vision of the Celestial Chariot (Ezek. 1 and others) and Isaiah's vision of God on His throne (Isa. 6), Rava asserted that these two prophets had experienced identical visions. He then cryptically explained why two prophets experiencing the same vision would express themselves so differently—Isaiah wrote but a few verses, whereas Ezekiel described his vision at great length.

Rambam offered two interpretations of Rava's imagery of the "villager" and "townsman": Isaiah's audience may have attained a higher spiritual level than Ezekiel's audience. Consequently, Isaiah did not need to elaborate on the details of the vision because his generation understood him immediately. Alternatively, Isaiah reached a higher level of prophecy than Ezekiel, and therefore was not as overwhelmed by his vision as was Ezekiel.[24]

For Rambam, the language, style, and formulation of a prophet are partially contingent on his historical setting and audience. At the same time, the objective experience of a prophet influences his reaction to and formulation of his prophecy. Therefore, it is necessary to understand each prophet on his own terms.

III. Allegorical vs. Literal Readings

Rambam maintained that if logic or scientific knowledge contradicts the literal sense of a biblical text, that text must not be taken literally:

I believe every possible happening that is supported by a prophetic statement and do not strip it of its plain meaning. I fall back on interpreting a statement only when its literal sense is impossible, like the corporeality of God: the possible however remains as stated.[25]

Rambam included considerably more than God's corporeality among the "impossible." Consequently, he allegorized many biblical passages as a result of his philosophy. Warren Zev Harvey recently noted that when Rambam deviated from the literal meaning of a biblical passage, he almost invariably had earlier precedents in traditional Jewish sources to support his readings.[26] That being said, Rambam certainly pushed the boundaries of allegorical interpretation in traditional exegesis. Louis Ginzberg has aptly described Rambam as "the head and front of all philosophical allegorism among the Jews in the Middle Ages."[27]

A. Angelic Encounters

Rambam maintained that all angelic encounters must have been experienced in prophetic visions.[28] There are occasions where this principle has proven helpful in explaining difficult texts. For example, when Joshua encountered an angel "in Jericho" (Josh. 5:13-15), that city had yet to be captured. Rambam's explanation, that Joshua saw the angel in a prophetic vision, eliminates this difficulty. In a prophetic vision, Joshua *could* have been standing inside of Jericho.[29]

On other occasions, however, Rambam's principle may present difficulties on the textual level. For example, Rambam maintained that Abraham's encounter with the three angels in Genesis 18 must have been in a prophetic vision.[30] Ramban[31] censured this position. If this were only a vision, why did the Torah offer so many details with regard to Sarah's preparation of food? Did Lot and the wicked people of Sodom experience prophetic revelation when they encountered the angels in Genesis 19? And if *that* were a vision, Lot historically should still have remained in Sodom, since the entire episode was experienced only in Lot's prophetic dream! While several later commentators defended Rambam's view, Ramban believed that Rambam had favored his philosophical beliefs over the actual meaning of the Torah.[32]

Rambam's premise about angels also became a potentially dangerous precedent. Abarbanel expressed outrage that some writers were applying Rambam's principle to argue that the entire *akeidah* narrative occurred only in Abraham's prophetic vision. Abarbanel considered this view a gross misapplication of Rambam's philosophy. It was heretical to deny the historicity of the *akeidah*.[33]

B. Unusual Commands to Prophets

Throughout *Tanakh*, God ordered prophets to perform symbolic actions, including several that appear shocking. For example, God instructed Hosea to marry an *eshet zenunim* (commonly translated as "prostitute"[34]) to illustrate Israel's infidelity to God. The ensuing narrative reports that Hosea did so, and fathered three children with her (Hos. 1:2-9). Similarly, God commanded Isaiah to "untie the sackcloth from his loins" to foretell that the Assyrians would lead the Egyptians and Ethiopians away as naked captives; Isaiah faithfully obeyed, and walked around *arom* (literally "naked") and barefoot (Isa. 20:2-6).

Disturbed by these and similar prophetic commands, Rambam asserted that God never would order a prophet to do anything irrational. Therefore, Hosea and Isaiah performed these actions only in prophetic visions:

> Therefore the multitude think that these actions, transportations, questions, and answers, occurred all of them in a state in which they could have been perceived by the senses, *not in a vision of prophecy*...God is too exalted than that He should turn His prophets into a laughingstock and a mockery for fools by ordering them to commit acts of disobedience... In the same way when He says, *Like as My servant Isaiah hath walked naked and barefoot*, this only happened *in the visions of God*...The position is similar with regard to the words addressed to Hosea: *Take unto thee a wife of harlotry and children of harlotry*. All this story concerning the birth of the children and their having been named so and so happened in its entirety *in a vision of prophecy*...This is a thing that can only be doubted or not known by him who confuses the possible things with the impossible ones.[35]

Thus, Hosea did not actually marry a prostitute,[36] nor did Isaiah walk around naked in public.[37] As noted earlier, when a conflict arises between the personal perfection of a prophet and his mission to the people,

Rambam favored the element of personal perfection.

Abarbanel criticized Rambam for contradicting biblical texts, which state explicitly that Hosea and Isaiah performed their respective actions:

> One must be extremely astonished at these learned authors [i.e., Ibn Ezra and Rambam]—how could they advance this kind of sweeping principle in prophetic narrative...If the text testifies that the action occurred, we have no right to depart from its plain sense, lest we interpret the verses incorrectly...In truth, it is infidelity and a grave sin (*zimmah va-avon pelili*) to contradict the plain sense of the verses; if this is what we do to them, this disease (*zara'at*) will spread over all verses and reveal interpretations that contradict their veracity.[38]

Abarbanel reiterated his view that a prophet's mission to the people is more important than his personal perfection and dignity. Therefore, if God decides that these shocking symbolic actions would have a positive religious effect on the people, He will order prophets to perform them.

Despite Abarbanel's protests in these two instances, however, he himself applied Rambam's view elsewhere. For example, God commanded Ezekiel to lie on his sides for a total of 430 days (Ezek. 4:4-8), and to shave off all of his hair (Ezek. 5:1-4). The former command is physically difficult to fulfill, and the latter appears to violate the Torah prohibition against shaving the "corners of one's beard" (Lev. 19:27). Rambam included these commands among those that occurred in prophetic visions, not in a waking state. Even Abarbanel agreed that these events occurred in prophetic visions, since the text does not explicitly report that Ezekiel performed these actions.[39] Abarbanel did not countenance Rambam's view in cases that entailed contradicting explicit verses; however, he employed Rambam's reasoning in those instances that did not flatly contradict biblical verses.

C. Anthropomorphism and Anthropopathism

Rambam dismissed attributions of corporeality and human emotions to God, and certainly exerted a profound impact on Jewish thought in this arena. Nevertheless, some writers rebuked him for ignoring the force of the biblical texts that employ this language. While accepting that God is infinitely beyond human comprehension, these writers insisted that *Tanakh* deliberately employs this terminology so that we may build a relationship with God.

As R. Samson Raphael Hirsch commented:

For so long people have philosophied all round these expressions
to remove the danger of the slightest thought of any materiality or
corporality of God that at the end one runs very nearly into the
danger of losing all idea of the personality of God. Had that been
the purpose of the Torah, those kind of expressions could easily
have been avoided. But this last danger is greater than the first...
The Ra'avad already, one of the most Jewish of our thinkers, is of
the opinion that such consciousness of the personality of God is of
much greater importance than speculating about it, as to whether
this or that can be asserted of God.[40]

D. Messianic Visions

The wolf shall dwell with the lamb, the leopard lie down with
the kid...In all of My sacred mount nothing evil or vile shall be
done; for the land shall be filled with devotion to the Lord as water
covers the sea (Isaiah 11:6, 9).

Insisting that nature will not be altered fundamentally in the messianic
era, Rambam adopted Ibn Ezra's reading and interpreted this prophecy
(and many related prophecies) as a poetic reference, i.e., all nations will
live together in peace.[41]

While agreeing that prophetic visions about the messianic age
may contain poetic imagery, some exegetes offered interpretations they
believed were closer to the biblical text. For example, Radak noted that
in the messianic age, there would be peace in the *entire world*, not only in
Israel. Isaiah, however, refers to the lack of destruction "*be-kol har kodshi,*"
i.e., in Israel. Therefore, Radak interpreted that aspect of the prophecy
literally: wild animals will not cause damage within the Land of Israel.[42]
Yet, he maintained that carnivores still would eat meat in the messianic
era—accepting Rambam's allegorical reading.

Significantly, Rambam himself entertained the literal reading of
Isaiah 11:6-9:

You must realize that I am not at all positive that all the promises
and the like of them are metaphorical. No revelation from God
has come to teach me they are parables...I will only explain to you
what impels me to speak this way...I try to reconcile the Law and
reason, and wherever possible consider all things as of the natural
order. Only when something is explicitly identified as a miracle,
and reinterpretation of it cannot be accommodated, only then I
feel forced to grant that this is a miracle.[43]

Although there were issues that Rambam considered outright irrational, there were others where he allegorized because he considered that possibility more likely. In those latter instances, he was willing to entertain the more literal reading.

Similarly, Rambam believed that Job was most likely a parable, but did not feel confined by his opinion.[44] He stressed that the importance of Job lies in the philosophical issues it raises, not in discussions about its historicity:

> To sum up: *whether he has existed or not*, with regard to cases like his, which always exist, all reflecting people become perplexed; and in consequence such things as I have already mentioned to you are said about God's knowledge and His providence.[45]

Rambam emphasized that biblical texts must be probed for their religious truths. Too much attention to historical issues may distract readers from using *Tanakh* as a means of developing their relationship with God. Rambam's views on allegorization, and subsequent responses to his positions, have paved the way for contemporary discussions of this topic.[46]

IV. Setting of the Torah

Although the divinely given Torah is an eternal covenant, it was revealed to a certain society at a particular time. Rambam attempted to understand how the ancient setting in which the Torah was given influenced the narratives and style of the Torah, and even the *mizvot*.

A. Setting of Patriarchal Narratives

Although he lived long before the Torah was given, Judah observed the laws of levirate marriage (Gen. 38:8). Several Midrashim suggested that Judah must have instituted the laws of levirate marriage, which the Torah subsequently codified (Deut. 25:5-10).[47] However, on the textual level, Judah appears to have been following a known practice. Upholding the impression yielded by the narrative, Rambam asserted that levirate marriage must have been an ancient procedure.[48]

In a similar vein, several Midrashim attempted to explain Tamar's death sentence by burning (Gen. 38:24) in light of later Torah legislation. The only relevant sexual crime that receives death by burning in the Torah is when a priest's daughter is promiscuous (Lev. 21:9). Therefore,

Tamar must have been the daughter of a priest.[49] Rambam, however, followed the pattern of many exegetes in asserting that the patriarchs did not observe the entire Torah before the Torah was given.[50] Rather, they practiced those laws that were prevalent at that time (e.g., Mesopotamian, Hittite). In this case, there must have been a law that called for death by burning.[51]

Rambam learned this historical approach from his father, who had suggested that the ancient world must have had some hierarchal system for levirate marriage. If no brothers were available, then the daughter-in-law could marry her father-in-law. This would explain Tamar's efforts to bear children through Judah.[52]

B. Deliberate Omissions from the Torah

Rambam maintained that the Torah deliberately omitted important ideas as a consequence of its historical setting. For example, Rambam enumerated the Resurrection among the thirteen tenets of Jewish faith in his *Introduction to Perek Helek*. Yet, the Torah never refers explicitly to that miraculous occurrence; Rambam considered Daniel 12:1-3 the only unambiguous reference to the Resurrection in *Tanakh*. Why would the Torah never express this tenet clearly? Rambam proposed that the Resurrection was too sophisticated a concept for the ancient, primitive Israelites. They first needed to develop faith in prophecy and in miracles; then, God could expose them to the idea of a Resurrection.[53]

Likewise, the Torah never names Jerusalem explicitly, a surprising omission given the repeated emphasis on "the site where the Lord your God will choose" in Deuteronomy.[54] Rambam suggested that were the Torah to have identified the chosen site in advance, the Canaanites would then either fortify it or destroy it. Moreover, the Israelite tribes would have fought to have it included in their inheritance. By keeping the identity of Jerusalem hidden, God avoided these consequences.[55]

C. The Reasons for *Mizvot*[56]

Rambam's most significant (and controversial) use of the ancient setting of the Torah came in the context of explaining the rationale behind some of the Torah's commandments. In general, he maintained that all decrees of the Torah have reasons. Many of the laws were given in order to draw the Israelites away from pagan culture to the service of God.[57]

For example, having spent so long in pagan Egypt as idolaters,[58] the Israelites had a strong predilection to offer animal sacrifices. God recognized this propensity and therefore instituted animal sacrifices in the Israelite religion. God further prescribed specific boundaries for this form of worship by insisting that animals could be sacrificed only in the Temple. Thus, prayer, the higher form of serving God, was encouraged as a substitute for animal sacrifices.[59]

Ramban attacked Rambam on this assertion: "Behold, these words are worthless, they make a big breach, raise big questions, and pollute the table of God." [60] He maintained that the Temple, sacrifices, and related laws were ideal means of communing with God, not concessions to the ancient Israelites' historical condition.

In addition, Rambam's view raised the fundamental question: now that we have become more sophisticated than the ancient Israelites, what would be the relevance of these ritual commandments in our times?[61] Living in the 19th century, R. Samson Raphael Hirsch lamented the terrible misapplication of Rambam's thought among assimilating German Jews. Many were using Rambam's logic in the *Guide* as precedent for abandoning other *mizvot* as well.[62]

In some writings, though, Rambam did stress the value of animal sacrifices, considering them among the *mizvot* that we cannot fully understand.[63] Rambam likely had several reasons for stressing the aspect of weaning away from paganism, including: a) Rambam feared that overemphasis on Temple worship might misrepresent ideal religion.[64] b) Rambam favored placing maximum religious responsibility on each individual; the Temple service could lead people to think that they could expiate their sins without working at self-improvement.[65]

Rambam further believed that were we to have access to more documents from the ancient world, we would be able to determine the reasons behind *all* of the *mizvot*:

> If we knew the particulars of those practices and heard details of those opinions, we would become clear regarding the wisdom manifested in the details of the practices prescribed in the commandments concerning the *sacrifices* and the forms of *uncleanness* and other matters whose reason cannot, to my mind, be easily grasped. For I for one do not doubt that all this was

intended to efface those untrue opinions from the mind and to abolish those useless practices, which brought about a waste of lives *in vain and futile things.*[66]

We now have access to a wealth of the ancient information that Rambam craved. Rambam's pioneering efforts in understanding the setting of the Torah have become all the more important in light of the archaeological findings of the previous two centuries.[67]

V. Conclusion

Tanakh, being the bridge that links God and humanity, serves as the basis for all discussions of Jewish faith. Rambam, although not a verse-by-verse exegete, has decisively influenced how *Tanakh* is to be interpreted and understood. Whether they accepted, rejected, or qualified Rambam's positions, all later exegetes took Rambam's ideas and assumptions of traditional learning into serious consideration. The tensions between close text reading and religious assumptions continue to play a central role in Bible study.

Perhaps the most important aspect of these debates is that the world's greatest *Tanakh* authorities have approached our most sacred text from a variety of angles and facets—often agreeing with each other, but just as often conflicting with one another. By studying the disputes of our greatest interpreters over the boundaries of biblical study, contemporary religious readers have the opportunity to read *Tanakh* anew, evaluate the arguments and evidence, and arrive at an ever-deepening understanding of the living word of God.

---

[1] See Shalom Rosenberg, "On Biblical Exegesis in the *Guide*" (Hebrew), *Jerusalem Studies in Jewish Thought* 1 (1981): 85-157. See also Hillel Fradkin, "Philosophy or Exegesis: Perennial Problems in the Study of Some Judaeo-Arabic Authors," and the response of Josef Stern, "Philosophy or Exegesis: Some Critical Comments," in *Judaeo-Arabic Studies: Proceedings of the Founding Conference of the Society for Judaeo-Arabic Studies*, ed. Norman Golb (Australia, 1997), 103-122, 213-228.

[2] See Menachem Kellner, "Maimonides' Commentary on *Mishnah Hagigah* II.1, Translation and Commentary," in *From Strength to Strength*, ed. Marc D. Angel (Brooklyn, 1998), 101-111.

[3] Much has been written on Rambam's system of biblical exegesis. See Jacob I. Dienstag, "Biblical Exegesis of Maimonides in Jewish Scholarship," in *Samuel K. Mirsky Memorial Volume: Studies in Jewish Law, Philosophy, and Literature*, ed. Gersion Appel (New York, 1970), 151-190; Shalom Rosenberg, "On Biblical Exegesis in the *Guide*." For a thorough

bibliographical listing, see Jacob I. Dienstag, "Rambam as an Exegete—A Bibliography," in *Sefer H.M.I. Gevaryahu*, ed. B.Z. Lurie (Jerusalem, 1989), vol. 1, 346-366. For a compilation of Rambam's teachings organized in the order of biblical verses, see Meir David Ben-Shem, *Torat ha-Rambam: Rambam's Interpretations on Torah, Nevi'im, and Ketuvim* (four volumes) (Jerusalem, 1988).

[4] For a thorough bibliographical listing, see Jacob I. Dienstag, "Prophecy in Rambam's Teachings— A Bibliography," *Da'at* 37 (1996): 193-228.

[5] E.g., *Bava Batra* 14b.

[6] *Guide* 2:45.

[7] *Bava Batra* 14b.

[8] R. Joseph Ya'abez, *Or ha-Hayyim*, chap. 12 (ed. Lublin, 1910), 96.

[9] For a discussion of the midrashic evidence and of Rambam's view, see Sid Z. Leiman, *The Canonization of Hebrew Scripture: The Talmudic and Midrashic Evidence* (New Haven, 1991), 56-66, and the notes on pp. 167-170, esp. n. 294.

[10] Translations of biblical passages in this essay are taken from the NJPS *Tanakh*.

[11] *Guide* 2:45.

[12] Commentary on *I Kings* 3:5.

[13] See discussions in Yaakov Medan, "*David u-Bat Sheva: ha-Het, ha-Onesh, ve-ha-Tikkun*" (Hebrew) (Alon Shevut, 2002), 7-24; Mosheh Lichtenstein, *Zir va-Zon* (Hebrew) (Alon Shevut, 2002), 235-257; Joel B. Wolowelsky, "'Kibbud Av' and 'Kibbud Avot': Moral Education and Patriarchal Critiques," *Tradition* 33:4 (Summer, 1999): 35-44.

[14] As noted above, Rambam argued in the *Guide* that Solomon (and David, for that matter) achieved only the lower level of divine inspiration (*Guide* 2:45). For a treatment of this apparent contradiction, see Sarah Klein-Braslavy, "Solomonic 'Prophecy' in Rambam's Writings" (Hebrew), in *Minhah le-Sarah: Studies in Jewish Philosophy and Mysticism, Presented in Honor of Prof. Sarah O. Heller-Wilensky*, ed. Moshe Idel, Devorah Diament & Shalom Rosenberg, (Jerusalem, 1994), 57-81.

[15] *Shemonah Perakim*, chapter 7. Translation from *The Eight Chapters of Maimonides on Ethics (Shemonah Perakim): A Psychological and Ethical Treatise*, edited, annotated, and translated with an introduction by Joseph I. Gorfinkle (New York, 1966), 81.

[16] *Hilkhot Issurei Bi'ah* 13:14,16.

[17] Commentary on *Judges* 13:5.

[18] Commentary on *I Kings* 3:3, 11:2.

[19] *Guide* 2:32-45.

[20] *Kuzari*, e.g., I:4; I:87.

[21] Commentary on *Amos* 1:1; 7:14.

[22] Commentary on *Amos* 1:1.

[23] *Haggigah* 13b.

[24] *Guide* 3:6.

[25] *Treatise on Resurrection.* Translation from *Crisis and Leadership: Epistles of Maimonides*, Abraham S. Halkin, trans. and D. Hartman (Philadelphia, 1985), 228.

[26] "On Maimonides' Allegorical Readings of Scripture," in *Interpretation and Allegory: Antiquity to the Modern Period*, ed. Jon Whitman (Leiden, 2000), 184.

[27] *Jewish Encyclopedia*, vol. 1, 408.

[28] *Guide* 2:41-42.

[29] Ralbag adopted Rambam's view on these verses. Alternatively, Joshua may have been standing in the Jericho area, not inside the walled city (Rashi, Radak, Yehudah Kiel, *Da'at Mikra: Yehoshua* [Jerusalem, 1970], 35).

[30] *Guide* 2:32.

[31] Commentary on Gen. 18:1.

[32] See further discussion of this debate in Shalom Rosenberg, "On Biblical Exegesis in the *Guide*," pp. 113-120.

[33] Commentary on Gen. 22:13. Avraham Nuriel ("Parables Not Designated Parables in the *Guide to the Perplexed*" [Hebrew], *Da'at* 25 [1990], 88-89) disagrees with the Abarbanel, and attempts to demonstrate that Rambam in fact believed that the *akeidah* all occurred in a prophetic vision.

[34] See, for example, *Pesahim* 87a-b, Kara, Ibn Ezra, Radak, Abarbanel, Malbim. Yehudah Kiel (*Da'at Mikra: Trei Asar vol. 1* [Jerusalem, 1990], 3, n. 6) suggests the alternative that the woman was not yet promiscuous, but would cheat on Hosea.

[35] *Guide* 2:46. Translation from *The Guide of the Perplexed*, Shlomo Pines, second edition (Chicago, 1963), 404-406.

[36] On this issue, Rambam followed Ibn Ezra (Hos. 1:1). Radak accepted Rambam's view in both cases.

[37] Several commentators who understood Isaiah's actions as having occurred in a waking state explained that "*arom*" can mean "with torn clothing," or "scantily clad," rather than outright "naked." See, for example, Targum, Rashi, R. Eliezer of Beaugency, Ibn Caspi.

[38] Commentary on Hos. 1.

[39] Radak followed Rambam in this instance as well; cf. Yehiel Moskowitz (*Da'at Mikra: Yehezkel* [Jerusalem, 1985], 26). In contrast, *Sanhedrin* 39a, Rashi, Kara, R. Eliezer of Beaugency, Ibn Caspi, and Malbim maintained that Ezekiel performed these actions in a waking state.

[40] Commentary on Gen. 6:6. Translation from *Pentateuch: Translated and explained by Samson Raphael Hirsch. Vol. 1 Genesis*, Isaac Levy, second Edition (Gateshead, 1982), 133.

[41] *Hilkhot Melakhim* 12:1; *Guide* 2:29.

[42] Cf. Lev. 26:6; Hos. 2:20.

[43] *Treatise on Resurrection. Crisis and Leadership: Epistles of Maimonides*, 223.

[44] See Shalom Rosenberg, "Job was a Parable: Philosophy and Literary Exegesis" (Hebrew), in *Mehkarim ba-Mikra u-ba-Hinukh: Presented to Prof. Moshe Ahrend*, ed. Dov Rappel (Jerusalem, 1996), 146-158. Cf. Shalom Rosenberg, "On Biblical Exegesis in the *Guide*," 98-103.

[45] *Guide* 3:22.

[46] For a recent discussion of the parameters of what is traditionally acceptable within the allegorization of biblical passages, see Joshua L. Golding, "On the Limits of Non-Literal Interpretation of Scripture from an Orthodox Perspective," *Torah U-Madda Journal* 10 (2001): 37-59.

[47] See *Gen. Rabba* 85:5, and further sources and discussion in *Torah Shelemah* Genesis 38:38.

[48] *Guide* 3:49. Hizkuni and Abarbanel agreed with Rambam, that levirate marriage must have been practiced in the surrounding society. Radak and Ramban suggested the possibility, but remained less confident than Rambam. See further discussion and sources in *Torah Shelemah* Genesis 38:78. Rambam's hypothesis has received much corroboration from ancient Near Eastern literature. See, for example, Nahum Sarna, *The JPS Torah Commentary: Genesis* (Philadelphia, 1989), 266: "The levirate institution long antedated the Pentateuchal legislation. In fact, it is widely documented in one form or another in several extrabiblical sources."

[49] See *Gen. Rabba* 85:10, and further sources and discussion in *Torah Shelemah* Genesis 38:96.

[50] For a survey of medieval exegetes who shared this position, see Uriel Simon, "*Peshat* Exegesis of Biblical History—Between Historicity, Dogmatism, and the Medieval Period" (Hebrew), in *Tehillah le-Moshe: Biblical and Judaic Studies in Honor of Moshe Greenberg*, ed. Mordechai Cogan, Barry L. Eichler & Jeffrey Tigay (Winona Lake, IN, 1997), Hebrew section, 171*-203*.

[51] *Guide* 3:49. Yehudah Kiel (*Da'at Mikra: Bereshit vol. 3* [Jerusalem, 2003], 88) observes that the Code of Hammurabi (paragraph #110), legislates death by burning for adultery (cf. *Torah Shelemah* Genesis 38:96). It is conceivable that the bond created from levirate marriage was viewed by that society as the equivalent of being legally married. Therefore, Tamar had committed adultery. See, e.g., Rashbam, R. Avraham ben ha-Rambam, and Radak on Gen. 38:24.

[52] Quoted by R. Avraham ben ha-Rambam in his commentary on Gen. 38:13. In the Hittite Laws (James Pritchard ed., *Ancient Near Eastern Texts* 3rd edition [Princeton, N.J., 1969], 196 paragraph #193), we find corroboration of R. Maimon's speculation; after brothers-in-law, a woman's father-in-law was next in the hierarchy for levirate marriage. See also Shalom Rosenberg, "Critical Bible Study in Contemporary Jewish Religious Thought" (Hebrew), in *ha-Mikra va-Anahnu*, ed. Uriel Simon (Tel Aviv, 1979), 86-119, esp. 95-99. Rosenberg cites the usage by R. Kook, R. Aviad Sar Shalom, and Zvi Graetz of Rambam's approach to the historical setting of *Tanakh*.

[53] *Treatise on Resurrection* (229-230). Abarbanel (beginning of *Behukkotai*) surveys and rejects six answers of his predecessors to this question before presenting his own hypothesis. The first two answers cited are attributed to Rambam. Regardless, it is noteworthy that *Tanakh* reflects a consistent belief in afterlife (both the soul world and the Resurrection), even as it almost completely avoids direct reference to it. See James L. Kugel, *The Great Poems of the Bible: A Reader's Companion with New Translations* (New York, 1999), 192-210.

[54] See Deut. 12:5, 11, 13, 14, 18, 21, 26; 14:23, 24, 25; 15:20; 16:2, 6, 7, 11, 15, 16; 17:8; 18:6; 23:17; 26:2; 31:11.

[55] *Guide* 3:45.

[56] For a thorough bibliographical listing, see Jacob I. Dienstag, *"Ta'amei ha-Mizvot* in Rambam's Teachings— A Bibliography," *Da'at* 41 (1998): 101-115.

[57] *Guide* 3:29.

[58] See Menachem Kellner, "Maimonides on the Nature of Ritual Purity and Impurity," *Da'at* 50-52 [2003]: p. xxiv, n. 63. See also Josh. 24:14; Ezek. 20:7-8 for biblical allusions to the idolatry practiced by the Israelites while in Egypt.

[59] *Guide* 3:32.

[60] Commentary on Lev. 1:9.

[61] Rambam himself was concerned with the possibility of the masses' losing respect for many *mizvot* were their reasons revealed by the Torah (*Guide* III:26). A thorough treatment of this issue is found in Isadore Twersky, *Introduction to the Code of Maimonides* (New Haven, 1980), 374-484. See also David Henshke, "On the Question of Unity in Rambam's Thought" (Hebrew), *Da'at* 37 (1996): 37-51.

[62] See the 18th of R. Hirsch's *Nineteen Letters.* Russel Jay Hendel ("Maimonides' Attitude Towards Sacrifices," *Tradition* 13:4-14:1 [Spring-Summer, 1973], p. 179, n. 48) observes: "Rabbi Hirsch praises the Rambam for preserving medieval Judaism but also severely criticizes him for the effect the *Moreh's* views were having at Rabbi Hirsch's time. There is a difference in tone between the Ramban and Rabbi Hirsch. Ramban although using quite strong language, nevertheless is basically criticizing the *view* of the Rambam. Rabbi Hirsch however criticizes the *methodology* of the Rambam."

[63] *Hilkhot Me'ilah* 8:8. For analysis of the extent of the debate between Rambam and Ramban, and of the apparent contradictions within Rambam's writings on the subject of sacrifices, see Russel Jay Hendel, "Maimonides' Attitude Towards Sacrifices," *Tradition* 13:4-14:1 (Spring-Summer, 1973): 163-179; David Henshke, "On the Question of Unity in Rambam's Thought."

[64] *Guide* 3:32. See, for example, I Sam. 15:22-23; Isa. 1:11-17; Jer. 7:1-11, 21-24; Amos 5:21-25. See further discussion in Roy Pinchot, "The Deeper Conflict Between Maimonides and Ramban over the Sacrifices," *Tradition* 33:3 (Spring, 1999): 24-33.

[65] See Menachem Kellner, "Maimonides on the Nature of Ritual Purity and Impurity," *Da'at* 50-52 (2003): p. xxvii, n. 68.

[66] *Guide* 3:49.

[67] For a recent article discussing some broader implications of the use of ancient Near Eastern sources in Orthodox biblical scholarship, see Barry L. Eichler, "Study of Bible in Light of Our Knowledge of the Ancient Near East," in *Modern Scholarship in the Study of Torah: Contributions and Limitations,* ed. Shalom Carmy (Northvale, N.J., 1996), 81-100.

Parent-Child Relationships and *Ta'amei ha-Mizvot* in Rambam*

Elimelekh M.S. Polinsky

Rambam consistently classifies the *mizvot* into groups of fourteen: fourteen books, classes, or categories. This scheme is first mentioned by Rambam in the *Sefer ha-Mizvot*[1] and is also used in the *Mishneh Torah*[2] and the *Guide for the Perplexed.*[3]

The *Mishneh Torah* is divided into fourteen books according to subjects or classes of laws.[4] For example, the laws of Shabbat and the annual holidays that fall in different seasons and times of the year are in *Sefer Zemanim*, the *Book of Seasons*. Each book is further divided into sections of *halakhot*. In the case of *Sefer Zemanim*, those sections are *Hilkhot Shabbat, Hilkhot Eruvin, Hilkhot Hamez u-Mazah, Hilkhot Shofar, Sukkah and Lulav*, etc.

In the third part of the *Guide*, Rambam devotes chapters 26–49 to explaining the reasons for the *mizvot*, *ta'amei ha-mizvot*. The *Guide* divides the *mizvot* into fourteen classes or categories of law. The fourteen classes in the *Guide* and the fourteen books in the *Mishneh Torah* are not an exact match; Rambam tells us in the *Guide* which books in the *Mishneh Torah* correspond to the classes in the *Guide*. For example, Rambam says that Book 14 of the *Mishneh Torah*, *Sefer Shofetim*, corresponds to the sixth class in the *Guide*:

> The sixth class is formed of precepts respecting fines, e.g., the
> laws on theft and robbery, on false witnesses, and *most of the laws*
> contained in the section *Shofetim* belong to this class. Their benefit
> is apparent; for if sinners and robbers were not punished, injury
> would not be prevented at all, and persons scheming evil would
> not become rarer. They are wrong who suppose that it would be

---

* Dedicated in loving memory and grateful respect: to my parents, Reb Yaakov Dov and Mrs. Rose Polinsky, of blessed memory.

an act of mercy to abandon the laws of compensation for injuries; on the contrary, it would be perfect cruelty and injury to the social state of the country. It is an act of mercy that God commanded "judges and officers thou shalt appoint to thee in all thy gates" (Deut. 16:18).[5]

In this essay, I will discuss the placement of the *mizvah* of *kibbud av va-em* in Rambam's organizational system. Rambam, in *Sefer ha-Mizvot*, enumerates two positive and two negative commandments related to the parent-child relationship:

> Positive Commandment 210: **Honor (Kibbud)** is based on: "Honor your father and your mother, so that your days may be long upon the land which the Lord your God gives you" (Ex. 20:12).
>
> Positive Commandment 211: **Reverence (Mora)** is based on: "Every man shall revere his mother and his father, and keep my Sabbaths; I am the Lord your God" (Lev. 19:3).
>
> Negative Commandment 318: **Do not curse (Lo tekalel)** is based on: "For every one who curses his father or his mother shall be surely put to death—he has cursed his father or his mother; his blood shall be upon him" (Lev. 20:9) and "He who curses his father or his mother shall surely be put to death"(Ex. 21:17).
>
> Negative Commandment 319: **Do not strike (Lo takeh)** is based on: "And he who strikes his father or his mother shall be surely put to death" (Ex. 21:15).

The prohibitions against cursing and hitting, *lo tekalel* and *lo takeh*, are prohibitions against injuring all people, not just parents; in cursing or hitting one's parents, however, one incurs the death penalty because of the severity of the sin. Therefore, only the punishment, and not the actual prohibition, is mentioned in the verses relating to parents.

Although Rambam's categorization in *Mishneh Torah* and the *Guide* appears quite orderly and systematic, the *mizvah* of honoring and revering parents and the prohibitions against mistreatment of them pose an apparent challenge to his organization. Strangely enough, in the *Mishneh Torah*, the *mizvot* regarding *kibbud av va-em* are included in *Sefer Shofetim*, the *Book of Judges*, in *Hilkhot Mamrim*. Why are the *halakhot* of this commandment included in a section that discusses court law and justice, and in the particular section dealing with rebellious judges? Additionally, the positive parent-child relationship *mizvot* are not rationalized in the chapter in the *Guide* dedicated to *Sefer Shofetim*. If these *mizvot* are indeed part of the sixth class of *mizvot* in the *Guide*, why are they not explained there?

It is my belief that through his mysterious categorization of these *mizvot*, Rambam attempted to teach us a crucial lesson regarding parent-child relationships, family, and society.

R. Nachum L. Rabinovitch analyzes[6] the way in which each of the fourteen books of the *Mishneh Torah* are weighted with positive and negative commandments in order to give it a unifying theme and a balanced amount of commandments, so that we would not be left with one book for miscellaneous commandments that do not have a common theme or connection to each other. In line with this, it behooves us to examine sources for this specific division of *Sefer Shofetim* and the placement and content of *Hilkhot Mamrim* in that book.

Sefer Shofetim contains the following *halakhot*: *Hilkhot Sanhedrin*, *Hilkhot Edut* (Testimony), *Hilkhot Mamrim* (Rebellious Judges), *Hilkhot Avel* (Mourning), and *Hilkhot Melakhim u-Milhamot* (Kings and Wars). *Hilkhot Mamrim* is further broken down into *mizvot* in this order:

1. To follow the rulings of the *Beit Din ha-Gadol*

2. Not to veer from the *Bet Din ha-Gadol*'s words

3. Not to add to the Torah, neither the written Torah, nor the interpretation we learned from tradition

4. Not to eliminate any *mizvot*

5. Not to curse father or mother

6. Not to strike father or mother

7. To honor father and mother

8. To revere father and mother

9. *Ben Sorer u-Moreh* (the gluttonous and rebellious son)

The Midrash derives the *mizvah* not to curse one's father or mother as follows:

> "For every one who curses his father or his mother shall be surely put to death; he has cursed his father or his mother; his blood shall be upon him" (Lev. 20:9). This is the punishment, where is the prohibition? In the verse, *elohim lo tekalel*—do not curse a judge (Ex. 22:27); if your father is a judge, he is included in the category of a judge, or if your father is a *nasi* he is included in the category of a *nasi*, or if he is a boor, *lo tekalel heresh*, do not curse the deaf (Lev. 19:14)…and you derive the law from the rule of interperetation, *binyan av mi-bein sheloshtan…ve-zeh ha-zad ha-shaveh ba-hen*. What do they have in common? They are part of your people and you are

prohibited from cursing them. So also, your father, who is part of your people, you are prohibited from cursing.[7]

This Midrash explains the flow of the contents of *Hilkhot Mamrim* and perhaps served as a rabbinic source for Rambam to connect and place the *mizvot* relating to parents in *Hilkhot Mamrim*. The flow of the Midrash corresponds to the list of *mizvot* as follows:[8]

• *Elohim* (judge) leads to the topic of *Beit Din ha-Gadol*; one must obey their words, the Torah and tradition.

• Discussion of the prohibition to curse a judge or *nasi* (*elohim*) brings us to cursing one's father or mother.

• Once on the topic of parents, the Rambam then continues with not striking one's father or mother, honoring them, revering them, and finally the *Ben Sorer uMoreh*, the gluttonous and rebellious son, who, by stealing from his parents and engaging in gluttony, is the antithesis of honoring and revering one's parents.[9]

Although this explains the placement of these *mizvot* in *Hilkhot Mamrim*, we are still left with the question of why they are not explained in the *Guide* along with the other *mizvot* found in *Sefer Shofetim* of the *Mishneh Torah*.

Honoring parents is given some rationale in the *Guide*, albeit indirectly, in the discussion of the fifth class of *mizvot* corresponding to *Sefer Nezikin*, the *Book of the Laws of Damages*:[10]

> The object of the law of restoring lost property to its owner[11] is obvious. In the first instance, it is in itself a good feature in man's character. Secondly, its benefit is mutual: for if a person does not return the lost property of his fellow-man, nobody will restore to him what he may lose, *just as those who do not honor their parents cannot expect to be honored by their children.*[12]

But the fifth class of *mizvot* is not the appropriate place for the placement of this *mizvah*, as it was included in *Sefer Shofetim*! The question is compounded by the fact that Rambam emphasizes twice in the chapter on the sixth class, that he has explained *all* of the commandments in *Sefer Shofetim*.[13] Moreover, elsewhere he states that the section includes *most* of the laws of *Sefer Shofetim*.[14] Prof. Isadore Twersky addresses a separate question regarding this statement: why are the laws of mourning completely absent from Rambam's treatment of this section? He concludes that Rambam viewed death as something positive, as in the case of Moshe who died by a kiss (or had death which is a kiss).[15] Hence, there is no room to discuss mourning or grief in the *Guide*, where death is viewed so positively.[16] Prof. Twersky does not offer an explanation specific to the discrepancy of the sixth class discussion in 3, 41, which omits the commandment of honoring parents.

Prof. Yaakov Levinger points out that there are other *mizvot* from *Sefer Shofetim* that are missing from the *Guide*, despite Rambam's claim.[17] He explains that the commandments of honoring and revering parents, as well as the other missing *mizvot*, are left out because the rationalization is obvious. The *mizvah* does not contain any secret matter and is out of place in a chapter alluding to secrets. Prof. Levinger follows Prof. Leo Strauss,[18] who puts great emphasis on this contradiction in Rambam. If Prof. Levinger is correct, then *lo takeh* should also be excluded from 3, 41 along with the other commandments regarding parents. But that is not the case:

> Death by the court of law is decreed in important cases: when faith is undermined, or a great crime is committed, such as idolatry, incest, murder, or actions that lead to these crimes. It is further decreed for breaking the Sabbath, because the keeping of the Sabbath is a confirmation of our belief in the Creation; a false prophet and a rebellious elder are put to death on account of the mischief which they cause; *he who strikes his father or his mother is killed on account of his great audacity, and because he undermines the constitution of the family, which is the foundation of the state.*[19]

I would suggest another answer as to why the *mizvot* of honoring and revering parents are not explained with the rest of the sixth class based on how the *halakhah* is presented by Rambam in *Mishneh Torah*. Rambam in *Hilkhot Mamrim* seems to follow the Talmud very closely. The Talmud states:

> Our Rabbis taught: What is "fear" and what is "honor"? "Fear" means that he [the son] must neither stand in his [the fathers'] place nor sit in his place, nor contradict his words, nor tip the scales against him. "Honor" means that he must give him food and drink, clothe and cover him, lead him in and out.[20]

Rambam writes:

> What is the distinction between reverence and honor? Reverence signifies that the son must neither stand nor sit in his father's place; must not contradict his father nor decide against him. What does honoring signify? The son must provide his father and mother with food and drink and clothing, paid for by the father. If the father has no money and the son has, he is compelled to maintain his

father and mother as much as he can. He must manage his father's affairs, conducting him in and out, and doing for him the kind of service that is performed by servants for their master; he should rise before him, as he should rise before his teacher.[21]

Similarly, Rambam follows the Talmud[22] in calling honoring and revering parents a *mizvah gedolah* and compares it to Man's relationship with God:

> It is a *great positive precept* to honor father and mother; so too, to pay reverence to father and mother. Scripture considers *the duty of honoring parents and revering them equal to the duty of honoring and revering God*. It is written: "Honor your father and mother" (Ex. 20:11) and it is also written, "Honor the Lord with your wealth" (Prov.3:9). Concerning one's father and mother it is written: "You shall each revere his mother and his father" (Lev. 19:3) and it is also written: "Revere the Lord your God" (Deut. 6:13). Just as God commanded us to honor and revere his great Name, so he has commanded us to honor and revere our parents.[23]

The idea that the honor and reverence given to parents by providing for their food and clothing or by not sitting in their seat is comparable to the honor and reverence due to God seems preposterous, if not heretical. This comparison in the model, therefore, must mean that the love and awe that we have for parents in the form of honor and reverence is similar to the love and awe that we have for God when we recognize that He is the Creator.[24] The goal in the parent-child relationship is to honor and revere in appreciation out of love and awe that goes beyond service out of duty and fear.[25]

R. Joseph B. Soloveitchik writes in *Halakhic Mind* that ta'amei ha-mizvot are usually seen as the attempt to rationalize commandments according to logic, common sense, or ethics. The problem is that *mizvot* have a logic all their own that may not appear to be rational by any other standards, or they may become oversimplified to the point of unimportance when rationalized. The question should not be: *Why* is this a *mizvah*? Rather, the question should be: *What* is the *halakhah*? Even if it confounds normal reasoning, *what* does the *mizvah* teach?

In R. Soloveitchik's words:

> For example, should we posit the question: why did God forbid perjury? The intellectualistic philosopher would promptly reply, "because it is contrary to the norm of truth." Thus he would explain a religious norm by an ethical precept, making religion the handmaid of ethics. Again, when the same philosopher attempts to sanction

dietary laws on hygienic grounds, the specific religious content and meaning are supplanted by a principle of foreign extraction. If the Sabbath is to be seen only against the background of mundane social justice and similar ideals, the intrinsic quality of the Sabbath is transformed into something alien. It serves merely as a means to the realization of a "higher" end. Maimonides' efforts foreshadowed failure from the very outset of his "how" approach. It is worthy to note that Maimonides, the halakhic scholar, came nearer the core of philosophical truth than Maimonides the speculative philosopher. In contradistinction to the causal method of the philosophical *Guide* [the *Mishneh Torah*] apprehends the religious act in an entirely different light. The *Code* does not pursue the objective causation of the commandment, but attempts to reconstruct its subjective correlative. It would seem the Maimonides of the *Halakha* was not intrigued by the "how" question. He freed himself from the generic purview and employed a descriptive method of expounding the content and symbolic meaning of the religious norm. The "what" question was his guide in the *Code*.[26]

This approach suits the analysis of the parent-child relationship very well. One must go beyond the utilitarian reason for the commandment, that if you are good to your parents your children in turn will be good to you, and explain the details of the *halakhah* and related *mizvot*. This method is also necessary to understand how *halakhah* deals with the growth of the child as he matures from obedience out of fear of parents to reverence and awe, from giving honor out of duty to giving honor out of respect and love. Conversely, how do the *mizvot* deal with deterioration in the parent-child relationship when a parent is ill or senile or when it involves neglect and abuse, whether physical or verbal?

Rambam writes:

To what lengths should the honoring of one's father and mother go? Even if they took a pocketful of gold pieces belonging to him and cast it into the sea right in his presence, he must not shame them or scream and be angry at them; instead, he should accept the divine decree and keep silent.

To what lengths should the duty of revering them go? Even if he wore costly clothes while presiding over a public assembly, and his father and mother came and tore his clothes, struck him on the head, and spat in his face, he must not embarrass them but keep silent. He should revere and fear the supreme King of kings who has thus commanded him. Had a mortal king laid a more painful restraint on him, he would be powerless to struggle against it; so much the more if the decree comes from him who spoke and the world came into being by his will.[27]

R. Soloveitchik, in *Family Redeemed*,[28] points out that this follows the Talmud very closely except for one very important difference, the injunction to heed the decree of the "King of kings." Both the commandments of *kibbud* and *mora* go beyond the rational and ethical that is evident in the obligation love your neighbor as yourself. We are commanded to accept waste and humiliation from our parents, even though they are generally intolerable. In *halakhah*, the *mizvah* is accepted without reservation as Divine decree. "How" or "why" is not the question—only the "what." In both the cases of *kibbud* and *mora*, man has to accept the Divine decree and learns, thereby, the true definition of honor and reverence. The commandment to revere, *mora*, becomes operative in the case of humiliation because it is the least rational and yet, *"Had a mortal king laid a more painful restraint on him, he would be powerless to struggle against it; so much the more if the decree comes from Him who spoke and the world came into being by His will."*[29]

The *Guide* could only leave us wanting a deeper answer to explain the detail and the symbolism that are by Divine decree. The need to explain the *mizvot* about parent-child relationship in this way prevented Rambam from giving a full exposition in the *Guide*. Only in *halakhah*, in the *Mishneh Torah*, is it possible to determine the ultimate meaning or deeper rationale of the *mizvah*.

I believe that Rambam offers another general approach to *ta'amei ha-mizvot* in the *Guide* that is neither utilitarian nor limited to the "how" method that relegates the *mizvah* to be the handmaiden of ethics. Rambam writes regarding the purpose of the *mizvot* in general:[30]

> The general object of the Law is twofold: the well-being of the soul, and the well-being of the body. The well-being of the soul (*tikkun ha-nefesh*) is promoted by correct opinions communicated to the people according to their capacity... The well-being of the body (*tikkun ha-guf*) is established by a proper management of the relations in which we live one to another.

> This we can attain in two ways: First by removing all violence from our midst: that is to say, that we do not do every one as he pleases, desires, and is able to do; but every one of us does that which contributes towards the common welfare. Secondly, by teaching every one of us such good morals as must produce a good social state... The true Law, which as we said is one, and beside which there is no other Law, the Law of our teacher Moses, has for its purpose to give us the twofold perfection.It aims first at the

establishment of good mutual relations among men by removing injustice and creating the noblest feelings. Secondly, it seeks to train us in faith, and to impart correct and true opinions when the intellect is sufficiently developed....

The purposes for the *mizvot* mentioned here correspond to the second and third of the four perfections that Rambam discusses in the *Guide*. Rambam writes as follows regarding the fourth level of *shleimut*:[31]

The fourth kind of perfection is the true perfection of man: the possession of the highest, intellectual faculties: the possession of such notions which lead to true metaphysical opinions as regards God. With this perfection man has obtained his final object; it gives him true human perfection; it remains to him alone; it gives him immortality, and on its account he is called man...The prophets have likewise explained unto us these things, and have expressed the same opinion on them as the philosophers. They say distinctly that perfection in property, in health, or in character, is not a perfection worthy to be sought as a cause of pride and glory for us: that the knowledge of God, i.e., true wisdom, is the only perfection which we should seek, and in which we should glorify ourselves. Jeremiah, referring to these four kinds of perfection, says: "Thus saith the Lord, Let not the wise man glory in his wisdom, neither let the mighty man glory in his might, let not the rich man glory in his riches; but let him that glorieth glory in this, that he understandeth and knoweth me" (Jer. 9:22-23).... Our Sages have likewise derived from this passage the above-mentioned lessons, and stated the same theory that has been explained in this chapter, that the simple term *hokhmah*, as a rule, denotes the highest aim of man, the knowledge of God; that those properties which man acquires, makes his peculiar treasure, and considers as his perfection, in reality do not include any perfection; and *that the religious acts prescribed in the Law, the various kinds of worship and the moral principles which benefit all people in their social intercourse with each other, do not constitute the ultimate aim of man, nor can they be compared to it, for they are but preparations leading to it...*

When the Rambam says that the *mizvot* and moral principles that benefit society do not "constitute the ultimate aim of man," he is referring to the second and third levels of *sheleimut, tikkun ha-guf* and *tikun ha-nefesh*, respectively. He is not denying the central role that *mizvot* play in attaining and achieving the fourth level of *sheleimut*, regarding which Rambam states:

The prophet...says, however, that man can only glory in the knowledge of God and in the knowledge of His ways and attributes, which areHis actions, as we have shown in expounding the passage, "Show me now thy ways" (Ex. 38:13). We are thus told in this passage that the Divine acts which ought to be known, and ought to serve as a guide for our actions are *hesed* [loving-kindness], *mishpat* [justice], and *zedakah* [righteousness].[32]

What is the Rambam teaching us about parent-child relationships, family, and society? First of all, according to Rambam, the *halakhot* regarding parents belong to the section of *Hilkhot Mamrim* in *Sefer Shofetim*. Based on the analysis of the Midrash, the prohibition of cursing or striking a judge is the same as cursing a parent, the only difference being the severity of the punishment. In the *Guide*, Rambam gives us the philosophical utilitarian purpose for the commandment, that the parent-child relationship is one of the pillars of a strong family unit that is at the core of a strong nation and society. There is a need to negate selfish and egotistical tendencies to have a more civil society. In the end, though, honoring and respecting parents is rationalized because treating parents well happens to serve self-interest when one becomes a parent himself. In the *Mishneh Torah*, Rambam teaches the "what" of the *mizvah*. From the detail of *halakhah* we learn about the relationship with parents and how to provide for them, honor and revere them: the *halakhah* indicates that man's relationship with his parents is modeled after man's relationship to God. We are to be in awe of the Creator and even accept humiliation at the hands of our parents because the Divine decree makes it obligatory. We would suffer no less from the decree of a human king.

The last section of the *Guide* is teaching us to reach the fourth level of human perfection—*sheleimut*. We need to get closer to God, the Creator, through the detail of the *halakhah* that teaches us how to emulate His ways. The command of *ve-halakhta bi-derakhav* (walking in God's ways) obligates man to emulate the attributes of *zedakah* and *hesed* of a personal God who cares about His creation. This command is the definiton and etymology of the very word "*halakhah*." The *mizvot* are the detail of following in God's ways of *zedakah* and *hesed*.

When Rambam published his first major work, the *Commentary on the Mishnah*, at the age of thirty,[33] he listed his ancestors going back seven generations in the colophon. He did not do this in any of his other books. Prof. S.D. Goitein[34] notes that Rambam did this not out of vanity, but to add to the authority of his work. His ancestors included four judges, and it was assumed that a man would try to live up to the high standards of his forefathers. I believe that he did this not only to establish his right as an authoritative link in the chain of tradition, but to give honor, respect, and gratitude to the chain of tradition from parent to child for seven generations. Rambam was heir to a great heritage in his family and he shared that heritage with all Jews for all time. We are all grateful to Rambam for making us heirs to that great tradition through his writings. As the Talmud says, "He who teaches Torah to his neighbor's son is regarded by Scripture as though he had fashioned him...."[35] Rambam writes:

> Just as a person is commanded to honor and revere his father, so it is his duty to honor and revere his teacher, even more than his father; for his father has secured him life in this world, while the teacher who has taught him wisdom secures for him life in the future world...There is no honor higher than that which is due the teacher, no reverence more profound than that which should be bestowed upon him. The Sages said: "The reverence for your teacher should be like the reverence for Heaven."[36]

In observance of the 800th anniversary of the *yahrzeit* of Rambam we give him honor as our teacher and stand in awe of his accomplishments. May God grant us the opportunity to continue to delve deeper into the writings of Rambam and to discover the intricacies and nuances of the *ta'amei ha-mizvot* from the detail of *halakhah* for parent-child relationships and all other *mizvot*.

---

[1] See Rambam's Introduction to *Sefer ha-Mizvot*.

[2] English translations for citations from *Mishneh Torah* are from Philip Birnbaum, *Maimonides' Mishneh Torah* (New York, 1944).

[3] English translations for citations from the *Guide* are from Michael Friedlander, *The Guide for the Perplexed*, (New York, 1956).

[4] The *Mishneh Torah* is also referred to as *Yad ha-Hazakah*, alluding to the fourteen books; the numerical value of the letters *Yud* and *Dalet* (*Yad*) equal fourteen. Many reasons have been offered for the use of this number in Rambam's writings. R. Yehoshua ha-Nagid (1310-1355, a descendant of Rambam), quoted by R. N.L. Rabinovitch in *Mishneh Torah im Perush Yad Peshutah, Hakdamah u-Minyan ha-Mizvot* (Jerusalem, 1997), 68, offers the following explanation:

> [The number fourteen] is an allusion to the positive and negative commandments. The numerical value of the 248 positive commandments in small numbers is as follows: 200 = 2, 40 = 4, and 8 = 8. 2+4+8 = 14. Similarly, the 365 negative commandments in small numbers are as follows: 300 = 3, 60 = 6, and 5 = 5. 3+6+5 = 14.

R. Rabinovitch questions this explanation in light of the fact that it was not customary to refer to the different numbers 248 and 365 as the breakdown between the positive and negative commandments in the time of Rambam.

Rambam's thirteen *ikkarim*, the Principles of Faith, are also actually fourteen. The fourteenth principle, not listed with the others but nonetheless underlying them all, is the belief in free will. Rambam says in *Hilkhot Teshuvah* 5:3 that free will is an important principle and it is the pillar on which the Torah and the *mizvot* stand. Perhaps, R. Rabinovitch argues, Rambam therefore chose the number fourteen as the numerical scheme for his writings.

[5] *Guide* 3, 35.

[6] *Yad Peshutah*, 66.

[7] *Mekhilta, Parashat Mishpatim, Masekhet Nezikin, Parashah* 5. See *Sifra, Parashat Kedoshim, Perek* 10, with some variations in the text.

[8] Interestingly, *Mamrim* 5:4 cites the *derash* according to R. Akiva for the prohibition against cursing parents. R. Akiva holds that *lo tekalel heresh* is the source for not cursing parents. The Midrash we quoted is the Mekhilta according to R. Yishmael and includes the judges and a *nasi* as part of the derivation for the prohibition. See the *Kesef Mishneh ad loc.* who notes that this is based on R. Akiva's opinion, not R. Yishmael, as cited in the *Mekhilta* and *Sifra*. The *Lehem Mishneh* questions the *Kesef Mishneh* on the exclusive reliance of Rambam on R. Akiva as the source for this, since the Rambam in *Hilkhot. Sanhedrin* 26 quotes R. Yishmael as well: "…Why would Rambam enumerate them [these mizvot] here [in *Mamrim*] if not for this [*derashah* of R. Yishmael]…." I would suggest that perhaps the source for the ruling and the source for organizing the *Mishneh Torah* may be different without being contradictory.

[9] The child/parent relationship requires rising above the ego and individual selfishness and pleasure seeking.

[10] *Guide* 3, 40.

[11] Deuteronomy 22:1-3.

[12] Emphasis mine. R. Yosef Kafah, *Moreh ha-Nevukhim* (Jerusalem, 1972), notes in the *Guide* 3, 40 n. 16 that there is another similarity in the comparison of returning a lost object and honoring parents, i.e. negation of egotistical tendencies and selfishness.

[13] *Guide* 3, 41:

> The precepts of the sixth class comprise the different ways of punishing the sinner. Their general usefulness is known and has also been mentioned by us. I will here describe them one by one and point out their nature in detail……Although I have shown the reason of *all the laws contained in* ""*the Section of Judges*" (*Sefer Shofetim*), I find it necessary, in accordance with the object of this treatise, to explain a few of these laws, e.g., the laws concerning a rebellious elder…

> We have thus shown the moral lessons contained in these laws, and we have explained *the reason of every precept of this section*….

[14] *Guide* 3, 35.

[15] *Guide* 3, 51.

[16] Isadore Twersky, *Introduction to the Code of Maimonides (Mishneh Torah)* (New Haven, 1980), 307.

[17] See his *Ha-Rambam ki-Philosof u-ke-Posek* (Jerusalem, 1989), 239-240. Other *mizvot* left out in 3, 41 that are in *Shofetim* are: Positive 236: Burying the executed on the same day; Negative 66: Prohibition against prolonged hanging; Negative 57: Prohibition against cutting down fruit trees in war; Negative 362: Against choosing a convert as king; Negatives 363-365: relating to prohibitions for kings.

[18] See his *Persecution and the Art of Writing* (Connecticut, 1952), 62. Prof. Strauss was a leading exponent of the dualistic method of interpreting Rambam that is popular among academic scholars. This secular approach attempts to show that Rambam was hiding his true opinions and belief through a system of self-contradiction, allusion and symbolic language to avoid persecution from the religious community. For example, in the case of a contradiction between the *Guide* and the *Mishneh Torah*, Prof. Strauss would say the true belief of Rambam is expressed in the *Guide* where he may not confirm traditional belief and practice as expressed in the *Mishneh Torah*. I believe that this approach is antithetical to a correct interpretation of Rambam. Rambam was not a split personality divided by two different sets of belief in philosophy and Judaism, espousing belief in one book and heretical doctrine in another. Rather, Rambam wrote for two different audiences with different questions and attitudes in the *Guide* and the *Mishneh Torah*. As they say in Yiddish, *der Rambam fun der Moireh Nevukhim un der Rambam fun der Mishneh Toire iz der zelbe Yid*: the Rambam who wrote the *Guide* and the Rambam who wrote the *Mishneh Torah* is the same Jew.

[19] *Guide* 3, 41. Emphasis mine.

[20] *Kiddushin* 31b.

[21] *Hilkhot Mamrim* 6:3.

[22] *Kiddushin* 30b.

[23] *Hilkhot Mamrim* 6:1. Emphasis mine.

[24] *Yesodei ha-Torah* 2:1-2. Also, see R. Joseph B. Soloveitchik, *Family Redeemed: Essays on Family Relationships* (Hoboken, N.J., 2000), 132-133.

[25] In contrast to *Mishneh Torah*, see *Sefer ha-Mizvot*, Positive Commandment 4, where we are told that the meaning of *yir'ah* is to be in fear of His punishment at all times for disobedience.

[26] R. Joseph B. Soloveitchik, *Halakhic Mind* (New York, 1986), 93-94. R. Soloveitchik illustrates this point with three examples: 1) Shofar, 2) Catharsis (*tum'ah* and *taharah*, the change in status of purification as a result of *tevilah*, ritual immersion in a *mikvah*) and 3) Shabbat. An explanation of parent-child relationships according to this method without making reference to the theory behind it can be found in *Family Redeemed*. See the essay "Kibbud u-Mora: The Honor and Fear of Parents," pp. 126-157.

[27] *Mamrim* 6:7.

[28] Pp. 149-152.

[29] *Hilkhot Mamrim*, ibid.

[30] *Guide* 3, 27.

[31] *Guide* 3, 54.

[32] *Guide* 1, 54.

[33] A project Rambam started at the age of thirteen.

[34] See *A Mediterranean Society*, vol. III, pp. 3-4.

[35] *Sanhedrin* 99b.

[36] See *Avot* 4:12, *Hilkhot Talmud Torah* 5:1-2.

Rambam: A Man of Letters

Moshe Sokolow

Rambam was surely one of the most accomplished and influential figures in all of Jewish history. Better known for his Halakhic and philosophical works, he was also the author of numerous monographs, in which he addressed some of the critical issues of his day. In this essay, we will focus on the Islamic intellectual and cultural milieu in which Rambam flourished and how he responded to its unique challenges. Through selections from his multifarious correspondence, we will explore the following themes:

- Muslim antagonism and persecution (*Iggeret ha-Shemad*, c. 1165)
- False messianism (*Iggeret Teiman*, c. 1172)
- Resurrection and the World to Come (*Ma'amar al Tehiyyat ha-Meitim*, c. 1191)[1]

Conventional wisdom regards the Mishnah commentaries and the *Guide for the Perplexed* as intended primarily for an intellectual elite, *Mishneh Torah* as appealing to a broader social base, and the letters as popular compositions. The manner in which Rambam preserved his intellectual integrity while addressing the needs of the masses of the Jewish public reflects his singular coalescence of intellectual and communal leadership.[2]

I. The Muslim attitude towards Judaism, and Rambam's Attitude Towards Islam

It is well to consider, at the outset, the essential difference between the Christian and Muslim views of Judaism.[3] Whereas Christianity sees its "new" covenant as superseding the "old," Islam regards itself as complementary, not contradictory, to Judaism and Christianity.[4] Because Christianity consigned Judaism to oblivion and severed Torah injunctions from what it labeled the "spirit" of the law, it rejected Jewish ritual practice and advocated either the conversion or elimination of the Jews. Because Islam recognized the legitimacy of Judaism—for Jews, at least—it remained tolerant of its practice and its practitioners providing they kept within specific guidelines.

While the relatively frenetic history of the Jews of Christendom, characterized by exile and persecution, has been lamented as "lachrymose,"[5] the more stable and durable history of the Jews of Islam has been extolled as a "creative symbiosis."[6] In this symbiosis, Jews were granted protected status (*dhimma*)[7] by Muslim law (*shari'ah*),[8] and their payment of a special poll tax (*jizyah*) entitled them to practice their religion—provided it didn't infringe on their Muslim neighbors. Hence, while no new synagogues could be constructed, existing ones could be refurbished, yet no synagogue could be higher than a mosque.[9] While the law mandated various social constraints as well (e.g., Jews were forbidden to ride on horses or carry swords), it was not uncommon for individual Muslim rulers to overlook these prohibitions if it suited their financial or political purposes. In the first half of the tenth century, for instance, Samu'il ibn Nagrela—known as Shemuel ha-Naggid—served as commander of the army of the Muslim state of Granada in southern Spain, in which capacity he certainly rode a horse and carried a sword.

It is into such a symbiosis that Rambam was born and in whose midst he functioned and flourished. His rulings on the permissibility or prohibition of teaching Torah to Christians or Muslims, which we will study shortly, reflects the distinction he acknowledged between Christianity and Islam. While Islam is a thoroughly monotheistic religion, Muslims do not accept the text of the Torah as divine, arguing that it has been corrupted by the Jews to disguise the references to Muhammad they are certain it contained. Christians, while suspiciously polytheistic, accepted the sanctity of the "Old" Testament, while accusing the Jews of misinterpreting it.[10]

Here are the texts of his responsa:[11]

A. Christians

> It is permissible to teach the commandments to Christians and

to draw them close to our religion. This is prohibited regarding Muslims, because, as you know, they reject the divine origin of Torah and if they are taught Scripture it would contradict the version of events that they have either invented or confused...

Christians, on the other hand, believe the text of the Torah is immutable although they interpret it improperly in their commentaries. If they were presented with the correct interpretation, however, it is conceivable that they would recant; and even if they don't recant, it will cause us no harm since their scriptures are the same as our own.[12]

B. Muslims

These *Yishmaelim* [i.e., Muslims] are not idolaters at all. [Idolatry] has been eradicated from their mouths and hearts. They unify God without question... Likewise all contemporary Muslims, including women and children, have eradicated idolatrous beliefs and their errors and foolishness are manifest in other maters... In respect of the unity of God, they are in no error at all.[13]

A resident alien [*ger toshav*], namely one who has accepted the seven [Noahide] commandments... we may not drink his wine but we may benefit from it...

Similarly, any non-Jew who does not serve idols, such as the *Yishmaelim* [Muslims], though their wine may not be drunk, it is permitted to benefit from it. So have all the *Geonim* ruled. We may derive no benefit, however, from the wine of idolaters.[14]

The practice of religious tolerance cited above is almost the invariable rule in Muslim history. Indeed, in nearly 1,400 years of Muslim sovereignty (reckoning from the start of the Muslim era in 622 and ending with the termination of the Ottoman Empire at the close of World War I) there have been only three recorded incidents that amount to government-sponsored anti-Jewish persecution. We shall deal here with the earliest of them, one of two which occurred within Rambam's own lifetime.[15]

The incident involved a movement known to historians as the al-Mohades (Arabic: *al-Muwwahadun*, from the word *wahad* meaning one), a radical fundamentalist sect that emphasized God's absolute unity.[16] They originated among the Berber tribes of North Africa early in the twelfth century and spread across the Gibraltar straits to Spain, demanding that the Jews (and Christians) they encountered convert to their brand of Islam. The Maimon family, along with many Spanish Jews, fled from Cordova (in 1148) to the relative safety of Morocco (1159), and, later, to the security of Egypt (1164). Other Spanish and North African Jews, unable or unwilling

to flee, accepted conversion. Some of these forced converts returned to the
practice of Judaism when the al-Mohade threat subsided.

It was to the forced converts that Rambam addresses himself in the
epistle that has come to be known as either *Iggeret ha-Shemad* or as *Iggeret
Kiddush ha-Shem*. Prompted by his disenchantment with the treatment
of their predicament in a responsum issued by an unknown halakhist,
Rambam composed his own response to their quandary. The original
respondent condemned conversion to Islam even under pain of death,
and advised the converts that not only would they receive no reward for
keeping any of the *mizvot* in secret, but that every *mizvah* so observed
constituted a sin. Rambam retorts that such a position is untenable and
inexcusable, and he utilizes his and his family's personal experience
as a guide and precedent towards a more equitable treatment of their
predicament. The excerpts that follow underscore his attempt to treat a
critical and sensitive problem.

The normative force of the response is a matter of some controversy,
with no less an authority than Haym Soloveitchik arguing that Rambam
deliberately adopted a position contrary to *halakhah*:

> The *Iggeret ha-Shemad* is not a halakhic work, not a responsum,
> but to use a modern term, a propagandistic tract, written with a
> single purpose in mind—to counteract the effects of a letter of
> indictment that had gained great currency and threatened to
> wreak havoc on the Moroccan community.[17]

The opening paragraph of the letter provides the background of the
question and the response.[18]

> A contemporary of mine inquired regarding this persecution in
> which he is forced to confess that that man is God's messenger
> and that he is a true prophet. He addressed his query to one whom
> he calls a sage and who was not touched by the tribulations of
> most of the Jewish communities in this violence, may it pass soon,
> and he wished to learn whether he should make the confession
> in order not to die, although his children will be lost among the
> gentiles, or should he die and not acknowledge what he demands,
> seeing that in this way he does what he is required by the Torah of
> Moses, and that the confession leads to the relinquishment of all
> the commandments (15).

We will not deal, here, with Rambam's critique of that other sage,
save to note that Rambam is quite sharp in his criticism of one who
is so zealous that he would judge others without having been in their

position—a trait repudiated by rabbinic ethics.[19]

We will provide five excerpts from the letter corresponding to Rambam's own division:

1. laws that apply during a time of persecution

2. the desecration (*hillul*) of God's name and its sanctification

3. martyrdom versus submission

4. the distinction of this persecution

5. advice to the persecuted

> 1. One class of precepts, those concerning idolatry, incest and bloodshed, requires that whenever a person is forced to violate any of them, he is at all times, everywhere, and under all circumstances obliged to die rather than transgress... All the other commandments, any of which an oppressor may compel him to transgress, he is to judge. If the tyrant does it for his personal satisfaction... he may violate the Torah and escape death... If it is the aim of the oppressor to have him transgress, it is for him to deliberate: If it is a time of persecution he is to surrender his life and not transgress, whether in private or in public, but if it is not a time of persecution, he may transgress rather than die only in private; in public he may not violate even a minor rabbinic precept... (24-25)

> 2. Profanation of God's name is a grievous sin for which the inadvertent sinner and the deliberate sinner are equally punished... It is a more serious sin than any other. Neither the Day of Atonement, nor suffering, nor repentance procures forgiveness... As profanation of God's name is a grievous sin, so is sanctification of His name a most meritorious deed, for which one is generously rewarded. Every Jewish individual is required to sanctify God's name... (27)

> When a person fulfills one of the commandments and no other motive impels him save his love of God and His service, he has publicly sanctified God's name. So if he enjoys a good reputation he has sanctified God's name... (26-27)

> 3. A person to whom God grants the privilege of ascending to this high rank, in other words, to suffer a martyr's death, even if he is as sinful as Jeroboam ben Nebat and his associates, he is surely one of the members of the world-to-come, although he may not be learned... Now, if he did not surrender himself to death but

transgressed under duress and did not die, he did not act properly, and under compulsion he profaned God's name... He is not dubbed a transgressor, nor a wicked man... He simply did not fulfill the commandment of sanctifying God's name, but he can under no circumstance be named a deliberate profaner of God's name... Even if he worships idols under duress his soul will not be cut off [*karet*] and he is certainly not executed by court order (28-29).

4. Remember that in all the difficulties that occurred in the time of the sages, they were compelled to violate commandments and to perform sinful acts... But in this persecution they are not required to do anything but say something, so that if a man wishes to fulfill the 613 commandments secretly, he can do so. He incurs no blame for it, unless he set himself without compulsion to desecrate the Sabbath, although no one forced him. This compulsion imposes no action, only speech. They know very well that we do not mean what we say, and that what we say is only to escape the ruler's punishment and to satisfy him with this simple confession... When our rabbis ruled that a person is to surrender himself to death and not transgress, it does not seem likely that they had in mind speech that did not involve action... (30-31)

5. Anyone who suffered martyrdom in order not to acknowledge the apostleship of "that man"... His position is very high, for he has given his life for the sanctity of God, be He exalted and blessed. But if anyone comes to ask me whether to surrender his life or acknowledge, I tell him to confess and not choose death... A victim of this persecution should follow this counsel: Let him set it as his objective to observe as much of the Law as he can... He must not think that what he has already violated is far more grievous than what he observes; let him be as careful about observance as possible...(30-31)

Rambam's last piece of advice, however, is actually the first piece of advice (sequentially) that he would offer:

What I counsel myself, and what I should like to suggest to all my friends and everyone that consults me, is to leave these places and go to where he can practice religion and fulfill the Law without compulsion or fear. Let him leave his family and his home and all he has, because the divine Law that He bequeathed to us is more valuable than the ephemeral, worthless incidentals that the intellectuals scorn; they are transient, whereas the fear of God is eternal (31).

II. The Dangers of False Messianism: Rambam's Attitude towards Calculating the "End"

The appearance in Yemen during Rambam's lifetime of a particularly insidious messianic pretender caused the leaders of Yemenite Jewry to petition Rambam for a definitive statement on messianism, in general, and on the challenges they confronted, in particular.

They also requested and received, in his reply, a statement on the appropriate reaction to persecution. Rambam's position here is analogous to the one we reported in Part One. He distinguishes between three typologies of persecution and insinuates that the root cause of persecution of Jews is the desire to nullify the message of the Torah. As in the *Iggeret ha-Shemad*, Rambam recommends flight from persecution, for those who are able, and advises those who cannot flee to keep whatever *mizvot* they can and not fall prey to the misapprehension that their *prima facie* acceptance of Islam has cast them into an irremediable state of sin.

In this same context, Rambam also addresses himself to the charges that were being circulated in Yemen by a Jewish apostate[20] to the (aforementioned) effect that the Jews had falsified the text of the Torah to obscure its references to Muhammad. Rambam points out that the Torah was translated into other languages long before the advent of Islam yet these versions contain no such references:

> But the Muslims themselves do not accept these arguments; they do not admit nor cite them, because they are manifestly fallacious. Inasmuch as Muslims could not find a single proof in the entire Bible, nor a reference, or possible allusion to their prophet that they could utilize, they are compelled to accuse us, saying: "You have altered the text of the Torah, and expunged every trace of the name of Muhammad therefrom.
>
> They could find nothing stronger than this ignominious statement, the falsity of which is easily demonstrated to one and all by the fact that the Torah had been translated into Syriac, Greek, Persian and Latin hundreds of years before the appearance of the "prepostle"... [21] (107)

After the death of Muhammad in 632, the leadership of the Muslim nation ('*Umma*) was transferred to Abu Bakr, father of one of Muhammad's wives. After Abu Bakr's death, it passed to 'Umar, a close companion of Muhammad (who led most of the military conquests of that time), and then to 'Uthman, another companion (who oversaw the promulgation of a standard version of the Qur'an). When 'Uthman was murdered in 656, Muhammad's cousin and son-in-law 'Ali (husband to Muhammad's only child, Fatimah) asserted his leadership against significant opposition by the supporters of Mu'awiyya, governor of Syria, who had been promised the appointment by 'Umar and confirmed by 'Uthman.[22]

Civil war broke out and in 661, 'Ali was murdered. His partisans, the Shi'ites (*Shi'a* is Arabic for a faction), sided with his sons, Hassan and Hussein, while the majority Sunnis (*Sunna* is Arabic for tradition) followed Mu'awiyya (who began the 'Ummayyad dynasty that lasted for nearly a century, until it was replaced by the 'Abbasids). In 680, Hussein was killed in a massacre of Shi'ites at the Iraqi city of Karbala, an event that had "no great immediate political consequences,"[23] but was significant in initiating the Shi'ite tradition of martyrdom.[24]

Having lost political power, the Shi'ites looked to exercise religious influence and succeeded in rallying disaffected groups among the Muslims, particularly non-Arab converts. Whereas the Sunni Muslim credo is "There is no God but *Allah* and Muhammad is His prophet," Shi'ites add: "And 'Ali is the friend of *Allah* and heir to the prophet of Allah."[25]

Muslims have no institution comparable to the *Beit ha-Mikdash* [Temple] and, consequently, experienced nothing comparable to the *hurban* [destruction]. Since their attempts at conquest were rewarded with success that remained unchanged over most of their early history, neither did they ever experience anything comparable to *galut* [exile]. As a result, Sunni Muslims are generally unconcerned with either the concept of "redemption," in general, or with the "messiah," a redeemer, in particular.[26]

Shi'ism tells a different story. Because its roots lie in the historical failure to realize its political aspirations, and on account of the cruel massacre of its early leaders in Karbala, Shi'ism developed a tradition of suffering, torment and affliction (including even self-flagellation) and, alongside it, the aspiration towards future and ultimate redemption. The most important religious idea of Shi'ism is—arguably—the belief in a messiah-like figure called the *Mahdi* (Arabic for "the [divinely] guided one"), who will restore Muslim rule to the descendants of Muhammad through 'Ali and will usher in the equivalent of the "end of days."[27]

Geonic and early medieval Jewish history in the orbit of Islam are replete with episodes of sectarianism and false messianism, occurring primarily (although not exclusively) in areas under Shi'ite influence, such as Yemen and Persia.[28] The twelfth century, in particular, saw a veritable outbreak of messianic fervor due, in large part, to the disruption of ordinary Jewish life on account of the Crusades, the clash between East [Christendom] and West [Islam] serving as a backdrop for considerable speculation and anticipation.[29]

While there were Messianic pretenders before and throughout the Middle Ages,[30] we shall limit our discussion here to four who are referred to explicitly by Rambam in the letter.

(a) Abu 'Issa al-Isfahani

The first of these is known as Abu Issa of Isfahan, who lived in the Persian city of Isfahan towards the close of the seventh century.[31] As Rambam writes:

> ... One of these is the exodus of a multitude of Jews, numbering hundreds of thousands from the East beyond Isfahan, led by an individual who pretended to be the Messiah. They were accoutered with military equipment and drawn swords, and slew all those that encountered them... (127)

According to the continuation of the narrative, when this army reached the outskirts of Baghdad, the Caliph summoned the heads of the Jewish community and charged them with the task of determining whether the leader was the genuine Messiah (in which case, he was prepared to negotiate with him peacefully) or a pretender (in which case, he would wage war against him). The Jewish scholars spoke to them and ascertained that they came from "across the river,"[32] and were led by a virtuous man, a descendant of David, whose major messianic qualification was that he was cured overnight of leprosy.[33] The Jewish sages disabused them of his messiahship and persuaded them to return home peacefully. (The Caliph even bestowed valuable gifts upon them, for which he later exacted recompense from his Jewish subjects.)

(b) Moses al-Darri[34]

Al-Darri traveled to the Academy of Joseph Ibn Megash at Lucenna, around 1130, and later to Fez, in Morocco, foretelling certain events and predicting that the Messiah would arrive on the first day of Passover. Many Jews sold their possessions in anticipation of their departure for the Land of Israel. When the Messiah failed to arrive, he fled to Israel, where he died. Rambam writes of him in a particularly positive, almost nostalgic, vein:[35]

> About fifty years ago or less, a pious and virtuous man by the name of Moses al-Darri came from Darral to the province of Andalusia to study under Rabbi Joseph ha-Levi ibn Migash... People flocked to him... He informed them that the Messiah was about to come, as was divinely revealed to him in a dream... My father and master, of blessed memory, endeavored to dissuade and discourage people from following him. However... most, nay nearly all, clung to R. Moses. Finally he predicted events that would come true no matter what was going to occur...
>
> Once he foretold a vehement rain for the coming Friday and that the falling drops would be blood[36] ... This episode took place in the month of Marheshvan... This miracle convinced all the people that he was undoubtedly a prophet. In itself this is not inconsistent with the tenets of the Torah, for prophecy, as I have explained, will return to Israel before the messianic advent...
>
> When Passover came and nothing transpired, the people were ruined, as most of them had disposed of their property for a trifling sum, and were overwhelmed with debt... As this Muslim country no longer offered him protection, he left for Palestine where he died, may his memory be blessed. (128-129)

(c) Ibn Arieh

For this messianic episode we have only the evidence of the *Iggeret*:

> My father of blessed memory told me that about fifteen or twenty years before this episode [of Moses al-Darri, i.e. c. 1110-1115] some respectable people in Cordova, the center of Andalusia, among whom a number were given to the cult of astrology, were all of one mind that the Messiah would appear that year. They sought a revelation in a dream night after night, and ascertained that the Messiah was a man of the city. They picked a pious and virtuous person by the name of ibn Arieh, who had been instructing the people. They wrought miracles and made predictions just as al-Darri did, until they won over the hearts of all the people.
>
> When the influential and learned men of our community heard of this, they assembled in the synagogue, had ibn Arieh brought there, and had him flogged in public... because by his silence he gave assent to the professions of his adherents, instead of restraining them and pointing out to them that they were contradicting our religion.... The Jews escaped the wrath of the gentiles only with

the greatest difficulty. (129-130)

(d) Lyons

According to the *Iggeret*, about forty years prior to ibn Arieh (c. 1070) there appeared a messianic pretender in the French city of Lyons, who claimed the ability to fly like a bird.[37]

> Many who witnessed the miracle became his votaries. The French discovered this, pillaged, and put many of his followers to death, together with the pretender. Some of them maintain however that he is still in hiding until this very day.[38]

The episodes recounted above, as well as those recorded in the notes, make it abundantly clear that the medieval Jewish world—particularly the Jews in the orbit of Islam[39]—were frequently fixated on the advent of the Messiah.[40] Calculating the advent was no less of an obsession and, as Rambam notes with some asperity, even such luminaries as R. Sa'adyah Gaon (in his commentary on the Book of Daniel, in particular) participated.

Rambam negotiates a difficult strait here, steering clear of the shoals of creating false expectations on the one hand and plummeting into the abyss of dubiety on the other.

> You have adverted to the computations of the date of the redemption, and Rabbi Saadiah's opinion on the subject. First of all, it devolves upon you to know that no human being will ever be able to determine it precisely... Furthermore God has communicated through His prophets that many people will calculate the time of the advent of the Messiah, but they will be disappointed and fail. He also cautioned us against giving way to doubt and distrust because of these miscalculations. The longer the delay the more fervently we hope...[41] (114-115)

To illustrate his point, Rambam refers to the exodus from Egypt. Even though God specified in His covenant with Abraham that his descendants would be enslaved and oppressed for "four hundred years," it proved impossible for the Israelites to calculate their redemption. Witness the erroneous calculations of the Ephraimites who attempted an exodus prematurely[42] and were slain for their efforts.[43] In order to prevent similar mishaps, messianic calculations were proscribed.

> Now if such uncertainty prevailed in regard to the date of the emancipation from the Egyptian bondage, the term of which was fixed, it is much more so with respect to the date of the

final redemption, the prolonged an protracted duration of which appalled and dismayed our inspired seers...

Inasmuch as Daniel has proclaimed the matter a deep secret,[44] our sages have interdicted the calculation of the future time of the future redemption, or the reckoning of the period of the advent of the Messiah,[45] because the masses might be mystified and bewildered should the Messiah fail to appear as forecast. (115-116)

As we noted above, Sa'adyah Gaon had dealt extensively with the issues of the Messiah and the redemption, in both his commentary on the Book of Daniel and his philosophical magnum opus, *Sefer ha-Nivhar ba-Emunot ve-ha-De'ot*. If messianic calculations were "interdicted," as Rambam reported, how was Sa'adyah able to justify his own calculations? And if Sa'adyah was justified in defying the rabbininc interdiction, could not others claim a like justification? Rambam provides just such a rationalization on behalf of Sa'adyah and, by extension, provides himself with the justification for his own calculation.

As for Rabbi Saadiah's calculations, there are extenuating circumstances for them though he knew they were disallowed. For the Jews of his time were perplexed and misguided. The divine religion might have disappeared had he not encouraged the pusillanimous, and diffused, disseminated and propagated by word of mouth and the pen a knowledge of its underlying principles. He believed, in all earnestness, that by means of the messianic calculations he would inspire the masses with hope to the Truth. (116)

In other words, Rambam excuses Sa'adyah on grounds that the Talmud labels "*Et la-asot la-ha-Shem hefeiru toratekha;*"[46] theological exigency sanctions violation of an interdiction. Faced with the predicament of a querulous Jewish public growing increasingly skeptical over the viability of the messianic redemption, Sa'adyah offered his calculations in order to boost their flagging morale and shore up the crumbling edifice of the doctrine of divinely vouchsafed redemption.

Arguing that current conditions in Yemen resemble those that confronted Sa'adyah,[47] Rambam then proceeds to offer a calculation of his own—one that he implies has been a tradition in his family since the time of the exile following the destruction of the first Temple:

The tradition is that a covert indication lies in the prediction of Balaam to the future restoration of prophecy in Israel... By this method of cryptic allusion it was transmitted to me that Balaam's statement "Jacob is told at once (*ka-et*), yea Israel, what God has planed" (Numbers 23:23), contains a veiled hint as to the date of the restoration of prophecy to Israel. The sentence means that after the lapse of an interval equal to the time that passed from the six days of creation to Balaam's day, seers will again tell Israel what God had planned.

Now Balaam uttered his prediction in the thirty-eighth year after the Exodus, which corresponds to the year 2485 after the creation of the world, for the Exodus took place in the beginning of the year 2448. It is doubtless true that the reappearance of prophecy in Israel is one of the signs betokening the approach of the messianic era....[48]

This is the most reliable tradition concerning the advent of the Messiah. I call it reliable, although I have admonished against it, and strictly prohibited blazoning it abroad, lest some people deem it unduly postponed... (122-123)

According to this tradition,[49] prophecy, the harbinger of the redemption, was "scheduled" to be restored 2485 years after Balaam. In other words, the date of its restoration could be calculated to 4970 AM, corresponding to 1210 CE.[50] Given that the *Iggeret* was written c. 1172, and that Rambam died in December of 1204, he was, so to speak, "cutting it very close." Taken together with Sa'adyah's "erroneous" calculation, it appears as though Rambam, like Sa'adyah, was prepared to sacrifice a portion of his own credibility to the cause of maintaining the precarious balance between the imminence of the redemption and its utter unpredictability. By running the self-acknowledged risk of erring, Rambam was proving the fundamental futility of messianic calculation. Yet, by offering his own calculation, keyed to a relatively imminent date, he was providing the ingredient of hope in a desperate situation that kept hope depressed.

III. Resurrection of the Dead: *Ma'amar Tehiyyat ha-Metim*

The title of this epistle (i.e., *ma'amar* vs. *iggeret*) constitutes its distinction. Whereas the previous two texts are entitled "letters," the third translates better as "treatise," indicating that it was written at Rambam's initiative rather than in response to the specific request of a second party.[51] As such, it reveals a good deal about his personality and his concern over whether he was exerting effective influence over his coreligionists. We shall first treat the substantive issue of resurrection and then display some of the more individualistic elements in the composition.

An excerpt from the Shabbat morning service mentions several terms that figure prominently in our discussion:

> None is Your equal... *ba-Olam ha-Zeh*, in this world
>
> There is none but You... *le-hayei ha-Olam ha-Ba*, in the life of the world to come
>
> None exists without You... *li-yimot ha-Mashiah*, in the days of Messiah
>
> None can compare to You *li-t'hiyyat ha-meitim*, at the resurrection of the dead.

To these, we may add *le-atid la-vo*, the future to come, *Gan Eden*, Garden of Eden or Paradise, and *Gehennom*, Gehinnom or Hell. The operative question is: What do all these different terms designate? While some may overlap and others have been left deliberately ambiguous, there is a consensus among the vast majority of informed Jews regarding their sequence and interrelationship.

A. *The Days of the Messiah* (Messianic Era) designates the period of time at which the present historical era will terminate with the rule in Jerusalem of a scion of the Davidic monarchy who will revive and unify the Jewish nation (Ezekiel 37) and free them once and forever from gentile subjugation. As reported by the Amora, Shemuel, "*Ein bein ha-olam ha-zeh li-yimot ha-Mashiah elah shi'abud malkhuyot bilvad*"—The only distinction between this world and the Messianic era is subjugation by gentile kingdoms.[52]

B. *The Future to Come* can refer to the Messianic Era or, more generally, to any later point in time.

C. *Paradise* is the reward vouchsafed to the righteous after death. Some sources refer to this as *olam ha-neshamot*, the World of the Souls, a term that does not appear in the Talmud.

D. *Hell* is the punishment that is threatened to evildoers after death. In Hell, they can atone for their sins in this life after which they, too, become eligible for the reward for the good things they did.

E. *The World to Come* is an ambiguous term and it sits at the root of one of the several controversies surrounding Rambam's views on resurrection.

According to Rambam, the soul after death goes to either Paradise or Hell. Following bodily resurrection, people will live for a period of time after which the soul will again depart the body, this time to live forever in the World to Come, the World of the Souls. According to Ramban,[53] however, *Olam ha-Ba* refers to the eternal condition of resurrection, since he maintains that once the body and soul are reunited they so remain in perpetuity.

The views of Rambam and Ramban on this subject are abstracted by R. Joseph Albo in *Sefer ha-Ikkarim*:

> However it will come to pass, will the resurrected live, drink, bear children and die—as is the way of the [present] world?[54] We have explained that this is debated by the great scholars of recent times.
>
> Rambam, and other Jewish scholars, say that the resurrected will utilize all their senses, as is the way of the [present] world, after which they will die [again] and return to dust.[55]
>
> R. Meir haLevi and Ramban say that after resurrection, the resurrected will live as long as naturally possible, after which their bodies will be purified like that of Elijah and they will subsist in body and soul after which they will no longer utilize their senses and will not eat or drink or die. Rather, they will exist eternally without food or drink.
>
> This [later] appears to be the opinion of some of our Sages who said (*Sanhedrin* 92): "The righteous whom God will resurrect will not return to dust."[56]

The importance of the doctrine of the resurrection of the dead is epitomized by its prominent position in the well-known Mishnah that addresses the question of what articles of faith are required of Jews.

> All Jews have a share in the world to come.... The following have no share in the World to Come: One who says that the [doctrine of] resurrection of the dead is not [mandated by] the Torah; that Torah is not divine, and a heretic...[57]

While the Mishnah does not specify just what that doctrine comprises, it appears to have been the unanimous opinion of the sages of the Talmud and the Geonim that it refers to the return of the souls of the deceased to a corporeal form during the Messianic age. Witness its formulation by R. Sa'adyah Gaon (882-942):

> The author of this book declares that, as far as the doctrine of the resurrection of the dead is concerned... it is a matter upon which our nation is in complete agreement. The basis of this conclusion is a premise... namely, that man is the goal of all creation. The reason why he has been distinguished above all other creatures

is that he might serve God, and the reward for this service is life
eternal in the world of recompense.

Prior to this event, whenever He sees fit to do so, God separates
man's spirit from his body until the time when the number of souls
meant to be created has been fulfilled, whereupon God brings
about the union of all bodies and souls again...We consequently
do not know of any Jew who would disagree with this belief... [58]

On the one hand, Rambam made explicit reference to the doctrine
of resurrection in his "13 articles of faith," part of his commentary on
the very Mishnah cited above. Although the formulation that appears
in contemporary *siddurim* is not originally his (it is, essentially, a
"bowdlerization"), the "standard" version is close enough to the original
to serve our purpose:

[Article 13:] I believe with consummate faith that there will be a
resurrection of the dead whenever it pleases the Creator...[59]

In the *Mishneh Torah*, however, his formulation of the doctrine tends
sharply to the metaphorical:

The World to Come contains no corporeality, only the souls of
the righteous without bodies—like the ministering angels. Since it
contains no bodies it also contains neither eating nor drinking or
anything that is required by human beings in this world including
such activities that require corporeality such as sitting, standing,
sleeping, death, sorrow, happiness and the like. As our earliest
sages have said: "The World to Come has no eating, drinking or
cohabitation, just the righteous sitting—adorned with crowns—
enjoying the radiance of the Presence."[60]

The absence of corporeality is clarified by the fact that there will be
no eating or drinking; the reference to the righteous being "seated"
is metaphorical namely, that they will experience neither labor nor
exertion; the reference to the adornment with crowns symbolizes
their awareness [that it is by virtue of their righteousness] that
they are enjoying the World to Come...; and the reference to the
radiance of the Presence denotes an awareness of God of which
they were incapable while they were corporeal.[61]

This highly metaphorical treatment caused Rambam's intent to be
misunderstood, as illustrated by the accompanying stricture of his critic,
R. Abraham ben David (Ra'avad):

"The World to Come is incorporeal." Said Abraham [ben David]:
These words of that person [Rambam] appear to me to be similar
to one who says that there will be no corporeal but only spiritual
resurrection, and I swear that this is not the opinion of the Sages

who said: "The righteous will eventually stand clothed..." (*Ketubot* 111), and who would instruct their children: "Do not bury me in either white or black garments, should I merit..." (*Shabbat* 114). They also said: "The righteous will not be interred in the ground but they will arise bodily" (*Sanhedrin* 92), and: "They will arise with their infirmities and be cured" (*Sanhedrin* 91). All this proves that they will be resurrected bodily, although it is possible that God will grant them bodies that are as strong and as healthy as those of the angels, or of Elijah[62] and the crowns [too] should be taken literally and not metaphorically.[63]

Criticism such as that of the Ra'avad originated in large measure from R. Samuel ben Ali, *Gaon* (dean) of the yeshiva in Baghdad, a contemporary of Rambam (1164-1193) and one of his most implacable opponents. From Rambam's reference to it early in the treatise, we can see that it was, to an extent, typical of its time: R. Samuel relied on the unadorned and unexplained lore of the Talmud and Midrash, while Rambam argued for the necessary qualification of rabbinic legendary material in the light of contemporary philosophical sensibilities.

> But this year, 1191, a letter arrived from some of my colleagues in Baghdad, in which they wrote that an individual from Yemen inquired regarding these selfsame issues of Samuel ha-Levi, the incumbent head of the Academy—may God protect him—who at present resides in Baghdad. He composed an essay on resurrection, and in it he calls some of my views an error and a sin, and others defensible... I found it was a collection of the homilies and legends that he had gathered. Everyone knows that scholars are not expected to rehearse the homilies and the curious tales, of the sort that women tell one another in their condolence calls. What is wanted is their interpretation, and an exposition of their implied meaning, so that they conform to a rational position, or at least approximate it. (217-218)

Rambam attributes the misunderstandings to a certain oversimplification of the doctrine of resurrection on the part of the "masses:"

> However, all this is an inescapable consequence of premature misconceptions in the minds of the masses. They do not recognize true existence other than in a body... For this reason, most of them believe that God is corporeal, because in their judgment He would not be in existence if He were not. (215)

This point of view is absolutely rejected by Rambam who devotes another of his 13 principles to its refutation:

> I believe... that the Creator... is not corporeal; neither can he be
> described through corporeal attributes.

In *Mishneh Torah* he elaborates:

> Since we have clarified that He is not corporeal, neither can
> he be affected by corporeal activities. He cannot be connected
> or separated, He has neither space nor size, neither ascent nor
> descent, right or left, front or rear, standing or sitting. Neither does
> He exist within time such as to have a beginning, an end or an
> age...[64]

Because they cannot conceive of existence other than in a corporeal form, however, these "ignorant" people also regard angels as having bodies and even capable of eating. After all, does the Torah not say of Abraham's guests that "[they sat] beneath the tree and ate" (Genesis 18:8)? And if angels are corporeal, why should the members of the World to Come be any different?

To this Rambam replies:

> ... I do not mind. I would this were the extent of the ignorance
> of any of them. I hope their view of the Creator is free from any
> acceptance of corporeality. There is no harm in their assuming it
> for the separated beings [angels]. (215)

IV. Afterword

As we noted at the outset, the treatise on resurrection, while composed in response to a particular challenge, also represents Rambam's attempt to evaluate the extent of his influence on the Jewish public. In this latter regard, the treatise reflects a significant doubt over the effectiveness of his grand plan for public education. Pay close attention to the following excerpts—one of which appears at the very beginning of the treatise and the other, at its conclusion. Note the nobility of Rambam's expressed intentions, on the one hand, and to the disparaging way in which he dismisses his opponents, on the other.

> It is not rare that a person aims to expound the intent of some
> conclusions clearly and explicitly, makes an effort to reject
> doubts and eliminate far-fetched interpretations, and yet the
> unbalanced will draw the reverse judgment of the conclusion he
> sought to clarify... The same thing came to pass when some in our
> religious community challenged my understanding of one of the
> fundamentals of the Torah.
>
> I sought to call people's attention to the sorely neglected basic
> tenet that they doubted... When I concentrated on a compilation

of the law of the Torah and an exposition of its statutes [i.e., the *Mishneh Torah*], my object was to find favor with God, not to look forward to honor or reward from people. I wished to the best of my ability to provide guidance, understanding, and comprehension to whomever is not qualified to grasp the teachings of the scholars of the law who lived before me...

When I applied myself to this task, I realized that it was not correct to strive to explain the ramifications of the religious law, and to leave its roots neglected, unexplained, and its essentials undiscussed, providing no guidance. This is especially urgent since I have met some who think they are among the sages of Israel... [who] are in fact the most ignorant, and more seriously astray than beasts, their minds filled with the senseless prattle of old women and noxious fantasies, like children and women... (211-212)

No intelligent person has the right to blame me for the repetition in this essay, the additions to the main idea, or for the extensive clarification of what does not really require further light. I wrote this tract only for the common people who had begun to doubt what I had stated explicitly, and for those who reproached me for brevity when I spoke of the Resurrection... discourse with the wise stands in need of neither repetition nor elucidation... But the common people need both... [The] right thing to do is to address each group according to its capacity. (233) The essay is finished with the help of God, blessed be He and blessed be His name. (ibid.)

---

[1] While nearly all of Rambam's letters were composed in Arabic, there are both Hebrew and English editions of the three letters we have chosen. The Hebrew edition is vol. 20 in the רמב"ם לעם series published by Mossad ha-Rav Kook, and the English edition is *Crisis and Leadership: Epistles of Maimonides* (Philadelphia, 1985), translations by Abraham Halkin and discussion by David Hartman.

Throughout this essay, we will utilize excerpts from the English edition—keyed to its own page numbers—with reference made to either the Hebrew translation or Arabic original as the need may arise.

[2] Leo Strauss, *Persecution and the Art of Writing* (Chicago, 1988), 38-94, introduced the idea that the *Guide* has both "exoteric" and "esoteric" dimensions, addressing both broad and narrow constituencies. His work has been supplemented recently by his student Ralph Lerner, *Maimonides' Empire of Light* (Chicago, 2000). The fusion of intellectual and communal leadership is discussed in Hartman's introduction to *Crisis and Leadership*.

[3] An excellent overview of medieval Jewish life in both the Christian and Muslim orbits is Mark R. Cohen, *Under Crescent and Cross* (Princeton, N.J., 1994). On their respective attitudes towards Judaism and Jewish law, cf. chapter 2, "Religions in Conflict," 17-29.

[4] The Qur'an regards both Moses and Jesus as true prophets who paved the way for

Muhammad, "the seal of prophecy" (*hatim al-anbiya'i*), who restored the original true religion inspired by Abraham—ancestor to the Arabs, as well as to the Jews.

[5] The term is attributed to Salo W. Baron.

[6] Goitein, S.D., *Jews and Arabs* (New York, 1964), *passim.*, and Bernard Lewis, *The Jews of Islam* (Princeton, N.J. 1984). For a critique of the concept, cf. Steven M. Wasserstrom, *Between Muslim and Jew; The Problem of Symbiosis Under Early Islam* (Princeton, N.J., 1995).

[7] Cf. Bat Ye'or, *The Dhimmi: Jews and Christians Under Islam* (Rutherford, N.J., 1985).

[8] So were Christians and even Zoroastrians. The basis for their mutual designation was their designation in the Qur'an as "people of the book" (*ahl al-kitab*), which signified their religious organization under the guidance of a revealed scripture.

[9] Cf. "The Pact of Umar," in Norman Stillman, *Jews of Arab Lands* (Philadelphia, 1979), Vol. I, 157-8.

[10] Hava Lazarus-Yafeh, *Intertwined Worlds: Medieval Islam and Bible Criticism* (Princeton, N.J., 1992), Chapter One.

[11] *Teshuvot ha-Rambam*, ed. Joshua Blau (Jerusalem, 1986), vol 1, 284-85; vol 2, 726.

[12] Responsa 149.

[13] Responsa 448.

[14] *Mishneh Torah, Hilkhot Ma'akhalot Assurot* 11:7.

[15] The second occurred in Yemen and is treated in Rambam's *Iggeret Teiman*. The third transpired in the Iranian city of Meshhed in 1839.See Raphael Patai, *Jadid al-Islam: The Jewish New Muslims of Meshhed* (Detroit, 1997).

[16] They denied the independent existence of the attributes of God as incompatible with his unity, and therefore polytheistic. To place their activities in perspective, it should be noted that they did not reserve their zeal for Jews; they expended a great deal of their invective on fellow Muslims (particularly the al-Moravid [alMurabitun] dynasty) whom they regarded as doctrinally deficient.

[17] H. Soloveitchik, "Maimonides's *Iggeret ha-Shemad*: Law and Rhetoric," in *Rabbi Joseph H. Lookstein Memorial Volume* (New York, 1980), 306. Soloveitchik's position is disputed by David Hartman in his discussion of the letter. *Crisis and Leadership*, 46 ff.

[18] All citations are from *Crisis and Leadership*; the page numbers appear in ( ) following each selection.

[19] *Avot* 2:4.

[20] Individual Jews had already converted to Islam during the lifetime of Muhammad. They brought with them a knowledge of Biblical and post-Biblical (i.e., Talmudic and Midrashic) tradition that is reflected—albeit, at times, indistinctly—in the Qur'an and the Hadith, the corpus of legends about Muhammad that supplements the Qur'an in matters of faith and practice. A number of these Jews are known by name, including Ka'b al-Ahbar [Hebrew: חבר, an honorific title] and Wahb Ibn Munabbih, who were responsible for the genre of Hadith known as *Isra'iliyyat*, legends about Jews.

21 In Arabic, Muhammad is called *rasul Allah*, the "apostle" of Allah. Jews (even while writing in Arabic) habitually punned on the title, calling him *pasul*, or disqualified. Halkin manufactured the word *"prepostle,"* a combination of preposterous and apostle, that retains the linguistic flavor of the Hebrew original.

22 Together, Abu Bakr, Umar, Uthman and Ali are known as *al-Khulafa' al-Rashidun*, the rightly guided Caliphs, thereby distinguishing them from all their successors.

23 Bernard Lewis, *The Arabs in History* (New York, 1966), 67.

24 Note the following excerpt from a report by USA Today, dated 4/23/2003:

> Karbala is the site of the seventh-century martyrdom of Hussein Ibn Ali, a grandson of the prophet Mohammed. The pilgrimage marks the end of the traditional 40-day mourning period that Shiites observe each year to mark his death.Shiites see Hussein and his father, Ali, as the rightful heirs to the prophet. The battle in which Hussein was killed was one in a series of violent clashes between Sunnis, who dispute the Ali-Hussein claim, and Shiites.Saddam [Hussein], a Sunni, ordered the killing of thousands of Shiites during his time in power. He banned mass pilgrimages and the flagellations that some Shiites endure to show their grief over the killing of Hussein. Ali, the father, is buried in Najaf.
>
> www.usatoday.com/news/world/iraq/2003-04-22-shiite-pilgrimage_x.htm

25 Cf. Yitzhak Nakash, *The Shi'is of Iraq* (Princeton, N.J., 1994), 59.

26 Cf. Hava Lazarus-Yaffe, "Al ha-Ra'ayon ha-Mishihi be-Islam," in *Mishihiut ve-Esketologiah* (Jerusalem, 1984), 169 ff.

27 Such a descendant is called an *Imam*. (Sunnis use the term to designate a prayer leader.) The extensive doctrine of the "twelfth" Imam, and its current use by Islamists in Iran, Iraq and Lebanon, is another of the several significant links between early Muslim history and current Middle Eastern events.

28 Cf. Israel Friedlaender, "Jewish-Arabic Studies: Shi'ite Elements in Jewish Sectarianism," *JQR* (NS) 1 (1910-11): 183-215; 2 (1911-12): 481-516; 3 (1912-13): 235-300. On "ordinary" messianic expectations of Jews living in the orbit of Islam, see S. D. Goitein, "Meeting in Jerusalem: Messianic Expectations in Letters of the Cairo Geniza," *AJS Review* 4 (1979): 43-57.

29 Mordekhai Akiva Friedman, *Ha-Rambam, ha-Mashiah be-Teiman, ve-ha-Shemad* (Jerusalem, 5762), 158.

30 A survey of false messianism can be found in the *Jewish Encyclopedia*, s.v. "Pseudo-Messiahs."

31 Arab sources date him according to the reign of the Ummayad Caliph, 'Abd al-Malik ibn Marwan (684-705).

32 A reference to the legendary river *Sambatyon* [related to the noun Sabbath], which was believed to surround the territory of several of the lost tribes of Israel. The river is better known from the legend of *Eldad ha-Dani* who, as his name indicates, maintained his descent from the tribe of Dan [see Elkan N. Adler, *Jewish Travellers* (New York, 1966), 4 ff.]. It also features in the title of a recent book on the search, in northern India, for

the remnants of the tribe of Menasheh, cf. Hillel Halkin, *Across the Sabbath River* (New York, 2002).

[33] The belief that the Messiah would be a cured leper was based on the verse (Isaiah 53:4): "Surely our diseases he did bear, and our pains he carried; whereas we did esteem him stricken, smitten of God, and afflicted."

[34] In the actual historical sequence of messianic appearances, Abu Issa was followed early in the eighth century by his disciple, Yudghan [Persian for Yehudah] of Hamadan [also in Persia], who taught his followers an ascetic regimen including no meat or wine, frequent prayer and fast days. Another early eighth century pretender was named Sereni (or Serenus, Sheria or Sonoria). Motivated, perhaps, by increased proselytization under the Caliph Omar II and a heavy tax burden imposed on the Jews of Spain, he promised to rid the land of Israel of Muslims and restore it to the Jews.

[35] It should be noted that Rambam's authorship of these four episodes [al-Isfahani, al-Darri, ibn Arieh and Lyons] is questioned by some scholars on several grounds. They appear as a coda to but a single manuscript, they utilize language and literary forms uncharacteristic of him, and—as we see here—depict the events in an entirely too sympathetic fashion.

[36] This was regarded as a messianic portent, based upon the verse in Joel 3:3:"And I will show wonders in the heavens and in the earth, blood, and fire, and pillars of smoke."

[37] This ability was believed to be a messianic portent, based on Daniel 7:13-14.

[38] The doctrine of the "hidden Messiah"—acknowledged with regard to Abu Issa and Yudghan as well—is also well-known among Shi'ites, particularly among the "twelvers" (cf. n. 21, above).

[39] See Gerson D. Cohen, "Messianic Postures of Ashkenazim and Sephardim," in *Studies of the Leo Baeck Institute* (1967).

[40] S.D. Goitein, who has studied the question from the vantage point of thousands of documents from the Cairo Genizah, writes: "The preceding survey demonstrates that the belief in the sudden and miraculous appearance of the Messiah was a fact of life. The great event had to be miraculous, not natural, because thus it was foretold by the prophets and expounded in minute detail by the theologians, especially Saadya Gaon, whose writings dominated most of the Geniza period." *A Mediterranean Society*, vol. V (California, 1988): 397.

[41] Based upon Habakuk 2:3: "For the vision is yet for the appointed time, and it declareth of the end, and doth not lie; though it tarry, wait for it; because it will surely come, it will not delay."

[42] The Ephraimites began their calculations with the *berit bein ha-betarim* (Genesis 15) rather than with the birth of Isaac 30 years later. This discrepancy is also cited to account for the contradiction between the "promise" of 400 years and the "actual" sojourn in Egypt, which is reported in Exodus 12:40 to have been 430 years.

[43] Rambam cites Psalms 78:9 for the fate of the Ephraimites:

> The children of Ephraim were as archers handling the bow, that turned back in the day of battle.

In the Midrash (*Mekhilta* 13:17 [ed. Rabin p. 76]), it is derived from I Chronicles 7:21:

Whom the men of Gat that were born in the land slew... And Ephraim
their father mourned many days.

It is widely assumed that the legend of Messiah ben Joseph (a military leader who is
destined to die preparing the way for Messiah ben David) derives from the presumptive
Ephraimite experience.

[44] Daniel 12:9: "And he said: 'Go thy way, Daniel; for the words are shut up and sealed
till the time of the end.'"

[45] *Sanhedrin* 97b: "May calculators of the end come to grief."

[46] *Berakhot* 54a, *inter alia.*

[47] "Remember, God has informed us through Isaiah... that the prolongation of the
adversities of exile will impel many of our people to believe that God has relinquished and
abandoned us—far be it from Him—but He assured us that He would not abandon and
would not relinquish us..." (120-121).

[48] Based on Joel 3:1: "And it shall come to pass afterward, that I will pour out My spirit
upon all flesh, and your sons and your daughters shall prophesy..."

[49] There are those who maintain that the entire passage is an outside interpolation into
the *Iggeret* and not original to Rambam at all! In addition to the internal inconsistencies
between this tradition and Rambam's stalwart reluctance to countenance any such
calculations, they point to the fact that what is presented here as a "family" tradition is
actually an explicit passage in the Jerusalem Talmud *Shabbat* 6:9 (43a) and was cited by
at least two of Rambam's contemporaries, R. Judah Barceloni and R. Abraham bar Hiyya.
Cf. *Crisis and Leadership*, p. 145, n. 223, and Rabinowitz, p. 174, n. a.

[50] Illustrating the complexity of messianic calculations, there are several versions of
the text of the *Iggeret* at this point and, consequently, several different outcomes to the
calculation. In addition to the version reproduced here by Hartman and Halkin, there
is the translation of Samuel Ibn Tibbon, who reckons the vision of Balaam to have been
in the fortieth year after the Exodus, corresponding to 2488 AM. That would render
the restoration of prophecy in 4976 AM=1216 CE. The matter is rendered even more
confusing by the fact that Halkin, in his critical edition of the *Iggeret* and its Hebrew
translations (New York, 1952), hews consistently to 1216!

[51] Rambam did respond to a request by Ibn Jabbar, a student of the academy in Baghdad,
to reply to the criticisms of the dean of the academy, R. Samuel ben Ali, but the relative
sequence of the two responses is not unambiguous.

[52] *Sanhedrin* 99a.

[53] See Ramban, *Kitvei ha-Ramban, Torat ha-Adam: Sha'ar ha-Gemul* (Jerusalem, 1964),
vol. II, 295 ff. Also see R. Meir ha-Levi Abolafia (Ramah), in his commentary, *Yad Ramah*,
to the Talmud in *Sanhedrin* and in a series of letters on the subject that he wrote to the
scholars of Lunel in Provence.

[54] The debate concerns the following passage in *Berakhot* 17 a:

> Rav would recite a pearl [of wisdom]: The World to Come does not resemble
> this world. In the World to Come there is not eating, drinking, intercourse,
> business, jealousy, enmity, or competition. Rather, the righteous are seated

with crown upon their heads and enjoy the luminescence of the Presence [of God]. To wit: "They viewed God, ate and drank" (Exodus 24:11).

[55] See Rambam's treatment of this passage in *Hilkhot Teshuvah* 8:2.

[56] *Sefer ha-Ikkarim* 4:35.

[57] *Sanhedrin* 10:1.

[58] Sa'adyah devotes the entire seventh treatise of *Emunot ve-De'ot* to resurrection. There are two versions of this treatise extant; we have utilized the one that appears in *The Book of Beliefs and Opinions*, ed. Samuel Rosenblatt (New Haven, 1948), 264. In addition to dealing with the sources of the doctrine in the Bible and Talmud, Sa'adyah discusses the physics of resurrection: how the dead will be dressed, will they be resurrected with the same physical infirmities they had while alive, will they be recognizable to relatives and to one another, and what will they do thereafter.

[59] Similarly, in enumerating 24 categories of individuals who, although Jewish, have no share in the world to come (*Hilkhot Teshuvah* 3:6), Rambam lists: "those who deny the resurrection of the dead" (*ha-koferim bi-t'hiyat ha-metim*).

[60] *Berakhot* (17a). The reference to "radiance" is highly reminiscent of the work of Dr. Raymond Moody on "near-death," one of whose characteristic features is known as the "tunnel" experience, which is described as: "being drawn into darkness through a tunnel, at an extremely high speed, until reaching a realm of radiant golden-white light." Several of Moody's observations (*Life after Life* [1975]) are related to resurrection by Marc Angel, "Life after Death," *Body and Soul in Judaism* (New York, 1991), 10-13. Angel bases his article on a lengthy essay by R. Hayim David Halevi in *Aseh Lekha Rav* (Jerusalem, 1978), vol. II, 17-94.

[61] *Hilkhot Teshuvah* 8:2.

[62] Angels, of course, are incorporeal and have no need to fortify themselves with food and drink. Elijah was able to survive with little sustenance during his 40 day sojourn at Mt. Horeb—just as Moses was able to do atop Mt. Sinai—because God ostensibly granted them supernatural good health.

[63] *Ra'avad, Hilkhot Teshuvah* 8:2.

[64] *Hilkhot Yesodei ha-Torah* 1:11. In the *Guide*, Rambam asserts that on account of God's incorporeality such phrases as "God spoke" are metaphorical. God "communicates" in a manner that we, accustomed to verbal communication, assume to be audible speech. In truth, however, it could well transpire through an inarticulate medium, such as we call "mental telepathy."

ORAL LAW AS INSTITUTION IN MAIMONIDES*

Gerald J. Blidstein

I

In the course of his investigation of the concept *"Torah min ha-Shamayyim,"* Abraham Heschel pointed out that Maimonides rejected the notion that the Oral Torah in its entirety was delivered by God to man at Sinai.[1] Maimonides stresses the rabbinic, human authorship of much of the Oral Tradition. The claim that the entire Oral Torah was given at Sinai is, of course, an aggadic claim; it is, perhaps, the dominant aggadic claim about the origins of the tradition. The actual content of this claim is none too clear, and we would be wise in not reading it in a one-dimensional literal fashion. But whatever it does mean, this claim was staked out in the language of heavenly origins. Maimonides, in contrast, does not present his claim as to the tradition's significance in this aggadic language.

Actually, this is not quite the case; snatches of these *aggadot* do enter into his presentations, as we shall see. But even when they do appear, they seem pallid or pared down as compared to their originals, and they are balanced off, often immediately, by contrasting statements on rabbinic authorship. The Maimonidean thrust, then, is not in the direction of Sinai as the origin of the Tradition in its entirety, either as a literal description or as a rhetorical device. Indeed, by refusing to read the *aggadah* as rhetoric, Maimonides is forced to read it (or to use it) as history; and as history it must be whittled down to realistic and rational dimensions.

---

* In Memory of Sandy Braverman. Originally published in *The Thought of Moses Maimonides: Philosophical and Legal Studies*, eds. Ira Robinson, Lawrence Kaplan, Julien Bauer (Lewiston, N.Y.:Edwin Mellen Press, 1990), 167-182.

Actually, the proper foil for the Maimonidean presentation is not the aggadic tradition *per se*, but rather the uses to which this tradition was put by Maimonides' contemporaries and the broader debate of which this was a part. The central questions, then, will be: What are the historical and intellectual implications of Maimonides' rejection of the claim that the Tradition, in its entirety, is from Sinai? And, second, what alternative sanction did Maimonides provide for the Tradition once its heavenly source was compromised?

II

Let us first survey the ways in which the idea of the rabbinic authorship of Oral Tradition is expressed in Maimonides' halakhic work and sensibility. Indeed, the deployment of this idea indicates that we are justified in describing it as an element in Maimonides' halakhic sensibility, and not merely as a detail of technical significance.

(1) The term *torah she-be'al peh* (Oral Law) is used in a number of different ways by Maimonides, but he makes it clear that in its most precise sense the term describes the Sinaitic Oral Law alone, as distinguished from the body of traditional law created by the rabbis. Thus, rabbinic law is set over the divine Oral Law at the basic level of terminology.[2]

(2) Maimonides takes great pains to categorize the Oral Law in terms of its origins—its different and varied origins. Here the idea of rabbinic authorship is pinned down in very concrete ways. Alongside the Oral Law delivered to Moses at Sinai as explanation of Scripture or as supplementary to it, we have the rabbinic exposition of Scripture (*midrash*) and rabbinic legislation (*takkanot* and *gezerot*). We are not concerned, at the moment, with the varied uses to which Maimonides puts his catalogue of origins nor with the vexing question as to how origins determine halakhic status; we rest satisfied with the fact of varied origins alone. We also note the scope of Maimonides' interest in the topic, which was pursued throughout his life and was expressed in his major halakhic writings. Central segments of the Introduction to his Mishnah Commentary, as well as the first two of the Principles upon which the *Sefer ha-Mizvot* is structured, are devoted to this issue. *Mishneh Torah*, seemingly a code distinguished by its seamless anonymity, doggedly categorized the specifics of the Oral Law according to their Sinaitic or rabbinic origins.[3]

(3) Scripture, in a number of places, warns that nothing may be

added to its norms just as nothing may be subtracted from them. The Talmudic tradition to which Maimonides is heir refuses to read these prescriptions as threats to the rabbinic enterprise itself (so ready to add its enactments to the biblical law), understanding *bal tosif* on the level of individual observance only: a Jew must not add a string to the required number of *zizit*, and so on. (From a systematic point of view, this Talmudic reading is, of course, fully justified. Since God, in the rabbinic tradition, has commanded the rabbis to legislate beyond the Scripural norm, he cannot also demand that nothing be added to Scripture!) Karaites, on the other hand, found these verses to be a perfect weapon in their battle with the rabbinic Oral Law. Maimonides decides to confront the issue head-on in his Code: in a most paradoxical fashion he claims that so long as the addition to Scriptural norm is clearly identified as rabbinic, one has not violated the terms of Scripture. The issue is virtually set on its head; it is the *identity* of revelation that is to be protected, not its *singularity*, and the more blatantly the non-Scriptural law is identified as such—the less it offends. All this is possible only for a sensibility that has absorbed the distinction between rabbinic and Sinaitic law at a very basic level.[4]

(4) Another central Karaite argument revolves around the existence of *mahloket*, the thousands of disagreements found in rabbinic texts: these are certainly proof that the rabbinic tradition is not sacred, since it is not divine. Maimonides' reply relies once again on the question of origins: disagreements will be found, he claims, only within the range of law authored by rabbis themselves. That which was bestowed at Sinai has been transmitted intact.[5] Once again the fact of rabbinic authorship functions for Maimonides in a powerful and decisive way.

III

The picture I have sketched is not exactly novel, as we shall yet see, but it is also not a commonplace. Indeed, ever since David Nieto,[6] Maimonides has been portrayed as a conventional figure on the issue of Oral Law, one more distinguished apologist in the rabbinate camp.[7] This portrayal draws, fundamentally, on two Maimonidean positions. First, Maimonides does seemingly repeat midrashic claims as to the revelation of the Oral Law in its entirety to Moses. Second, Maimonides on *mahloket* asserts that Sinaitic Oral Law was transmitted intact. In so doing, he deliberately and pointedly rejects the geonic view that blocs of Oral Law were forgotten, with disagreements being engendered in the struggle to recapture the original tradition. Maimonides, on the contrary, argues for the purity of the Tradition and rejects the view that its transmission was subject to normal human lapses and failings. In taking this position (for its anti-Karaite value), Maimonides thus renders ever more formidable the fortress of divine Oral Law.

I cannot analyze, in this limited context, all the texts in which Maimonides seemingly reproduces the midrashic claim. Let me state, so as to balance my continued stress on the idea of the rabbinic authorship of law, that Maimonides does announce over and over again that Oral Law was given at Sinai and that Moses received the law's interpretation as well as its text. The Code itself, in hundreds of cases, notes that a given interpretation of Scripture is "of the tradition," and what is doubtless meant is "of Mosaic tradition."[8] This attribution runs a distinct, if minor, counterpoint through the entire Code; it cannot be missed. Yet that is still not the heart of the matter, and despite the quantity of such assertions, I would argue that Maimonides side-steps the crux of the midrashic claim, which is that the Oral Law *in its entirety* is Sinaitic.[9] By stating, for example, that "each command given to Moses by God was given with its explanation...everything contained by that wondrous verse" was delivered to Moses, Maimonides does not exactly enter the midrashic claim intact and whole. For the basic questions remains unanswered: What did the verse and its explanation contain? In a sense, Maimonides' statement is a tautology; it says no more than that the text contained what it contained. More significantly, Maimonides' massive stress on rabbinic authorship of Scriptural exposition (*midrash*) contrasts bluntly with a conventional reading of such texts—and this is the heart of the Maimonidean position. As he himself notes, "the majority of the law ... is derived from the thirteen modes of Scriptural interpretation,"[10] and this is clearly law authored by rabbis in their exposition of Scripture; it is law about which rabbis may disagree.

Much the same is true of Maimonides' treatment of *mahloket*. The crucial point here is *not* his insistence that no part of the true Sinaitic tradition was forgotten, but rather that this tradition is a limited component of the Jewish heritage, and that much of this heritage is not Sinaitic at all, but is subject to the normal human processes of argument. In effect, Maimonides does not seem to counter the Karaite challenge at all; indeed he seems to concede its major point—that the presence of disagreement in the rabbinic tradition proves that it is not revealed, not sacred. We shall of course return to this major problem further on. At this point, though, we wish to note that Maimonides mounts, in essence, a frontal attach on geonic tactics by responding as he does.

The geonic position, to recapitulate, was that the Oral Law was given in its entirety at Sinai, and that subsequent rabbinic activity was an attempt to recover aspects of the tradition lost by forgetfulness or error. More broadly, the geonic position would deny all novelty in rabbinic literature; this literature either restores what was lost, expounds what is implied, or formulates what is universally known—all these are the basic posture of Sherira's *Iggeret*, for example. Sa'adyah will even say that no creative rabbinic *midrash* exists, that *midrash* relates to the Bible as rules of grammar relate to the text from which they are drawn. The *Iggeret*, again, does not mention the possibility of rabbinic legislation.[11] Maimonides rejects these positions one by one: rabbinic Midrash does create law; rabbinic legislation does exist; rabbis disagree because they are working out problems on their own. "The notion that even law given at Sinai is subject to *mahloket*...due to error or forgetfulness...is—by God—perverse, peculiar, and incorrect... Those holding this worthless idea were brought to it by their defective grasp of Talmud..." True, Maimonides will, more generously, suggest that geonic description of halakhic facts are sometimes polemical and apologetic, and that the *geonim* knew better themselves.[12] Similarly, we wonder whether we do not read the *geonim* too simple-mindedly or too literally. The idea of forgetful sages hardly seems to be useful in polemical argument, after all. More profoundly, the implication that the Talmud is a project whose certain conclusions can never be more than hopeful, unconfirmable approximation of a forgotten revelation is, indeed, a provocative and surprising image. But all this aside, the Maimonidean message is clear: the geonic description of the Tradition—perhaps a transformation of aggadic rhetoric into literal descriptive prose—is rejected. The security offered by the belief that the entire tradition is God-given must be abandoned. In a sense, Maimonides rejects halakhic *kalaam*.

IV

Though Maimonides has often been placed in the geonic camp, his views on rabbinic authority of Law have also been appreciated. Heschel was not the first to realize that Maimonides rejected either the aggadic ideology or its language. I wish to survey briefly the career of this aspect of Maimonidean scholarship which, as we shall see, throws at least as much light on the scholars surveyed as it does on Maimonides himself.

We may well begin with Nahmanides. Although he certainly does not hit our nail squarely on its head, Ramban relates to the Maimonidean posture in two, somewhat contrasting, ways. First of all, he is displeased with the ostensible *status* of law derived from midrashic methods. In the Maimonidean view, rabbinic *midrash* is a human enterprise, and so its results will not have Scriptural status. This upsets the Talmudic system, Ramban claims, and it is difficult to know whether he refers to the academic dialectics of the Talmud or to its religious sensibility—in which case he would be pointing to the antinomian dangers implied by the Maimonidean assertion.[13] But Ramban also learns from Maimonides, I believe. His own view of rabbinic *midrash* is that it in fact creates law with Scriptural status. This carries him beyond Maimonides, but it may also reflect the permission granted by Maimonides to see the rabbi as creative. For the Scriptural status of rabbinically derived law is not achieved by assuming that they recapture in some way what was originally revealed at Sinai, but by asserting that their reading of Scripture becomes the normative reading. Ramban himself offers a number of explanations for his posture, but there is no reason to overlook its Maimonidean coloration.[14] Nahmanides' view of the authority of the Great Court as base of its institutional status ("for the Torah was given...according to the Court's understanding of it"),[14a] rather than on its charismatic infallibility, certainly owes much to Maimonides, as we shall see.

Subsequent comments on the Maimonidean posture tend to become more pointed as we approach the modern era. The seventeenth century Rabbi Yair Bachrach complained that although Maimonides attempted to defend the Oral Law, he achieved the opposite result, "for practically the entire Mishnah is not from Sinai" in his presentation.[15] It is difficult to know whether Bachrach was concerned with any actual historical threat or simply evaluated Maimonides' system in terms of its own announced goals. But Bachrach's younger contemporary David Nieto was clearly involved in actual polemic with erstwhile Marranos when he strenuously denied that Maimonides allowed the rabbi any significant role in creating Jewish law. It is difficult to understand how Nieto missed so much in Maimonides, but it is safe to say that he understood to what uses an admission of human rabbinic authorship would be put.[16]

It may well be the case that my choice of the term "human" as the proper implication of the term "rabbinic" is anachronistic for much of the medieval period; the contrast between the "heavenly" and the "human" may reflect a modern sensibility and its problems more than it faithfully interprets our medieval authors. But this reading is clearly adopted in the nineteenth century by the Italian Isaac Samuel Reggio. Reggio was an advocate of moderate reform, opposing both the extreme Aaron Chorin as well as the defenders of every rabbinic custom. His statements on Maimonides often seem inaccurate (and contradictory); actually, they are exaggerations of points that possess some validity if taken generally and modestly. Reggio attacks Maimonides for duly stressing the Sinaitic origin of the Oral Law, as though Maimonides invented the doctrine.[17] But in his *Torah and Philosophy* Reggio wrote:

> The contents of the Mishnah are not of uniform status...some matters are traditions held for Moses our Master...others are laws rationally derived, hence one finds disagreement about them; some are enactments made by prophets and the Patriarchs of every generation; and some enactments of the Sages. And Maimonides has already explained this at length...

> Now consider, wise reader, how much we must labor so as not to confound the divine matter with the human, and just as the Torah has distinguished the holy and the profane, so too must we devote all our energies to distinguishing the traditions that derive from a divine source...from those produced by argumentation...and we shall be able to do this if we are attentive to the rule laid by Maimonides...[18]

Reggio draws out to the full the Maimonidean distinction between the Sinaitic and the rabbinic, and he parallels this distinction with another one, that between the heavenly and the human. All this, of course, is not of academic interest alone—it has become a tool for moderate religious reform. Reggio asserts in his *Behinat ha-Dat* that "we must cleanse the Divine Laws from all accretions, so that they become sacred," though that which is Divine Torah must not be tampered with.[19] Maimonides thus becomes a model figure in the attempt to maintain a balance between the inviolability of the Law and its reform.

The twentieth century has seen similar approaches. We opened by noting Heschel's reference to Maimonides. M.S. Feldblum of Bar Ilan University is more explicit. The assertion that "all details go back to Sinaitic tradition," he notes, "minimizes the value of investigating the historical and socio-economic forces that may have been important factors in the shaping of the *halakhah*." For Maimonides, on the other hand, "more than 90% of the Oral Law as we know it is a product of the halakhic process," and recognition of this fact ought to enable the rabbinate to "more easily assimilate the results of modern scholarship." It is fairly clear that Feldblum's thrust is not toward the proper understanding of the role of historical forces in shaping *halakhah* as an academic enterprise alone, but towards the possibility that this Maimonidean perspective will affect concrete decision-making. Thus, he suggests that the vexed issue of disqualified witnesses (on which center other issue such as "marriages, divorces, and conversions as well as the issue of the ordination of women in the Conservative movement") would be handled more flexibly if the varied origins of such disqualification could be considered.[20]

V

Having seen the ideological impact of Maimonides' ideas on some modern traditionalists, let us return to Maimonides himself. Early on in this discussion I stated that our central questions would be about the historical and intellectual implications of the Maimonidean position and what alternative sanction he provided for the Tradition once its heavenly source was compromised. We have already seen, as partial answer to our first question, that taken in his own terms and period, Maimonides mounted a frontal attack against the geonic version of the origin of the Oral Law. But we also know that the version was meant to counter the Karaite claim that the rabbinic tradition had no roots and was a patent fabrication. Maimonides, now, seems to accept that Karaite claim by urging the concept of rabbinic authorship; in asserting that rabbinic authorship explains the plethora of rabbinic arguments, Maimonides seems to win the battle but lose the war.

Maimonides, I believe, was moved by a combination of strategic and intellectual considerations. First, he was saying, I think, that the geonic position was based on Karaitic premises, thus conceding the case before it began its counter-argument, so to speak. By claiming that the entire Oral Law was literally Sinaitic, a most difficult assertion to sustain convincingly, rabbanites accepted the Karaitic premise that *only* that which had heavenly historical origins was sacred, significant, normative, and obligatory. But the Tradition itself as revealed in the Talmud did not make this assumption. Maimonides urged rabbanites, therefore, to break loose of the Karaite model ideologically, to neutralize it, just as they hardly accepted it halakhically. We may even proceed one step further: the Karaite assertion that only ancient revelation bestowed legitimacy is an apt assertion for a young revolutionary movement; it makes it the equal of its older traditional rival, and indeed gives it the upper hand, for it has no inexcusable spiritual debris to explain. But let the older tradition argue that sanctity also devolves on that which has developed through the centuries, that spiritual wealth is accumulated through the ages—and its younger rival is put on the defensive. This was what Maimonides may have been doing as *his* answer to the Karaite challenge.

Second, Maimonides rejected the geonic model because it was intellectually untenable in terms of the Talmudic literary tradition. Whatever certain *aggadot* said, the Talmud taken as a whole, the warp and woof of its thousands of pages and myriad discussions, said the opposite. The very structure of halakhic decision-making is reared on the distinction between the Scriptural and rabbinic, though this distinction is sometimes hard to pin down in specific cases. Maimonides found it impossible, I believe, to silence this testimony. He even insisted that the halakhic structures themselves, rather than the aggadic brethren, serve as ideological counters, that the Tradition be presented halakhically and not rhetorically, with all the intellectual maturity that such a step demanded. For it was no small matter to announce that the Oral Law was not delivered, in its entirety, to Moses.

How, in fact, did Maimonides hope to convince Jews that the entire Oral Law obliged them, even if much of it was of human invention? The aggadic claim, whatever its defects, possessed profound religious logic and superb psychological power, as a Maimonidean contemporary like Halevi understood full well.[21] Indeed, one may well concede at the start that the Maimonidean answer, however satisfying systemically, must fight an uphill battle to convince religiously. Briefly put, Maimonides argued that the Oral Tradition is an institutional structure, and that what legitimates it is neither its content nor its heavenly origin. It is anchored in Sinai and legitimated by the Sinaitic imperative that quickened it and called it to life. From that original Sinaitic moment on, it is sanctioned by the rules that govern it. Rather than argue this claim explicitly and in these abstract terms, Maimonides—in typical halakhic mode—presents the Oral Tradition and its processes in this perspective, and leaves the interpretation to us.

The linchpin in this structure is the Sanhedrin, the Great Court, and the system it engenders and authenticates. The Sanhedrin does not merely *function*, as it does even in its Mishnaic description as that "from which Teaching goes forth to all Israel;" it is reified and made into the "incarnation" of Oral Law: [22]

> The Great Sanhedrin of Jerusalem is the root of the Oral Law. The members thereof are the pillars of instructions; from them go forth statutes and judgments to all Israel....Whoever believes in Moses our teacher and his law, is bound to ground the act of religion on them.

Moreover, *all* pronouncements of the Court are of equal weight, all sustained by the biblical verse which commands obedience, its enactment is as normative as its interpretation of Scripture—a position rejected by many other halakhists, incidentally.[23] Maimonides is fond of reminding us that the blessing on rabbinic ordinances ("Blessed be our Lord...who has sanctified us with His commands and commanded us to light the Hanukkah candles," for instance) really means that God has commanded us to obey the Sages who have, in their turn, commanded us to light the candles.[24] The structure is divine, not the content; but the content is thereby sanctified. The Sadducees, Maimonides tells us, "doubted the Tradition and explained Scripture as each saw fit, without being subject to any Sages at all, despite God's command, 'According to the law which they teach you...'"[25] The last phrase is most telling; for only by his institutional authentication does the Pharisee-Rabbanite differ from the Sadducee-Karaite.

Indeed, the basic characteristic of the Oral Law, its non-reducibility to a written text, was designed (claims Maimonides) to mesh with this institutional structure. For a written law is available to all, engendering the divisive sects which compete in their differing interpretations of the law. But an Oral Law must remain the possession of those who teach it to their chosen disciples, thus guaranteeing a necessary accord. The oral-ness of Oral Tradition, then, is an instrument of institutional control.[26]

We are now in a position to re-evaluate the famous Maimonidean discussion of Prophet and Sage, and his insistence that only the Sage may enter the halakhic process.[27] This distinction has often been read as another expression of Maimonidean rationalism, as Maimonides again prefers the discursive Sage to the irrational Prophet. Yet Maimonides hardly disavows revelation as an instrument of legislation. The distinction has also been read as an expression of Maimonidean respect for individual judgment as over against authoritarian ukase (a point that goes well the first reading, of course). But whatever processes utilized by the Sage himself, he demands obedience no less than his prophetic counterpart.[28]

The perspective developed in our discussion allows a different reading of the Maimonidean insistence that only the Sage engage in the halakhic process. The statement is basically sociological, or better yet, reflects the sociology of knowledge. The Sage is not reason; he is institution. And the prophet is not unreason—he is the individual who is not authenticated by any institution. Recall that the Sage has a double function; he engages in rational discussion but he is also a link in the transmission of the inherited tradition to a next generation. Both functions are equally significant and both require institutional frameworks. (Indeed, it may well be that Maimonides defends the purity of the Sinaitic Oral Law not so much for the sake of that Law but for the sake of its tridents: were *they* guilty of lapses then *nothing* they did would be credible.) The prophet fulfills neither function of the Sages: first, he does not engage in discussion, or demonstrate his truth to his community. He also need not *receive* a tradition from his masters because he has direct access to the source of tradition; nor will he transmit this traditional knowledge to his disciples, each of whom will be prophet in his own right. It is this fundamentally sociological demand that Maimonides makes, then; it is the demon of the charismatic individual, who does not function within normative institutions, which he exorcises from the halakhic process. I would not go so far as to say that the tradition exists to preserve the institution, rather than the reverse. But we must admit that each contributes to the viability and the content of the other.

Maimonides' posture is historically and temperamentally appropriate. From a historical perspective, he is challenging the Karaites rather than responding to them as the *geonim* had done. By explicating the Oral Tradition as an institutional structure, and by asserting that God had commanded this structure and indeed founded it, he asserted that the Karaites, who lacked such a structure (and indeed prided themselves on that lack), were religiously delinquent and were ignoring a basic requirement of Judaism. Indirectly, he is accusing geonic orthodoxy of allowing itself to be placed in a defensive position which was both difficult to maintain intellectually and inattentive to the basic reality of Talmudic literature. Finally, the heavily authoritative nature of institutionalized law seems to be an appropriate expression of the Maimonidean temperament, which recognizes full well the need for social and religious control over an often backsliding humanity.

---

[1] A. Heschel, *Torah Min ha-Shamayyim ba-Aspaklariyyat ha-Dorot* (Heb.) II (London, 1965), 231-233; Heschel neglects to point out, though, that much Oral Law is Sinaitic for Maimonides.

[2] *Introduction to Mishneh Torah*, ed. Y Cohen (Jerusalem, 1964), 1, lines 1-9; *Hilkhot Mamrim* 1:2, 3:1-3. "Oral Law" will, of course, also be used in the broader sense of the entire non-Scriptural tradition: *Introduction*, line 164; *Hilkhot Mamrim* 1:1, *Hilkhot Talmud Torah* 1:13; *Hilkhot Tefillah* 7:10.

[3] Maimonides' distinction between Sinaitic and non-Sinaitic tradition will function as the conceptual framework of this paper. The idea of Sinaitic tradition could itself be the subject of scrutiny, both in terms of the philosophical problematics of the meaning of revelation for Maimonides in general, and in terms of a number of distinct problems raised by various Maimonidean statements on biblical law, the relationship of Sinaitic tradition to the "plain sense" of biblical texts, and so on. Nonetheless, the texts discussed in this paper are all predicated on the distinction of Sinaitic and non-Sinaitic tradition, and I believe that they can be discussed meaningfully within this framework.

[4] *Hilkhot Mamrim* 2:9. For a survey of the Talmudic references, see, *Enzyklopedia Talmudit* (Heb.), 3:326-330. Other medievals treated the matter much as one would expect from the perspective of the rabbinic materials; see R. Yehudah ha-Levi, *Kuzari*, 3:40-41; Ra'abad at *Hilkhot Mamrim* 2:9, and others. It should be noted, however, that ha-Levi does adopt the Maimonidean solution in *Kuzari* 3:51.

[5] *Introduction to Commentary on the Mishnah; Hilkhot Mamrim* 1:3.

[6] See note 16 *infra*.

[7] See, e.g., M. Zucker, "Le-Ba'ayat ha-Mahloket," *S. Baron Jubilee Volume* (Heb.) (Jerusalem, 1975); Y. Faur, *Iyyunim be-Mishneh Torah la-Rambam* (Heb.) (Jerusalem, 1978), 80-98; Y. Levinger, in U. Simon, ed. *Ha-Mikra ve-Anahnu* (Tel Aviv, 1979), 120-132, and in *Darkhei ha-Mahshava ha-Hilkhatit Shel ha-Rambam* (Jerusalem, 1965), 65.

[8] See *Hilkhot Mamrim* 1:2-3; *Hilkhot Ma'akhalot 'Assurot* 17:5, and *Kessef Mishneh; Hilkhot Tefillah* 14:11; *Hilkhot Sukkah* 7:4.

[9] It ought to be noted that Maimonides does also cite the *beraita* of the *Sifra*, which presents the aggadic claim in its most specific form, twice: *Introduction to Mishneh Torah*, 65, lines 503-5, and *Introduction to the Mishnah Commentary*: "these 613 commandments were given, they and their generalizations and particularizations." Yet this too ought to be seen against the background of the total picture discussed in the paper. See, as well, my comments in *Jewish Law Annual*, I (1978): 113.

[10] *Sefer ha-Mizvot*, Principle II (J. Kafah, trans. [Jerusalem, 1972], 11).

[11] For the geonic view that lapses in the tradition due to forgetfulness are responsible for *mahloket* (a view adopted by Rashi as well; cf. *Eruvin* 12b *s.v. ve-yoter*), see S. Abramson, *Sinai* 88 (1981): 214-5 (R. Samuel b. Hofni Gaon; though M. Zucker, *Op. cit.*, attributes the passage to a contemporary Karaite); A.S. Halkin, *Louis Ginzberg Jubilee Volume, Hebrew Volume* (New York, 1946), 153 (R. Sa'adyah; Sa'adyah, though, speaks of factors other than forgetfulness); M. Zucker, *Surah* 2 (1956-7): 324, note 36 (Sa'adyah's comparison of *midrash* and grammar). See also *Mavo ha-Talmud*, currently attributed to R. Samuel b. Hofni, which claims that only authoritative *halakhot* were in fact given at Sinai, a view warranting further analysis, to be sure. For Sherira's *Iggeret*, see my preliminary study in *Da'at* 4 (Winter, 1980): 9. Maimonides was not alone, incidentally, in rejecting these geonic views; see R. Hananel at *Megillah* 3a, *Hagigah* 12b, *Sukkah* 44a; R. Nissim Gaon as cited in S. Abramson, *Rav Nissim Gaon* (Jerusalem, 1965), 353-4; in *Arukh s.v. namek*; and by Y. England in *Shenaton ha-Mishpat Ha-Ivri* 1 (1974): 51. They merely hint at the point, though; Maimonides is brutally explicit.

[12] *Commentary to Mishnah, Rosh Hashana* 2:7, regarding R. Sa'adyah on the calendar. (Geonic tradition itself, incidentally, had treated Sa'adyah's claims as polemic and nothing more: see R. Hai, in *Ozar ha-Geonim, Yom Tov*, pt. 1, p. 4.) Of course, Maimonides will himself be hard-pressed to explain away disquieting Talmudic legends; he assigns the story that thousands of *halakhot* were forgotten after the death of Moses (*Temurah* 16a) to *halakhot* generated by *midrash* alone (*Sefer ha-Mizvot* [op. cit.], 13).

[13] Nahmanides in his comments to Sefer HaMizvot, Principle II:

עיקר זה עוקר הרים גדולים בתלמוד ומפיל חומות בצורות בגמרא, והענין ללומדי הגמרא רע ומר.

[14] The Maimonidean element had been noted by M.S. Feldblum, *Perushim...ba-Talmud* (New York, 1959), 5, note 9. For Nahmanides' general indebtedness to the Andalusian tradition, see B. Septimus in *Nahmanides*, ed. I. Twersky (Cambridge, 1983), 11-35.

[14a] See note 13.

[15] *Responsa Havvot Ya'ir*, 192, end:

הנה הרב בנה חומה בצורה סביב תורה שבעל פה...אף כי יוצא שכרו בהפסדו...כמעט כל סדרי המשנה אינם כלל מסיני.

[16] *Matteh Dan*, ed. J.L. Maimon (Jerusalem, 1958), 312-14; 4:276. Nieto's reading *Sefer ha-Kabbalah* into Maimonides had been noted by I. Twersky, *Introduction to the Code of Maimonides* (New Haven, 1980), 100, note 5.

[17] *Behinat ha-Kabbala* (Gorizia, 1852), 107, 122-6. Reggio also claims (125-6) that Maimonides uses the idea of Sinaitic origins as a Platonic myth.

[18] *Ha-Torah ve-ha-Philosophia* (Vienna, 1827), 120-121.

[19] *Behinat ha-Dat* (Vienna, 1853), 94.

[20] M.S. Feldblum in *Jewish Law and Current Legal Problems*, ed. N. Rakover (Jerusalem, 1984), 29-36.

[21] For Halevi, all authoritative rabbinic acts issue from a Sanhedrin sitting in the Temple and enjoy a holy prophetic spirit: see E.E. Urbach, *Tarbiz* 18 (1947): 20-21, and N. Arieli, *Da'at* 1 (1978): 43-52 (both in Hebrew).

[22] *Hilkhot Mamrim* 1:1.

[23] Ibid., 1:2.

[24] *Hilkhot Berakhot* 11:3; *Hilkhot Lulav* 7:15 (as opposed to 7:22); *Hilkhot Hannukkah* 3:5.

[25] *Commentary to Mishnah, Avot* 1:3. Maimonides also points out (*Guide*, III:36) that the command to honor the sage is not only a reflection of the honor due the Torah, but is designed to bolster his authority; thus the sage is seen as an authoritative figure similar to the king and high priest, and the tradition must find ways to inculcate the habits of obedience towards him. See also at *Avot* 4:7.

[26] *Guide* I, 71.

[27] *Hilkhot Mamrim* 1:4, interpreting the Talmudic statement dating the rise of *mahloket* to the "multiplication of students of Hillel and Shammai who had not studied" enough – a statements Maimonides repeats literally in the Introduction to the Mishnah Commentary. Compare, too, *PhM Kiddushin* 4:1 with Rashi, *Kiddushin* 69b *s.v. mesayah*.

[28] See D. Hartman, *Maimonides: Torah and Philosophic Quest* (Philadelphia, 1976), Chapter 3.

Worship, Corporeality, and Human Perfection: A Reading of Guide of the Perplexed, III:51-54[*]

David Shatz

Interpreters through the ages have explored a rich variety of philosophical, historical, and literary aspects of Maimonides' discussion of human perfection in part III, chapters 51-54 of the *Guide*. The very first sentences of those climactic sections, however, contain a remark that has not been given the attention and interpretive weight it deserves. In the opening lines of III:51, Maimonides provides the following characterization of the ideas he is about to present:

> This chapter that we bring now does not include additional matter over and above what is comprised in the other chapters of this Treatise. It is only a kind of conclusion...(III:51, 618)[1]

Maimonides applies the description "[kind of] conclusion" specifically to "this chapter," i.e., chapter 51.[2] Yet part III of the *Guide* contains three chapters *after* this conclusion. It what sense, then, is III:51 the conclusion of the *Guide*? Why isn't III:54 given that designation?[3]

I believe that Maimonides' use of the term "conclusion" for III:51, as distinct from III:54, is perfectly apt: III:51, and not III:54, is the real end of the *Guide*. If we examine closely the content of these chapters, we find that III:51 and III:54 are markedly different from each other. III:54 presents a highly *simplistic* and *misleading* picture of Maimonides' views on human perfection; III:51, on the other hand, is fraught with complexities, tensions, ambiguities, and uncertainties that better reflect Maimonides' thinking. These complexities, tensions, ambiguities, and uncertainties have been present in the *Guide* all along, in "the other chapters of this

[*] Originally published in *The Thought of Moses Maimonides: Philosophical and Legal Studies*, eds. Ira Robinson, Lawrence Kaplan, Julien Bauer (Lewiston, N.Y. :Edwin Mellen Press, 1990), 77-129.

Treatise"; however, they come to a head when Maimonides articulates his account of human perfection.

In this paper I would like to (1) lay out the evidence for taking the treatment in III:51 to be more advanced and sophisticated than that in III:54; (2) construct an explanation of why Maimonides jumbled the sequence of his final chapters; and (3) explain the significance of my interpretation for our understanding of human perfection in the thought of Maimonides.

I

In what way is III:54 simplistic and misleading? I begin with two impressions conveyed by III:54 that are contradicted by statements in III:51. The two impressions are the following: (1) intellectual apprehension is the end of a human being; (2) performance of all the commandments plays no role in the life of an individual who has achieved intellectual apprehension, since the commandments are but preparation for intellectual perfection. As we shall see, the contrast between III:51 and III:54 on these issues is but a symptom of a deeper difference between the chapters.

1. The Human Telos

Upon careful reading, it becomes plain that the stage of human development that Maimonides describes in III:54 *precedes* the stage of human development that he describes in III:51. In III:54, Maimonides describes four kinds of human perfection: the perfection of possessions, the perfection of bodily constitution and shape, the perfection of moral virtues, and the perfection consisting in the acquisition of rational virtues ("I refer to the conception of intelligibles, which teach true opinions concerning the divine things," p. 635). The last of these four perfections is described as "the ultimate end." Later in that chapter Maimonides expands his characterization of what is known by those who attain true perfection, so that it now includes apprehension of God's *providence*: "The perfection of man that may truly be gloried in is the one acquired by him who has achieved, in a measure corresponding to his capacity, apprehension of Him, may He be exalted, and who knows His providence extending over His creatures as manifested in the act of bringing them into being and in their governance as it is" (III:54, 638).

The argument given in this chapter for the supremacy of intellectual perfection is that by achieving intellectual perfection one realizes his true self.

> This [i.e., intellectual perfection] is in true reality the ultimate end; this is what gives the individual true perfection, a perfection belonging to him alone; and it gives him permanent perdurance; through it man is man. (III:54, 635)

The lineage of this argument extends back to Book X of Aristotle's *Nichomachean Ethics*. Intellectual perfection constitutes *eudaemonia* because the human being's "true self" is intellectual.[4]

Now, in III:51, Maimonides speaks of a class of people who, "after having attained perfection in the divine science, turn wholly toward God,...renounce what is other than He, and direct all the acts of their intellect toward an examination of the beings with a view to drawing from them proof with regard to Him, so as to know His governance of them in whatever way it is possible" (III:51, 620). Thus far, the stage under discussion (identified as "the rank of the prophets," as distinct from "the men of science") *seems* identical with "the perfection of man that may truly be gloried in" as depicted in the lines we quoted from III:54. But it is not. III:54 makes no reference to "turning wholly toward God," "renouncing what is other than He," and "directing *all* acts of the intellect toward an examination of the beings." Apprehension, not concentration, is the focus of the closing lines of III:54; and the "fourth perfection" as defined earlier in that chapter makes no mention of anything beyond "conception of the intelligibles" and "true opinions concerning the divine things."

The significance of this omission becomes clear as we read on in III:51. For Maimonides goes on to describe a stage *beyond* apprehension: the stage of *worship*. At this level, one not only apprehends, but, in addition, concentrates—as totally, exclusively, and continuously as possible—on the object of apprehension. It is eminently clear that worship is the *next* goal of one who has achieved apprehension:

> If, however, you have apprehended God and His acts in accordance with what is required by the intellect, you should afterwards engage in totally devoting yourself to Him, endeavor to come closer to Him, and strengthen the bond between you and Him—that is, the intellect...(III:51, 620)
> The Torah has made it clear that this last worship...can only be engaged in after apprehension has been achieved...after love comes this worship...after apprehension, total devotion to Him

> and the employment of intellectual thought in constantly loving
> Him should be aimed at...(III:51, 621)
>
> Know that even if you were the man who knew most the true
> reality of the divine science...you would cut that bond existing
> between you and God if you would empty your thought of God
> and busy yourself in eating the necessary or in occupying yourself
> with the necessary. (Ibid.)

Here we have a portrait of "the worship peculiar to those who have
apprehended the true realities" (620), a worship engaged in "after he
has obtained an apprehension of what He is" (618), a worship neglect
of which can lead to a severance of the bond between the individual
and God. In sum, worship, the subject of III:51, comes *after* intellectual
apprehension, the subject of III:54.[5] In fact, Maimonides, in III:51,
contradicts his portrayal of perfection as given in III:54, for he writes that
this worship "is the end of man" (618). Providence is enjoyed to the fullest
extent only by those who have achieved this later stage, a sure mark of its
supremacy (III:51, 622-26).

Thus, an examination of the contents of III:51 makes clear why it,
and not chapter 54, represents the "conclusion" of Maimonides' *Guide*.
Insofar as III:54 makes no explicit mention of worship, it not only presents
a misleading picture of what human perfection is, but also (given the
difficulties an individual encounters in trying to sustain the state of worship)
encourages an overly generous estimate of the prospects for attaining human
perfection. My point here is not a purely literary or structural one about the
sequence in which the *Guide*'s chapters should be read. Rather, my thesis
is that we cannot construct an accurate theory of what human perfection
is for Maimonides and of whether it is attainable unless we start with the
recognition that III:54 is not Maimonides' last word on the subject.

I wish to acknowledge one respect in which III:54 appears to go
beyond III:51. After describing "the perfection of man that may truly be
gloried in," Maimonides writes that

> The way of life of such an individual, after he has achieved
> this apprehension, will always have in view loving-kindness,
> righteousness, and judgment, through assimilation to His actions,
> may He be exalted, just as we have explained several times in this
> Treatise. (III:54, 638)

It is generally agreed that Maimonides is here referring to political
activities—governance of the people—and possibly to the activity
of legislation. The perfect individual apprehends God's attributes as

manifested in "His actions," i.e., nature, and uses those attributes as a model for his own activity.[6] Should we say, then, that III:54, since it includes reference to political activity, tells us more about human perfection than III:51, and that III:51 contains this simplistic formulation, not III:54? No. For there *is* a passage in III:51 which makes reference to political activity, specifically that of Moses and the Patriarchs, the end of whose efforts was "to bring into being a religious community that would know and worship God" (624). The full interpretation and significance of this passage will be explored later, but its existence quashes the notion that III:54 is more advanced than III:51[7] by virtue of referring to political activity.

Let us now turn to another respect in which the account of III:54 is inaccurate and misleading.

2. The Place of the Commandments in the Human Ideal

III:51-54 is preceded by a long section on the purposes of the commandments (*ta'amei ha-mizvot*) which begins at III:25 and extends through III:49. The relationship between this section and the sections that precede and follow it—respectively, the chapters on evil and providence (III:8-25) and on human perfection (III:51-54)—richly deserves study. For the moment, I should like to argue that III:54 presents ideas, themes, and even terminology that belong not to the immediately preceding chapters but to the section on *ta'amei ha-mizvot*; most strikingly, the key idea conveyed in III:54 concerning the aim of the commandments is inconsistent with the key idea concerning that subject in III:51.

The first chapter in the *ta'amei ha-mizvot* section (III:25)[8] begins by delineating four kinds of actions: (1) vain (an end is aimed at, but not achieved); (2) futile (no end is aimed at); (3) frivolous (an end is aimed at, but a low end); (4) good or excellent. A good or excellent action is one that not only aims at an end but aims at an end that is noble; furthermore, it achieves that end. Maimonides maintains that all of God's actions are good or excellent; and the chapters on the commandments are designed to verify this claim with respect to a specific class of divine acts, namely, acts of divine legislation. Accordingly, Maimonides (1) argues that all commandments have "causes," i.e., a purpose, and (2) identifies the specific intellectual and political benefits at which Torah legislation aims.

"The Law as a whole," Maimonides writes in III:27, "aims at two things: the welfare of the soul and the welfare of the body" (III:27, 510). The Law prescribes certain opinions to the multitude, and observance of the commandments inculcates correct opinions in them (welfare of the soul). As well, the Law brings about abolition of wrongdoing and fosters the acquisition by every human individual of moral qualities that are useful for life in society so that the affairs of the city may be ordered" (welfare of the body) (III:27, 510).

"Welfare of the soul" and "welfare of the body" do not exhaust the aims of the Law as depicted in III:27-28. Maimonides also speaks of "perfection" of the soul and "perfection" of the body.[9]

Perfection of the body, unlike *welfare* of the body, refers to "being healthy and in the very best bodily state"; perfection of this type (in contrast to welfare of the body) is in the first instance a benefit to the individual, though the only means of securing this benefit, the only means of obtaining "food," "shelter," and " bathing," is through political association. Again, *welfare* of the soul, as we have already noted, is a category that pertains to the multitude; the term refers to their acquisition of true opinions. *Perfection* of the soul, however, refers to the (individual's) ultimate perfection, which is "to have an intellect *in actu*" (III:27, 511). This perfection consists "only of [having] opinions towards which speculation has led and that investigation has rendered compulsory" (Ibid.).[10]

Clearly, perfection of the soul is achieved by the elite few and although it is "the ultimate perfection" (511), is not achieved directly by the Law (512). The Law provides directly for welfare—but not for perfection; it directs attention to theoretical opinions "in a summary fashion," but does not "direct attention toward them in detail" (III:27, 512).

When Maimonides enunciates "causes of the Law" in these chapters, he is not formulating reasons that are intended to motivate people to perform the commandments, or which motivated them to do so in biblical times. Nothing in the concept "welfare of the soul" precludes an individual's attaining "welfare of the soul" even if he or she does not know that the Law is aiming at that end.[11] Maimonides' concern is not with identifying motives of the *performer*, but with identifying motives of the *legislator*.[12] In fact, by demonstrating how wisdom is manifest in the commandments, he is showing that the Law is divine. As Warren Harvey has emphasized,[13] the divine law is identified as divine, or *proved* to be divine, by its ends and utility. As Maimonides explains in II:40:

> It is part of the wisdom of the deity with regard to the permanence
> of this species of which He willed the existence, that He put
> into its nature that individuals belonging to it should have the
> faculty of ruling. Among them [is]...the prophet or the bringers
> of the *nomos*...if you find a Law all of whose ordinances are due
> to attention being paid...to the soundness of the circumstances
> pertaining to the body and also to the soundness of belief...you
> must know that this guidance comes from Him, may He exalted,
> and that the Law is divine. (384)

III:25-49, then, establishes the divinity of the Law, by the special criteria
of "divinity" defined in II:39-40.

Now, the relevance of III:25-49 to our question—the relationship
between III:51 and III:54—is this. At first glance, Maimonides' discussion
of the commandments appears to terminate after III:49. Chapter 50 deals
with a different though loosely related subject (biblical narratives),[14]
and Chapter 51 begins with Maimonides' insistence that "this chapter...
does not include additional matter over and above what is comprised in
the other chapters of this Treatise" (III:51, 619). Notwithstanding this
instance, we *are* presented with "additional matter" in III:51, especially
a *new* explanation of the aim of the commandments which contrasts,
in particular, with the explanations given in III:25-49. This new and
different explanation is responsive to the peculiar goals of the worshipper
who is described in III:51. III:54, on the other hand, reverts back to
the older conception of III:25-49—ignoring altogether the account of
III:51.

What is the new conception proposed in III:51?

> Know that all the practices of the worship, such as reading the
> Torah, prayer, and the performance of the other commandments
> have only the end of training you to occupy yourself with His
> commandments, may He be exalted, rather than with matters
> pertaining to this world. (III:51, 622)

The same basic idea (with additional motifs) is encountered in III:52:

> It is by all the particulars of the actions [prescribed by the Law]
> and through their repetition that some excellent men obtained
> such training that they achieve human perfection so that they fear
> and are in dread and in awe of God, may He be exalted, and know
> who it is that is with them and as a result act subsequently as they
> ought to.... The actions prescribed by the Law bring about fear of
> God...love [of God is achieved] through the opinions taught by the

> Law...while fear is achieved by means of all the actions prescribed
> by the Law. (III:52, 629-30)[15]

According to these passages, the purpose of the Law is to provide "training," that is, a regimen through which the philosopher empties himself of other thoughts and concentrates exclusively (or as nearly exclusively as possible) on God; the commandments create a consciousness of "who it is that is with" him.[16] This conception is not found in III:25-49.[17] Thus, it appears that we are dealing with two neatly segregated discussions, one in III:25-49, the other in III:51; and so there appears to be a discrepancy between these two contiguous portions of the *Guide*.[18]

Before seeing how *ta'amei ha-mizvot* are treated in III:54, it is important to appreciate just why Maimonides might have made this shift. Notice, first, that Maimonides' two accounts of the commandments (III:25-49; III:51) are not inconsistent. III:51 sets down an *additional* dimension of the commandments, one that is the exclusive reserve of the philosopher who aspires to love. In III:52, Maimonides speaks only of "*some* excellent men" who "achieve human perfection" through the particulars of the actions prescribed by the Law (III:52, 628-29). The philosopher who aspires to love or who develops fear utilizes the commandments in a *special* way, as a regimen for concentrating on all he knows, for occupying himself with God rather than with "matters pertaining to this world" ("buying and selling," "the building of your habitation"); and through such concentration he achieves "nearness to God and being in His presence." The fact that the commandments serve this purpose for the exceptional individual does not preclude their serving other, more preliminary purposes for the multitude, nor their having served those same purposes for the philosopher-worshipper at an earlier stage of his development, when he was not yet a philosopher. In III:25-49, Maimonides is explaining the Law as it pertains to the community, the multitude; in III:51, the Law as it pertains to exceptional individuals. The Law can obviously operate on multiple levels, corresponding to the multiple stages of human development.[19]

But even if we have shown that the two treatments of the commandments are *consistent with* each other—we have explained how a shift *could* take place—we still need to understand why it *does* take place. What induced Maimonides to abandon the account of III:25-49 when discussing the higher levels of worship?

In all likelihood, Maimonides is anticipating, and responding to, two arguments for antinomianism that grow out of his discussion in III:25-49.

The philosopher has *already* acquired correct opinions and has *already* perfected the moral habits. For him, the Law no longer achieves the ends of "welfare of the soul" and "welfare of the body" set down in III:27. As for "perfection" of the soul, that is achieved through philosophical speculation, independently of any specific performances. If the Law is to be saved from falling into disuse *for the philosopher*, it must serve some *other* set of ends. What it serves is a new, higher telos: the commandments assist him in directing his thought to God.[20]

In addition, the shift to the training conception of III:51 may be viewed as a response to another antinomian implication of the reasons stated in III:25-49. Idolatrous practices are no longer extant; hence, the many commandments whose aim it is to efface idolatry no longer achieve their aim—they become pointless. We may sharpen the difficulty as follows. To fulfill the human telos, a person must understand the natural order. However, God's legislation of the commandments is part of the natural order.[21] Hence, to understand the natural order (and thereby fulfill the human telos) one must understand the reasons for the *mizvot*. But anyone who understands those reasons will also realize that God's legislation of the commandments is conditioned by the historical circumstances in which the commandments were legislated. Such a person, assuming he is living in post-biblical times, will ineluctably abandon the Law because the Law is irrelevant to *him*. Achievement of the human telos, then, results in abandonment of the Law.[22]

By developing his conception of the commandments as training, Maimonides is able to respond to this argument. He can now maintain that the commandments retain their value for the philosopher long after the benefits they provided for the masses in biblical times are no longer needed. As Warren Harvey put it,[23] III:25-49 is concerned with what the commandments meant "then"; III:51 tells us what the commandments mean now.[24]

A third, and simpler, explanation of the shift in III:51 is possible. We have already seen that, in III:25-49, Maimonides is concerned not with motives of the performer, but with motives of the legislator. Now in III:51, Maimonides' mandate to the philosopher is to concentrate only on God, at least to the extent that this is humanly possible. For one who devotes himself exclusively to intellection, however, performance of a bodily activity (a commandment) without proper attention to God can result in a break in concentration. The training conception is introduced because only that conception guarantees that the worshipper will not fail to focus on God while performing the commandment:

> If, however, you pray merely by moving your lips while facing a wall, and at the same time thinking about your buying and selling; or if you read the Torah with your tongue while your heart is set upon the building of your habitation and does not consider what you read; and similarly in all cases in which you perform a commandment merely with your limbs—as if you were digging a hole in the ground, or hewing wood in the forest—without reflecting either upon the meaning of that action or upon Him from whom the commandment proceeds or upon the end of the action, you should not think that you have achieved the end...
> (III:51, 622)

The requirement that Maimonides introduces here is *reflection.* To achieve "the end"—constant occupation with God—you must focus upon "the end of the action." I take this last term to refer to the end of focusing on God, as distinct from the ends set out in III:25-49. On either reading of the phrase, however, the doer of the action must be aware of the end of the action; hence, the "end" in this passage is one that motivates an individual to perform the action. Maimonides has altered the *contents* of the reason for the Law (for the philosopher, the commandments serve a purpose distinct from inculcation of actual opinions, abolition of wrongdoing, and so forth), because he must alter the *type* of reason in question. It must be a reason that is a motive for the performer *and* incorporates reference to God.[25]

So, a genuine shift takes place in III:51 with respect to *ta'amei ha-mizvot,* yet it is a shift which Maimonides not only can make with consistency, but is, furthermore, impelled to make. If we now turn to III:54, though, we find there the very approach to the commandments which Maimonides had abandoned in III:51 in the case of the philosopher![26] For the utility of the commandments in fostering moral virtue and preparing one for intellectual protection—a motif of III:27—looms prominent in III:54 after having been missing from III:51:

> The third species...is the perfection of the moral virtues. Most of the commandments serve no other end than the attainment of this species of protection. But this species of perfection is likewise

a preparation for something else and not an end in itself. (III:54, 635)

...All the action is prescribed by the Law—I refer to the various species of worship and also the moral habits that are useful to all people in their mutual dealings—that all this is not to be compared with this ultimate end [intellectual perfection] and does not equal it, being but preparations made for the sake of this end. (III:54, 636)

The difficulty is plain. By now, the conception of *mizvot* advanced in these lines has been *superseded* by the explanation given in III:51—that the philosopher uses the commandments as a regimen by which he occupies himself exclusively with God. Even after the commandments have aided the individual in achieving intellectual perfection and are no longer needed for *that* purpose, they serve as a means of training the individual to concentrate his attention on God. The conception in III:54 harks back to III:27-28, and it represents a striking retrograde step. It is, furthermore, a step which carries antinomian implications.

The reason for the retrogression should by now be obvious. III:54 conceptually precedes III:51. The commandments cannot be conceived in III:54 as furnishing a regimen for concentration on God, for this conception of their purpose is appropriate only for people who are on the level of *worship* described in III:51. That level, which demands total concentration on God, has not yet been achieved in III:54.

In light of the fact that III:54 appropriates the conception of *ta'amei ha-mizvot* given in III:25-49 rather than the conception given in III:51, it is intriguing that III:54 also contains other literary and conceptual links to III:25-49. For example, after describing four kinds of human acts in III:25 (vain; futile; frivolous; good or excellent), Maimonides ends with a discussion of divine wisdom as manifest in the divine acts. Thus, the chapter exemplifies the following pattern: four kinds of human acts, then divine wisdom. Then, in III:54, Maimonides again begins with a fourfold classification: he describes four sorts of human wisdom. The end of the chapter discusses divine acts. Thus the chapter exemplifies a reversal of the pattern in III:25: four kinds of human wisdom, then divine acts. To take another example of a literary connection between III:25-49 and III:54, Maimonides distinguishes between "the rational matter of the Law" that is received through tradition and is not demonstrated, and wisdom, through which the rational matter received from the Law is demonstrated. "And this should be the order observed: the opinions in question should first be known as being received through tradition; then they should be demonstrated..." (633-34).[27] This distinction parallels that drawn in III:27-28 between welfare of the soul and perfection of the soul.[28]

Apart from these intriguing literary ties, we may note a conceptual connection between III:54 and III:25-49. Maimonides' argument for the goodness or excellence of the Law (in III:25-49) contains a significant lacuna that is filled by III:54. Maimonides has asserted and then shown that the Law aims at certain ends. However, there is a difference between (1) showing that the Law achieves certain ends, and (2) providing a *reasoned argument* for the conclusion that those ends are noble. Legislation that aims at welfare of the soul and welfare of the body and that has, as its ultimate aim, perfection of the soul and perfection of the body—such legislation is certainly not futile; it is purposive. But is that legislation good or excellent? That depends on whether the aims achieved are noble. And until chapter 54, Maimonides provides no *argument* for the contention that these ends are noble; instead we have encountered only assertion or presupposition. Hence, until chapter 54, Maimonides has not demonstrated his thesis that Torah legislation is good or excellent.[29]

III:54 supplies the missing argument. Perfection of the soul was said to be an aim of the Law; now intellectual perfection is *shown to be* a noble end. Furthermore, if perfection of the soul or intellectual perfection is a noble end, so is anything that leads to perfection of the soul. Welfare of the soul (acquisition of correct opinions) is necessary for perfection of the soul; welfare of the body and perfection of the body are likewise propaedeutic to intellectual attainment. Thus, in III:54, Maimonides finally completes the argument for the thesis he set out in III:25. And so, we may say that chapter 54, which bears literary connections to chapter 25, also completes the argument for the thesis stated in III:25.[30]

There is also a more straightforward and familiar connection between III:54 and the *ta'amei ha-mizvot* section. As already noted, the individual described at the end of III:54 who imitates God's actions in nature may be the transmitter of the legislation. It has been argued that certain specific categories of explanation given for the commandments in III:25-49 exemplify the divine attributes.[31] If this interpretation is correct, the end of III:54 circles back to III:25-49. In light of the other connections we noted between III:54 and earlier chapters, this more familiar observation must be seen as part of a larger, more comprehensive pattern.

It is difficult to know with certainty whether these literary symmetries and conceptual ties between III:25 and III:54 are intended by Maimonides. Nevertheless, we cannot dismiss the possibility that Maimonides deliberately spiced III:54 with themes and terminology from III:25-49 in order to let the astute reader know that the chapter "belongs" in that section—and hence before III:51. My case, however, need not rest on establishing this possibility. Rather, I have shown that III:54 leaves the casual reader with two mistaken impressions: that intellectual apprehension is the end of man, and that the commandments play no role in the life of the one who has achieved intellectual perfection. The first impression is dispelled in III:51 through Maimonides' assertions that worship (together with love and fear of God) is the end of man; the second, through the "training" conception of the commandments. Clearly, III:54 is not an accurate indication of Maimonides' views.

The task before us now is clear. We need to explain why Maimonides jumbles the sequence of chapters, putting his real "conclusion" before the end of the book.

II

Before proceeding, a word of clarification. I have been speaking as if III:51 is the last word of the *Guide* on human perfection. In truth, the structure of these chapters is more complex than that; in particular, I have not touched as yet on the place of chapters 52 and 53.

I believe that 52 continues 51. Chapter 52 begins with a variation on the palace metaphor and proceeds to emphasize love and fear of God. Thus, it is not really 51 alone which is the end of the *Guide*, but the tightly integrated unit III:51-52. Maimonides labels III:51 the "conclusion" only to signal that III:54 is not deserving of that designation.

Chapter 53, which explicates the attributes of *hesed, mishpat,* and *zedakah,* is clearly a prelude to the concluding portion of III:54, which states that the actions of the perfect individual will imitate these divine characteristics. I have already stated that the end of III:54 must be integrated into the brief discussion of political activity in III:51 (623-24). Indeed, an additional reason for thinking that III:54's first part (on the four perfections) is out of place is that III:53 belongs immediately before this section on *imitatio dei* at the end of III:54; the section on the four perfections interrupts the flow from 53 into the final part of 54.

III

Why did Maimonides jumble the sequence of his final chapters, so as to make it appear that III:54 gives his final view on human perfection? The most plausible answer, I believe, is that he wished to conceal complexities, tensions, and uncertainties in his thinking. These are totally absent from III:54; they find subtle expression, however, in III:51.[32]

What are these "complexities, tensions, ambiguities, and uncertainties" that emerge in III:51, but whose significance is veiled by III:54? Basically, what III:51 suggests is that the argument used in III:54 to generate the thesis that the fourth perfection is supreme—namely, the argument that man's "true self" is intellectual—is highly simplistic in Maimonides' own mind.

> This [i.e., intellectual perfection] is in true reality the ultimate end, this is what gives the individual true perfection, a perfection belonging to him alone; and it gives him permanent perdurance; through it man is man. (III:54, 635)[33]

The deepest differences between III:51 and III:54 are related to the following question: can a human being transcend corporeal limitations and realize a purely intellectual "true self," as III:54 suggests? Or is corporeality a constant, ineliminable impediment to realizing a purely intellectual self?

The most obvious loci for an intellectualist, *anti*corporeal conception of a human being are the first and last chapters of the *Guide*.[34] According to I:1:

> The term "image" is applied to the natural form, I mean to the notion in virtue of which a thing is constituted as a substance and becomes what it is. It is the true reality of the thing insofar as the latter is that particular being. In man that notion is that from which human apprehension derives. It is on account of this intellectual apprehension that it is said of man, "in the image of God created He him." (22)

> Now man possesses as his proprium something in him that is very strange as it is not found in anything else that exists under the sphere of the moon, namely, intellectual apprehension. In the exercise of this, no sense, no part of the body, none of the extremities are used; and therefore this apprehension was likened unto the

apprehension of the deity, which does not require an instrument, although in reality it is not like the other apprehension, but only appears so to the first stirrings of opinion. (23)

Again, in III:54 Maimonides insists on the supremacy of intellectual perfection by deploying the true self argument.

What is striking about the chapters which contain these passages is that they include no acknowledgment of the arduous nature of intellectual attainment, and in particular no acknowledgment of the impediments that matter puts in the path of those who seek this goal. Nor do they attend to the difficulties incurred by one who is attempting to *sustain* intellectual focus and see the light of the truth on a *continuing* basis, not merely in brief flashes. These difficulties are noted in Maimonides' introduction (7), but the closest Maimonides comes to stating them in I:1,2 and III:54 is when he says that Adam was punished for indulging his imagination and senses by being deprived of intellectual apprehension (I:2, 25) and when, in III:54, he admonishes a reader over whom corporeal faculties have gained dominion (III:54, 635-36). The possibility of apprehending but briefly and then losing what one has attained is at one point almost denied: "Therefore you ought to desire to achieve this thing [intellectual apprehension], which will remain permanently with you" (III:54, 635). The prospect for realizing and sustaining an intellectual self are here made to appear bright, the task almost easy.

Yet, in some places, Maimonides seems to regard matter as an inherent, insurmountable aspect of human beings. Statements along these lines arise in epistemological contexts. In I:49, Maimonides acknowledges that "it is very difficult for man to apprehend, except after strenuous training, that which is pure of matter and absolutely devoid of corporeality" (I:49, 109). Very difficult—but is it impossible? At least one passage suggests so.

> Matter is a strong veil preventing the apprehension of that which is separate from matter as it truly is....Hence, whenever our intellect aspires to apprehend the deity or one of the intellects, there subsists this great veil interposed between the two.... The apprehension of His true reality is impossible for us because of the dark matter that encompasses us and not Him, may He be exalted; for He, may He be exalted, is not a body. (III:9, 437-38)

That a person's being endowed with matter makes human knowledge of "His true reality" and knowledge of *any* beings that are "separate from matter" "impossible," has been emphasized by Shlomo Pines in an article[35] that has stimulated numerous other scholars to clarify and rethink Maimonides' epistemology, psychology and metaphysics.[36] Pines severely restricts the metaphysical knowledge that is accessible to man according to Maimonides and draws, from this interpretation, the conclusion that political, not theoretical, activity is the highest perfection of a human being. For Pines, the "great veil" is not to be lifted; escape from corporeality is impossible. Pines perhaps does not do justice to contrary evidence.[37] Nevertheless, the corporeal picture of human beings emerges forcefully in III:8-12. Perhaps it is too much to say that Maimonides definitely thought that human beings cannot transcend corporeal limitations. We must say, nonetheless, that he was uncertain whether they can, and that this uncertainty accounts for divergent statements he issues on the subject.

Interestingly, of all the lexicographical chapters in the *Guide*, only one begins with the words, "the equivocality of the term..." That chapter is devoted to the term "Adam."[38] Besides referring to the first man, "Adam" may refer either to the species or to the multitude (I:14). The three texts cited by Maimonides to illustrate the former use of the term include "my spirit shall not abide in man" (Gen. 6:3), and "so that man hath no preeminence over the best" (Eccl. 3:19), both of which are pejorative to the "species" and express pessimism about its religious capacities. The third text (Eccl. 3:21) at best suspends judgment about whether the destiny of the human spirit differs from that of the animals. Thus, among the three definitions of "Adam" are two that affirm the existence of an elite group of humans (since "Adamites" denotes the multitude in the third definition, and "Adam" the first man in the first sense), but also one that groups human beings with animals. Here, too, we find uncertainty and ambiguity about the nature and potentialities of human beings.

What does III:51 suggest concerning Maimonides' assessment of human potentialities? Which conception does he adopt there? The crucial point to grasp is that, for Maimonides, commandments are necessary because of human corporeality. "All man's acts of disobedience and sins are consequent upon his matter and not upon his form, whereas all his virtues are consequent upon his form. ...A man committing an act of disobedience does it only...because of the accidents consequent upon his matter..." (III:8, 431, 434). "Also, the commandments and prohibitions are only intended to quell the impulses of matter" (III:8, 433). Maimonides implies that, if God were to change the nature of human beings, there would be no need for "commandments and prohibitions, rewards and punishments," and hence "sending of prophets and all giving of a Law would have been useless" (III:32, 529). Since the aspect of man's nature that produces disobedience is its materiality (III:8), it seems fair to say that "commandments and prohibitions" are necessitated by human corporeality. Similarly, we read: "For all the hindrances keeping man from his ultimate perfection, every deficiency affecting him and every disobedience, comes to him from his matter alone" (Introduction, 13). We may safely assume that the commandments lead a person to perfection by overcoming limitations and deficiencies that are due to matter. Hence only an individual who has not transcended corporeality will have need for the commandments.[39]

Now Maimonides' trainee must perform the commandments. He, therefore, has not transcended corporeality, has not actualized a non-corporeal self. In III:54, where we are led to believe that realization of the intellectual self is possible through intellectual apprehension, we are also led to believe that commandments are not necessary for those who have attained intellectual perfection.[40] In III:51, where we learn that commandments *are* necessary for the trainee, we must conclude that the trainee has *not* escaped corporeality. (Notice that, as we saw earlier, the trainee *has* attained the level of intellectual perfection described in III:54; he is now seeking to go further, to achieve the level of worship.) The differing values placed on performance of the commandments in III:51 and III:54 reflect differing assessments of the prospects for freeing oneself from corporeal limitations. According to III:51, and contrary to III:54, intellectual knowledge alone does not permit one to achieve such a rank.

Without referring to the fact that the philosopher of III:51 is a corporeal creature, it is difficult to see why Maimonides insists on performance of the commandments by the philosopher in III:51. Earlier I said he introduced the trainee conception partly because the conception of *ta'amei ha-mizvot* in III:25-49 led to antinomianism. But what of it? What philosophic consideration restrains Maimonides from taking an antinomian step, which seems anyway legitimized by his formulation in III:54 (the commandments are "but preparations" for the fourth perfection)? It is his recognition that even the philosopher has not gone beyond the *need* for commandments.

This interpretation receives support from III:52. In III:52, the actions prescribed by the Law not only serve as a regimen to enhance focusing on God and God alone, but also to bring it about that some excellent men "fear, and are in dread and awe of God, and know who it is that is with them and as a result subsequently act as they ought to" (III:52, 630). Earlier in the chapter Maimonides speaks of "perfect men" achieving humility, awe, reverence, fear, and shame. Shame is associated with the sense of touch and materiality (III:8, 433), and an immediately succeeding line refers to sexual conduct and speech, which are likewise implicated in Maimonides' discussion of matter in III:8, 435. Fear of God would seem to arise out of recognition of one's peculiar status as matter joined with intellect.[41] It is specifically the *actions* prescribed by the Law—associated with corporeality—that instill fear, while the *opinions* instill love. Through acquiring truth, one attains love; knowledge of the truth, in turn, then instills fear. Thus, in III:52 knowledge and then concentration leads to a recognition of corporeality—an implication altogether absent from III:54.

Hence, the continuing need of the philosopher to observe the commandments (in III:51) signals a naivete in the conception of the true self set out in III:54. III:51 reveals a human being as an essentially corporeal creature even after he has attained the "fourth perfection." Perhaps not wishing to make this implication plain, Maimonides made it appear that chapter 54's optimistic portrait of human potentialities is the *Guide*'s last word on the subject.

IV

It may easily be argued that this "corporealist" reading of III:51 is highly partial and selective. For, if we merely read on in III:51, we amass strong evidence that some exceptional human beings can transcend corporeality. Maimonides' description of Moses and the Patriarchs appears to tell us precisely that. I want to address this claim by subjecting the rest of III:51 to a close reading. My reading will suggest a deliberate and sustained conflict in Maimonides' thought when he assesses the lives of Moses and the Patriarchs.

As set out in III:51, Maimonides' mandate to the philosopher is not only to acquire knowledge, but also to *concentrate* exclusively on what he knows to the extent that this is possible. It would seem, however, that, for one who devotes himself exclusively to intellection, concentration on any sort of bodily activity is an impediment—it interferes with intellection. Performing commandments involves bodily activity. Hence, one problem with performing the commandments when one has achieved the higher level is the possibility of losing intellectual focus through concentration on physical action. Not only does performing a commandment while thinking about *worldly* things break the attention of the would-be worshipper, but even performing a physical act required by the Law seemingly requires a break in attention, since one must focus on one's movements.

Maimonides takes stock of this difficulty in III:51. The commandments "have only the end of training you to occupy yourself with His commandments...rather than with matters pertaining to this world" (III:51, 622). By placing himself in the right motivational state, the performer will be able to execute bodily movements without abandoning his intellectual focus. Far from impeding intellectual concentration, the commandments promote it, provided that they are executed with the right measure and mode of reflection.[42]

> If, however, you pray merely by moving your lips while facing a wall, and at the same time thinking about your buying and selling; or if you read the Torah with your tongue while your heart is set upon the building of your habitation and does not consider what you read; and similarly in all cases in which you perform a commandment merely with your limbs—as if you were digging a hole in the ground, or hewing wood in the forest—without reflecting either upon the meaning of that action or upon Him from whom the commandment proceeds or upon the end of the action, you should not think that you have achieved the end.

One who is concentrating exclusively on God will not perform commandments "with the limbs only."

After implicitly resolving the problem of diverted concentration as it pertains to acts of worship, Maimonides raises a parallel question about the political activities and daily life of Moses and the Patriarchs. These men achieved the "union with God—I mean apprehension of Him in love of Him"; "also the providence of God watching over them in over their posterity was great" (III:51, 624). Yet they engaged in practical pursuits:

> Withal they were occupied with governing people, increasing their fortune, and endeavoring to acquire property.

How shall we explain this paradox?

> Now this is to my mind a proof that they performed these actions with their limbs only while their intellects were constantly in His

presence. (III:51, 625)

Thus Moses and the Patriarchs exemplify Maimonides' depiction of a special sort of person, one who attains a rank that Maimonides suggests even he cannot be guided to attain.[43] This is a rank of

> a human individual who, through this apprehension of the true realities and his joy in what he has apprehended, achieves a state in which he talks with people and is occupied with his bodily necessities while his intellect is wholly turned toward Him...while outwardly he is with people. (III:51, 623)

This phenomenon—the existence of special individuals who (in contrast to the trainee) perform physical or political activities "with their limbs only, while their intellects are constantly in His presence"—can be understood against the backdrop of I:72. There Maimonides writes that "the relation obtaining between God, may He be exalted, and the world" may be compared to "that obtaining between the acquired intellect and man; this intellect is not a faculty in the body but is truly separate from the organic body and overflows toward it" (193). Now the acquired intellect is just "the perfect intellect *in actu*."[44]

What the passage suggests, therefore, is that the perfect intellect "overflows" toward the body and determines human actions.[45] If we put this idea of I:72 together with the notion that Moses and the Patriarchs did certain things with their limbs only, we come up with the following explanation of how they did these actions: the actions in question were done with the limbs only because these actions, *like all human actions done by those whose intellects are perfected*, were merely an overflow from the acquired intellect, and this overflow operates through a causality that more closely resembles mechanical causality than it does intentional human action, i.e., action that results from the exercise of practical reason.[46]

This understanding of the Moses/Patriarchs phenomenon dissolves an otherwise puzzling contradiction. Maimonides states:

> In all these actions their end was to come near to Him.... For the end of their efforts was to bring into being a religious community that would know and worship God.... Thus it has become clear to you that the end of all their efforts was to spread the doctrine of [God's unity] and to guide people to love Him. (624)

Now one would think that, if the end of their activity of governance was "to bring into being a religious community that would know and worship God...to spread the doctrine of the unity of [God's name] and to guide people to love Him," then the one activity that would decidedly *not* be performed "with the limbs only" would be governing the people. And yet, Maimonides explicitly lumps "governing people" together with "increasing fortune," ("tending cattle, doing agricultural work, and governing the household") and "endeavoring to acquire property," as actions they performed "with their limbs only."

A possible explanation of this fact is that *all* physical activities done by one who has achieved the highest level are done with the limbs only since these activities are the result of the overflow from the intellect. It has already been observed by others[47] that, at the end of the *Guide*, Maimonides distinguishes between (1) "the perfection of man that may truly be gloried in," which consists in apprehending God and His providence over his creatures, and (2) "the way of life of such an individual," which "will always have in view lovingkindness, righteousness, and judgment, through assimilation to His actions." "The way of life" probably refers to political governance.[48] Based on a principle Maimonides advocates in II:11 ("Know that in the case of every being that causes a certain good thing to overflow from it according to this order of rank, the existence, the purpose, and the end of the being conferring the benefits, do not consist in conferring the benefits on the recipient. For pure absurdity necessarily would follow from this assumption" (II:11, 275), we may say that the actions referred to are not part of the *essence* of human perfection but rather part of the *overflow*.[49] And based on III:51 (the "limbs only" passage), we might take a further step: action resulting from this overflow does not represent anything like ordinary deliberative behavior, because the explanation of it is so different from the explanation of the ordinary deliberative behavior. Indeed, there is nothing special about the fact that political governance was carried out by Moses and the Patriarchs with the limbs only. *Any* bodily activity performed by them had to be performed with the limbs only.[50]

The section on Moses and the Patriarchs, as just interpreted, has an obvious bearing on Maimonides' conception of the human self. If the philosopher's continuing need for the commandments and his need to focus on God *through* bodily activity is a mark of *his* corporeality, the phenomenon of Moses and the Patriarchs, who performed bodily actions with their limbs only, would appear to confirm that rare human beings *can* transcend corporeal limitations. The true self of an individual who is on the level of Moses and the Patriarchs is purely intellectual. Because their "true selves" were intellectual, *any* bodily activity they would execute could be performed with the limbs only. For the body is merely a corporeal entity, and not part of the essential person.

The passage immediately after the one on Moses and the Patriarchs augments the case for this claim about human potentialities. Here Maimonides interrupts the flow of exposition in order to divulge an "extraordinary speculation" that "has occurred to me just now" (624). The speculation is that providence operates over an individual according to the degree to which he is occupied with divine matters without distraction.

> If the man's thought is free from distraction, if he apprehends Him, may He be exalted, in the right way and rejoices in what he apprehends, that individual can never be afflicted with evil of any kind. For he is with God and God is with him. (625)

Apart from the literary peculiarity of Maimonides' discussion—a chapter of which he expressly attests that it contains nothing new is also one in which Maimonides remarks that an idea has just occurred to him[51]—the conception of providence just advanced has seemed to commentators to contradict the naturalistic account of providence developed by Maimonides in earlier chapters. In earlier chapters, Maimonides had maintained that a person who has developed his intellect may enjoy providence in two ways:

> (1) He may utilize his (practical or scientific) knowledge to articulate and protect himself from potential harms; (2) he may utilize his (philosophic) insight that material goods and evils are insignificant as compared to intellectual goods, in order to remain untroubled through periods of adversity.

In both cases, providence is "operating" in an entirely naturalistic manner. Yet, in III:51, Maimonides writes of the individual who is exclusively occupied with God that "no evil at all will befall him" (626), neither floods nor pestilence nor wars nor any physical calamity.

> If you should happen to pass...a widely extended field of battle... even if one thousand were killed to your left and ten thousand to your right, no evil at all will befall you. (627)

Samuel ibn Tibbon sought to explain why the philosopher enjoys this extravagant degree of protection; it seems difficult to explain, save by shifting from a naturalistic theory to a supernatural one: God must directly protect the individual from harm. Thus, the naturalist theory of III:11-12, 17-23 seems to give way to, and be contradicted by, a supernatural theory in III:51.[52]

Of the solutions proposed to Samuel's query, the most compelling appears to be that offered by Moses Narboni.[53] Narboni, in effect, italicizes the word "him": "no evil will befall *him*." If the individual's "true self"—his true form—is the intellect, then, indeed, neither floods nor pestilence nor war can affect *him*; only the material body is affected, while the intellect, the real person, emerges unscathed. To be sure, the protection of the true self is limited to those moments at which the individual's intellectual potentialities are being actualized. Still, at those moments, if only at those moments, the individual becomes one with the separate intellect and thus separate from matter.[54]

While Narboni's interpretation does not exclude the operation of the other types of naturalistic protection identified by Samuel ibn Tibbon (Shem Tov lists all these forms of protection in his construal of Maimonides), the interpretation does force us to say that III:51 anticipates, or, rather, presupposes, the view that man's "true self" is intellectual—a view that will not explicitly be forwarded until III:54.[55] The same view may underlie Maimonides' statement at the end of III:51 that Moses, Aaron, and Miriam achieved salvation from death because they were in a state of passionate love when their bodily faculties were extinguished.[56] And that same view may be invoked to explain why Moses and the Patriarchs must be said to have acted with their limbs only. The limbs are not part of their essential being. The proximity of the two paragraphs; the strong suggestion that the Moses/Patriarchs passage inspired the doctrine about providence; the explicit "proof" that Moses and the Patriarchs must have acted with their limbs only *because* they enjoyed providence—all these render it virtually certain that the two passages are tightly connected and mutually dependent.

The foregoing represents a rather strong case in support of the claim that, for Maimonides, in III:51, rare human individuals can actualize a purely intellectual self, just as claimed in III:54. However, the issue cannot be settled so simply. Reading the Moses/Patriarchs and providence passages as we have leaves us with nagging questions. For example, if, as per Narboni, the "true self" argument of III:54 is needed to explain the phenomena described in III:51, why wasn't that argument introduced in

III:51 instead of three chapters later?[57] In addition, the true self argument of III:54 was applied to someone who possessed the fourth perfection; and the fourth perfection is achieved through intellectual knowledge alone. The trainee of III:51, therefore, *by the definition of the fourth perfection given in III:54*, has *already* actualized his true self through knowledge and should not be subject any longer to corporeal limitations; yet he *is* still subject to these limitations and would have to attain the level of Moses and the Patriarchs to transcend them.

In addition to these unresolved problems, some of the evidence in III:51-52 suggests that the portrait of Moses and the Patriarchs, as well as of the man of providence, is presented by Maimonides as only a possibility, not as an actuality. He himself was uncertain about whether the possibility could be and was actualized; and he presents us, in III:51-52, with ingredients of a competing picture, a picture in which no human individual can transcend all corporeal limitations.

First, Maimonides thinks that one cannot be *guided* to attain the rank of Moses and the Patriarchs.

> This rank is not a rank that, with a view to the attainment of which, someone like myself may aspire for guidance [Pines records two alternative meanings: to be guided, and to guide others]. But one may aspire to attain that rank which was mentioned before this one through the training that we described. (III:51, 624)

In contemporary philosophical parlance, the Moses/Patriarchs phenomenon is a "nomological dangler": Maimonides has no way of explaining *how* it can evolve within his own theories. The level of Moses and the Patriarchs is not continuous with that of the trainee. To concentrate on God, the trainee must occupy himself with concentration, on bodily activities, i.e., the *mizvot*; and when performing mundane tasks he is to focus on worldly activities, apparently to the neglect of concentration on God (III:51, 613). As I will later show (see appendix below), Maimonides does not even intend the training he prescribes to serve as training for the level of Moses and the Patriarchs, but only, on the contrary, to serve as training for the ability to meditate properly when *not* engaged in bodily activities. How anyone living in the way prescribed for the trainee could *develop* into a Moses is a puzzle Maimonides cannot resolve, and that anyone can enjoy the degree of providence he describes is "an extraordinary speculation" that would not have occurred to him were it not for the existence of Moses and the Patriarchs. Lacking a theory to explain how one could *become* a Moses, Maimonides lacks a theory to explain how Moses could be as he appears. Doubts about the ability to *guide* one to this level easily generate doubts about the ability to *attain* the level.

Second, we read in III:51, 627 that "in the measure in which the faculties of the body are weakened and the fire of the desires is quenched, the intellect is strengthened, its lights achieve a wider extension, its apprehension is purified, and it rejoices in what it apprehends." Apprehension and love wax as bodily capacities wane in old age. This passage yields a powerful argument for the possibility of *immortality*— survival of the soul *after* death—in Maimonides' thought. But its implications for the possibility of transcending corporeality *while* soul and body are one—in other words, the possibility of achieving worship in the here and now—are pessimistic. The fullest flowering of the intellect must await the extinction of desire. If even the Active Intellect "sometimes gets an impediment that hinders its act" (I:68, 166), the prospects of a corporeal creature remaining in a state of unimpeded intellectual activity would appear to be dim indeed. If the passage on old age is to be read as I have just suggested, III:51 contains a counterpoint to the optimistic picture of human possibilities painted in the passage on Moses and the Patriarchs and the passage on providence. This illustrates my claim that III:51 recapitulates the tensions in Maimonides' conception of the person that have run through the *Guide* all along.

Third, the passage on Moses and the Patriarchs, in which Maimonides describes the special sort of individual who can do physical activities while concentrating on God and who enjoys the fullest extent of providence, does not make that sort of individual appear *too* rare. Not only Moses, but Abraham; not only Abraham, but even Isaac and Jacob, are said to have attained this exalted level (III:51, 623-24).[58] Maimonides here abandons the idea that Moses was singular, an idea that is found in scattered places in the *Guide* and even earlier in III:51, 620. Any claims for the uniqueness or near uniqueness of Moses are undermined still more at the end of the chapter, when Aaron and Miriam suddenly surface as individuals who achieved passionate love and secured salvation from death. They seem to rank even above the Patriarchs.[59] By conceding that Moses was not singular, and that even individuals whose achievements as prophets and leaders are surpassed by those of Moses can appropriately be grouped with him, Maimonides is perhaps subtly suggesting that even Moses did not achieve perfection.

Fourth, III:52, I said earlier, caps the discussion initiated in III:51 and is, in my view, the last word of the *Guide*. Here, emphasis is on man's *lesser* status. "The one who has apprehended the true realities" seeks to liberate himself from all potentiality, and not merely to actualize a potential for moral conduct or to actualize the potential of the rational faculty (which, unlike the acquired intellect, resides in matter; see I:72). *Fear results from the realization that this escape is not possible.*

Here, in III:52, we find a counterpoint to III:51, 624-26. In fact, even *within* III:52, one finds both acknowledgment of corporeality (as we have just seen) and contrasting sentences about "the bond between us and him." Maimonides begins the chapter by stating that one does not "sit, move, and occupy himself when he is alone in the house, as he sits, and occupies himself when he is in the presence of a great king" (III:52, 629). We know from the lexicographical chapters that such verbs may be used for both corporeal and noncorporeal beings; in context the ambiguity is most appropriate.

Fifth, skepticism about the Moses example is warranted even as regards *apprehension*. As Pines points out, Maimonides gives expression to two contradictory interpretations of "my face shall not be seen" (Exodus 33:23). His official, stated view in I:38 is that Moses apprehended "*all* things created by me," which would include the separate intellects; but in I:37 he quotes an interpretation of Onkelos to the effect that human beings can know only "things endowed with matter and form". Pines argues that Onkelos's interpretation is the one Maimonides believes (since he had no other reason to cite it) and that the statement in I:38 is made for political reasons.[60] Josef Stern, on the other hand, has argued, more convincingly, that Maimonides is presenting contradictory alternatives between which he cannot adjudicate given his own epistemological theory. In other words, Maimonides himself suspends judgment.[61] Limitations to human knowledge are also conceded in I:21, 31, 32, 54 and in III:9, without Moses appearing to be an exception. A similar agnostic attitude may characterize III:51: Maimonides lays out for us two conflicting pictures.

The situation is analogous to one we encounter when we try to assess the place of matter in Maimonides' metaphysics. As Alfred Ivry has shown,[62] Maimonides on the one hand accepted the Aristotelian definition of substance as including matter and thus saw matter as a necessary part of being—a substratum for form and individual existence, as well as a principle of change and potentiality; on the other hand, he was attracted to certain aspects of the rival Neoplatonic approach, for example, its negative *evaluation* of matter and its view of matter as privation. The conflict that characterizes the evidence in the *Guide* concerning the nature of human beings and the scope of human potentialities mirrors the conflict that characterizes Maimonides' understanding of the place of matter in the world. Multiple approaches to human beings have been said to account for the several and diverse theories of providence found in part III of the *Guide*.[63]

Maimonides tells us in I:17 that philosophers and learned men, in discussing the topic of matter and form, used only riddles, figurative language, and similes. It would be surprising if Maimonides furnished us with a ready, clear statement on the subject of matter and form as those concepts serve to elucidate his conception of the human being. A deliberate ambiguity in III:51-52, a presentation of conflicting pictures, would fit in perfectly with Maimonides' views on the need for care in exposition.

Thus, III:51-52 brings to a head the clash between two pictures of human beings that has been waged in "the other chapters of this Treatise." Maimonides leaves us with a fourfold knot of problems whose resolution depends upon which view of human beings emerges triumphant. These problems are (1) the possibility of knowing immaterial beings; (2) the possibility of enjoying providence to the fullest degree; (3) the possibility of transcending the need for commandments; (4) the possibility of anyone living in the style ascribed to Moses and the Patriarchs. The absence of any explicit assertion of the "true self" argument in III:51 may be due to Maimonides' uncertainty about the possibility of this true self being actualized. III:51 is the *Guide*'s real conclusion; but Maimonides chose to end with a formulation (III:54) that is blissfully free of tensions.

One other consequence of our discussion should be noted. Pines believes that, *because* theoretical perfection is impossible for human beings, and the only positive knowledge of God of which man is capable is knowledge of the attributes of action, *therefore* the life of practical, political activity, in which one imitates God's attributes of *hesed*, *mishpat*, and *zedakah*, is the highest perfection of a human being.[64] But, if the individual described at the very end of III:54 who imitates God's attributes of action is identified with or is exemplified by Moses (as is suggested by I:54), *and* we take III:51 as articulating the *nature* of Mosaic governance, then political activity *as defined by Maimonides* is dependent upon theoretical perfection. Any political activity not achieved by escaping corporeality will be different from the political activity of the ideal Moses of III:51. Even in III:54 itself, we must hold that only the individual for whom political activity represents an "overflow" of his perfection satisfies the description of the ideal personality, for only such an individual rises to the level of Moses and the Patriarchs and rules as they are said to have ruled in III:51—with the limbs only. Thus, if man is precluded from attaining theoretical perfection because matter is an ineliminable impediment, he cannot attain practical perfection as Maimonides defines it; at best he can attain practical perfection in some other sense. The two perfections, theoretical and practical, would appear to stand or fall together.

This consequence follows provided that we take the Moses passage in III:51 and the passage on *imitatio dei* in III:54 to be describing the same phenomenon. From the connection between I:54 and III:54, on the other hand, it would seem that knowledge of God's actions, i.e., knowledge of nature, even without positive knowledge of immaterial beings, can generate (overflow into) a distinctive political way of life modeled on imitation of God's attributes as manifested in nature. III:54 nowhere states explicitly that political activity is not ideal unless it satisfies the account given of Moses and the Patriarchs in III:51; the account in III:51, on the other hand, makes no reference to *imitatio dei*. Thus, our lack of clarity as to whether Maimonides is describing, in III:51 and III:54, a single type of political life, or instead two different types, leaves us uncertain as to whether political perfection is dependent on escaping corporeality.

V

My reading of III:51-54 contains several distinct elements, and a reader is not obliged to accept all of these by virtue of having accepted one. A point that I think is beyond controversy is that

> (I) III:51 differs from III:54 in its characterization of the human *telos* and in its assessment of the purpose of *mizvot*.

Also beyond controversy, I think, is that

> (II) III:51 describes a stage of human development that comes after the stage described in III:54.

More debatable is whether

> (III) The chapters differ in another respect as well: viz., they differ in their assessments of whether human beings can transcend all corporeal limitations and actualize a purely intellectual self.

Lastly, even assuming one grants (I), (II), and (III), there is the question of why Maimonides placed III:54 after III:51. Perhaps

> (IV) By placing 54 at the end, Maimonides wishes to conceal the tensions and uncertainties which characterize his real position.

I concede that (IV) is speculative. What is not speculative is that there is a problem about the placement of III:54 and III:51 that must be explained somehow.

The approach to III:51-54 advocated in this paper is significant, I believe, for several reasons.

(1) Scholars who have turned their attention to these final chapters of the *Guide* have tended to rivet their gaze on the question: which is the highest end of a human being, theoretical perfection or practical perfection? Certainly the importance of this issue to our understanding of Maimonides must not be denigrated; and certainly the work that has been produced on this issue is valuable. Nevertheless, focusing exclusively on this question of how to rank the two perfections has led to neglect of other problems with which Maimonides was grappling in these final chapters. Chief among these are problems concerning the nature of a human being, which in turn bear on the prospects for attaining perfection, whether intellectual or practical. Indeed, the salience of these problems throughout the *Guide* needs to be emphasized more than it has been.

(2) Chapters 51-54 have often been treated as a seamless web. The differences between them have been ignored, and as a result chapter 54 has been taken at face value. I have sought to correct this perspective and to caution against taking chapter 54 superficially.

(3) Some of the literary features of chapter 51 that have often been remarked on can now be understood. In particular, Maimonides' insistence that chapter 51 contains nothing new perhaps is meant to divert attention from the significance of the chapter. Interestingly, the heart of the chapter is the segment beginning with "additional matter," viz., the passage on the training conception of the commandments, the passage on Moses and the Patriarchs, and the "extraordinary speculation"

about providence which has "occurred to me just now." Attending to this new material helps us define the problematic nature of III:51. To a certain extent, though, Maimonides' remarks about introducing nothing new rings true: the chapter plays out—brings to a climax—themes that have been broached before, indeed have run throughout the *Guide*.

(4) That Maimonides devoted twenty-five chapters to *ta'amei ha-mizvot* suggests that this topic was central to the philosophic outlook of the *Guide*. This centrality, I believe, traces to Maimonides' view that the commandments represent a way of dealing with human corporeality and the limitations it imposes on human achievement—a problem which, on my reading, is a focal concern of the *Guide*. On my reading, furthermore, Maimonides' handling of *mizvot* in III:51-54 provides an interpretive key to the chapters, since the conception of *mizvot* in III:54 serves as an indication that III:54 precedes III:51.

(5) The place of the commandments in Maimonides' conception of the human ideal has often struck readers of the *Guide* as highly tenuous and problematic. For, first, the notion that "all the actions prescribed by the Law" are "but preparations made for the sake of this end [intellectual perfection]" (III:54, 636) implies that the commandments are of no value at all for the individual who has achieved the end for which the commandments are designed, and hence that the commandments can occupy no niche in the life of the philosopher. And second, the fact that certain commandments originated in specific historical circumstances would seem to entail that they may be abandoned in changed circumstances.

What has often been overlooked is that the two sources of antinomianism just identified are problems to which Maimonides, as we have seen, presented a reasonably explicit answer in III:51, when he introduced the idea that the commandments train the philosopher to be occupied with God. Preoccupation with the means/ends argument and the argument from historical origins is unfortunate, because it has crowded out interest in certain other problems that Maimonides cared about and addressed, albeit with characteristic ambiguity. Compounding the error, some readers of the *Guide* work with the pat assumption that Maimonides consistently defended the Law outwardly while rejecting it inwardly, when in truth, it is his *open* declaration that the commandments are but preparations that may be seen from III:51 to be a poor gauge of his real position. In truth, the philosopher, too, must observe the law (III:51, 622).

In this paper, then, I have sought to stimulate a reorientation of perspective and emphasis as regards the key questions we must ask about Maimonides' accounts of the commandments, of human perfection and of the figures who seek to create a "religious community that would know and worship God" (III:51, 624). Our discussion has taken us to problems that lie at the deepest levels of Maimonides' psychology and epistemology, and to hard questions about what to make of the peculiar literary features of the *Guide's* climactic chapters. We are left, at the least, with a new agenda.

APPENDIX

In section IV I called attention to the following question: does the philosopher's conception of the bodily movements associated with *mizvot* preclude his concentration on God while he is performing the commandments? Maimonides' implicit reply, I indicated, was no; and that negative answer underlies his entire conception of the commandments (in III:51) as a regimen through which the philosopher trains himself to be occupied with God. More argumentation is needed, however, to support our taking Maimonides at face value when he implies that no conflict is incurred by the philosopher while performing the commandments; indeed, an interesting line of thought can be wielded against this reading. In this appendix I wish to defend my exoteric reading of the passage against this line of thought.

The problem of diverted concentration that is raised by the examples of Moses and the Patriarchs parallels the problem of diverted concentration that is raised by the example of the philosopher who performs acts prescribed by the Law. In both cases, Maimonides is aware of the possibility that attention to bodily activities will interfere with intellectual concentration. But Maimonides' *solution* to the problem of diverted concentration in the case of Moses and the Patriarchs is the *opposite* of his solution to the problem of diverted concentration that he proposed in the case of the commandments. In the trainee's case, Maimonides had cautioned that, while concentrating on God, one should *not* perform actions (commandments) "only with your limbs." In the Moses passage, by contrast, he holds that, while performing bodily actions— "governing people, increasing fortune, endeavoring to acquire property";

"tending cattle, doing agricultural work, governing their household"—
Moses and the Patriarchs *did* act "with their limbs only." They *had to*,
for otherwise they could not remain constantly in the presence of God.
What does Maimonides wish to convey by repeating the phrase ("with
the limbs only") that he used in the passage on the commandments? One
possibility is that the repetition of the phrase should be taken innocuously,
i.e., Maimonides repeats the phrase in order to *contrast* the two situations.
Performing the commandments of praying, reciting the *shema* and
benedictions, and reading the Torah, readily lead one to concentrate on
God, while the mundane activities of Moses and the Patriarchs do not.
But could he perhaps be intimating, through repetition of the phrase, that
the activity of one who performs the commandments as training is more
analogous to the activity of Moses and the Patriarchs than appears at
first? Might his real view be that the philosopher, too, must split between
his mental concentration and his bodily activity when he performs the
commandments?

Maimonides' selection of examples—reading the Torah and
prayer—might be read in a way that supports a reading of this esoteric
kind. As Josef Stern has pointed out,[65] these activities are problematic
for the philosopher because they involve the use of anthropomorphic and
anthropopathic expressions.[66] Hence, when Maimonides instructs his
readers to

> cause your soul, whenever you read or listen to the Torah, to be
> constantly directed—the whole of you and your thought—toward
> reflection on what you are listening to or reading (III:51, 622)

and to practice the same with regard to discourses of the prophets and
benedictions, or when he advises:

> give heed to all that you are reading ... aim at meditating on what
> you are uttering and at considering its meaning (Ibid.)

he cannot possibly mean that you should focus on the anthropomorphic
and anthropopathic language and the affirmative attributes. Doing
so would lead you down the wrong path, that of "the affections of the
imagination" (III:51, 623). Quite the contrary, what the philosopher
must do is split his concentration from his action; he must think about
philosophic truths, and these are radically different in content from the
assertions in verbal prayer. Note that when advising his reader to engage
in "intellectual worship" while upon his bed, Maimonides stresses that
this worship consists in "nearness to God and being in His presence *in*

that true reality that I have made known to you and *not by way of affections of the imagination"* (III:51, 623)—not, that is, in the way stimulated by affirmative attributes. On this reading, doing the commandments in the way Maimonides prescribes doesn't merely train you to occupy yourself with God. Rather, it trains you to occupy yourself with God *while engaged in activity that to some extent interferes with exclusive occupation with God.* And in that way performance of the commandments trains the gifted individual to act in a manner more nearly approximating the way of Moses and the Patriarchs, who could remain in God's presence while doing other things, though in fact their rank may not be attainable by others.

The same possibility comes out forcefully in a passage that contains a remarkable ambiguity. Maimonides has allowed one who is free from distraction while performing acts of worship to also occupy his thoughts with worldly things for "many and long stretches of time":

> Thus, I have provided you with many and long stretches of time in which you can think all that needs thinking regarding property, the governance of the household, and the welfare of the body. On the other hand, while performing the actions imposed by the Law, you should occupy yourself *only with what you are doing, as we have explained.* (III:51, 623)

What are you "doing" when you perform the commandments? Are you "doing" the action—that is the exoteric reading—or are you concentrating on God? With which of these should you "occupy yourself"? What, precisely, have you "explained"?

According to the esoteric reading, in which Maimonides is encouraging a split between mental focus and bodily movement, Maimonides has chosen the examples of prayer and reading the Torah because in those cases the conflict between concentration on God and concentration on the activity is *maximal.* In fact, since anthropomorphic and anthropopathic concentrations are "affections of the imagination," and imagination is a corporeal faculty, the conflict is one between mind and body. If this reading is correct, then the philosopher is not really concentrating on doing the commandments if he concentrates on God.

However, the selection of examples and the intent of the passage could be explained differently. Reading the Torah and prayer involve minimal bodily movements and maximal possibility of concentrating on God. By choosing these examples, so this reading goes, Maimonides is able to mute the conflict that could arise between the twin demands of occupation with God and concentration on the bodily movements demanded by a particular precept. In short, Maimonides picked examples in which the problem of diverted concentration is *minimal*, not (as in Stern's reading) examples in which the conflict is *maximal*. As for the problems posed by affirmative attributes, the philosopher is to reflect on what those attributes mean within Maimonides' theory of attributes, or on why such attributes are used. Thus the philosopher keeps a distance from the literal meaning of prayers but still uses the texts as an opportunity to reflect on truths pointed to, if only allusively and misleadingly, therein, or on truths which explain why the texts are used. He need not split his thought from his actions. Maimonides saw no conflict between thought and behavior here.

Which reading is correct? On behalf of the second, let us return to a passage quoted earlier only in part:

> If, however, while performing these acts of worship, you are free from distraction and not engaged in thinking upon any of the things pertaining to this world, cause your soul—after this has been achieved—to occupy your thought with things necessary for you or superfluous in your life, and in general with worldly things, while you eat or drink or bathe or talk with your wife and your small children, or while you talk with the common run of people. Thus, I have provided you with many and long stretches of time in which you can think all that needs thinking regarding property, the governance of the household, and the welfare of the body. On the other hand, while performing the actions imposed by the Law, you should occupy yourself only with what you are doing, as we have explained. (III:51, 623)

Maimonides here wants to contrast property, household, and body on the one hand, with actions imposed by the Law on the other. However, in the case of the mundane activities, he seems to be advising that while engaging in one thing (eating, drinking, bathing, conversing) one should concentrate on *other* things, viz., *other worldly things*. He is suggesting a way of cutting down on the time spent thinking about mundane matters.[67] But if the mundane cases require a split between concentration and action, then the actions imposed by the Law, which are being contrasted with the mundane actions, cannot require such a split.

There is another, more fundamental reason to support the second, non-esoteric reading. On the first reading (which demands a split between concentration and action during performance of the commandments), the training of which Maimonides speaks is training in the following: doing one thing while concentrating on another. Now, the whole notion of training through the commandments is paradoxical *if* (1) one must not do *mizvot* with the limbs only; (2) the training is intended as training designed to elevate one to the level of Moses and the Patriarchs. How can one train for a level at which one acts with the limbs only, by performing certain activities that must *not* be done with the limbs only? If one is training for the level of Moses and the Patriarchs, then the "diverted concentration" understanding of Maimonides' examples (prayer and Torah reading) is the only one feasible. However, Maimonides implies quite strongly that one is *not* training for *that* level, but instead for the ability to meditate properly when alone "upon your bed."

> In my opinion this end ["intellectual worship consisting in nearness to God and being in His presence in that true reality that I have made known to you and not by way of the affections of the imagination"] can be achieved by those of the men of knowledge who have rendered their souls worthy of it by training of this kind. (III:51, 623)

We also have an explicit statement on 624:

> But one may aspire to attain that rank which was mentioned before [i.e., the rank lower than that of Moses and the Patriarchs] through the training that we have ascribed.

In this passage we have the sense that there is a lack of transition between the lower level and the level of Moses and the Patriarchs. One cannot *be guided to* the rank of Moses and the Patriarchs (624). If by performing the commandments one were doing one thing while concentrating on another, one *would* thereby be guided to the rank of Moses and the Patriarchs, contrary to Maimonides' rejection of this possibility. Since no such guidance is possible, Maimonides' repetition of the "limbs only" phrase is better read as contrasting two levels: a (higher) level at which one *can* concentrate on God while engaged in other things, and a (lower) level at which one can not. The higher level is not continuous with the lower level; rather, attaining it involves a quantum leap.

Even if we reject an esoteric reading which sees prayer and Torah reading as involving a split between thought and action, a modified esoteric reading may yet be proposed. Granted that Maimonides did not intend the examples of prayer and Torah reading to epitomize cases of conflict between mind and body, his selection of examples, one may nonetheless say, is calculated to conceal the problem that arises when we try to extend the training model to other commandments. The examples he chooses are too convenient; they make it too easy for him to illustrate his claim that performance of the commandments does not interfere with intellectual concentration. When it comes to *other* commandments, the way in which we are to apply this approach is not clear. Maimonides' catch-all phrase "and the performance of the other commandments," it will be argued, masks the fact that his "new" explanation of the commandments works only for a select few of them.[68] For instance, social laws seem to have no place in the training conception, though they are prominent in III:54.[69]

Interestingly, although Maimonides' examples—prayer, Torah reading, benedictions—are taken from the commandments in the *Mishneh Torah*'s Book of Love that he itemized in III:44,[70] Maimonides does not here refer to the most physical of the commandments mentioned in III:44, to wit, phylacteries, *mezuzah*, and acquiring a Torah. Also intriguing is the fact that Avicenna, who arguably influenced Maimonides' conception of prayer in III:51, declares that "all the other ordinances of the religion are explicable along the lines" which he sketched for prayer, but then writes: "We would have desired to expound each act of worship separately: but it was impossible for us to enter upon matters which may not fitly be communicated to every man."[71] Avicenna's reluctance to explicitly extend his model to other practices might encourage the notion that, for Maimonides, the performance of the other commandments cannot be explicated along the same lines as his primary examples; at the level of worship, performance of the *other* commandments would interfere with attainment of the human telos.

I do not find this argument on behalf of an esoteric, antinomian reading of the "training" conception persuasive. It is true that, in III:51, Maimonides picks examples that best fit the conception, just as in III:54 he picks examples (social laws) that best illustrate the propaedeutic conception he advocates there. However, this does not mean that he thought the conception in III:51 cannot be applied to any commandments but those in his examples. In other passages in which love and fear are said to be the end of the commandments, no examples are given at all (III:24, 501). As for the Avicenna reference, Maimonides may be following Avicenna's lead (of not discussing other precepts), but not because these do not fit his model. Perhaps he is wary of people applying the model incorrectly and paying insufficient heed to the details of the actions. No such danger exists in the cases of prayer and Torah reading.

It would be instructive to compare Maimonides' discussion here with discussions by Jewish writers in the Neoplatonic and Sufi tradition, such as Bahya ibn Pakuda. Like Maimonides, Bahya argues vigorously for the supremacy of interior religious attitudes—love, awe, cognition— over external performances. At the same time, he recognizes that most duties prescribed by Jewish law are external in character, and attempts to specify the proper attitude with which these commandments should be performed.[72] Maimonides was addressing the same problem, but unlike Bahya refrained from specifying appropriate interior attitudes for *all* external performances. Bahya's own attempt[73] to furnish proper motivations for such acts as taking a *lulav* and wearing *zizit* illustrates the point that interior attitudes might be defined so broadly as to lose their connection to the *particular* actions that supposedly must be performed with those attitudes.

I see no reason, at any rate, to doubt that Maimonides wanted his trainee to perform *all* commandments in the manner he suggests, that is, with a unity between mental focus and bodily act. We saw earlier that Maimonides' repetition of the "limbs only" phrase may be taken either as (1) accentuating the contrast between, on the one hand, the individual engaged in "training" through the commandments, and, on the other, Moses and the Patriarchs; or as (2) *blurring* that contrast—the trainee is more like them than appears, because he, too, must split himself between mental focus and bodily action. I have argued against this second possibility. Indeed, if, in accordance with the possibility I raise in the text, Maimonides could not adequately understand how the Moses/Patriarchs phenomenon is possible, then perhaps any similarity between the trainee and them works in the opposite way: they, like the trainee, do not fully divert their attention from their physical movements, because to do so they would need the overflow.

Though I do not accept an esoteric reading of Maimonides' remarks on using commandments as the regimen for concentrating on God, it must be admitted that the problem of how the philosopher can concentrate on God *through* prayer and Torah reading, practices which utilize anthropomorphic and anthropopathic conceptions, is an interesting one. In my view Maimonides' reference to activities which utilize these conceptions serve as yet another signal that the trainee has

254 The Legacy of Maimonides

not transcended corporeality and therefore has continued need for *miẓvot*. What he *can* achieve, in a constructive way, through these conceptions is, however, not clear for Maimonides' account.[74]

---

[1] Page references to the *Guide* are to the translation by Shlomo Pines (Chicago, 1963).

[2] I will henceforth drop the qualification "kind of" in citing this passage.

[3] Struck by the oddity of having three chapters come after a conclusion, Shlomo Pines has written that the designation of III:51 as "conclusion" "may, but does not necessarily, mean" that at first Maimonides intended III:51 to be the concluding chapter, but later changed his mind and added 52, 53 and 54. See Pines, "The Philosophical Purport of Maimonides' Halachic Works and the Purport of the *Guide of the Perplexed*," in *Maimonides and Philosophy*, edited by Shlomo Pines and Yirmiyahu Yovel (Dordrecht, Boston, Lancaster, 1986), p. 9. Unfortunately, the suggestion that these chapters were introduced as an afterthought is not at all plausible. The chapters include such important themes as fear of God (52), the divine attributes manifested in nature (*hesed, mishpat, zedakah*) (53), the four perfections (54), and the imitation of God (end of 54). Furthermore, the passage on *imitato dei* in III:54 rounds out a discussion provided in I:54, as pointed out in Pines, "Translator's introduction," cxxi-cxxii, his "The Limitations of Human Knowledge According to Al-Farabi, Ibn Bajja and Maimonides," in *Studies in Medieval Jewish History and Literature*, edited by Isadore Twersky (Cambridge, 1979), pp. 82-109, esp. 98-100, and also in Eliezer Goldman, "The Worship Peculiar to Those Who Have Apprehended the True Realities" (Heb.), *Annual of Bar-Ilan Studies in Judaica and the Humanities* VI (1968), 287-313. The notion that Maimonides thought of these themes only after having set down in writing the themes of III:51 strains credulity. Pines himself uses very guarded language in broaching the possibility of a change of mind, and we would be wise to look for other explanations.

Steven Harvey, in "Maimonides in the Sultan's Palace," in *Perspectives on Maimonides*, ed. Joel L. Kraemer (London, 1996) pointed out that "*al-khatima*," translated as "conclusion," can also mean "seal," and that "in *heikhalot* writing seals are what the adept need to journey safely and successfully through the heavenly palaces." Maimonides "would then be saying that III:51 is the decisive clue to understanding his treatise." I certainly will agree that III:51 is the "conclusion" in this sense, but hope to show why it is the "conclusion" of the *Guide* in the straightforward sense as well.

[4] For a classic discussion of III:54 and its relationship to ibn Bajja's treatment, see Alexander Altmann, "Maimonides' Four Perfections," *Essays in Jewish Intellectual History* (Hanover, N.H., 1981), pp. 65-76. Cf. Goldman, "Worship," pp. 294 ff., who sees significant originality, at least in emphasis, in Maimonides' treatment.

[5] There is one passage in III:13, 451-52 that might be taken to indicate that worship precedes or is a means to perfection. Speaking of the views that "the final end of man is, as has been said, to worship God," Maimonides notes that "a question remains to be asked regarding the final end of this worship." The answer considered is that worship is a means to perfection. In that context, however, it is not clear either that the worship alluded to is that mentioned in III:51 or that the perfection referred to is purely intellectual, as opposed to being a state of perfection that is constituted by the state of worship.

[6] Pines, "Translator's introduction," cxxi-cxxii; Goldman, "Worship," 306 ff. Cf. Miriam Galston, "Philosopher King vs. Prophet," *Israel Oriental Studies* 8 (1978), 204-18.

[7] Maimonides says he has explained the political activity based on *imitatio dei* "several times in this Treatise." The passage on Moses and the Patriarchs in III:51 has as much claim to be among those chapters as does any other passage in the *Guide* with the exception of I:54, in which the *imitatio dei* motif is explicit. The absence of this motif in III:51 will be touched on later.

[8] Until III:25, Maimonides has devoted only two other chapters to *ta'amei ha-mizvot*: II: 39-40. These chapters contain the only cross reference in the *Guide* to the *ta'amei ha-mizvot* section. Their relevance to us will become clear later.

[9] While generally ignored, the distinction between welfare and perfection is noted by Miriam Galston, "The Purpose of the Law According to Maimonides," *Jewish Quarterly Review* 69 (1978), 27-51, and by Warren Zev Harvey, "Political Philosophy and Halakhah in Maimonides" (Heb.), *Iyyun* 29 (1980), 198-212.

[10] Maimonides also speaks of another class of opinions: those opinions belief in which is politically necessary—but (so he implies) need not be true (III:28, 513-14). Transmission of these opinions, evidently, falls under welfare of the body.

[11] The process by which the Law inculcates correct opinions is analogous to teleological processes in nature that "benefit" things that are not capable of cognizing and appreciating the processes. See, for instance, III:25, 503-4.

Two additional points support the idea that consciousness of God's ends is not necessary for the Law to achieve its ends as set out in III:25-49. First, some commandments, specifically those of the "second intention" (for example, sacrifices), are such that people in idolatrous times were not motivated by reasons Maimonides provides; indeed, it is evident, from a passage in III:32, 526, that people in idolatrous times were not even told of the reason for sacrifices. Second, even if people *had* been told the reasons for certain commandments—that they instill correct opinions or abolish reciprocal wrongdoing— they would not necessarily have been *motivated* by the ends. On the contrary, Maimonides believes that the masses are motivated by material rewards and punishments. See, e.g., *Guide* III:32, 529, where the use of material rewards and punishments is explained in terms of the frailties of human nature. The implication is that rewards and punishments (or promises and threats) are needed to motivate obedience, and motivation does not come through knowledge of the "reasons" Maimonides specifies. Also note I:36, 84: "For the multitude grasp only the actions of worship, not their meanings..." Shem Tov, in his commentary to III:51, correctly sees that in III:25-49, "*mizvot* do not require *kavvanah*."

[12] This terminology was suggested by Lawrence Kaplan. The same distinction, with different terminology, is central in Josef Stern, "The Idea of a *Hoq* in Maimonides' Explanation of the Law," in *Maimonides and Philosophy*, edited by Shlomo Pines and Yirmiyahu Yovel (Dordrecht, Boston, Lancaster, 1986), pp. 92-130. Much of this section is indebted to Stern's acute and sensitive analysis.

[13] "Political Philosophy and Halakhah."

[14] Stern, "Idea of a *Hoq*," p. 130, note 44, suggests that Maimonides interpolates this chapter precisely to conceal the contradiction between III:25-49 and III:51.

[15] Goldman, "Worship," pp. 290-91, effectively dispels the impression, created by this

passage, that fear of God relates only to actions and has nothing to do with opinions. See below, section IV.

[16] The conception, endorsed by Maimonides, that prayer is a means of "training" oneself to be occupied with God is found in Avicenna's treatise on prayer, to which Steven Harvey has referred me. As we shall later see, however, Maimonides' development of the conception contains significant twists.

[17] I am overstating matters. Yehudah Gellman has pointed out to me that the approach of III:51 is not new, having been foreshadowed in III:44. There Maimonides lists certain commandments whose end is "the constant commemoration of God, the love of Him and the fear of Him, the obligatory observance of the commandments in general, and the bringing about of such belief as is necessary for everyone professing the Law." His list includes prayers, recital of the Shema and reading of the Torah—the commandments showcased in III:51—as well as priestly blessings (he referred to benedictions in III:51). (The list also includes laws concerning phylacteries and *mezuzot*.) Nonetheless, I claim that III:51's approach is new, for in III:51 we find the idea that "the performance of the other commandments" (622) is to be understood along the same line as were the commandments from the *Mishneh Torah*'s Book of Love that were discussed in III:44. Interestingly, Maimonides concludes III:44 with these words: "All these are actions that bring about useful opinions. This is clear and manifest and does not require another discourse, for that would be nothing but repetition" (574). Even if Maimonides is here telling us that III:51's approach to the commandments is "nothing but repetition" and "includes nothing new," the fact he provided the "repetition" in III:51 needs explanation. The explanation, I think, is that in III:51 he is setting the approach of III:44 into a larger context (worship) and extending it to other commandments. For further discussion, see the Appendix below.

[18] The shift just described is pointed out by Yonah ben-Sasson, "A Study of the Doctrine of *Ta'amei ha-Mizvot* in Maimonides' *Guide*" (Heb.), *Tarbiz* 29 (1960):268-81; Goldman, "Worship," pp. 292-93; David Hartman, *Maimonides: Torah and Philosophic Quest* (Philadelphia, 1976), chs. 4-5, and *A Living Covenant* (New York, 1985), ch. 5; Yeshayahu Leibowitz, *The Faith of Maimonides* (Heb.), (Jerusalem, 1980); Josef Stern, "The Idea of a *Hoq* in Maimonides' Explanation of the Law." See also James H. Lehmann, "The Relationship of Love and Fear in the Writings of Maimonides," *Yavneh Review* VIII (1973), 7-24. Several of these writers characterize the shift as one from an anthropocentric to a theocentric explanation of the commandments, or from self-interested to disinterested worship. I am not happy with this formulation, partly because the argument given in III:54, 635 for the supremacy of intellectual perfection is boldly anthropocentric and self-interested, and partly because the aims of the Law set out in III:27-49 are not base or self-centered. See Hartman's critique of Yeshayahu Leibowitz on this point in *A Living Covenant*, pp. 117-24.

[19] Maimonides has in fact foreshadowed part of his new account in III:27, when he indicated that not only *welfare* of the soul but also *perfection* of the soul is aimed at by the Law. Though the element of concentration and training is not emphasized there, the connection between commandments and philosophic knowledge is.

[20] See Goldman, "Worship," p. 290. Maimonides does not use the term "worship" to refer to performances of the commandments until III:51. However, it is hard to know the precise significance of the term's not appearing earlier, for it appears in III:54 even though

III:54 is not referring to the training conception of the commandments but instead, as I shall presently argue, endorses the conception found in III:25-49.

[21] See Stern, "Idea of a Hoq" for an explanation of this remark. Note II:40, 382: "...the Law, although it is not natural, enters into what is natural."

[22] I owe this formulation of the argument to Stern, "The Idea of a *Hoq*," pp. 123-24.

[23] In discussion at the 1985 conference at which this paper was delivered.

[24] A similar reading is advocated by Josef Stern: "Knowing that content of the earlier chapters ... the philosopher will 'possess' the 'premises' from which he can now draw the 'conclusion' [III:51 is said by Maimonides to by a "only a kind of conclusion"] that for him the commandments only serve the end of 'training' Maimonides proposes here" (Stern, "The Idea of a *Hoq*," p. 124). Of course, on this reading, one must still uncover reasons for the *masses* to observe the commandments!

As Stern points out, (pp. 116-119, p. 129, note 36), the *Guide* contains other elements that combat the antinomian argument. The Law must be independent of time and place (III:34), and hence even prescriptions that are historically conditioned must continue in force. To be sure, it is not clear what issue Maimonides is addressing in III:34, and it is also unclear from his wording (p. 535, line 4-5) whether the claim of eternality (*a parte post*) applies to all laws or only those of the first intention (cf. Gerald Blidstein, "Maimonides on 'Oral Law'," in *Jewish Law Annual*, edited by B. Jackson, vol. I [Leiden, 1978], pp. 108-22, 117-21). Nevertheless, the fact that III:34 may contain a response to the antinomian threats, coupled with the fact that the philosopher would have ready access to this response, suggests that the shift to a new line of explanation in III:51 is not necessitated by the antinomian threat. On the other hand, it seems rather weak to say to the philosopher: "observe these practices because they once served a purpose for a different kind of society, and Law by nature must be eternal." He is likely to want an explanation that links up with his present interests. Thus, even if the antinomian threat could be met, a new motivation must be supplied for the philosopher.

[25] Contrary to my reading, Hartman argues that "reflecting upon the end of the action" means: reflecting upon the utility of the action as defined in III:25-49. The philosopher, on Hartman's understanding, realizes what God has done for the community of Israel by legislating the commandments, and this is a component of his love of God. See *A Living Covenant*, pp. 117 ff. Hartman's reading does have certain advantages. First, on my reading, there is no discernible distinction between "reflecting upon the end of the action" and "reflecting upon Him from whom the commandment proceeds," since on my reading the end of the action *is* "reflecting upon Him from whom the commandment proceeds." On Hartman's reading, the distinction between the two is clear (though on neither reading do we have a good idea of what "the meaning of the action" refers to). Second, nowhere else in the *Guide* do we find a statement enjoining the philosopher to reflect upon the ends in III:25-49 (the statement "marvel exceedingly at the wisdom of His commandments, just as you should marvel at the wisdom manifested in the things he had made," III:49, 605, is not an imperative to study and know the reasons, but to react to knowledge of them). Since, however, understanding those reasons is part of what is required to understand the natural order—the *mizvot*, as Stern emphasizes, being part of that order—we would expect a clear statement by Maimonides to the effect that the philosopher ought to reflect upon the reasons in III:25-49. The mere fact Maimonides devotes so much of the *Guide* to spelling out those reasons for his reader suggests that knowledge of them is crucial for

further religious and intellectual development. Hartman's reading gives us the imperative we expect, namely: reflect on the teleology of *mizvot* set out in III:25-49.

Despite these considerations, it strikes me as significant that on Hartman's reading the term "the end" shifts its meaning within the sentence. If we assume that it is preferable to hold the referent of the phrase constant, then, since the second occurrence of the phrase clearly refers to focusing on God, the first must too. Whether this consideration should outweigh those I adduced for Hartman's reading is, I suspect, a subjective matter.

[26] While I focus here on presence of the "preparation" conception in III:54, describing the shifts as we have—two neatly segregated treatments—oversimplifies matters in other ways: Maimonides' two treatments of the commandments are not neatly segregated. His explanation in terms of love and fear is not confined to the final chapters of the *Guide*: it also appears, if briefly, in III:24, 501, which is not part of the *ta'amei ha-mizvot* section, but instead (as Lawrence Kaplan observed) parallels III:52. This passage is significant, I think, because it implies that *all* commandments, and not merely those specifically mentioned in III:51 (such as prayer and Torah reading), aim at love and fear. In III:29, 518, we again encounter a conception like that in III:51-52, but there Maimonides' emphasis is not on love and fear *per se* but on the *opinion* that God is the one "who ought to be worshipped and loved and feared." Cf. Ben-Sasson, "A Study..."

[27] Cf. *Guide* I:33-34.

[28] However, two differences should be noted. First, one who achieves welfare of the soul need not be aware that the beliefs he has acquired are found in the tradition; and second, one who achieves perfection of the soul need not have started by setting for himself the project of proving beliefs X, Y, Z that he knows are found in the tradition.

[29] It is true that I:1 anticipates the true self argument that is used in III:54. However, not only is that chapter spatially distant from III:25-49, it is not directly concerned with the nature of perfection. Therefore, it is plausible to hold that III:54 is needed to complete the argument of III:25-49.

[30] It is true that III:54 is concerned with what a *person* should pursue, whereas Maimonides' proof that intellectual perfection is a good end would show that God had acted in "good or excellent" fashion in legislating the commandments. But both conclusions—that a person ought to pursue intellectual perfection, and that God's legislation is good or excellent—may be established from the same set of premises.

[31] See Goldman, "Worship," pp. 306ff. For example, laws of the second intention (e.g., sacrifices) are needed because of deficiencies in human beings that are due to their corporeal nature. Such laws exemplify *mishpat* as characterized in III:53.

[32] Historically, III:51 became better known in popular circles than III:54, thanks in part to the power of palace metaphor and the mystical quality of the chapter. On my view, all that this shows is that Maimonides did not always correctly anticipate what his audience would emphasize in reading him.

[33] Both Alexander Altmann, "Maimonides on the Intellect and the Scope of Metaphysics," in Altmann, *Von der Mittelalterichen zur Modernen Aufklärung: Studien zur Judischen Geistesgeschichte* (Tubingen, 1987), pp. 60-129, and Goldman, "Worship," note a paradox here. The immortal soul is one that loses its individuality; yet the activity that leads to immortality is advocated because it actualizes the true self. Altmann resolves the paradox

by inferring that the immortal soul retains a "modicum of individuality" (90).

[34] Lawrence Kaplan has pointed out to me that, by ending the *Guide* with III:54, Maimonides creates a symmetry between the first chapter of the work, which presents a portrait of man's essence as intellectual, and the last. The *Guide* has now come full circle. Interestingly, though, I:1, to my mind, is simplistic in just the way that III:54 is.

[35] Pines, "The Limitations of Human Knowledge."

[36] Altmann's lengthy paper, "Maimonides on the Intellect," originated as a response to Pines, and the University of Maryland devoted a 1987 conference to Pines' thesis. See also Warren Zev Harvey, "Maimonides on Human Perfection, Awe and Politics," in *The Thought of Moses Maimonides*, ed. Ira Robinson, Lawrence J. Kaplan and Julien Bauer (Lewiston, Queenston, Lampeter, 1990), [the volume in which the present essay originally appeared], 1-15; Barry S. Kogan, "What Can We Know and When Can We Know It?: Maimonides on the Active Intelligence and Human Cognition," in *Moses Maimonides and His Time*, ed. Eric L. Ormsby (Washington, D.C., 1988), pp. 121-37.

[37] Such as that marshaled by Altmann and Kogan (note 36).

[38] Noted by Warren Zev Harvey, *Hasdai Crescas's Critique of the Acquired Intellect*, Ph.D. dissertation, Columbia University, 1973, Excursus II.

[39] It is true that what "matter" will propel people to do in one historical period is not necessarily what "matter" will propel them to do at another. Consequently, even for "corporeal" men, not all the commandments will be necessary if the commandments were to quell only the impulses of matter at a particular time and place. Recall, however, Maimonides' views about the eternity of the Law and its applying equally to all individuals (III:34).

[40] Interestingly, whereas "being healthy and in the very best bodily state" is prized at III:27, 511, Maimonides, writing in III:54, 634-35, tells us of "the perfection of the bodily constitution and shape" that "utility for the soul is absent from this species of perfection." Although these two appraisals of bodily soundness are not strictly contradictory—III:54 is concerned with strength and proportionality of the limbs rather than health *per se*—the contrast may be very deliberate. Maimonides would have no reason not to advert to the positive, instrumental value he assigned to the body in III:27, especially since he is willing to acknowledge the instrumental value of another perfection, the third (moral virtues). By downgrading the body even more than he does in III:27-28, while preserving their instrumentalist view of the commandments as preparing one for intellectual perfection, Maimonides paves the way for a purely intellectualist conception of self.

[41] Throughout this paragraph I am indebted to Goldman, "Worship," pp. 289-93. The use I make of Goldman's observation is very different from the use he makes of it: his article accepts the possibility of transcending corporeality.

[42] Several scholars have noted the extensive influence of Sufi terms and themes on Maimonides' discussion. See for instance, Steven Harvey, "Maimonides and the Sultan's Palace" (referred to in n. 3).

[43] III:51, 624. Note, however, the two readings of the text cited by Pines in his note 32.

[44] Following Alexander Altmann, "Maimonides on the Intellect and the Scope of Metaphysics," p. 80.

[45] Ibid.

[46] It is puzzling, however (as pointed out by Lawrence Kaplan), that Maimonides states: "these actions were pure worship of great import."

[47] See Warren Harvey, "Maimonides on Human Perfection, Awe and Politics." Barry Kogan has called my attention to the resemblance between this portrait of Moses's activity and the account of the philosopher's actions in *Kuzari* I,1. The philosopher's organs or limbs behave "as if they were the organs of the Active Intellect" (Hirschfeld translation, New York, 1964).

[48] See I:54. For defenses of this reading, see Pines, "Translator's introduction," cxxi-cxii and his "The Limitations of Human Knowledge," esp. pp. 98-100; also Goldman, "Worship."

[49] Ibn Tibbon's translation slurs over the difference between "perfection" and "way of life," thereby, perhaps, reflecting his own reading of Maimonides as not sufficiently intellectualist.

[50] My reading clearly implies (or presupposes) that "overflowing" does not involve deliberate activity. That view would need to be tested by an examination of other "overflowings," such as those from the separate intellect toward that which is below them in rank. Cf. *Guide*, II:12, 279-80 and II:7, 266.

It is possible that Maimonides' inclusion of "acquiring fortune" implies a critique of the Sufis, for whom poverty was an ideal. On Maimonides' view, one could acquire fortune—or be engaged in any other activity—without leaving God's presence.

[51] Cf. III:22-23.

[52] See Z. Diesendruck, "Samuel and Moses ibn Tibbon on Maimonides' Theory of Providence," *Hebrew Union College Annual* XI (1936), 353-62.

[53] *Perush Le-Moreh Nevukhim*, ed. J. Goldenthal (Vienna, 1852), pp. 64-65. Narboni's view is accepted by Goldman, "The Worship Peculiar to Those Who Have Apprehended the True Realities," pp. 300 ff. See also Simon Rawidowicz, "Man and God" (Heb.), *Studies in Jewish Thought* (Jerusalem, 1959), pp. 297-331, 309-14. For a penetrating analysis of the whole issue of providence see Charles M. Raffel, "Providence As Consequent Union the Intellect: Maimonides' Theory of Providence," *AJS Review*, 12 (1987), 25-71.

[54] Note, however, that the importance of achieving *conjunction* should not be overstated. See Altmann, "Maimonides on the Intellect."

[55] Narboni himself does not cite III:54.

[56] See Goldman, "Worship," pp. 293-94.

[57] It is conceivable that Maimonides endorsed the argument fully, but wished to keep his "extraordinary speculation" about providence open to the kind of supernatural interpretation that Samuel ibn Tibbon, with puzzlement, raised. The "true self" argument would have exposed the naturalistic character of the theory; Maimonides therefore had a special motivation for postponing reference to it. The presence of the true self argument in I:1, however, casts some doubt about this explanation: the argument is already available to the reader of III:51.

[58] I am indebted to Warren Zev Harvey for this observation.

[59] "The other prophets and excellent men are beneath this degree; but it holds good for all of them that the apprehension of their intellects becomes stronger at the separation ..." (III:51, 628)

[60] "Limitations of Human Knowledge," p. 92. In these paragraphs, I assume that, if matter precludes complete *apprehension*, it also precludes complete concentration and worship. But I concede this premise needs further explanation.

[61] Stern, "Skeptical Themes in the *Guide of the Perplexed*," presented at the Maryland conference (note 36) in May 1987. For a similar approach, applied to other issues, see Sarah Klein-Braslavy, "The Creation of the World and Maimonides' Interpretation of Gen. i-v," in Pines and Yovel (eds.), *Maimonides and Philosophy*, pp. 65-78, as well as the papers by Ivry cited in note 62.

[62] Alfred Ivry, "Providence, Divine Omniscience, and Possibility: The Case of Maimonides," in *Divine Omniscience and Omnipotence in Medieval Philosophy*, edited by Tamar Rudavsky (Dordrecht, 1985), pp. 143-59; also see Ivry's "Islamic and Greek Influences on Maimonides' Philosophy," in Pines and Yovel, *Maimonides and Philosophy*, pp. 139-56.

[63] See Raffel, "Providence As Consequent Upon the Intellect." According to John Cooper in *Reason and Human Good in Aristotle* (Cambridge, 1977), cited by Raffel, the "true self" issue contains the key to understanding Aristotle's shifting pronouncements on the question of whether moral activity is integral to the good life. The importance of this issue in other writers would strengthen the case for reading Maimonides as concerned with the same issue.

[64] "Limitations of Human Knowledge."

[65] "Idea of a *Hoq*," p. 123. My development of Stern's points into the idea that prayer and Torah reading are paradigms of a split between act and concentration is not in his article; I am indebted to him for raising it, in conversation, as an interesting possibility. The problem is by no means contrived; mystics, too, had to maintain esoteric *kavvanot* while paying attention to the ideational content of the liturgy. See Joseph Weiss, "The Kavvanot of Prayer in Early Hasidism," *Journal of Jewish Studies* 9 (1958), 163-5. Cf. Lawrence Kaplan, "Response to Joseph Dan," in *Studies in Jewish Mysticism*, edited by Joseph Dan and Frank Talmage (Cambridge, 1978), pp. 121-28.

[66] See I:59.

[67] Lawrence Kaplan proposed this reading.

[68] On the this reading, Maimonides' injunction not to perform a commandment with your limbs as if you were hewing wood or digging a hole can be understood as follows. It is not that these actions are done absentmindedly; generally they are not. It is rather that they are so physical.

[69] Cf. Goldman, "Worship," pp. 292-93. The phrase translated by Pines, "Know that all the practices of the worship" is better rendered (as in ibn Tibbon and Kafah) "know that all *these* practices of the worship," which more clearly brings out the fact that "and the performance of the other commandments" is tacked on. Cf., however, note 25. If Hartman's view is correct, the difficulty is alleviated, since one is concentrating on the reasons God gave this specific commandment.

[70] Cf. note 17.

[71] *On Prayer*, in Arthur J. Arberry, *Avicenna and Theology* (London, 1951).

[72] See *Duties of the Heart*, V, 3 and X, 7.

[73] See especially V, 3.

[74] Both the general direction of this paper and numerous points of detail have been sharpened thanks to comments by David Berger, Warren Zev Harvey, Lawrence Kaplan, Barry Kogan, Charles Raffel, and Josef Stern. I also benefited greatly from discussion with Robert Brody, Yehuda Gellman, Steven Harvey, Arthur Hyman, Alfred Ivry, Sidney Morgenbesser, Aviezer Ravitzky, and David Sykes.

BIOGRAPHIES

Isadore Twersky

The late Isadore Twersky was the Nathan Littauer Professor of Hebrew Literature and Philosophy at Harvard University. He taught at the University for more than 30 years and served as director of the Center for Jewish Studies from 1978 until 1993. He was a prolific writer and was noted for his book, *An Introduction to the Code of Maimonides (Mishneh Torah)*, as well as numerous articles he wrote. He also edited *Harvard Studies in Medieval Jewish History and Literature, Volumes I, II, III*. Dr. Twersky won a Guggenheim Fellowship in 1989 and was a fellow of the American Academy for Jewish Research and the American Academy of Arts and Sciences.

Norman Lamm

Norman Lamm has served as rabbi, teacher, president of Yeshiva University and now as its chancellor and the *Rosh ha-Yeshiva* of its affiliated Rabbi Isaac Elchanan Theological Seminary. Dr. Lamm was the founding editor of the journal *Tradition: A Journal of Orthodox Thought* and has authored seven books, most recently *The Shema: Spirituality and Law in Judaism*, as well as numerous articles.

Arthur Hyman

Arthur Hyman serves as Distinguished Service Professor of Philosophy at Yeshiva University and is the dean of its Bernard Revel Graduate School for Judaic Studies. He has served as president of both the American Academy for Jewish Research and the Society for Medieval and Renaissance Philosophy. He has also served on the board of directors of the Association for Jewish Studies and is currently the editor of *Maimonidean Studies*.

Shalom Carmy

Rabbi Shalom Carmy is a Tenured Professor of Jewish Studies and Jewish Philosophy at Yeshiva University. He is a prominent Modern Orthodox theologian, historian and philosopher. He received his B.A. and M.S. from

Yeshiva University, and received his rabbinic ordination from its affiliated Rabbi Isaac Elchanan Theological Seminary. Rabbi Carmy has written many articles; he is the editor of *Tradition: A Journal of Orthodox Thought*, of *Modern Scholarship in the Study of Torah: Contributions and Limitations*, as well as several other works.

David Berger

David Berger is Broeklundian Professor of History at Brooklyn College and the Graduate Center of the City University of New York. He is also Visiting Professor of Jewish History at the Bernard Revel Graduate School of Yeshiva University, a Fellow and Executive Committee member of the American Academy for Jewish Research, and Co-chair of the Academic Advisory Committee of the National Foundation for Jewish Culture. He is the author of *The Jewish-Christian Debate in the High Middle Ages*, which was awarded the John Nicholas Brown Prize by the Medieval Academy of America, and co-author of *Judaism's Encounter with Other Cultures: Rejection or Integration?*, a Finalist for the Jewish Book Award in Jewish Thought. His book, *The Rebbe, the Messiah, and the Scandal of Orthodox Indifference*, which has recently been published in an updated Hebrew version translated by the author ("Ha-Rebbe Melekh ha-Mashiach," *Sha'aruriyyat ha-Adishut, ve-ha-Iyyum al Emunat Yisrael*), received the 2003-2004 Samuel Belkin Literary Award.

Norman E. Frimer

Norman E. Frimer served for nearly twenty five years as the Director of the Brookyn College Hillel Foundation and as the New York Regional Director of B'nai Brith Hillel. He later served as the International Director of B'nai Brith Hillel from 1975-1979 and the International Director of the Memorial Foundation for Jewish Culture from 1979-1984. Rabbi Frimer received his rabbinic ordination from Hebrew Theological College in Skokie, I.L. and his doctorate in Medieval Studies from Yeshiva University. His career also included service as the Dean of Students at Hebrew Theological College, Academic Dean and Professor of Ethics at Yeshiva University's Stern College for Women, Professor of Holocaust Literature at Brooklyn College, National Vice-President and member of the National Executive Committee of the Rabbinical Council of America, member of the Advisory Council on Higher Education of the New York State Senate, and Editorial Board Member of Tradition. His volume (co-authored with Prof. Dov Schwartz) entitled *The Life and Thought of Shem Tov Ibn Shaprut* was published in 1992 and his collected essays were published in a 1993 book entitled *A Jewish Quest for Religious Meaning*.

Dov I. Frimer

Dov I. Frimer is an attorney at law in Jerusalem, formerly Associate Professor of Law and Director of the Institute of Jewish Law at Touro College School of Law, Huntington, New York.

Roslyn Weiss

Roslyn Weiss is the Clara H. Stewardson Professor of Philosophy at Lehigh University. She has published extensively on ancient Greek philosophy and on medieval Jewish philosophy and has lectured widely in the U.S., Canada, Europe, and Israel.

Yamin Levy

Yamin Levy is academic director of Sephardic Studies at Yeshiva University and the founder of the Maimonides Heritage Center, a nonprofit organization dedicated to perpetuating Torat HaRambam to the lay public. Yamin Levy is author of internationally acclaimed *Confronting the Loss of a Baby: A Personal and Halakhic Perspective*, and *Journey Through Grief: A Sephardic Manual on Death and Bereavement* as well as numerous articles on Tanakh and Jewish Law.

Hayyim Angel

Hayyim Angel is the Rabbi at Congregation Shearith Israel, the Spanish-Portuguese Synagogue of New York. He also teaches Tanakh at Yeshiva University, and has published articles in various journals and collections of essays.

Elimelekh Polinsky

Elimelekh M.S. Polinsky is a Musmakh of the Rabbi Isaac Elchanan Theological Seminary and a *magid shi'ur* of Hevre Rambam, Young Israel of Avenue J, Brooklyn, New York.

Moshe Sokolow

Dr. Moshe Sokolow is Fanya Gottesfeld-Heller Professor of Jewish Education at the Azrieli Graduate School of Jewish Education and Adminstration at Yeshiva University. He is the Editor of *Ten Da'at: A Journal of Jewish Education*, and *Texts & Topics: Teaching Materials for Yeshiva High Schools*. From 1982-1985, Dr. Sokolow participated in the "Jerusalem Fellows" program. During that time, he assisted Prof. Nehama Leibowitz and conducted his own in-service training programs for teachers of Bible from both the United States and Israel. From 1985-1997, he served as the Director of Educational Services for the Department of Torah Education in the Diaspora of the World Zionist Organization. He has published and lectured widely on both Jewish Studies and Jewish Education.

Gerald Blidstein

Gerald Blidstein holds the Miriam Martha Hubert Chair in Jewish Law at Ben-Gurion University. He joined the faculty of Ben-Gurion University of the Negev in 1972 and has served in a number of senior positions including Dean of the Faculty of Humanities and Social Sciences, chairman of the Goldstein-Goren Department of Jewish Thought and Head of the Goldstein-Goren International Center of Jewish Thought. He has written six books and edited five, as well as publishing 150 articles. Dr. Blidstein was recently awarded the prestigious Israel Prize in Jewish Thought for the year 2006.

David Shatz

David Shatz is Professor of Philosophy at Yeshiva University, Adjunct Professor of Religion at Columbia University, editor of *The Torah u-Madda Journal*, and editor of the series *MeOtzar HoRav: Selected Writings of Rabbi Joseph B. Soloveitchik*. He has published eleven books and over fifty articles and reviews, dealing with both general and Jewish philosophy. He received his Ph. D in philosophy with distinction from Columbia University and was ordained by the Rabbi Isaac Elchanan Theological Seminary.

Index of Maimonides' Writings

General Index

gift, 151
inspiration, 149-50, 161 n. 14
inspiration vs. prophecy, 150
involvement in the universe, 74
law, 184, 209, 222-3
legislation, 221
omniscience, 74
oral law, 204, 206
origin of Torah, 181
providence, 33, 130
punishment, 177 n. 25
revelation, 91
science, 62, 220
things, 218-9
tradition, 205
unity, 49, 55
will, 54
wisdom, 131, 227
Divine Omniscience and Omnipotence in Medieval Philosophy, 261 n. 62
divinity, 223
divorce, 146 n. 30, 210
dogma, 73-8, 132
negative, 74
positive vs. negative, 75
drawn water, 32
dream, 153
drinking, 137
dues, 143
Duties of the Heart, 262 n. 72
duty, 171

E

eating, 137
forbidden foods, 137
live flesh, 104 n. 9, 105 n. 21
Ecclesiastes, 120, 150
efod, 7
egotistical tendencies, 174
Egypt, 32, 97, 104 n. 15, 181, 189, 200 n. 42
Egyptians, 154, 164 n. 57
Eichler, Barry L., 163 n. 50, 164 n. 66
Einayim la-Mishpat, 109 n. 62
Einstein, Albert, 92

Eldad ha-Dani, 199 n. 32
Elijah the Prophet, 85, 151, 193, 195, 202 n. 62
elimination of *mizvot*, 167
Elisha b. Abuya, 146 n. 27
Elman, Yaakov, 146 n. 29
Elon, Menachem, 104 n. 9, 110 n. 69
emancipation, 189
Emden, R. Jacob, 7
Emunot ve-De'ot, 202 n. 58
Encyclopedia Judaica, 109 n. 62
End of Days, 85, 130, 186
Engel, R. Joseph, 97, 105 n. 20
Englard, Y., 215 n. 11
Enlightenment period, 47 n. 101
Enzyklopedia Talmudit, 214 n. 4
Ephraimites, 189, 200 n. 42, 200 n. 43
epistemology, 232, 247
Epstein, R. Moshe Mordekhai, 105 n. 15
erudition, 2
eruvin, 165
Esau, 151
eschatological calculation, 80-1
Essays in Jewish Intellectual History, 254 n. 4
Essays on Maimonides: An Octocentennial Volume, 72 n. 6, 95 n. 5
eternal, 129
subjects, 28
eternity, 74
ethics, 32, 170-1
Aristotelian, 146 n. 31
ethical precept, 170
ethical quality, 136
ethicists, 33
Maimonidean, 146 n. 31
nature of, 138
rabbinic, 183
Ethiopians, 154
Eve, 122, 125 n. 17
Even ha-Azel, 108 n. 49, 108 n. 52, 108 n. 55, 110 n. 70

Judah, 157-8
Judaism, 88 n. 15
judges, 166, 174
  not cursing, 167-8, 174, 176 n. 8
  not striking, 174
  rebellious, 166
judgment, 220, 237
Jurewitz, R. Isaac Simcha, 59 n. 14
jurisprudence, 97
justice, 174

K

Ka'b al-Ahbar, 198 n. 20
kab ve-naki, 34
kabbalah, 26
  bridge with philosophy, 29
  kabbalistic circles, 29
  kabbalists, 26, 28, 30, 33
Kafah, R. Yosef, 46 n. 80, 176 n. 12,
  261 n. 69
kalaam, 207
Kalischer, R. Zevi Hirsch, 86, 88 n. 18
Kapasli, R. Elijah, 6, 19-20, 23
Kaplan, Lawrence J., 255 n. 12, 258 n.
  26, 259 n. 34, 259 n. 36, 260 n. 46,
  261 n. 65, 261 n. 67, 262 n. 74
Kara, 162 n. 34, 162 n. 39
Karaite, 205, 215 n. 11
  anti-Karaite value, 206
  assertions, 211
  challenge of, 206, 211
  challenging, 213
  claim, 210
  model ideology, 211
  premises, 210
Karbala, 186, 199 n. 24
karet, 184
Karlin, 14
Karo, R. Joseph, 14, 26, 29, 106 n. 31,
  107 n. 31
Kasher, R. M. M., 107 n. 33, 109 n.
  61, 110 n. 70
Katz, Hannah, 59 n. 20
Katz, Jacob, 86, 88 n. 17, 96-7, 103 n.
  4, 103 n. 7, 136, 146 n. 29

kavvanah, 255 n. 11
  kavvanot, 261 n. 65
Ke'arat Kesef, 45 n. 47
Kelal Kevod Elokim Hester Davar, 47
  n. 97
Kellner, Menachem, 88 n. 15, 130,
  145 n. 4, 145 n. 10, 145 n. 12, 148,
  160 n. 2, 164 n. 57, 164 n. 65
Kenesset ha-Gedolah, 47 n. 125, 104
  n. 7
Kerem Hemed, 44 n. 16
Kesef Mishneh, 26, 106 n. 29, 106 n.
  31, 108 n. 49, 147 n. 44, 176 n. 8,
  214 n. 8
Kesher Tefutsot, 107 n. 34
Keter David Kama, 109 n. 63
Ketuvim, 149-52
Kfar Chabad, 87 n. 7
kibbud, see honor
kiddushin, 100
Kiel, Yehuda, 162 n. 29, 162 n. 34,
  163 n. 51
Kimhi, R. David, see *Radak*
Kin'at Soferim, 60 n. 28
king, 32
  as an authoritative figure, 216
    n. 25
  human, 116
  King David, 33
  King of Kings, 171-2
  King Messiah, 33
  kingship, 33
  mortal, 171
Kirschenbaum, Prof. Aaron, 107 n. 43
Kiryat Sefer, 44 n. 14
Kitab al-Ras'il, 43 n. 12, 43 n. 13, 44
  n. 23
Kitvei ha-Gri Henkin, 104 n. 7, 110
  n. 66
Kitvei ha-Ramban, 201 n. 53
Klein-Braslavy, Sarah, 161 n. 14, 261
  n. 61
Knight, Daniel, 89
knowledge, 4, 63, 133

those of faith, 27
dissemination of, 25
engagement with, 30
exclusively authoritative, 38
Hebrew translations of the
Talmud, 38
home for all Torah, 32
impossibility of comparison to,
20
intended audience, 42
learning to become wise, 21
order and sequence of, 21
praise for, 30
primacy of, 29
role of, 37
seeking to understand, 39
single comprehensive treatise,
25
standing of, 27
subject, 6, 15
value of, 23
Mishneh Torah im Perush Yad Peshutah,
175 n. 4, 176 n. 6
mishpat, 229, 243, 254 n. 3, 258 n. 31
Mishpat ha-Melukhah be-Yisra'el, 104
n. 7, 109 n. 58, 109 n. 61, 110 n.
70
Mishpatim, 109 n. 61
Modena, R. Judah Aryeh, 13, 19, 30
moderation, 136-8
Modern Judaism, 88 n. 15
*Modern Scholarship in the Study of
Torah: Contributions and Limitations*,
164 n. 66
modernist, 90
modesty, 3
monotheism, 49, 139, 180
Montefiore, Moses, 17
Montpelier, R. Solomon, 18
Moody, Dr. Raymond, 202 n. 60
moon, 230
mora, see reverence
moral
activity, 261 n. 63

defect, 151
excellence, 137
habits, 225, 227
life, 123-4
matters, 117
perfection of values, 226
qualities, 3, 123, 222
sensibilities, 123
value, 121
virtues, 150
morals, 172
Morgenbesser, Sidney, 262 n. 74
Morocco, 181-2, 187
Moses, 11, 14-7, 19-20, 26-7, 32, 38,
41, 43 n. 4, 44 n. 34, 45 n. 42, 67-
8, 97, 105 n. 15, 105 n. 21, 116,
142, 149, 169, 172, 182, 197 n. 4,
202 n. 62, 204-6, 209, 211-2, 221,
234-45, 247-9, 251, 253, 255 n. 6,
260 n. 47
as prophet and legislator, 140
attending R. Akiva's school, 76
completeness of Mosaic
revelation, 74
death of, 215 n. 12
ideal, 244
Mosaic tradition, 206
Moses al-Darri, 187-8
Moses Maimonides and His Time, 259
n. 36
Mosheh Rabbenu, see Moses
Moskowitz, Yehiel, 162 n. 39
Moslem Almohads, 93
Mossad ha-Rav Kook, 197 n. 1
mourning, 168-9
Mu'awiyya, 186
Muhammad, 180, 182, 185, 198 n. 4,
198 n. 20, 199 n. 21, 199 n. 24
Munk, S., 66
Munkaczer *Rebbe*, 14
murder, 99, 104 n. 9, 169
indirect causation of, 99
Mussar Movement, 28
mysteries of the Law, 62